ISB 120
THE STORY

Acknowledgements

Thank you to everyone involved in the production of **ISB120 THE STORY** and to those who have supported the project.

Commissioners André and Silvia Cox, Territorial Leaders, and senior leadership of the United Kingdom Territory with the Republic of Ireland
Commissioners John and Betty Matear
Major Leanne Ruthven, Editor-in-Chief and Publishing Secretary, and members of the Territorial Literary Council

Photography: Anthony Graziano, Anthony Weil, John Matta, Doug Lyon, Val Cheesman, Nic Piper, Paul Dymott, John Stirzaker and Paul Harmer

Design: Andrew Wainwright

Compiling and Editing: Malcolm Quinn

Published by SP&S, a division of Salvation Army Trading Company Ltd.
66-78 Denington Road, Wellingborough, Northants NN8 2QH

© Salvation Army Trading Company Ltd
First published 2012
ISBN 978-0-85412-8617

Registered Company no.2605817 The Salvation Army registered charity no.214779 and in Scotland no.SC009359

CONTENTS

THE GENERAL 7
INTRODUCTION 8
REVIEWS:

    Former ISB bandsman 13
    Audience perspective 29
    UK Territorial leadership 43
    Overseas guest 59

THE BANDS 87

    Composer 169
    Central Hall, Westminster 183
    Buckingham Palace 199
    The Mall 213

FINAL REFLECTIONS 255

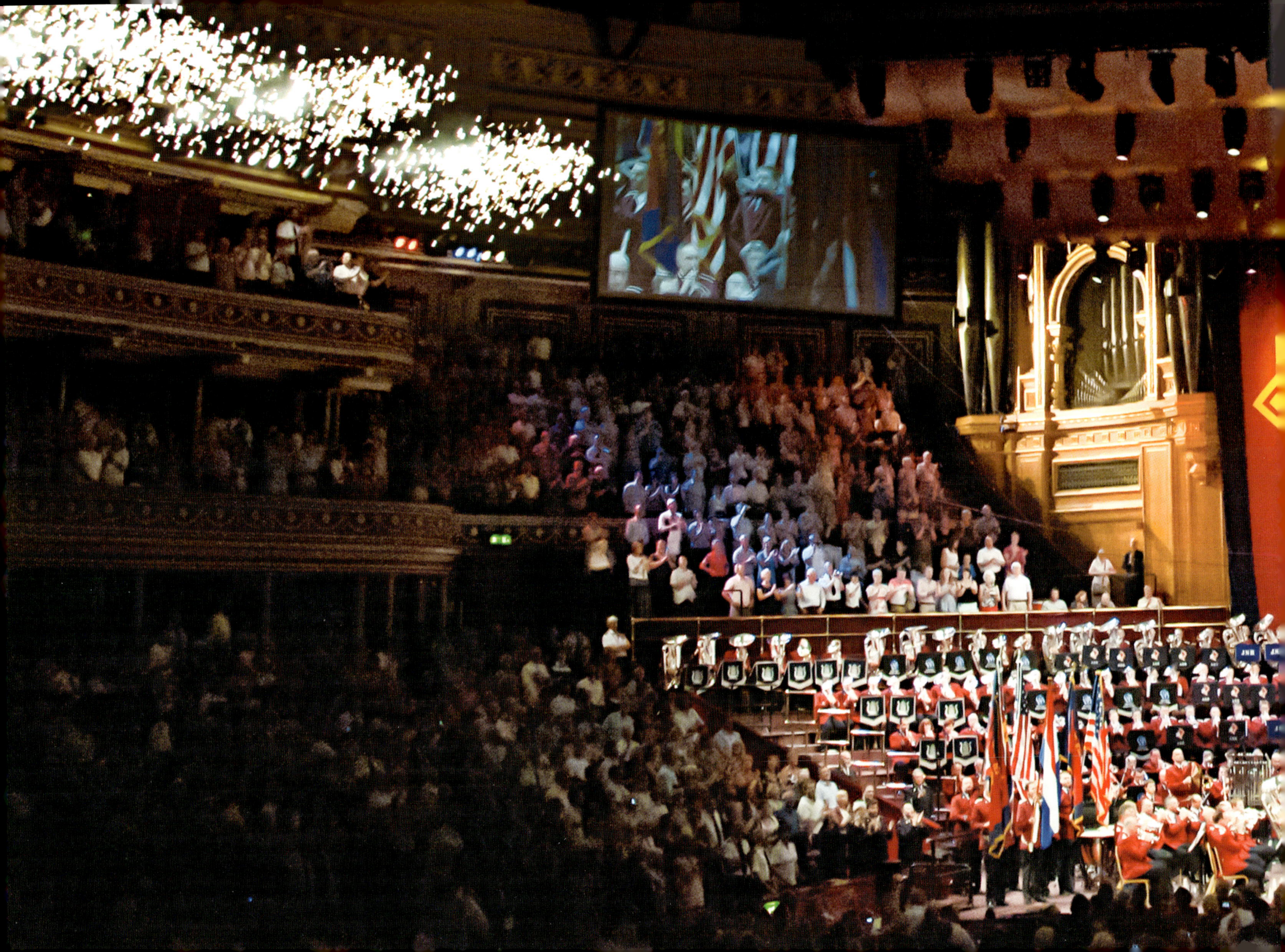

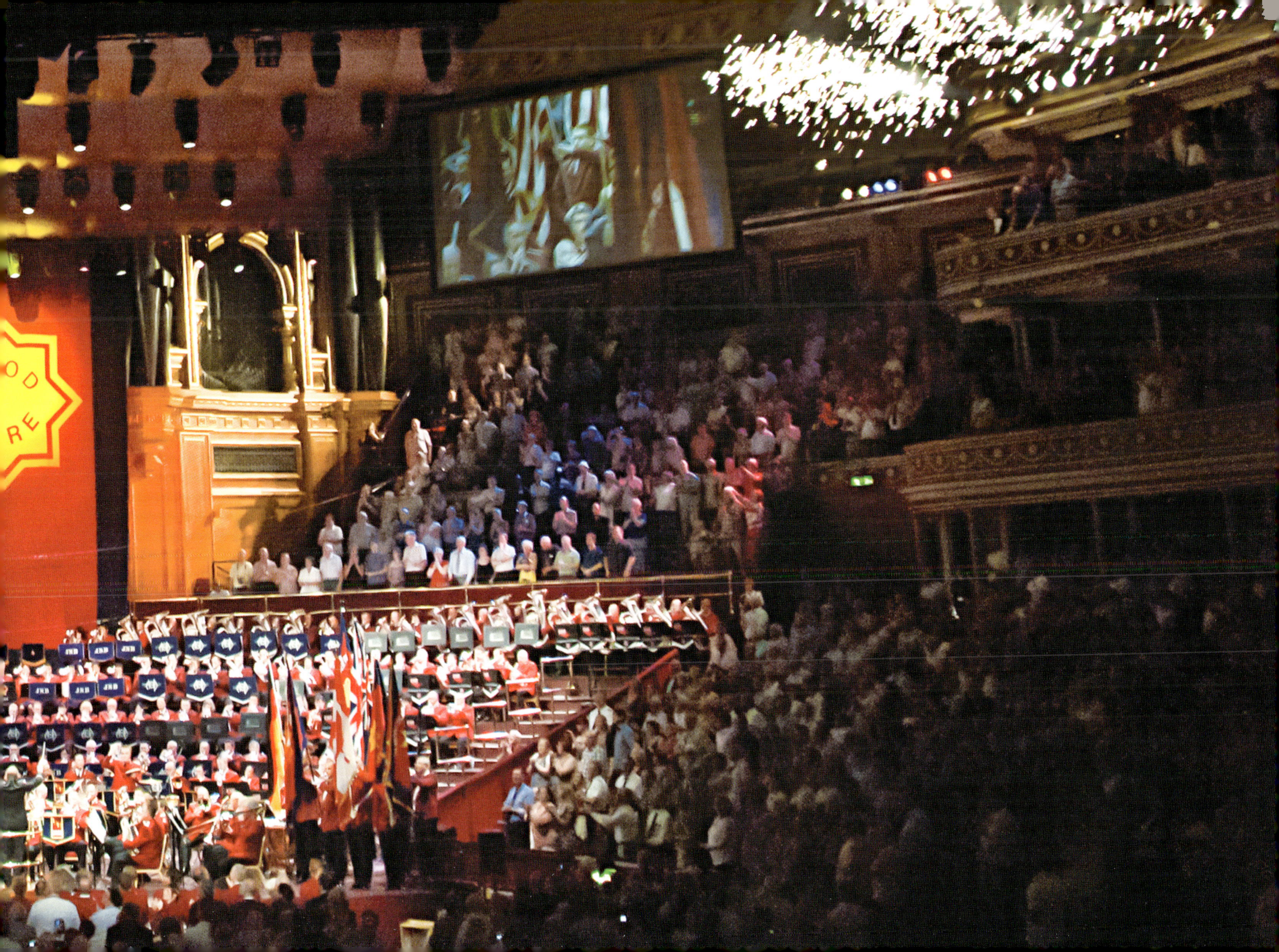

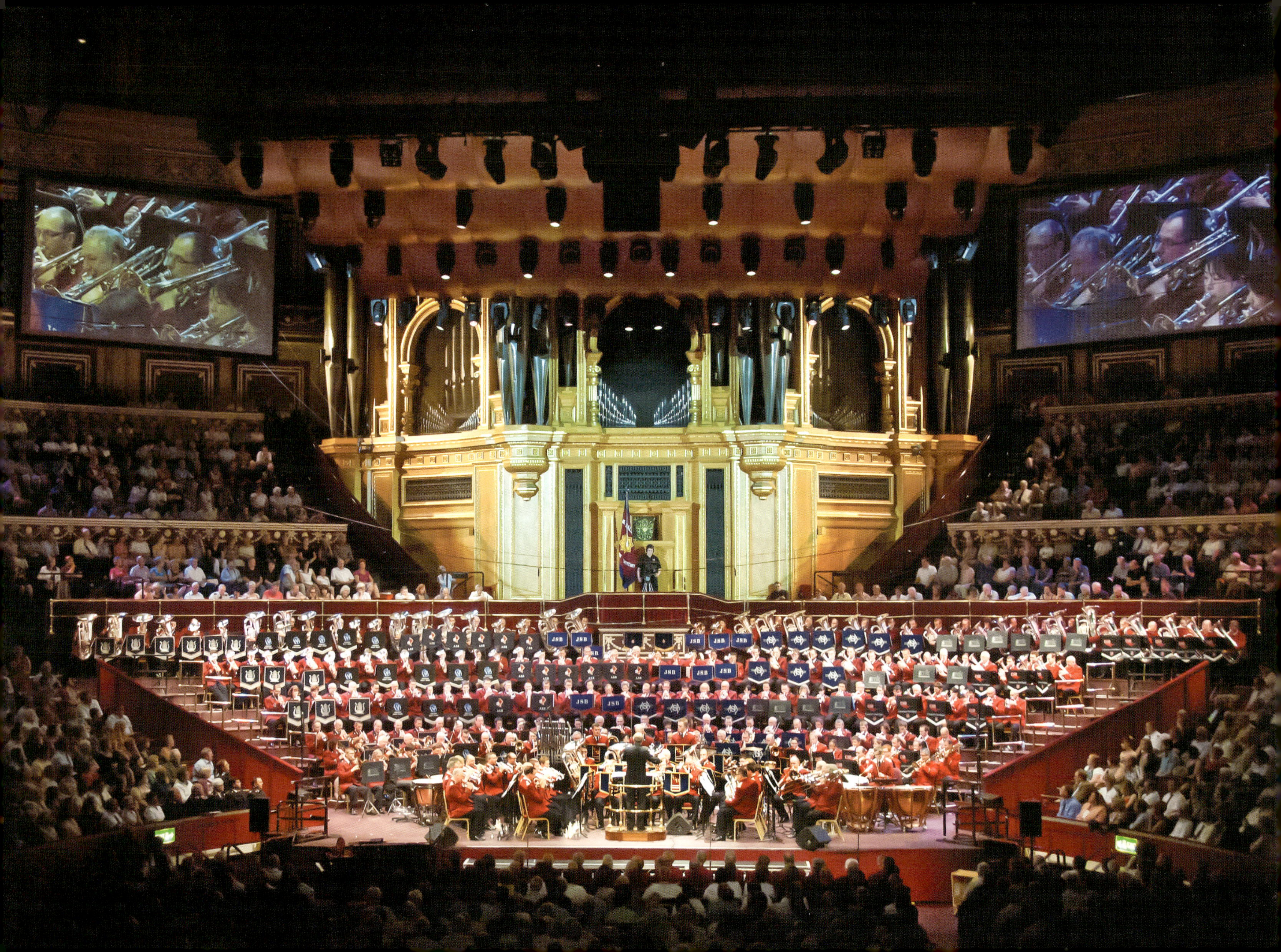
JSB

THE GENERAL

'*A picture is worth a thousand words!*', it is said. A single image can convey a wealth of ideas, tell a story and bring back memories of what has been seen or heard. This very special book visually captures an unforgettable weekend when seven Salvation Army Staff Bands came to London to join The International Staff Band in celebrating its 120th anniversary.

But this book offers more than a pictorial review of ISB120. First-hand reports from each participating band and testimonies from several who attended tell stories of the power of the ministry of music. This was no semi-professional brass band competition. This was no glorified massed band performance that was self-serving and insular in its influence. Quite the contrary! This is an account of Salvationist musicians from around the world, whose united focus was to offer their gifts for the glory of God and the spiritual inspiration of His people.

Accounts of the pre-anniversary weekend concerts, the Royal Albert Hall programmes and the march down The Mall give heart-warming descriptions of Christian camaraderie, excellence in music and a ministry blessed by God. One bandsman writes: 'In all the exuberance of the concerts and high profile performances the main objective is to tell the good story of Jesus'. Another speaks of it as 'God's wonderful music' being communicated in a 'very special way'.

An anniversary occasion by its very nature calls us to thanksgiving for the past, but it also positions us for the future and therefore sets the tone for dedicated service in the present. As one bandsman has written, 'Its legacy will not be measured in months or years, but in decades'. This certainly applies to The Salvation Army brass band impact but this brilliantly executed once-in-a-lifetime event went far beyond the borders of music making. The profit from ISB120 has gone to the opening of the Army's work in a new country in Africa.

So look at the pictures, read the stories and thank the Lord, the true Music Maker, for a weekend of praise and inspiration.

Linda Bond
General
October 2012

INTRODUCTION

The idea of the ISB120 event probably had its origins in 1994 in Toronto, Canada. Four staff bands participated in a superb weekend at Roy Thomson Hall and Toronto Temple. The feelings of camaraderie and fellowship were unique in my experience, as was the enthusiastic response to the weekend from participants and listeners alike. I congratulated Brian Burditt on arranging an absolutely outstanding weekend. His response was interesting. "Steve, you should do something like this in England one day!" At the time I laughed out loud and dismissed the idea, but I guess part of me took the comment as a bit of a challenge!

Fast forward several years to a morning coffee with my friend and colleague Trevor Caffull. What started as a business meeting became a conversation about arranging something special similar to the Toronto event, and the idea of bringing the eight active Salvation Army Staff Bands of the world together in London's Royal Albert Hall emerged. We decided that 2011 would be a great year as it marked the ISB's 120th Anniversary. At the end of our conversation we really believed that it could happen.

Having an idea is one thing. Making it happen is quite another challenge. I knew from the outset that I did not have the capacity or gifting to make such an event happen. However, I knew exactly the person who could! Malcolm Quinn and I have been friends for over 40 years; a friendship formed at Music School in the early '70s. Our paths had not crossed for some time, so I made a call to him with some apprehension. We then met and, after extensive discussion over a few weeks, he recommended a structure and process that would make it work. Subsequently, after careful consideration, he agreed to head up the team, and the rest is history. The significance of his role in making ISB120 happen should never be underestimated or forgotten. The ISB and the Band Board were also made aware of this initiative and were very enthusiastic about the possibility of ISB120.

Critical success factors were developed, not only to ensure the success of the event, but more importantly to express the mission value it needed to bring to The Salvation Army. We wanted to engage everyone in celebrating Salvation Army music ministry, in particular brass bands, but we also wanted to celebrate what it is to be part of the worldwide Salvation Army; to encourage and affirm, giving us real hope for the future of this movement that means so very much to us all, offering a strong evangelistic element to the weekend.

With the project broken down into eight distinctive teams, each with a leader (current, as well as former Staff Band members), the 'Programme of Events' team met to consider what the celebration might look like. For all teams, early meetings were necessarily robust and challenging, particularly when difficult and initially 'unpopular' decisions had to be made. Whilst striving for quality, the financial stewardship was also diligently managed, not only to ensure the event paid for itself, but also to optimise the potential for further revenue. The substantial profit realised would subsequently go towards opening the Salvation Army's work 'in yet another country', as well as supporting the Mission work of the United Kingdom with the Republic of Ireland Territory. With a very committed group of Staff Band members underpinning the project it is felt by many that the weekend turned out to be an outstanding success.

Excitement for the occasion built up as, throughout the UK and Ireland, 27 corps hosted four of the visiting bands in the two weeks prior to the event, and all bands converged close to London on the Friday night to give individual concerts, with the ISB and NYSB sharing a memorable concert at Cadogan Hall in London.

On Saturday, at the Royal Albert Hall, each band provided a 20 minute programme, reflecting music ministry in their part of the Salvation Army world, supported by a video presentation suggesting how music speaks into the life of their territory. The bands did this with creativity and integrity. The evening concert was an outstanding success and people were hugely encouraged by the possibilities for music ministry in the 21st century Salvation Army.

The Sunday morning service brought the eight bands together with music leaders from the UK Territory and countless Salvationist musicians were blessed and affirmed by General Linda Bond when she led our morning worship in a beautiful and meaningful meeting.

Sunday afternoon saw the eight bands marching down The Mall with uniformed Salvationists distributing Salvation Army publications and warmly greeting those who expressed an interest. We were told by the Police that they estimated in excess of 15,000 people witnessed the spectacle.

Without wishing to appear presumptuous, it would be fair to say that the ISB120 event was an outstanding and unequivocal success. How? Well, the Royal Albert Hall was packed to capacity throughout Saturday; Sunday morning's meeting and afternoon march down The Mall attracted great crowds; the event raised a substantial amount, £50,000 of which has gone to support The Salvation Army's work in Burkina Faso. However, and more importantly, each concert was a tremendous expression of worship, a re-affirmation of the power of Salvation Army music making, and all developed through a great sense of community!

That's almost it on ISB120... but not quite. You see, we did not plan for this weekend to be an end in itself, but to be a weekend that would have a ripple effect throughout the Salvation Army world. We believe this was achieved and even now, 18 months later, we are hearing new stories of people inspired by the weekend who have developed new initiatives in their part of the Salvation Army world.

We hope the ISB120 event continues to be a long and lasting memory for all who attended and for all who bought any of the CDs or DVDs. More importantly, our prayer is that ISB120 will have re-energised the belief that The Salvation Army, and its music ministry, has a vital role to play in our lives and the lives of those to whom we minister in the 21st century.

It is my wish that as you read this book you will not only enjoy the many pictures but also the words of those who have contributed in their own distinctive style.

Stephen Cobb
Staff Bandmaster

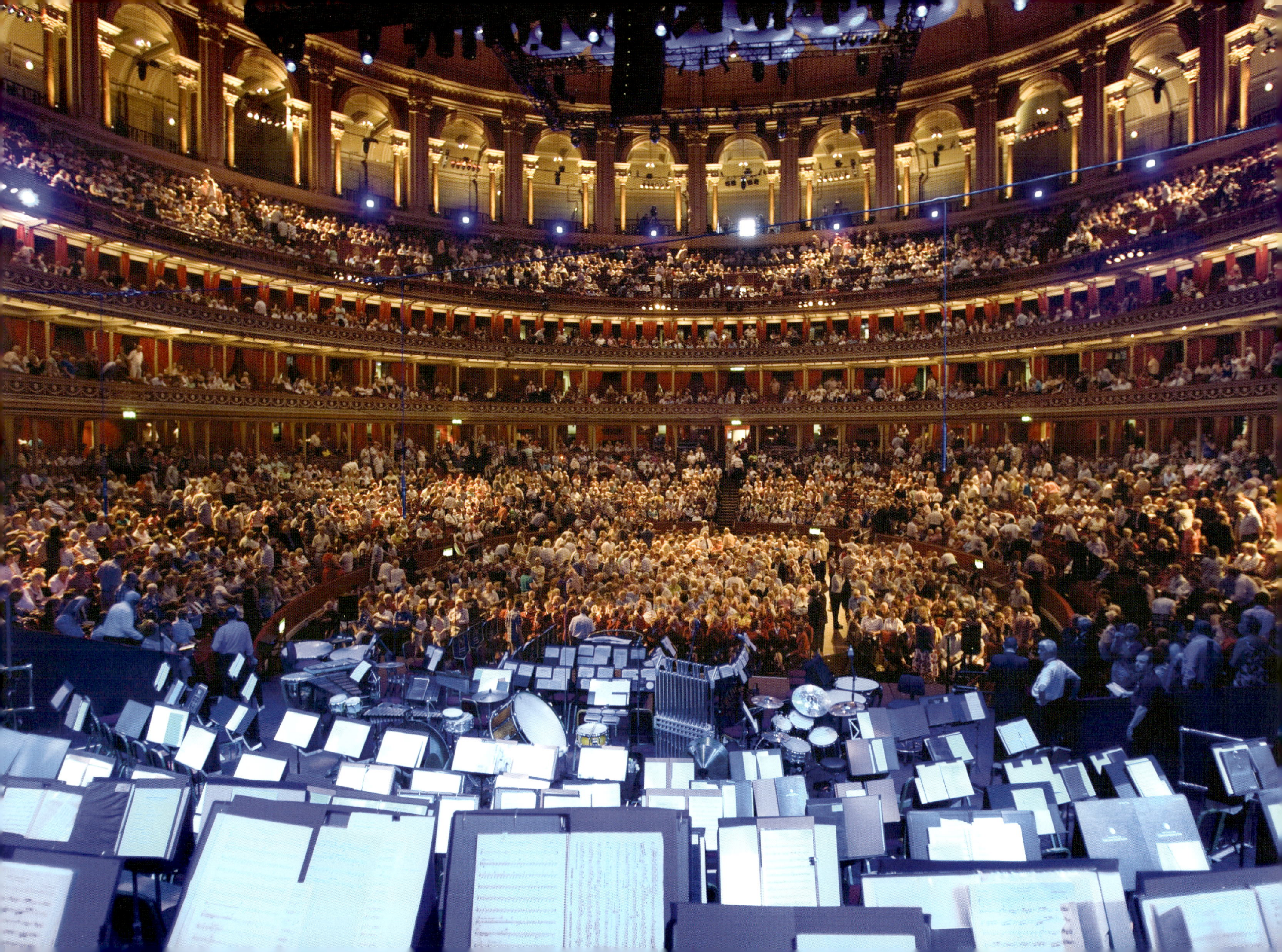

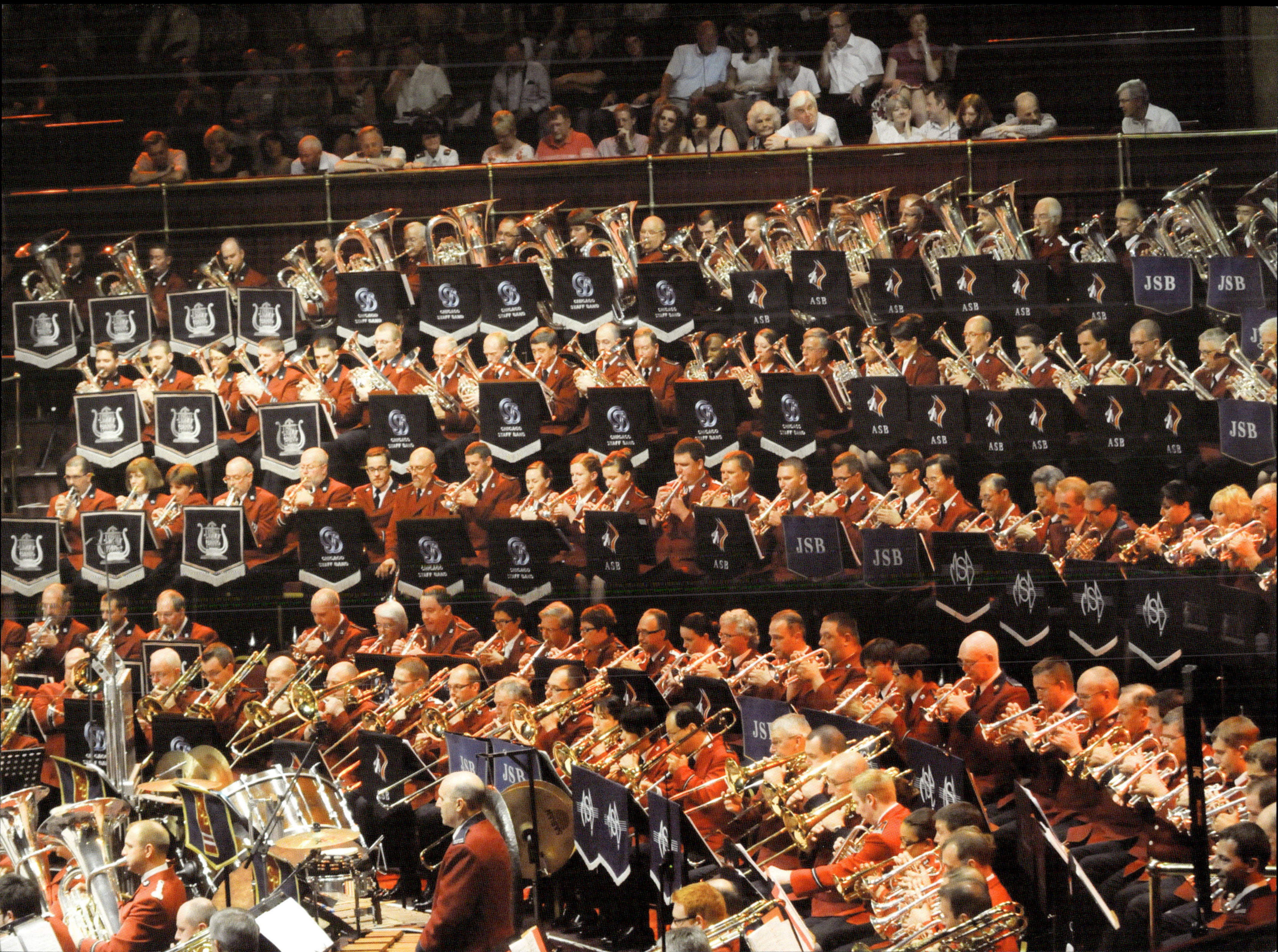
JSB
ASB

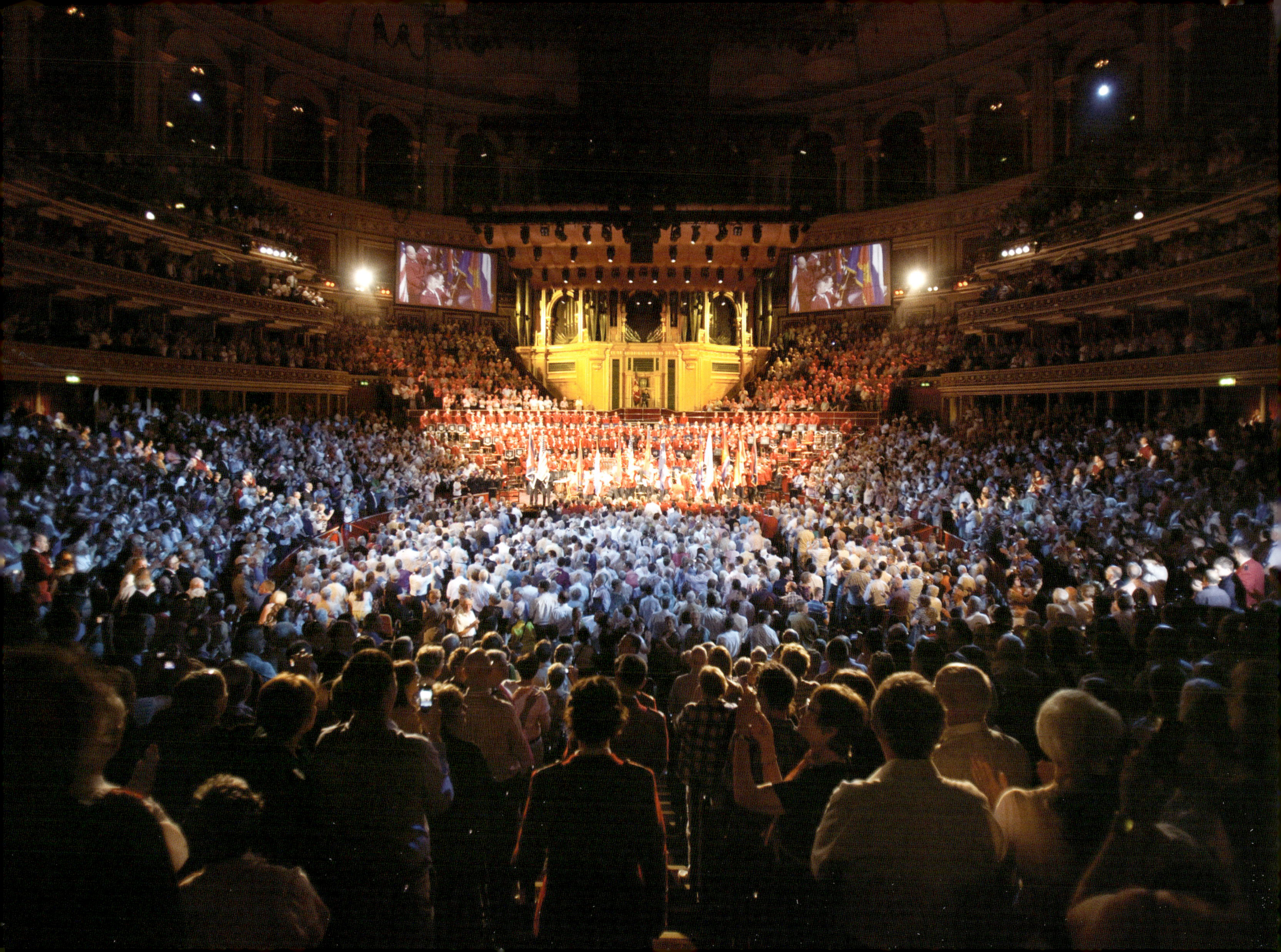

FORMER ISB BANDSMAN
Andrew Woodhouse

Having been brought up in a corps with a strong banding tradition and having spent more than 11 years as an ISB bandsman, I'm somewhat ashamed to admit that when I first heard about ISB120 I was in the 'it will never catch on' camp. I just didn't think enough people would be interested in a banding event on this scale. Now I have publicly confessed, I will explain my gradual conversion.

Even as communications started to appear about ticket allocations for former ISB members, I still couldn't seem to capture the vision. It was only when one wiser than I (my wife) convinced me that 'you will regret it if you don't go' that we eventually purchased tickets for the Saturday and Sunday events. In addition we decided that we would take our children (then aged eight and six) to their first big 'Army' event.

> In The Mall on Sunday I met friends, neighbours and relations, some of whom I had never seen at an Army event before. My doubts had disappeared, my faith had been rewarded and my conversion was complete. ISB120 was a success.

Now, as with any good conversion story, I still had my doubts. How would the children survive five hours of brass-banding? More importantly, how would my wife and I survive five hours of brass banding with two young children? As the months passed, news was breaking that the event had sold out! As a result I felt the first small pangs of excitement and the nagging doubts began to disappear. The excitement continued to build as my wife and I began to describe the Albert Hall to our children and what the event was all about. It seemed the more we tried to generate an atmosphere of excitement and anticipation for them, the more excited I became.

Eventually the ISB120 weekend arrived. Throughout the events on Saturday we cheered, clapped and cried (emotions usually reserved for my football team). In The Mall on Sunday I met friends, neighbours and relations, some of whom I had never seen at an Army event before. My doubts had disappeared, my faith had been rewarded and my conversion was complete. ISB120 was a success.

There were many highlights; the emotional reception afforded to the Japan Staff Band, as the whole congregation stood and applauded as if it had been rehearsed was quite remarkable, the marching in of the flags was spine-tingling and the drum head service was moving. I guess everyone who attended would have their own special moment.

For me, seeing my children at the end of a marathon banding event, standing and clapping above their heads as the march *Celebration* reached its finale, the giant flag unfurled and the fireworks sparkling and sizzling around the auditorium, will be a lasting memory. In this Olympic year there has been much talk of leaving a legacy. So what will be the ISB120 legacy?

I hope and pray that the legacy of ISB120 will be that we will treasure the gift of music and ensure that Salvation Army banding will hold as much excitement and satisfaction for our children as it has for us.

Bands entering the Royal Albert Hall – Saturday evening

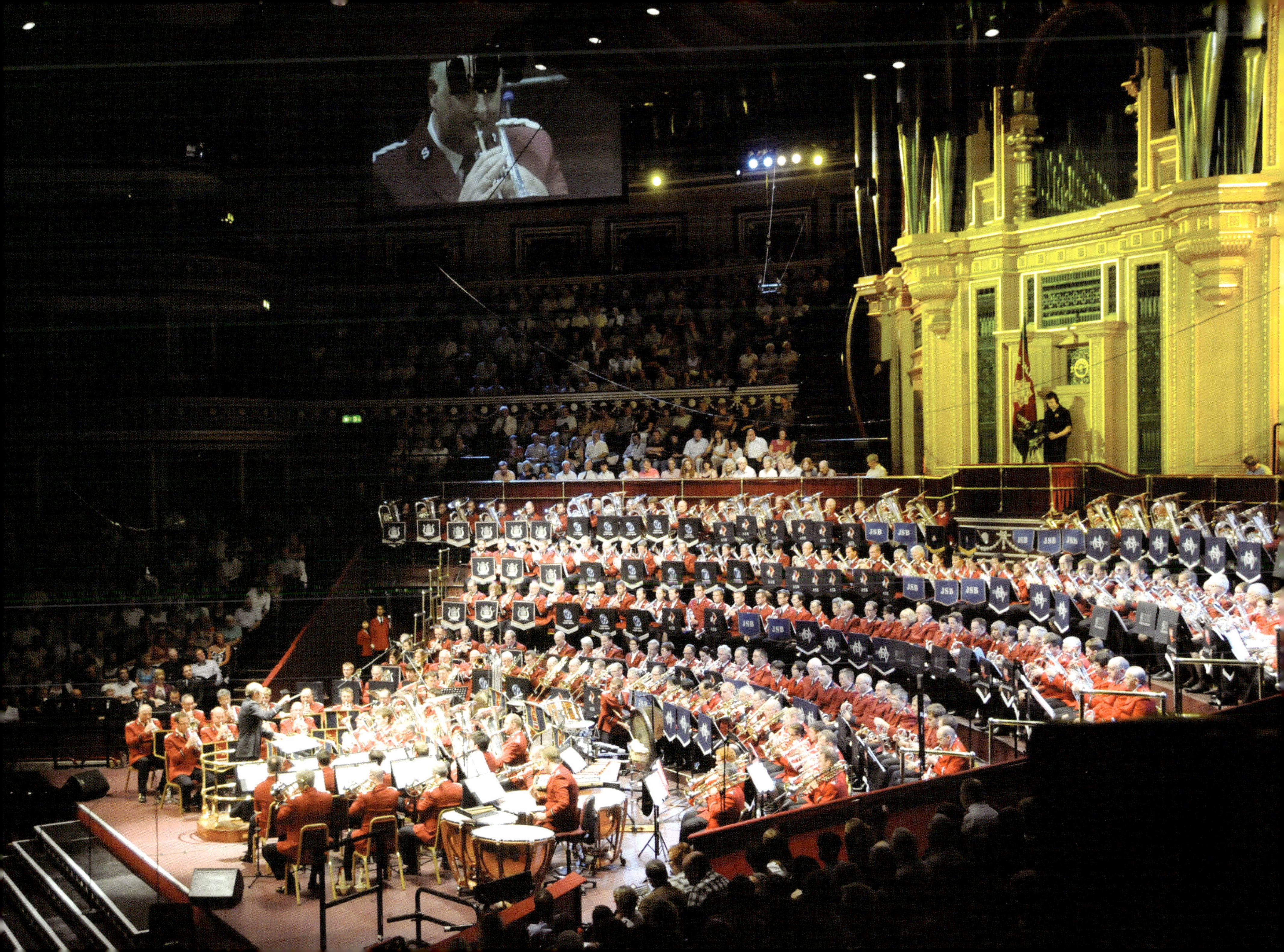
JSB

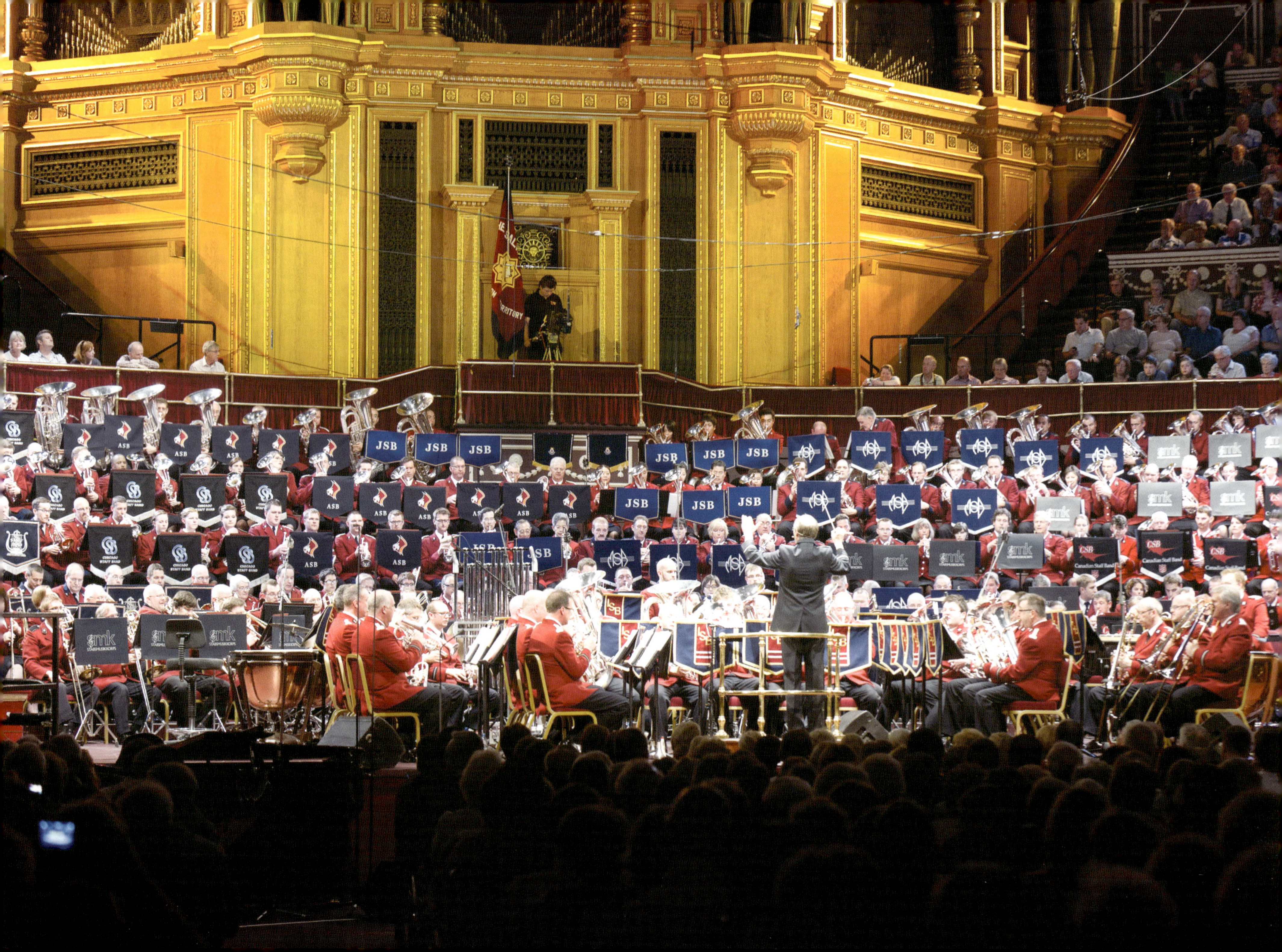
JSB
ASB
CSB
Canadian Staff Band

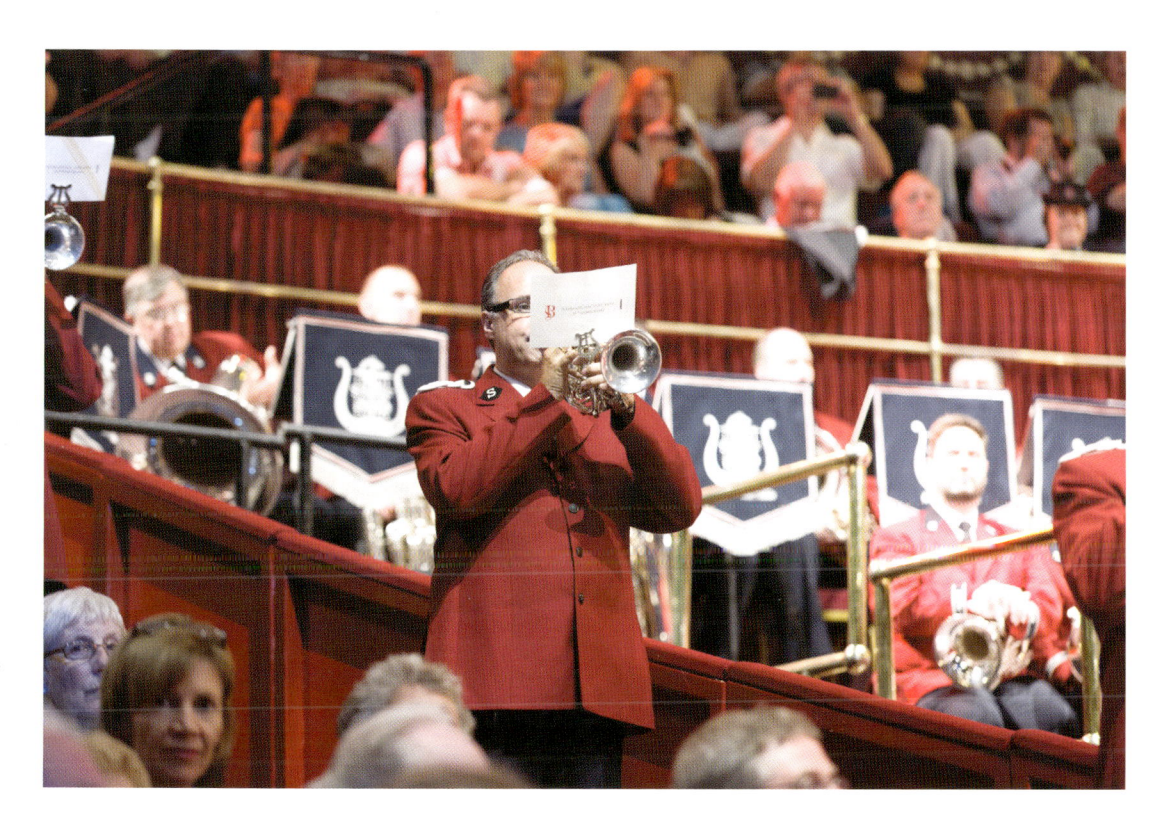

Opening *Fanfare, Prelude & Fugue on Sine Nomine* (Peter Graham)

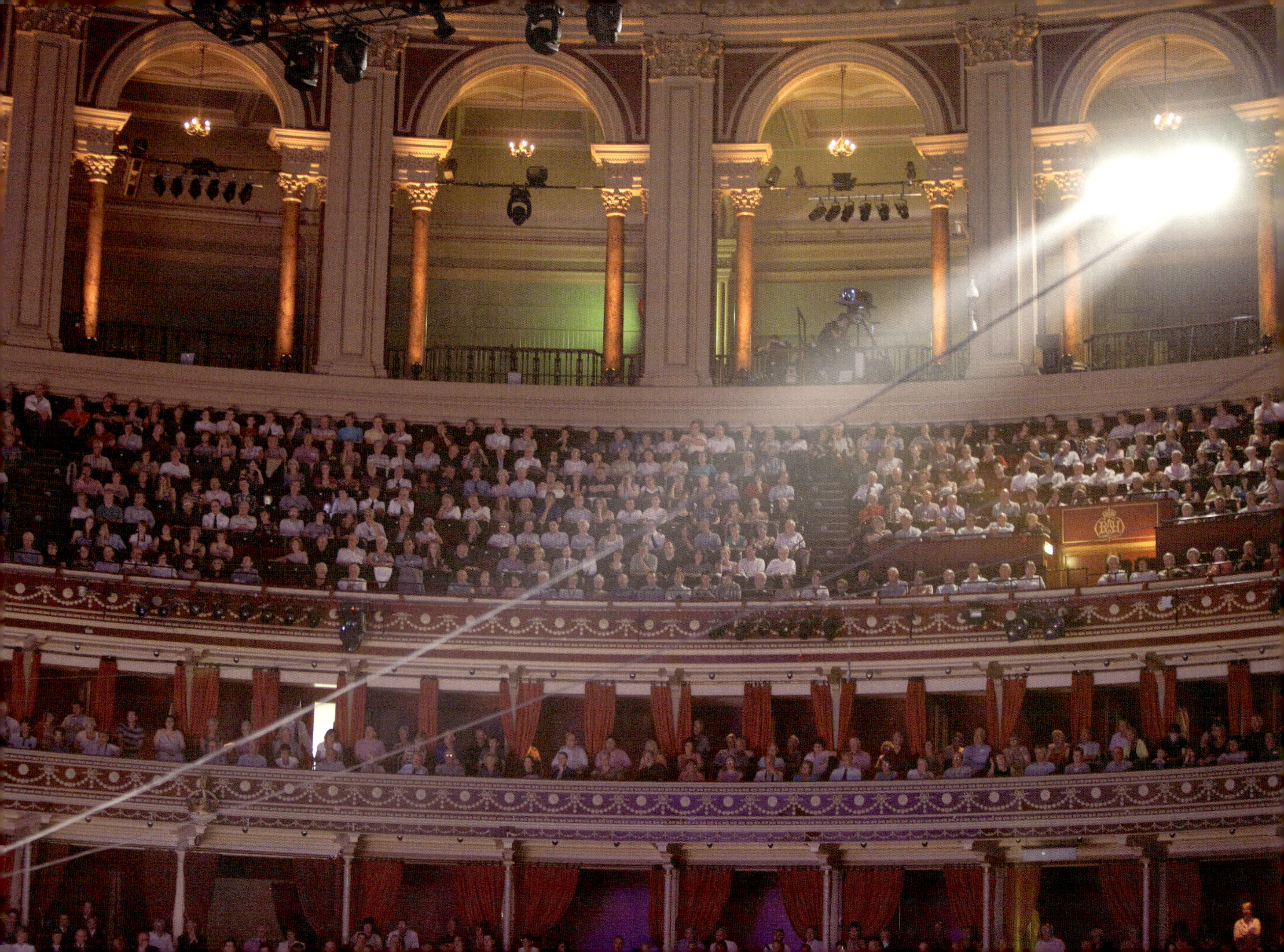

Flugel Horn feature *So Glad!* (William Himes)

Clockwise from top left:
Arthur Henry (New York Staff Band)
Philip Cobb (The International Staff Band)
Garry Todd (Melbourne Staff Band)

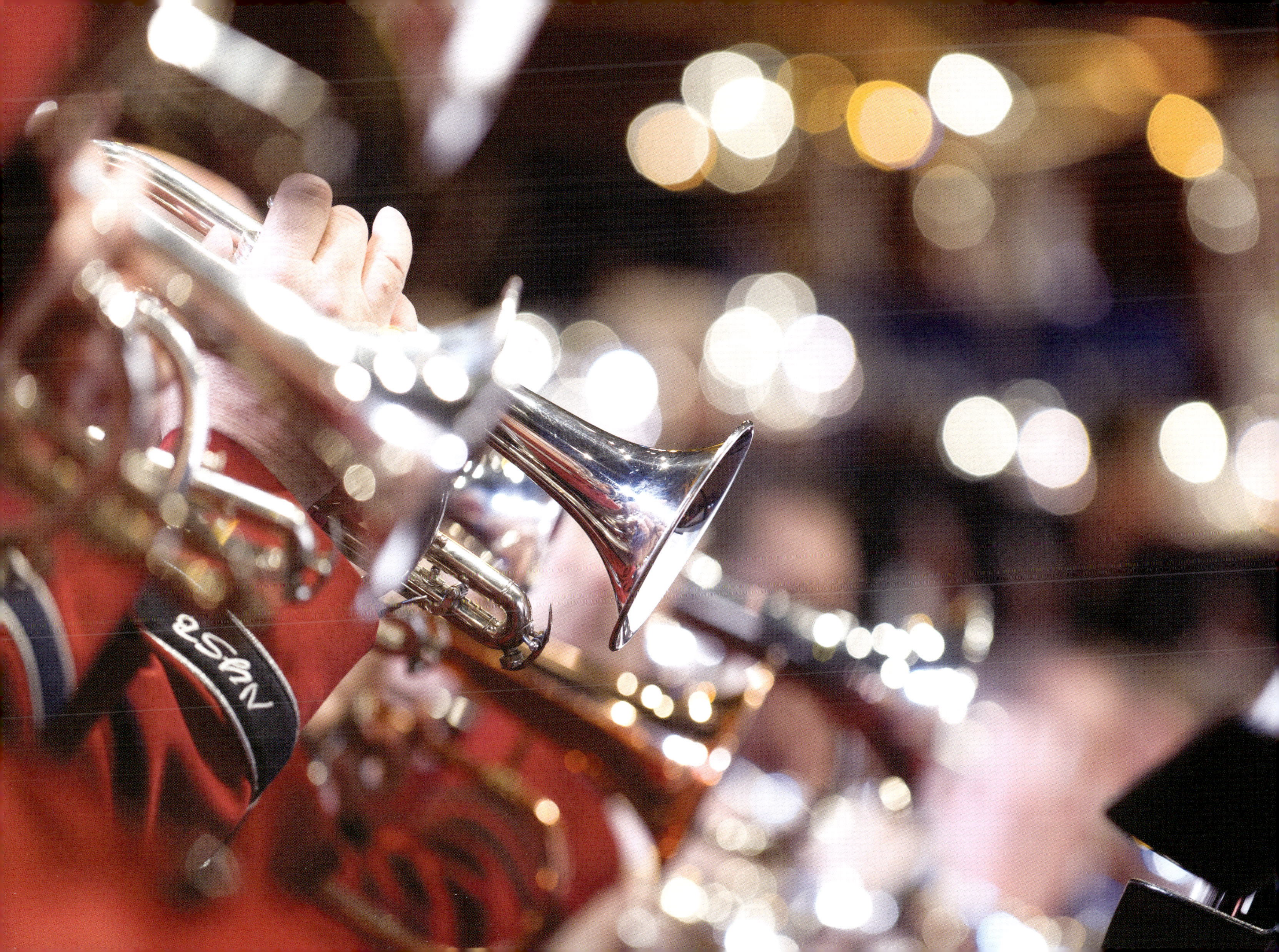

International Staff Bandmaster Stephen Cobb introducing the audience to former ISB members

Band Vocal *My Simple Prayer* (Music: Paul Lovatt-Cooper, Words: Rob Little arr. Kenneth Downie)

24

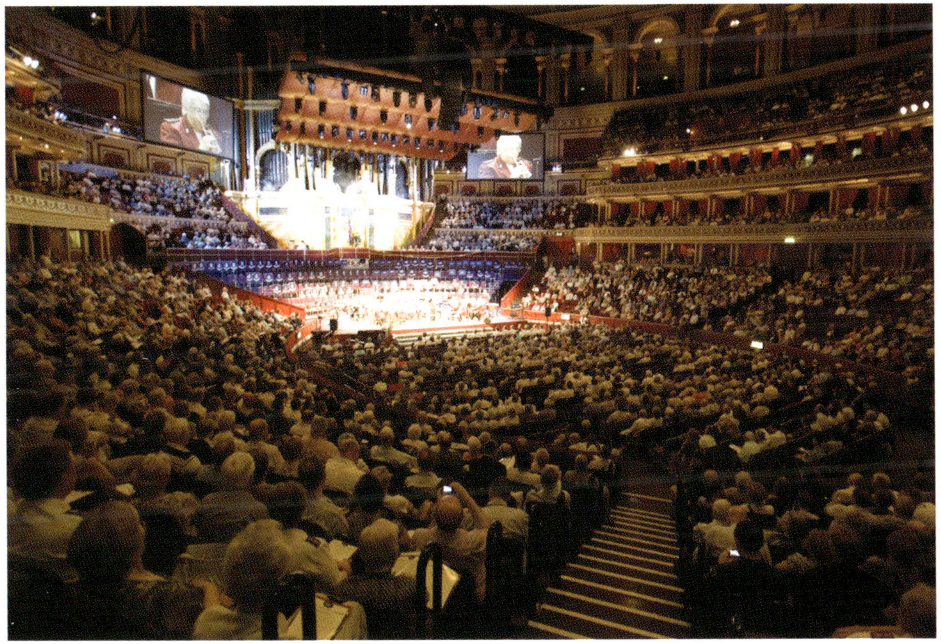

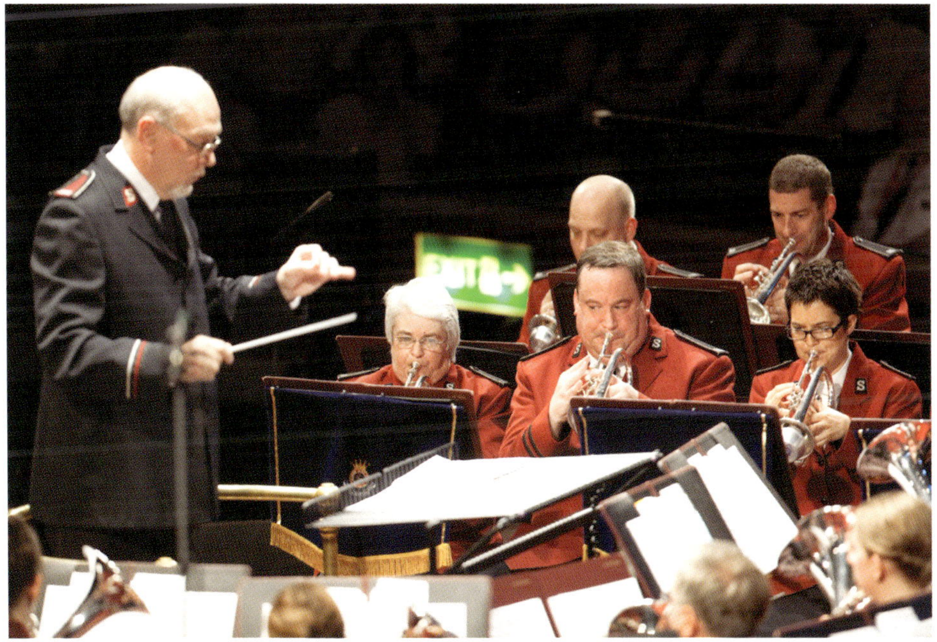

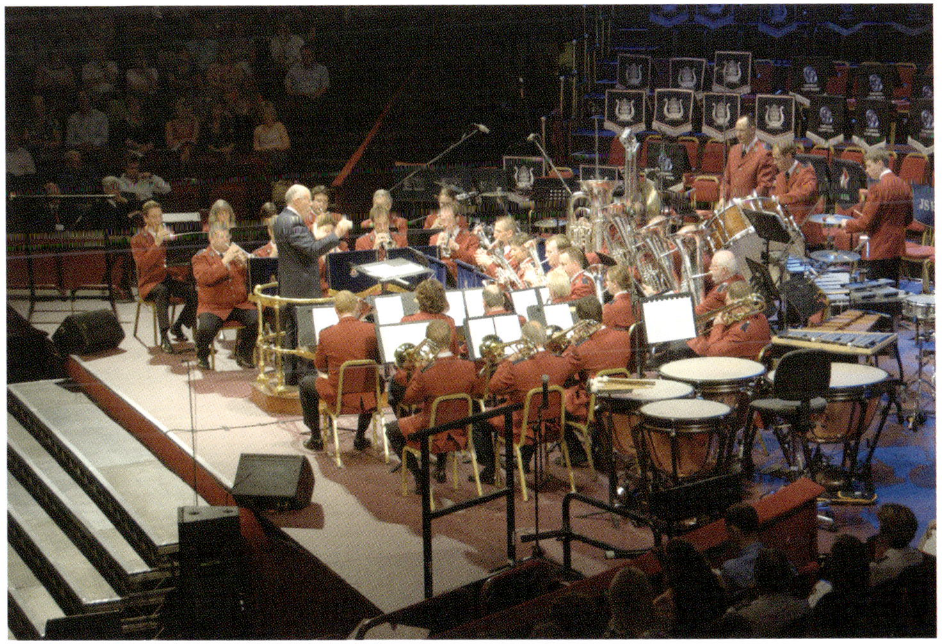

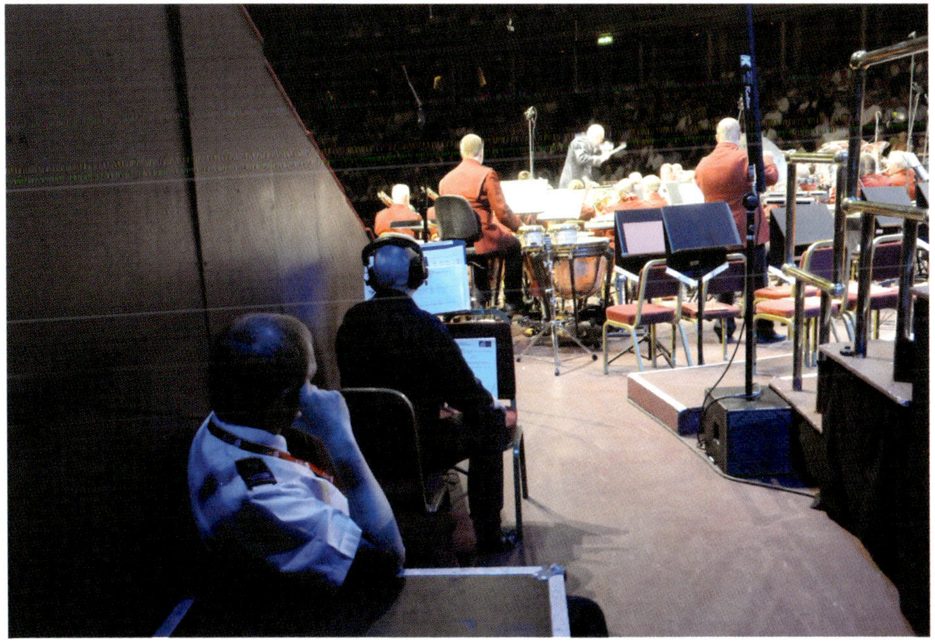

26

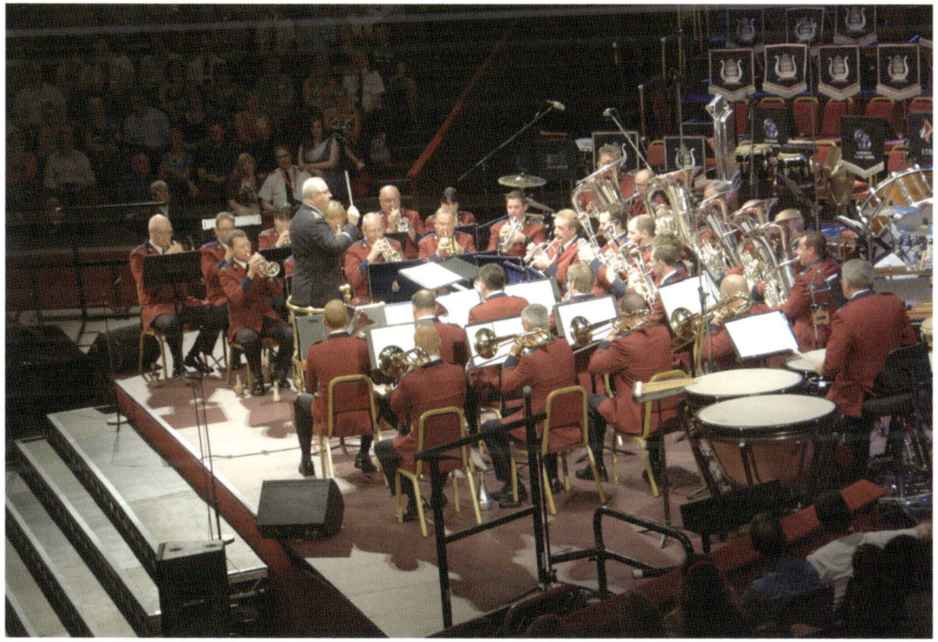
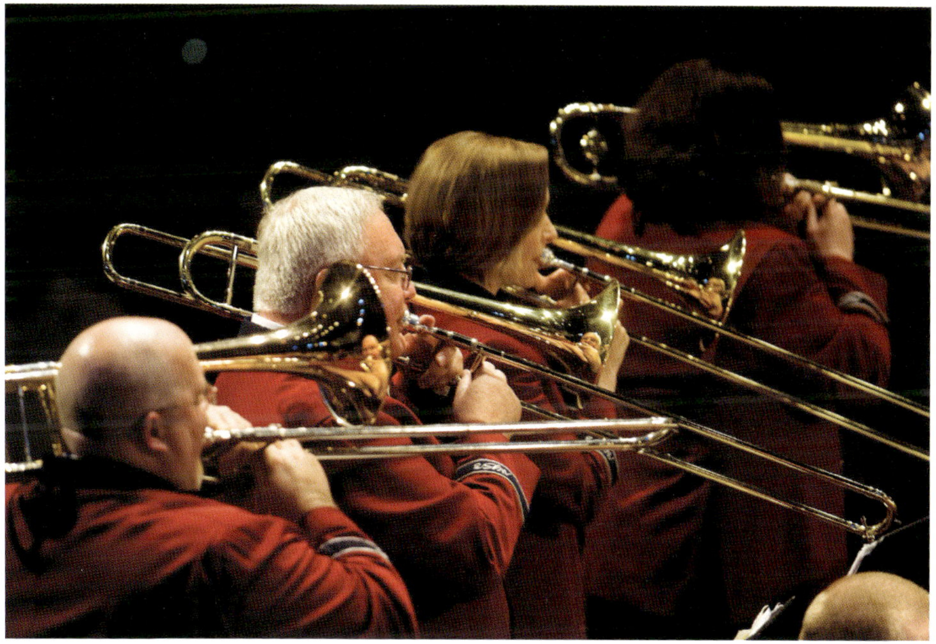
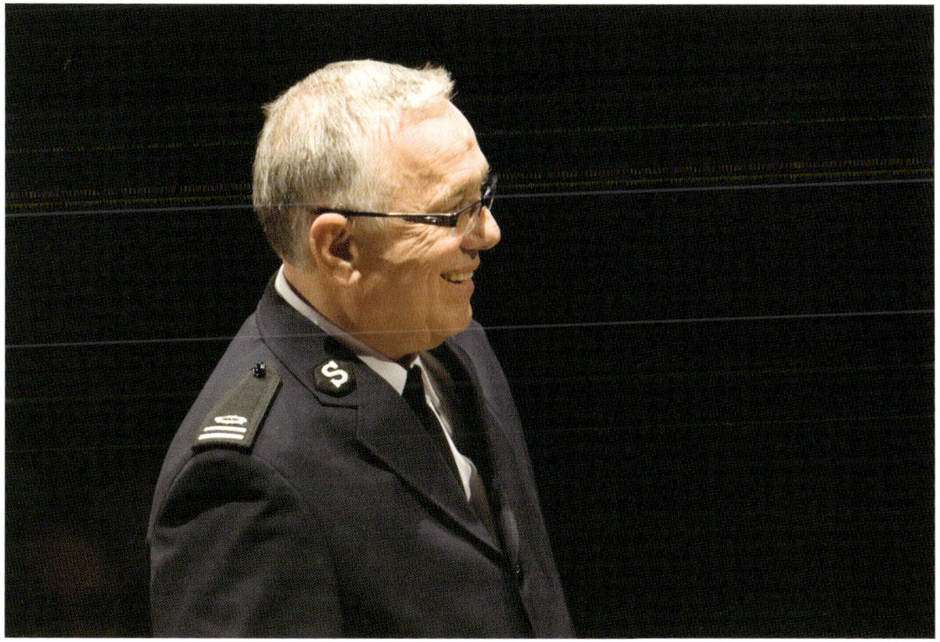
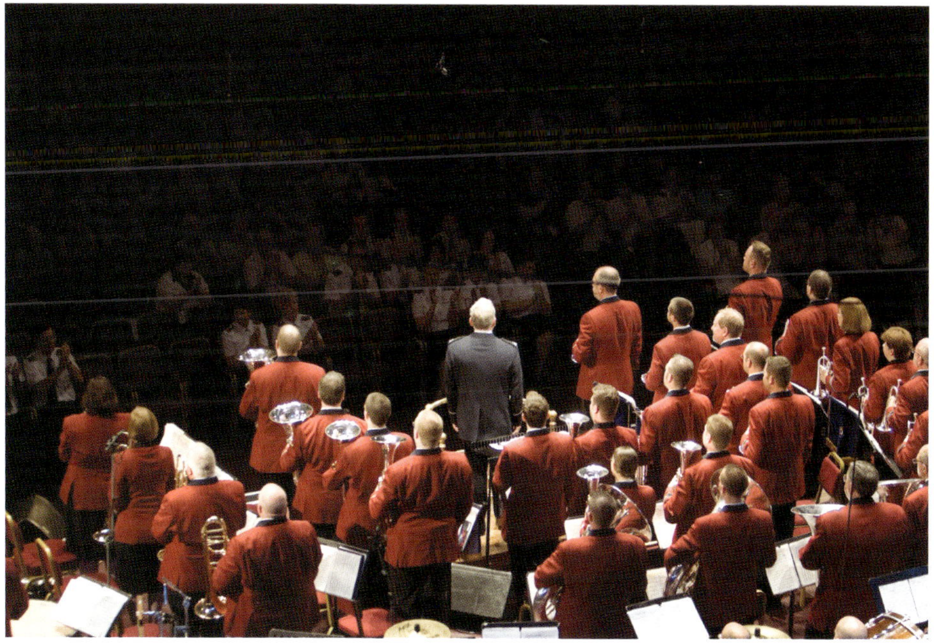

The massed bands of The International Staff Band and
New York Staff Band conducted by Bandmaster Ron Waiksnoris

AUDIENCE PERSPECTIVE
Philip Biggs

It was a balmy early June afternoon when I set off from Vienna Airport to travel to London for The International Staff Band's 120-year celebrations. I was leaving Austria and a fantastic brass festival which had featured James Morrison, Jens Lindemann and Mnozil Brass, but I firmly believed that ISB120 was a very special festival that could not be missed. It was to be a momentous celebration of the ISB's glorious history! The Friday curtain-raiser would feature two of my favourite bands, The International Staff Band and New York Staff Band, and my excitement really started to gather as I arrived at Gatwick Airport and headed for Victoria Station. Time wasn't on my side as I hailed a taxi to Sloane Square. It was less than half an hour before curtain-up, and the streets of London were busy. As my cab approached Cadogan Hall, I could see a huge queue, or should I say line, snaking around the corner from the hall entrance, all in shirtsleeve order.

Having collected my ticket, thanks to the ubiquitous Malcolm Quinn, I was quickly inside the hall and, looking around, it was like a who's who of SA banding from all four corners of the world. There were good friends such as Ron Holz and Carole Dawn Rheinhart from the USA and Germany respectively. Also in this huge turnout I spotted Derek Smith, Brian Bowen and Deryck Diffey and, closer to home, legends such as Roland Cobb, James Williams and George Whittingham.

The atmosphere was electric; a great feeling of anticipation hung in the hall as Bandmasters Stephen Cobb and Ronald Waiksnoris led their bands out and the evening was under way - and what an evening it turned out to be. The first half saw each band perform alternate works. The programme had obviously been carefully chosen as the balance was just right and the ISB's euphonium virtuoso, Derick Kane featured Norman Bearcroft's *The Better World*, which Derick had premièred over 30 years earlier at an International Congress. Derick brought the house down, as he has done on literally hundreds of occasions. The second half saw the ISB and NYSB play massed and *Symphony of Thanksgiving* (Dean Goffin), *The Cleansing Power* (Stephen Bulla) and *The Invincible Army* (Erik Leidzén) were the works that stayed in the mind of this writer. There were three 'guest' conducting appearances from Derek Smith and Brian Bowen, and with Peter Graham's *Shine as the Light* featured as the finale, this was the perfect way to conclude a great evening and set things up for the big day across London at the Royal Albert Hall.

After just a few hours sleep, I was London bound to attend what promised to be a day to remember, and it turned out even better than my expectations. Eight Staff Bands from across the world were assembled: New York, Canada, Germany, Chicago, Amsterdam, Japan, Melbourne and of course The International Staff Band of The Salvation Army, whose birthday the other bands and thousands of visitors to London were celebrating. The day was in two distinct parts with each staff band giving a 20 minute 'solo' programme showing off their unique style and musical performance. Special mention should be made of Trevor Caffull who was the expert 'link man'. The afternoon section was flawless and quite riveting as each band came and went, and the capacity audience, as well as myself, just loved what was served up.

The Evening Gala Spectacular saw the seven visiting Staff Bands sitting in massed formation with The International Staff Band seated on the platform as solo band. Add to this The International Staff Songsters and a mouthwatering evening was in prospect. The Massed Bands opened the evening with *Fanfare, Prelude and Fugue on Sine Nomine* by Peter Graham and then Bandmaster Stephen Cobb moved from the podium and walked around the Royal Albert Hall's arena to welcome one and all. This I found to be such a refreshing way to communicate with over 5,000 people and one particularly poignant moment occurred when Stephen stopped to acknowledge the presence of former members of the ISB - the spotlights shone onto the stars of previous years as they proudly stood for the generous and justifiable ovation they received.

The evening just flew by. The ISB's programme included Kenneth Downie's *King of Heaven* and Derick Kane was once again in the soloist's spotlight when he premièred *Scottish Folk Variants* by Stephen Bulla, whilst the massed bands performed *Dancebeat* by ISB solo cornet player Paul Sharman. The International Staff Songsters sang the Ray Bowes setting of *Jesus Loves Me* and the congregation sang *Stand Up and Bless the Lord* - a most stirring experience when sung by well over 5,000 voices in this vast historic auditorium. After the massed bands' performance of Leslie Condon's *The Call of the Righteous*, conducted by Ronald Waiksnoris, the evening finished in spectacular style with an indoor firework display at the conclusion of the march *Celebration*.

I left the Royal Albert Hall that Saturday evening knowing I had 'been there' at one of the most spectacular brass band events ever to take place and one that is unlikely to be repeated in my lifetime.

Rock of Ages (arr. William Bearchell) conducted by Dorothy Gates

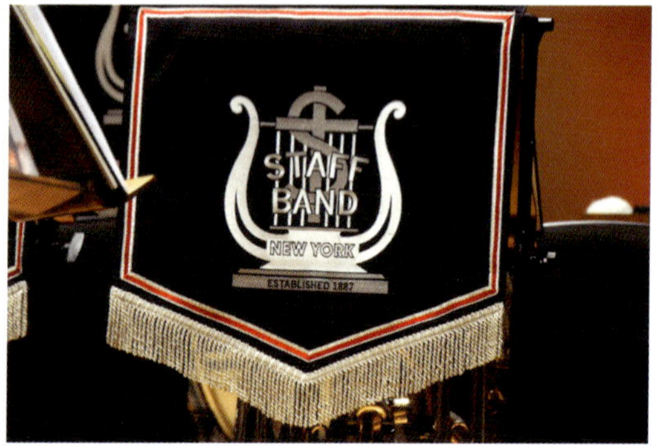
STAFF
BAND
NEW YORK
ESTABLISHED 1887

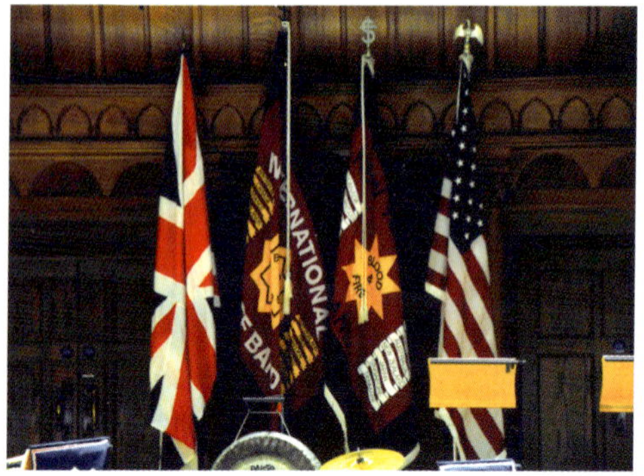

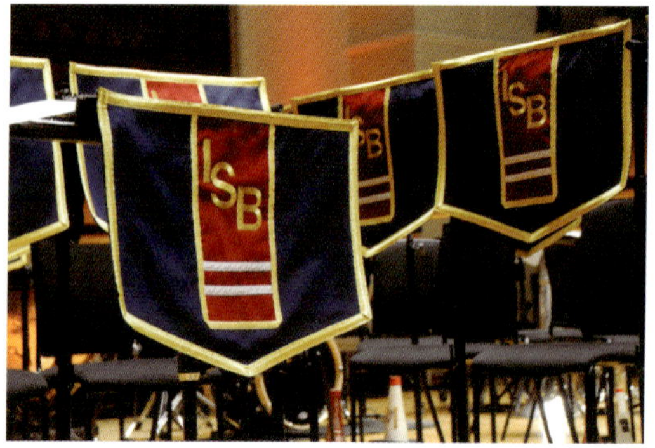
ISB

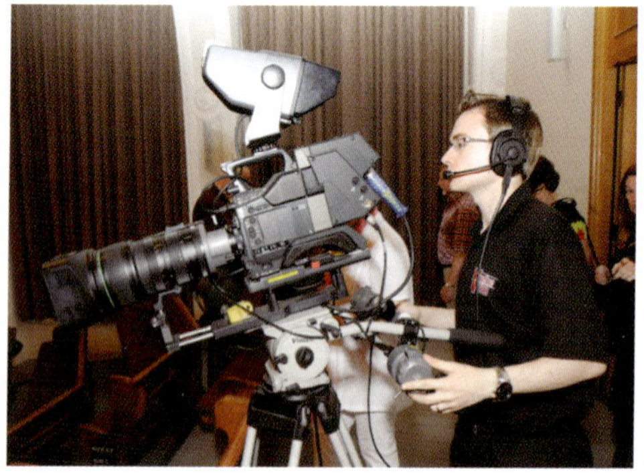

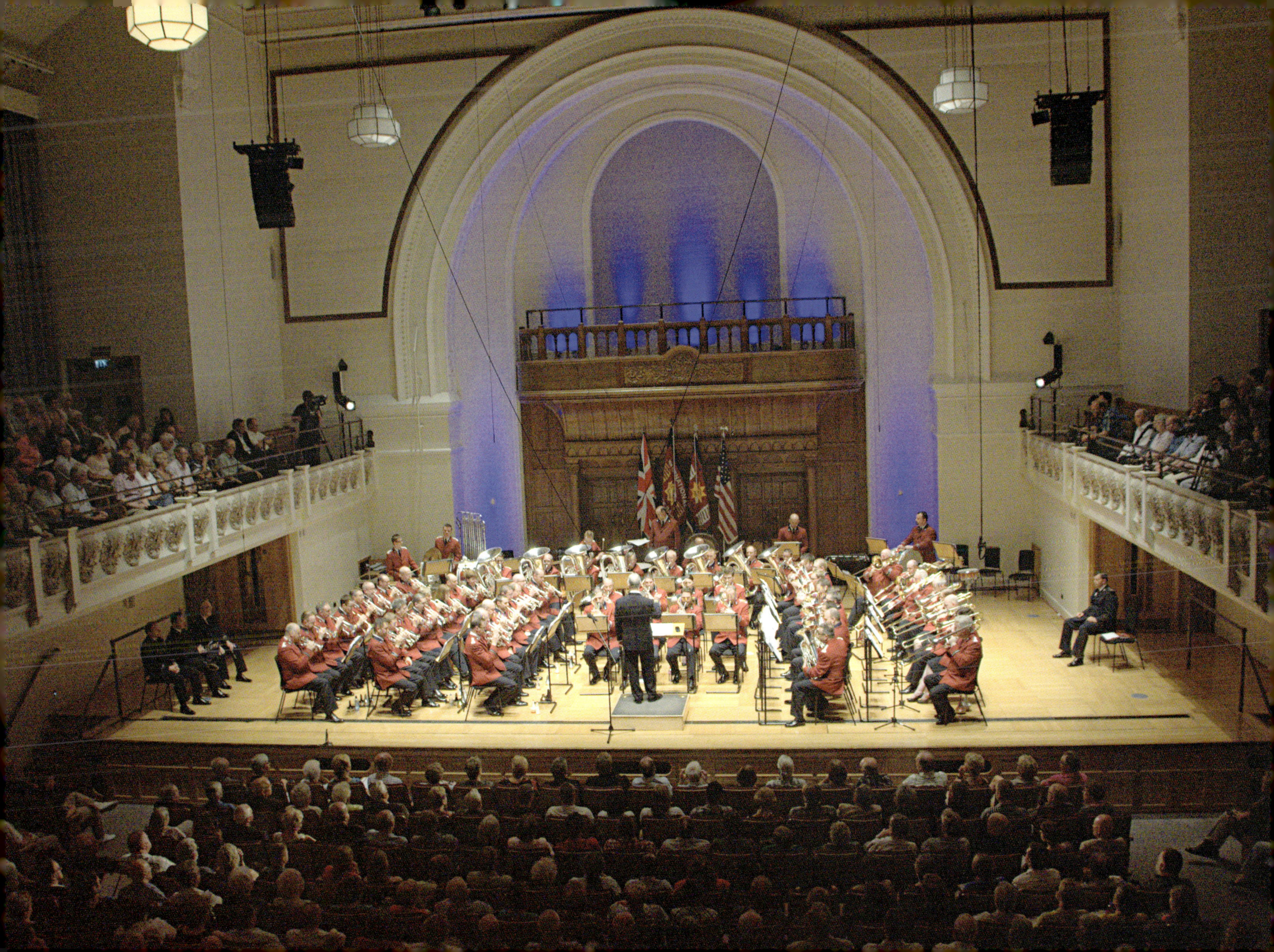

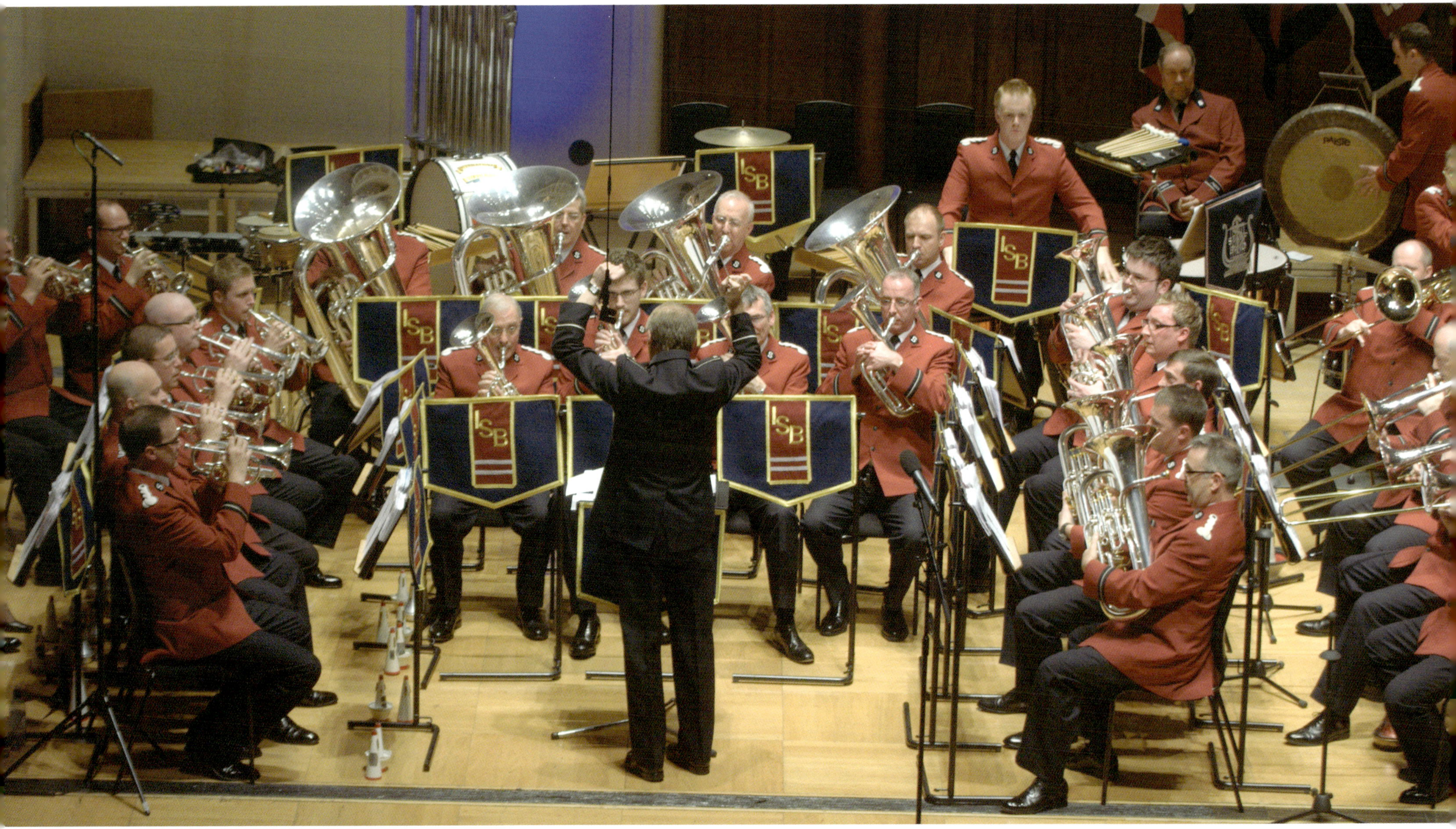
ISB

ISB soloists Derick Kane and Richard Woodrow

New York Staff Band 'star' percussionist Bob Jones

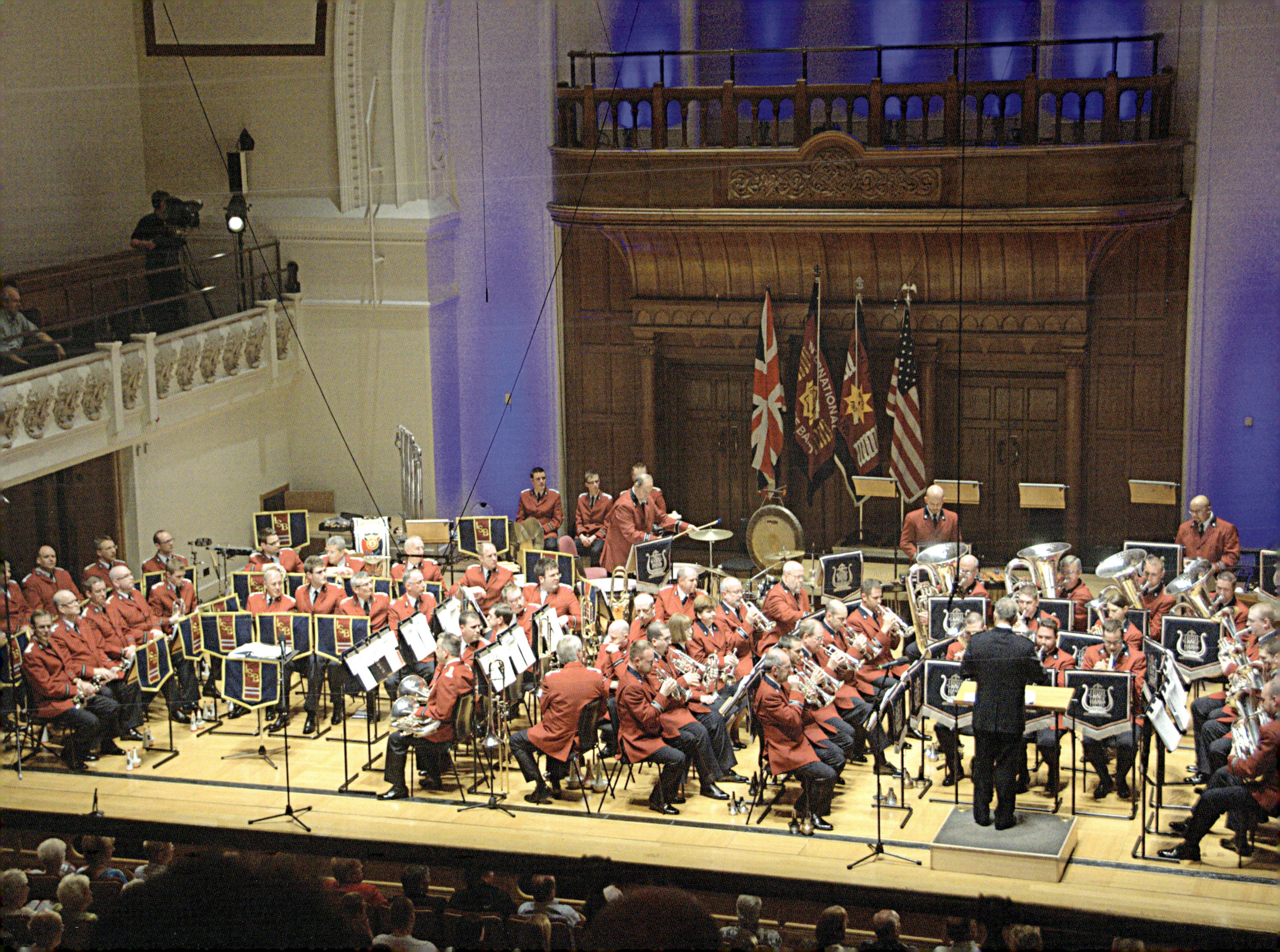

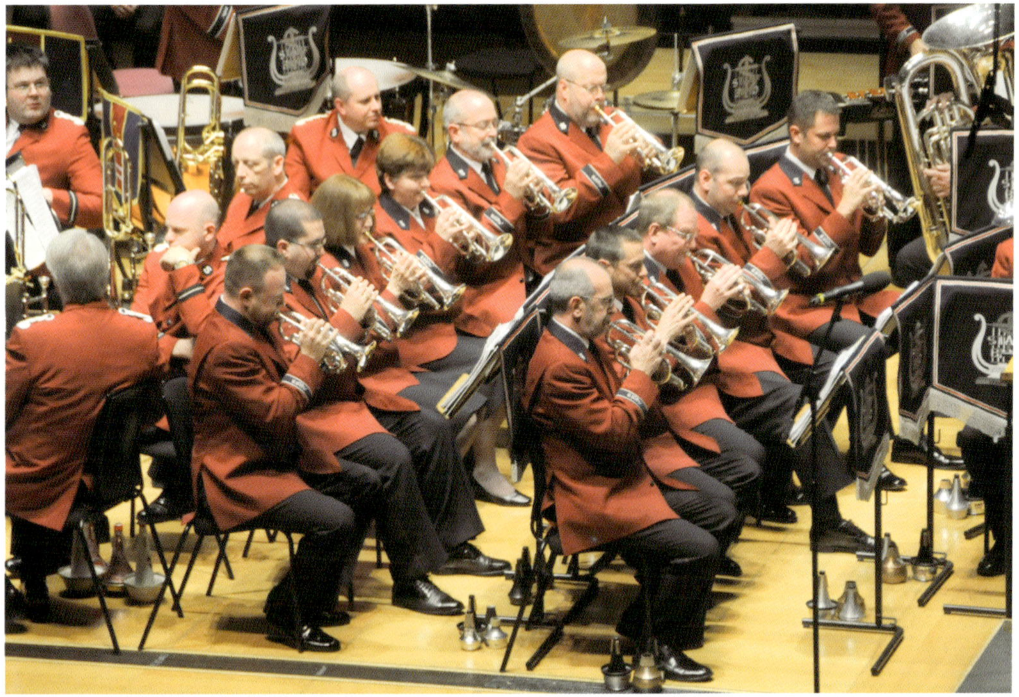

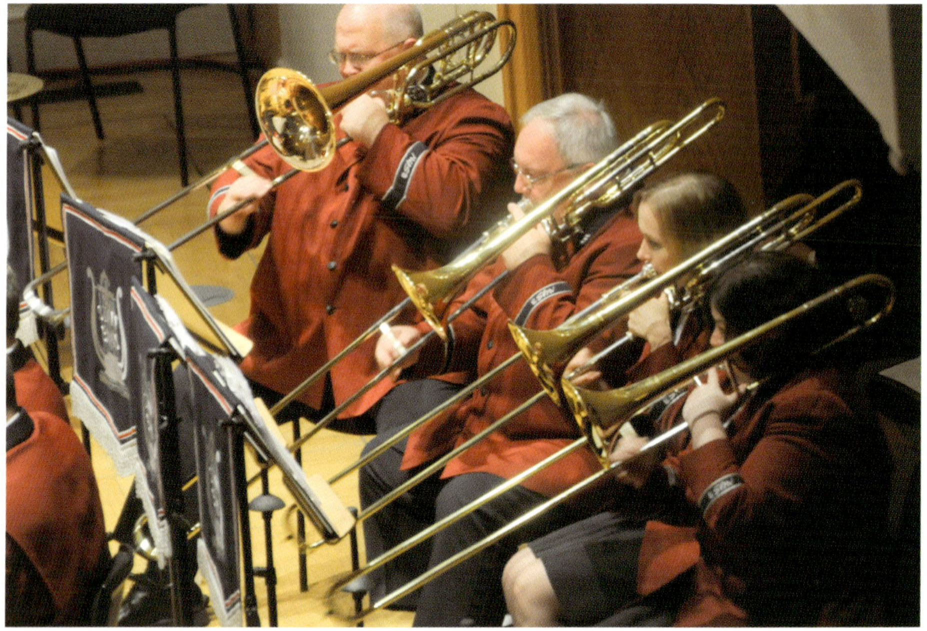

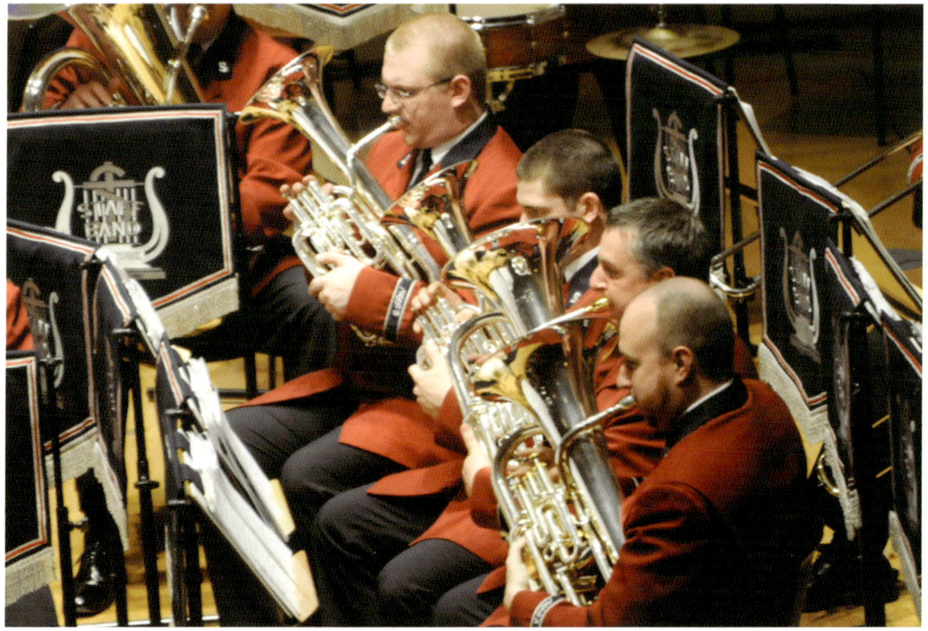

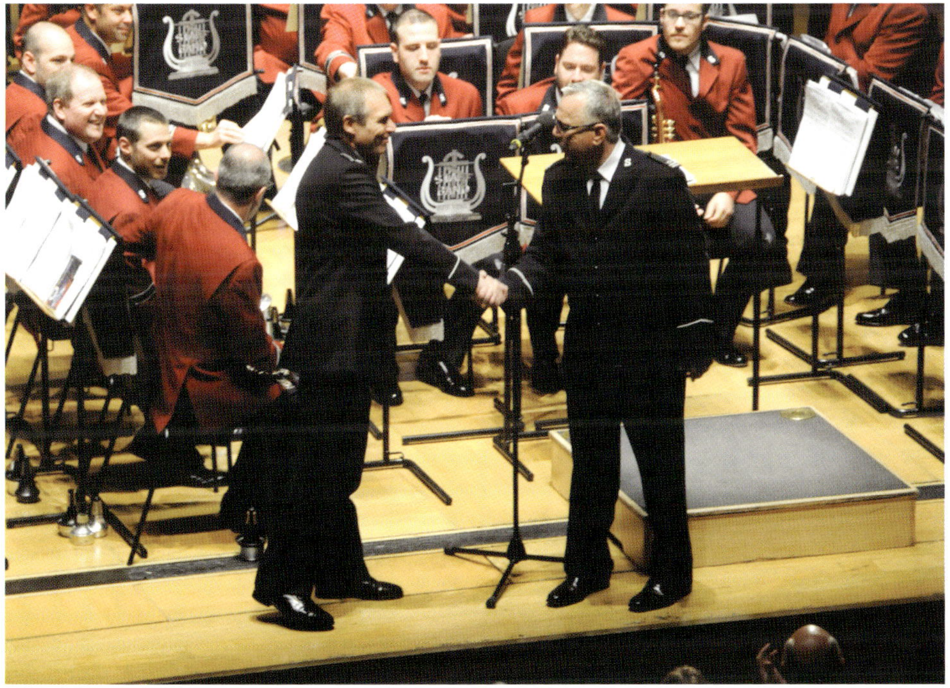

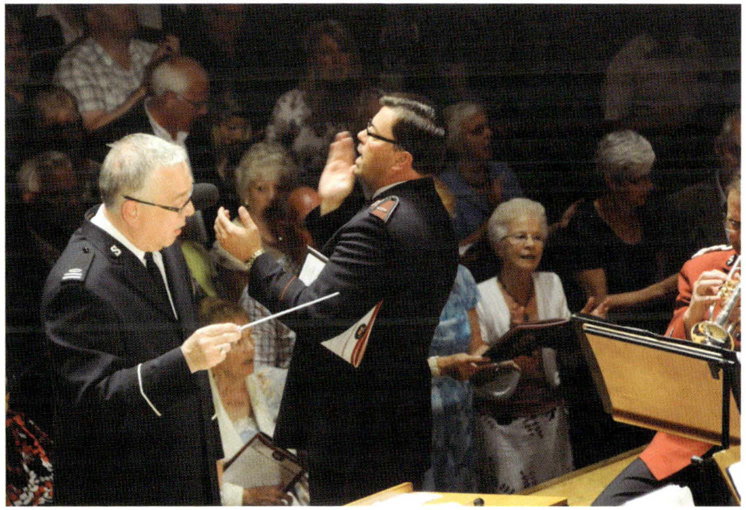

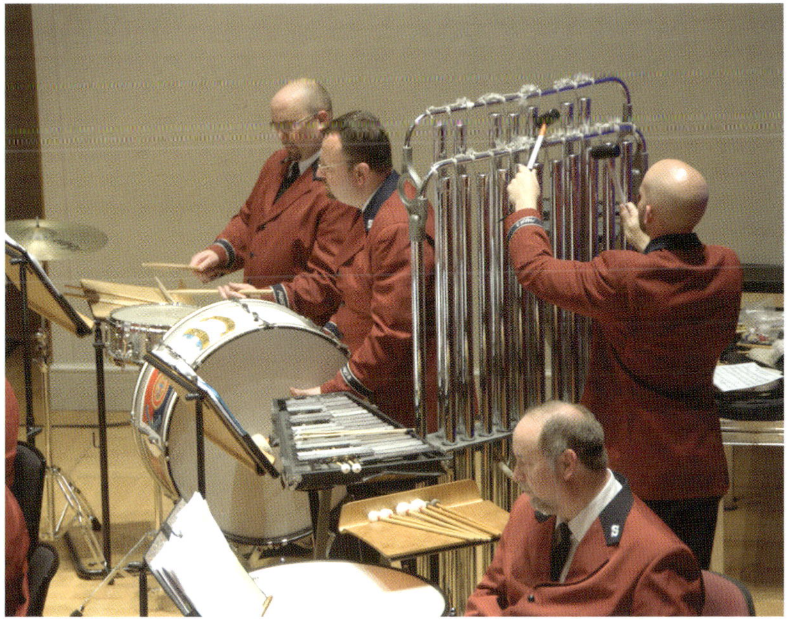

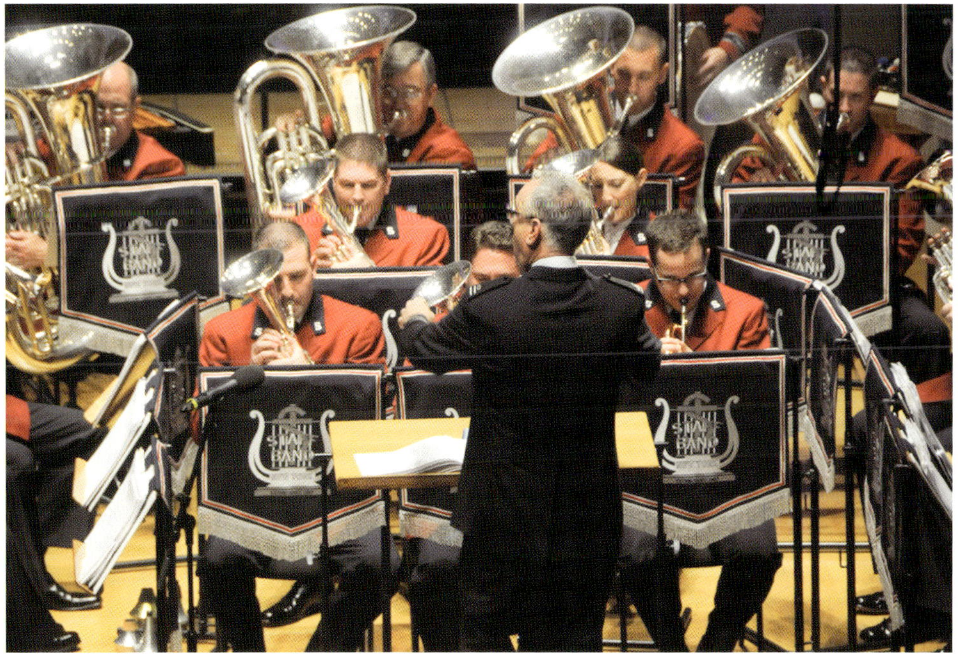

Clockwise from top: Guest conductors Derek Smith, Brian Bowen and Peter Graham

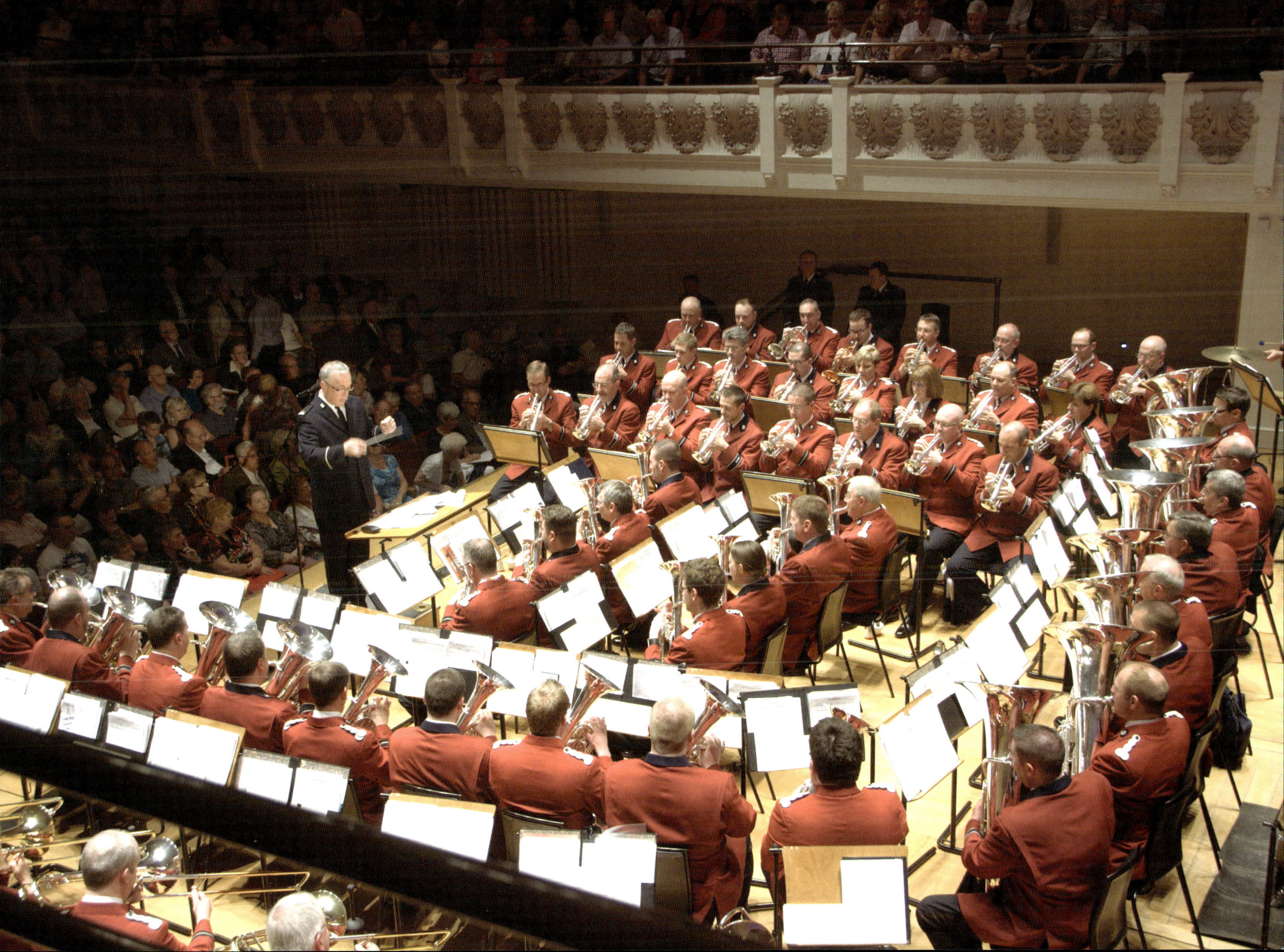

SA International leadership enjoying Saturday Evening *Brass Spectacular*

UK TERRITORIAL LEADERSHIP
Commissioner Betty Matear

Fire in the Blood seems to sum up all that we were about for ISB120. For me it was a weekend to anticipate from the discussions and plans many months before. It was a big idea that I have no doubt had the smile of approval from God. Hindsight confirms this event to be a marker for the Salvationist world.

Music covered the miles around the country as each of the eight Staff Bands ministered to thousands of people, in capacity audiences, before London opened its doors to even more thousands of Salvationists.

> While the event lasted for a few hours, there are still yet many outcomes because of it and this was the intent. I thank God that there are those who have reconnected and found again spiritual purpose and relationship with God... Fire in the blood is good for us, not only in the large gatherings but in the local context.

Salvationists love to be together. Music is in our hearts. Salvation is our song and when these come together the whole thing rings! I was thrilled to be in the street throng at Cadogan Hall and to meet friends and family from the USA, Australia and the UK, all united for a brief time. The music went beyond performance to dedication of talent and inspiration. There was too the immediacy of humour and camaraderie bound up in love and fellowship. From generation to generation there was a unity and harmony of spirits. It would be no understatement to liken this to the believers being together in one place and the Spirit came. God blessed us.

The coming together at the magnificent Royal Albert Hall, described by an American ticket holder as 'The Royal Albert Citadel', was not far off the mark. The hours of music did not seem like the marathon I thought it might be and that seemed to be shared by the rest of those in the auditorium.

Each band played to their strengths. Of course the welcome given to the Japan Staff Band, minutes of sustained applause, that reduced me and their cornet section to tears, is ever in the memory. We stood together identifying with the pain of a nation devastated by the earthquake. There was no sense of competitiveness, just everyone doing their utmost to give their best, a metaphor for our lives it seemed to me.

Sunday at Central Hall, Westminster was a spiritual season which undergirded all that music ministry must be. Music leaders filled the auditorium and participated in a wonderful morning of worship and praise. The climax for me was the singing of *Eternal God*, conducted by Lt. Col. Norman Bearcroft.

I had little inkling of the crowds of flag waving Salvationists packing into The Mall to cheer the Bands as they marched to Buckingham Palace where we stood to receive them. The light rain could not dampen the spirits of a people raised up to march and witness in the open air. The real impact of the day was to see the photographs of the throngs moving up the Mall. I wondered what the regular tourist must be thinking? The Army has come to town! We had fire in the blood.

While the event lasted for a few hours, there are still yet many outcomes because of it and this was the intent. I thank God that there are those who have reconnected and found again spiritual purpose and relationship with God. Young people have seen the potential and worth of this ministry and commitment, for this time. Fire in the blood is good for us, not only in the large gatherings but in the local context.

Beyond all that ISB120 has reached into the lives and communities of folk who never attended the London event. With all costs found the substantial surplus, as intended, was lovingly handed over to the emerging work and mission in Burkina Faso. The fire burns in our hearts.

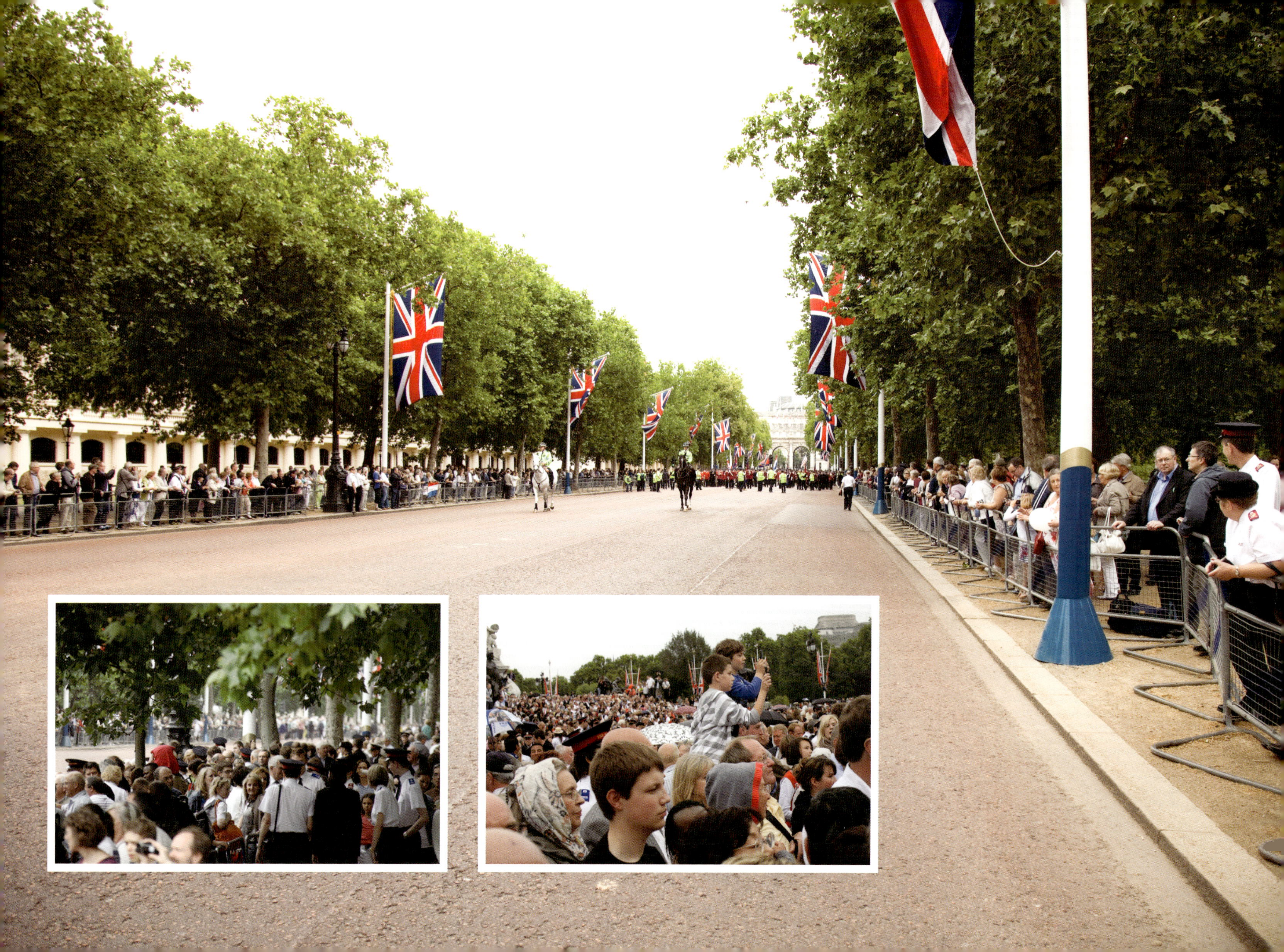

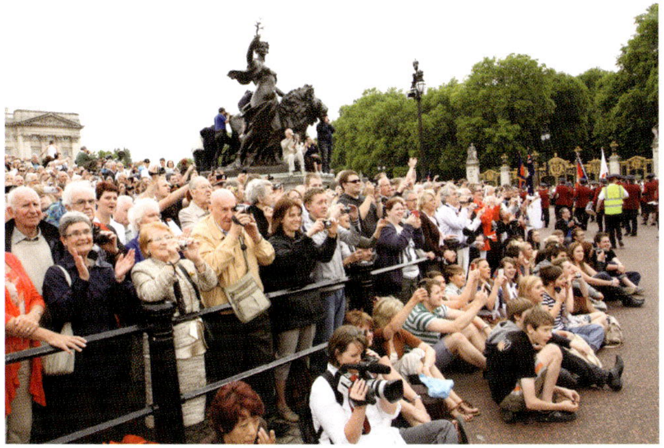
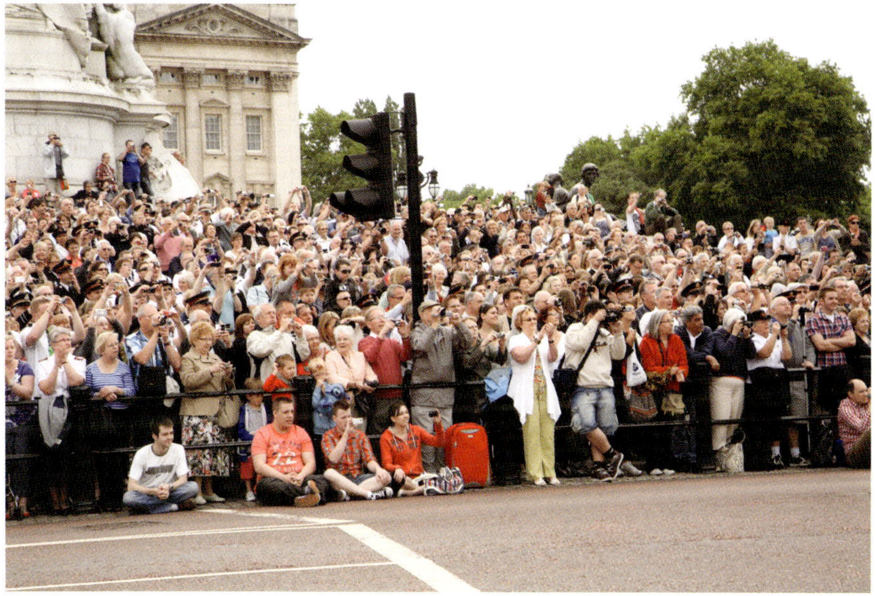
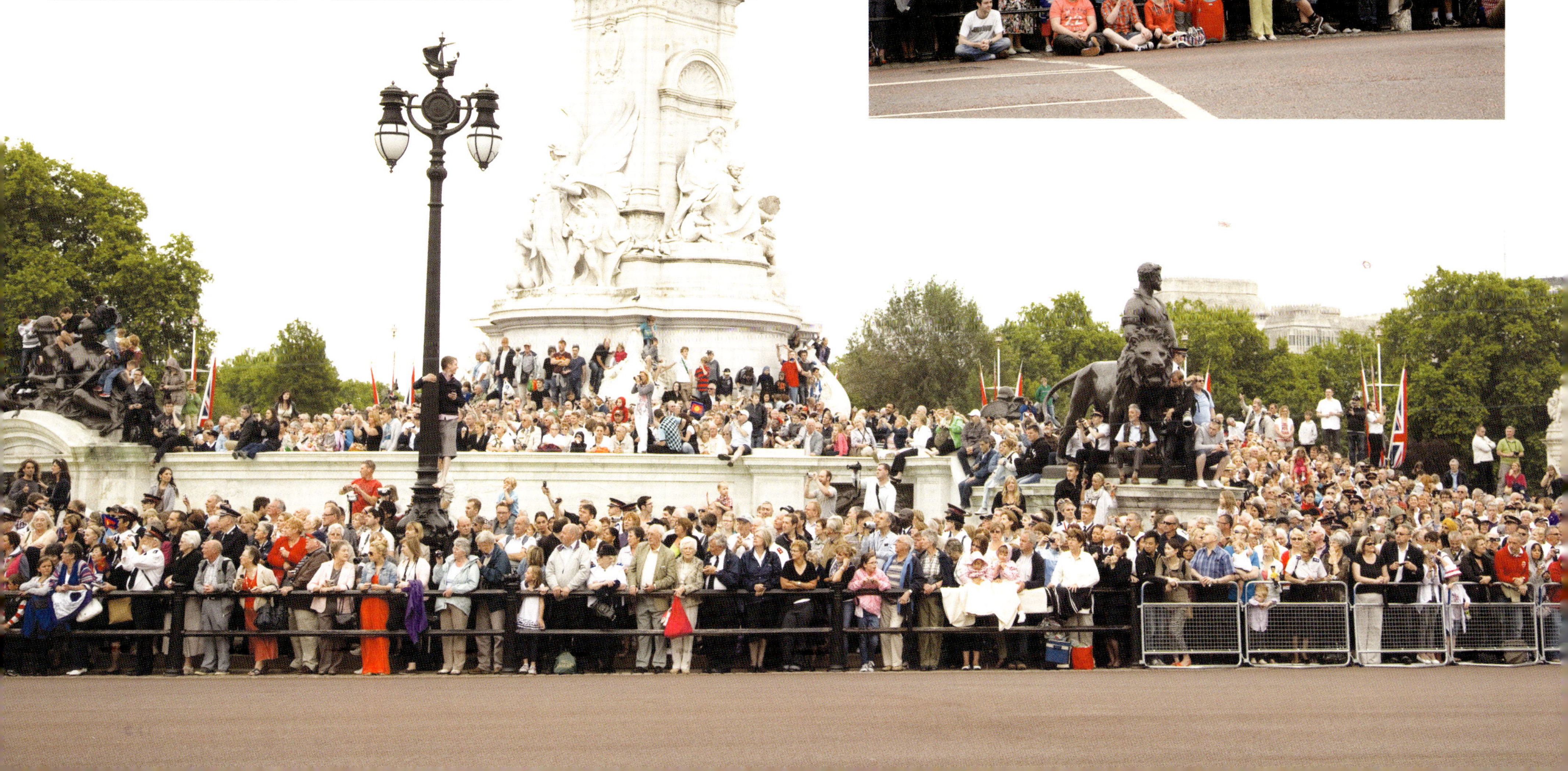

Friends and families enjoy the day!

Mrs Lt. Col. Florence Drury, now 100 years old, waving to the bands

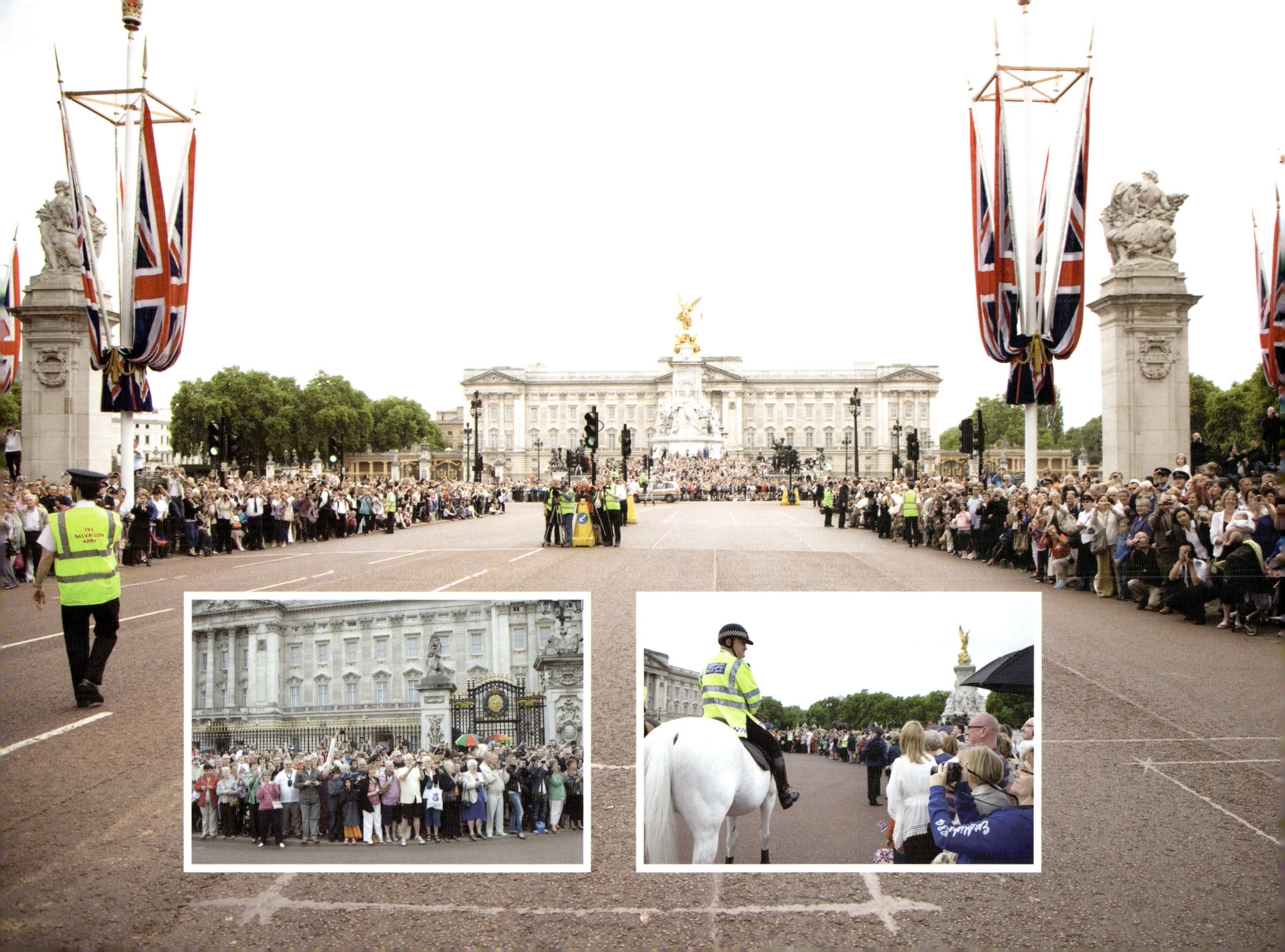
THE SALVATION ARMY

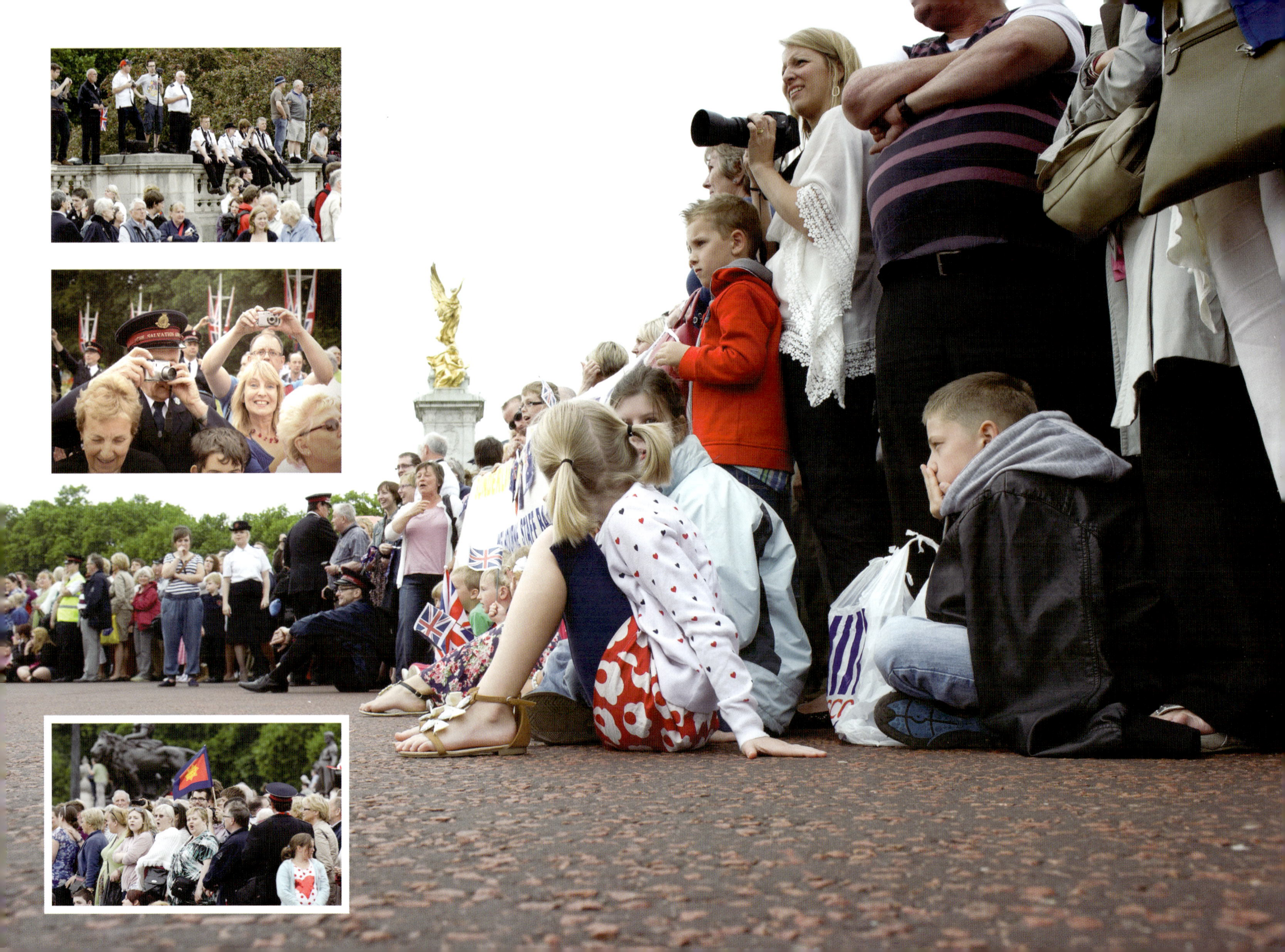

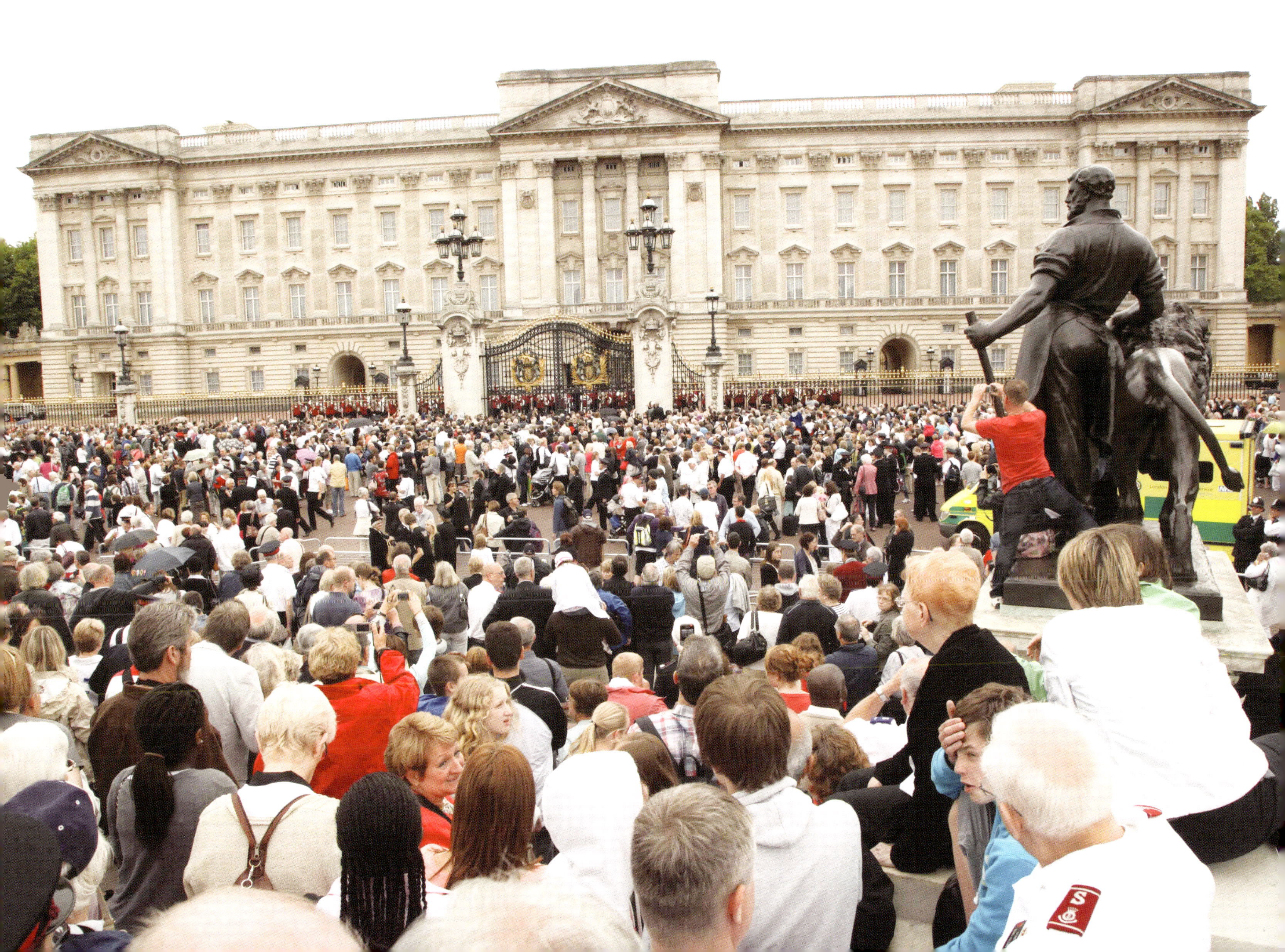

From left to right: Commissioner Sue Swanson, Commissioner Barry Swanson, General Linda Bond, Commissioner John Matear, Colonel Brian Peddle, Commissioner Betty Matear and Colonel Rosalie Peddle

Enjoying the massed bands' concert in the Buckingham Palace Forecourt

Salvation Army senior leadership joined by members of The Royal Household, Austin Burn, Lt. Col. Charles Richards (Deputy Master of The Household and Equerry to The Queen) and Ray Wheaton

The General waves to the crowd outside Buckingham Palace

The Salvation Army's international leadership with the eight Staff Bandmasters

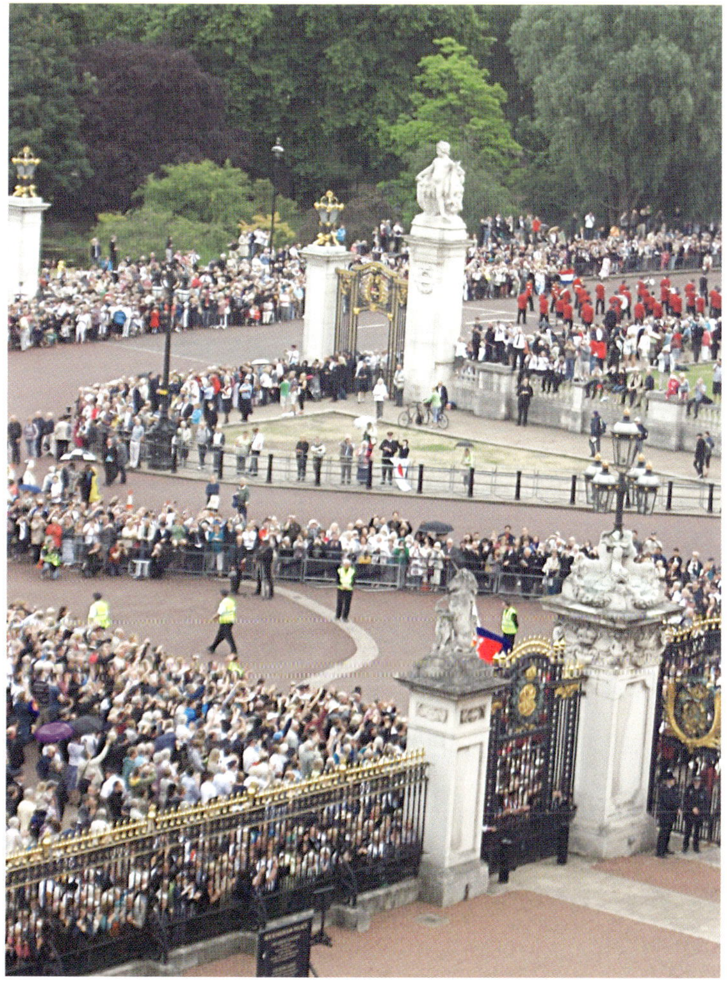

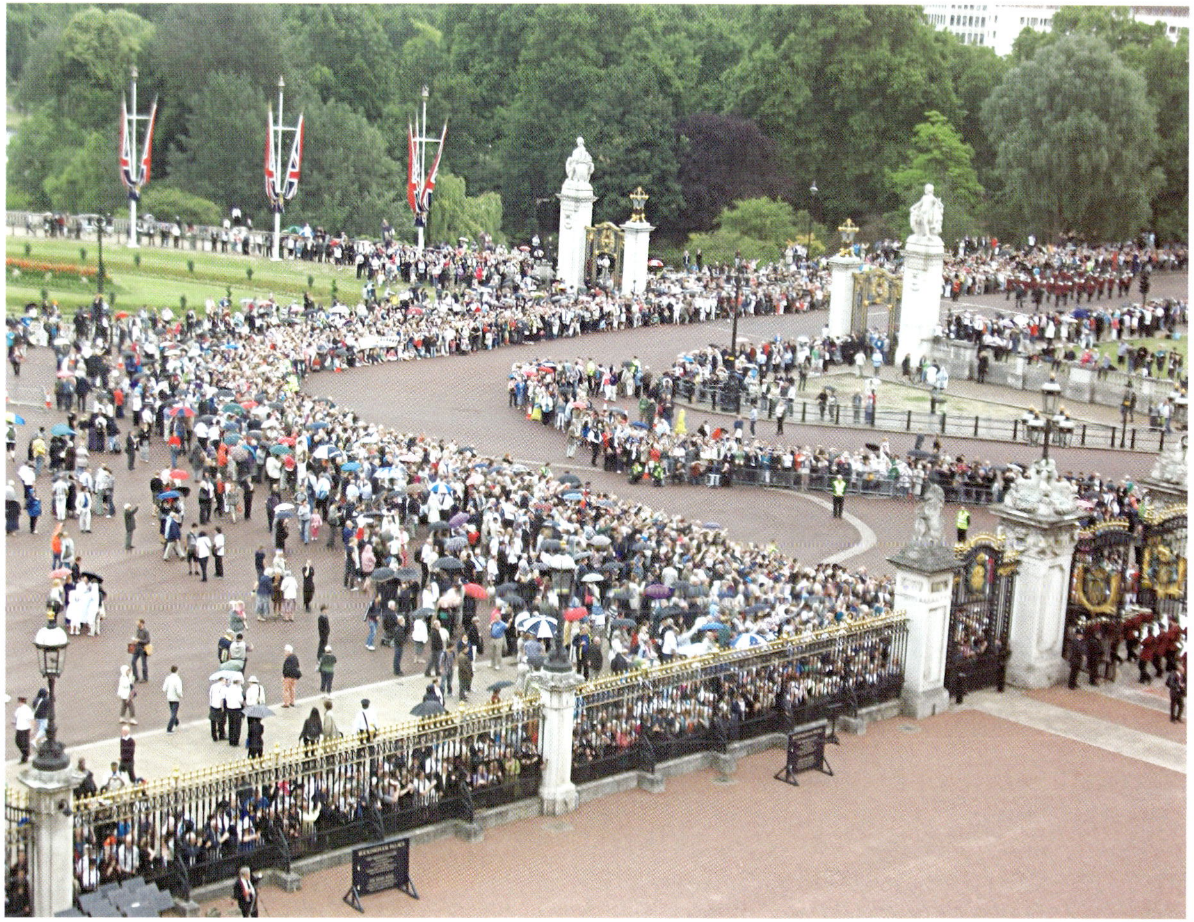

54

55

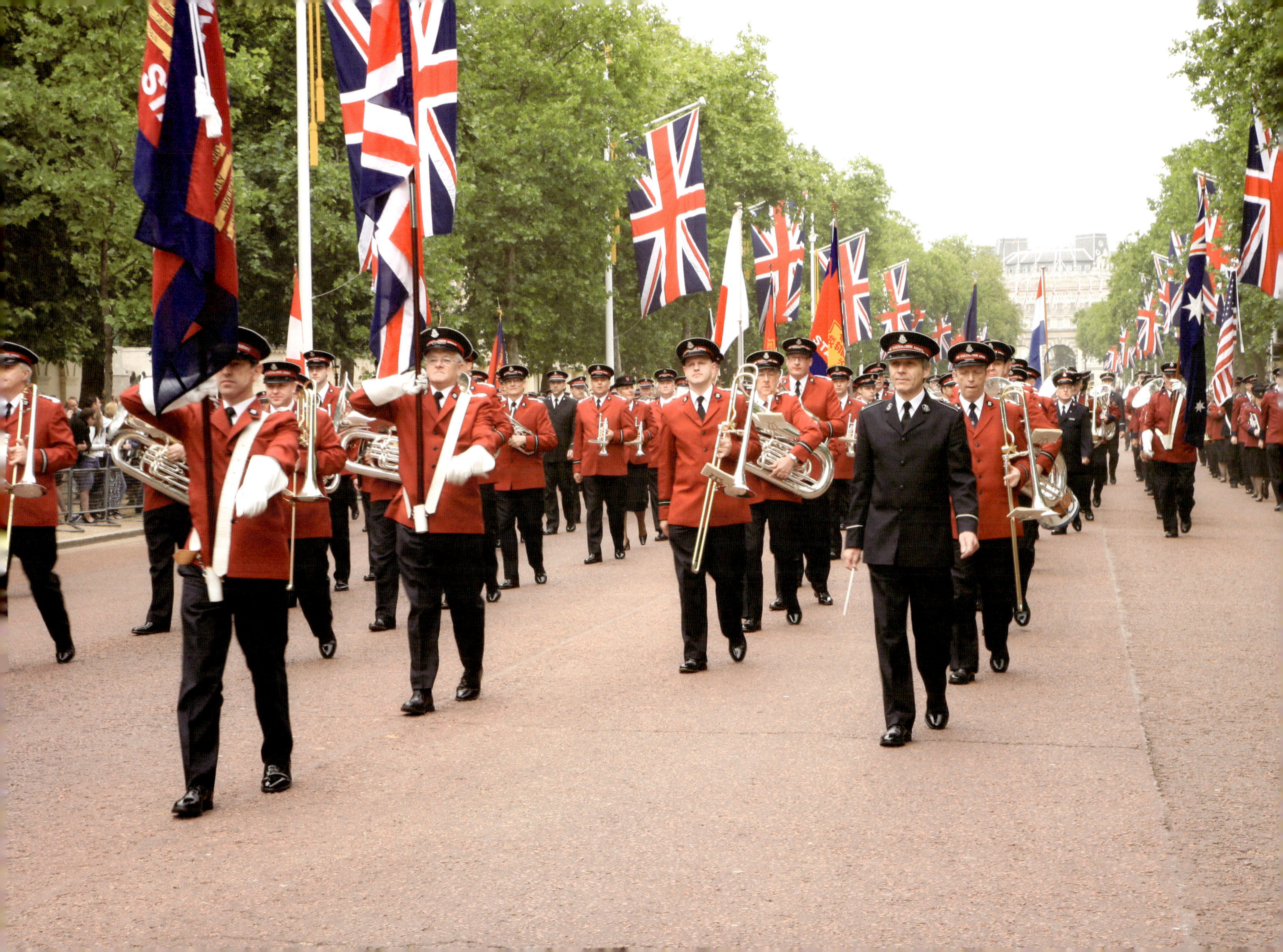

Bands waiting to be 'marched' into Buckingham Palace accompanied by The International Staff Band

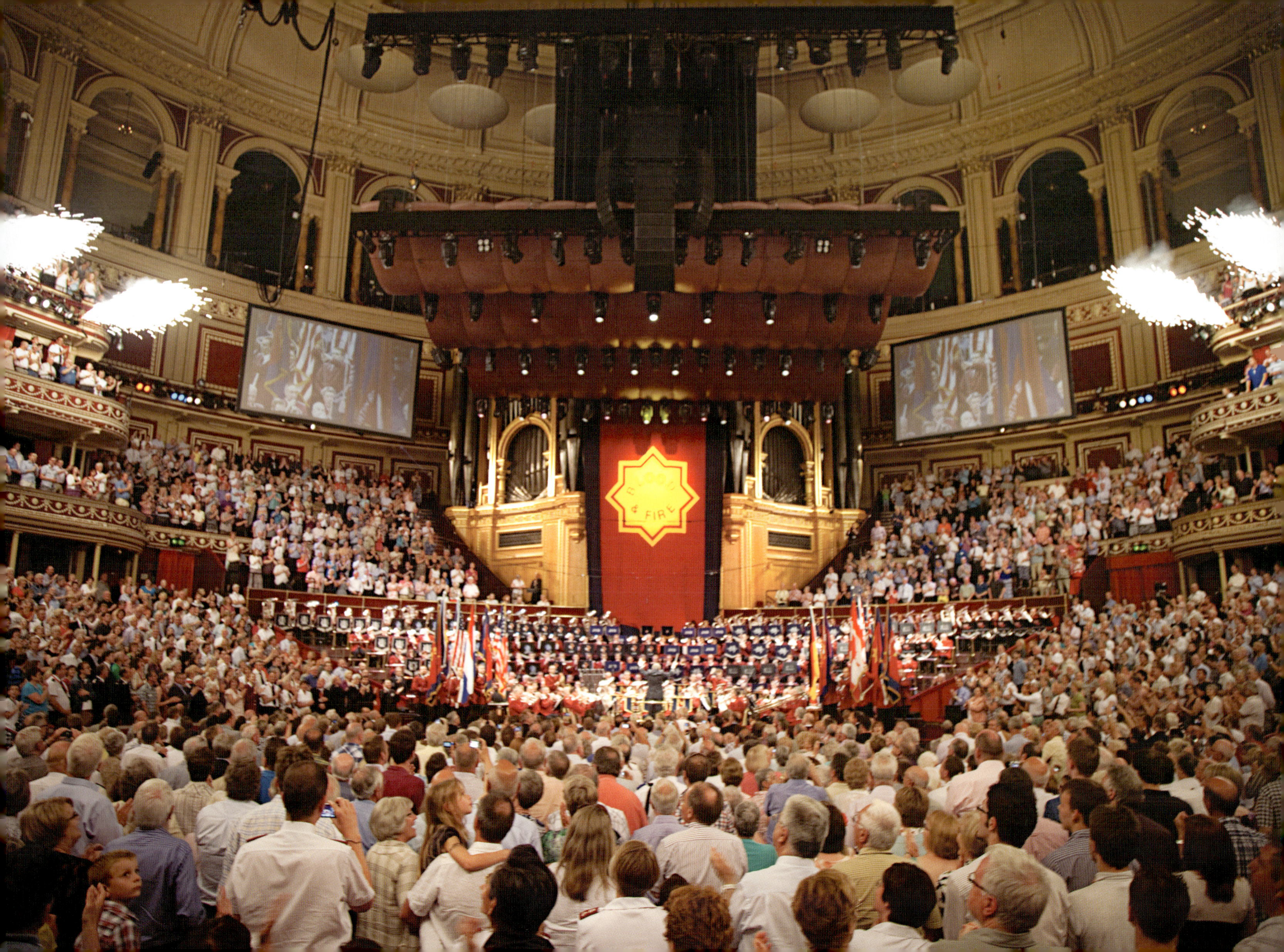
& FIRE

OVERSEAS GUEST
Dr. Ronald Holz

Over a year later, and after writing multiple pieces for and about ISB120, what else can I share?

First, I would emphasize that throughout the weekend I felt I was not only a part of something highly significant and remarkable in Salvation Army and brass band history, but that I was participating in a heightened experience of worship and thanksgiving. Beyond the gathering of friends, the buzz and excitement, the packed halls and the superbly organised concerts, I knew I was taking part in high praise for what God has wrought through the medium of SA brass bands and, in particular, the ISB.

> ...in the midst of challenging, brilliant sounds, exhilarating celebration, even dazzling fireworks, the organisers of the beautifully run event kept us focused on the purpose, the mission of SA bands - praising God and proclaiming the Gospel. That made all the difference to me, and I felt privileged to be a part of it all.

As a result, I found myself taking off the critic's hat, the music historian's scrutiny, and letting my heart and mind respond openly on different levels. I was spiritually nurtured and renewed, and I have a suspicion that happened to a lot of us hardened brass band enthusiasts.

Not that I did not revel in the technical and musical artistry of these bands, nor keep the critical faculties at bay for the entire time I heard the bands in Cadogan Hall and the Royal Albert Hall - and I listened to every note! As one who just days before had served as an adjudicator at a British brass band contest, I did not, at first, easily make that change. Perhaps it was natural for all of us to compare and contrast the styles, skills, sounds and literature shared by the eight staff bands in such an electric atmosphere. Well before the end of the Saturday night concert I had been able to abandon that 'seat of the scornful' that brass band types easily embrace even at SA sacred festivals – reader, you know what I am talking about, and we must be honest with ourselves!

Ultimately, I came away from the weekend with several observations about why this gathering resonated so much with my spirit and my hopes for the future of SA musical ministry.

First, the naysayers, those who have been proclaiming and seeking the demise of SA bands for the past six decades, must take another look at a weekend that represented a healthy sub-culture, not just a nostalgia trip or an embracing of a glorious past slipping away. Second, as I carefully reviewed the membership of these eight bands, the majority were young players providing ample evidence that bands still attract the best and finest of our youth. Third, Dr Cobb and the ISB stressed, other bands following their lead, NEW music. They did not just offer up old chestnuts, no doubt to the chagrin of some, but, ultimately for the vibrant health of our repertoire, rightfully emphasized 'new songs unto the Lord.'

Finally, in the midst of challenging, brilliant sounds, exhilarating celebration, even dazzling fireworks, the organisers of the beautifully run event kept us focused on the purpose, the mission of SA bands - praising God and proclaiming the Gospel. That made all the difference to me, and I felt privileged to be a part of it all.

ASB

CSB
Canadian Staff Band
THE SALVATION ARMY

CHICAGO
STAFF BAND

smk
STABSMUSIKKORPS

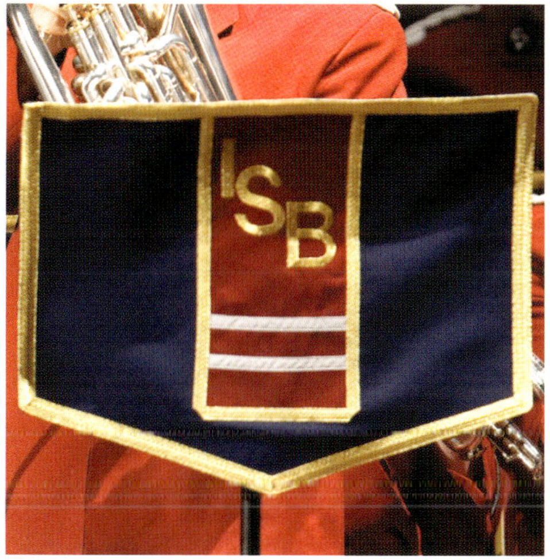
ISB
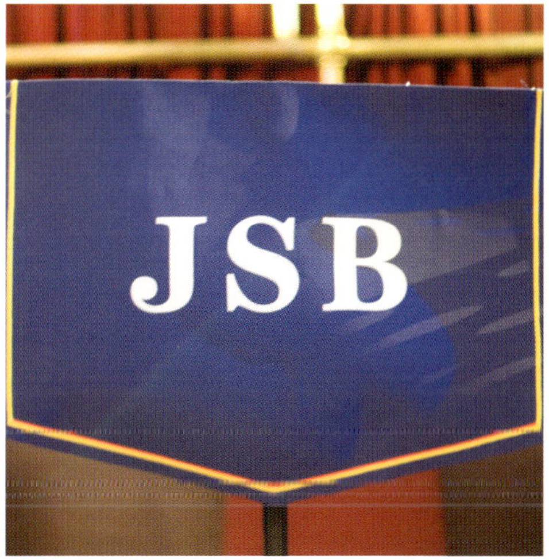
JSB
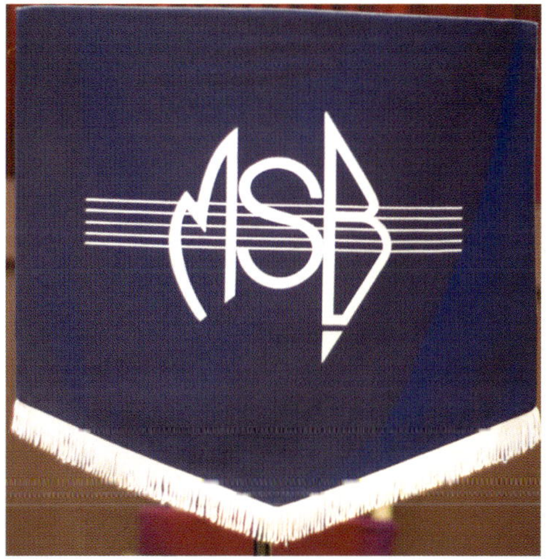
MSB
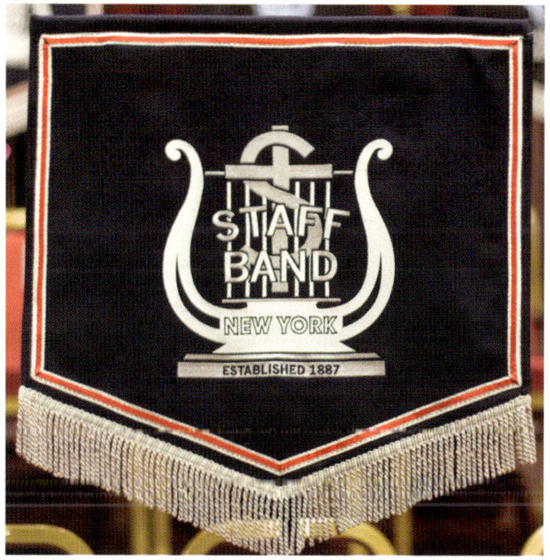
STAFF
BAND
NEW YORK
ESTABLISHED 1887

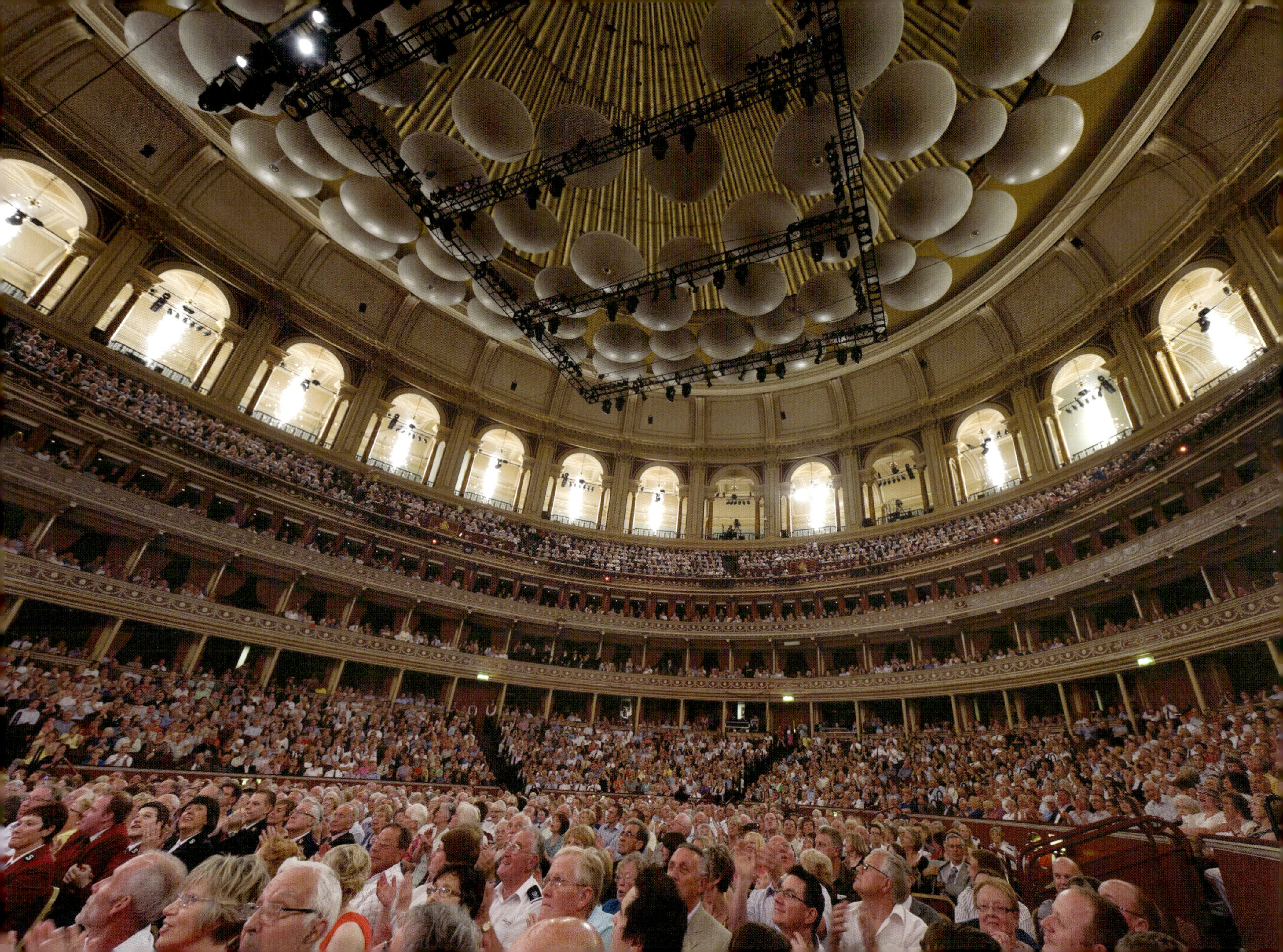

Saturday morning rehearsals

64

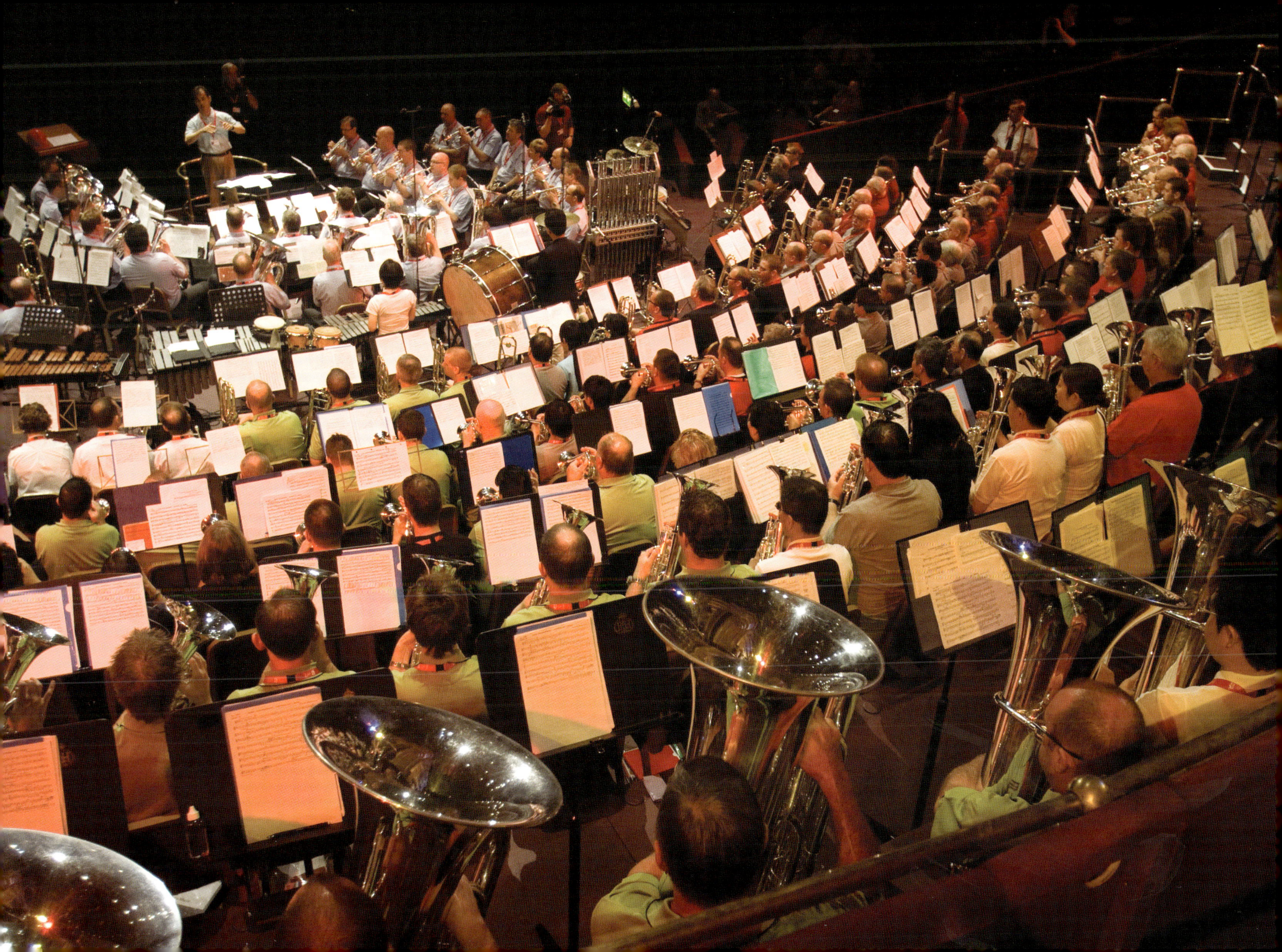

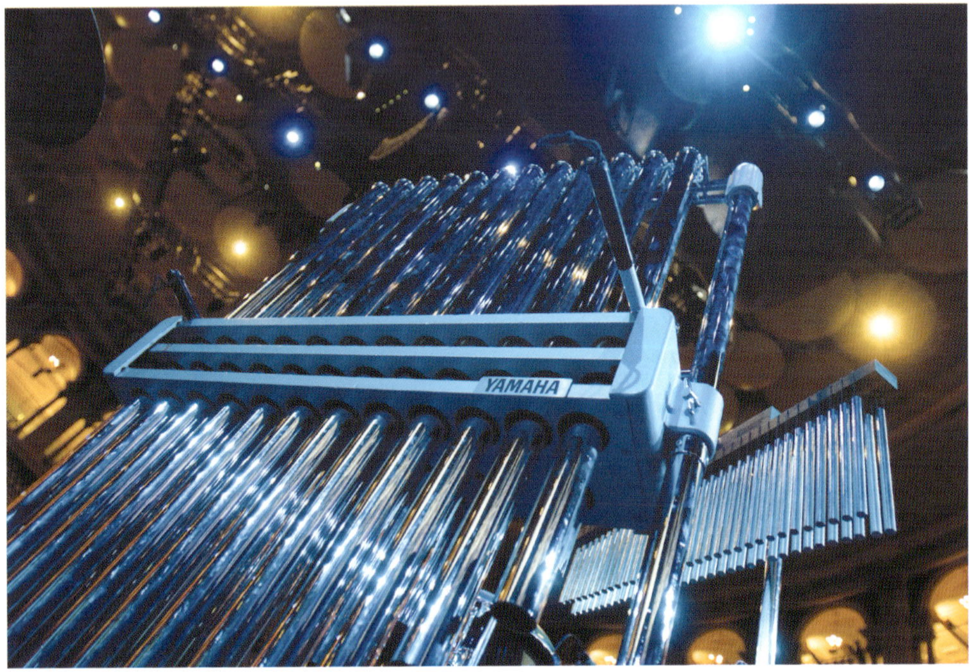
YAMAHA

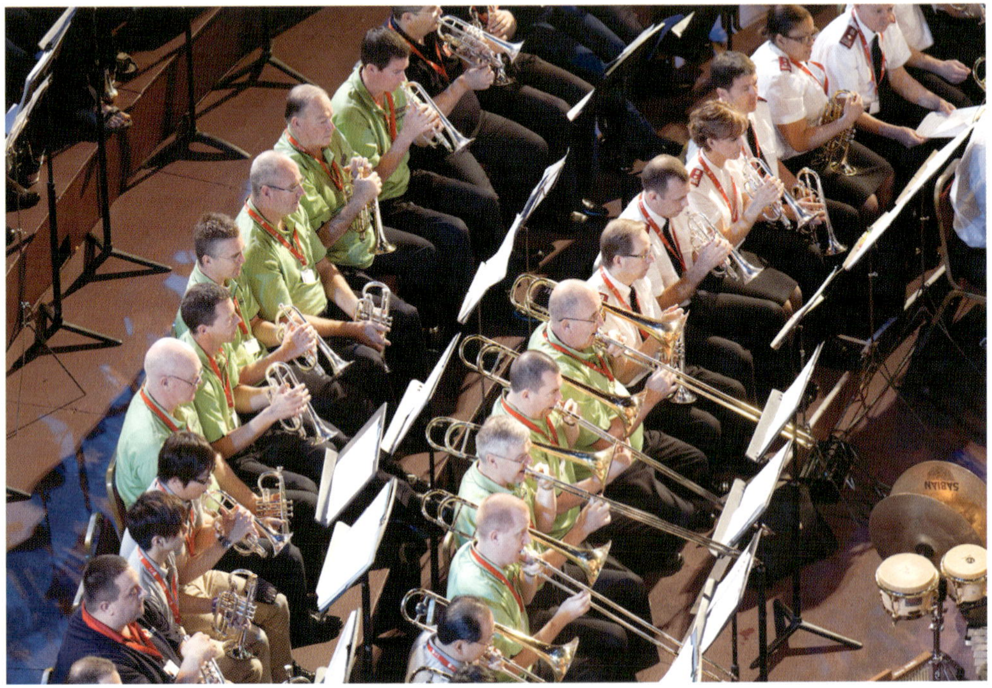

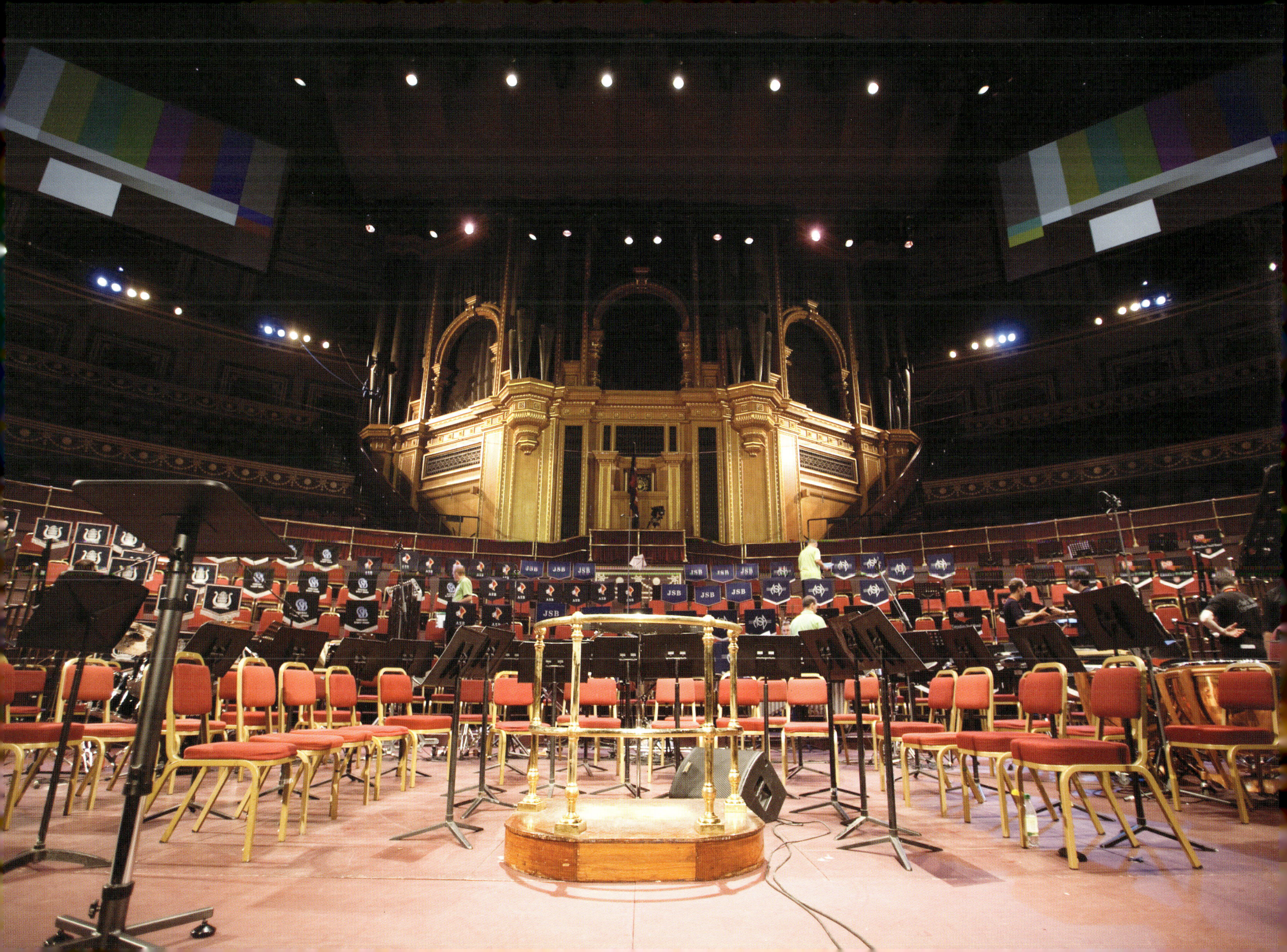
JSB

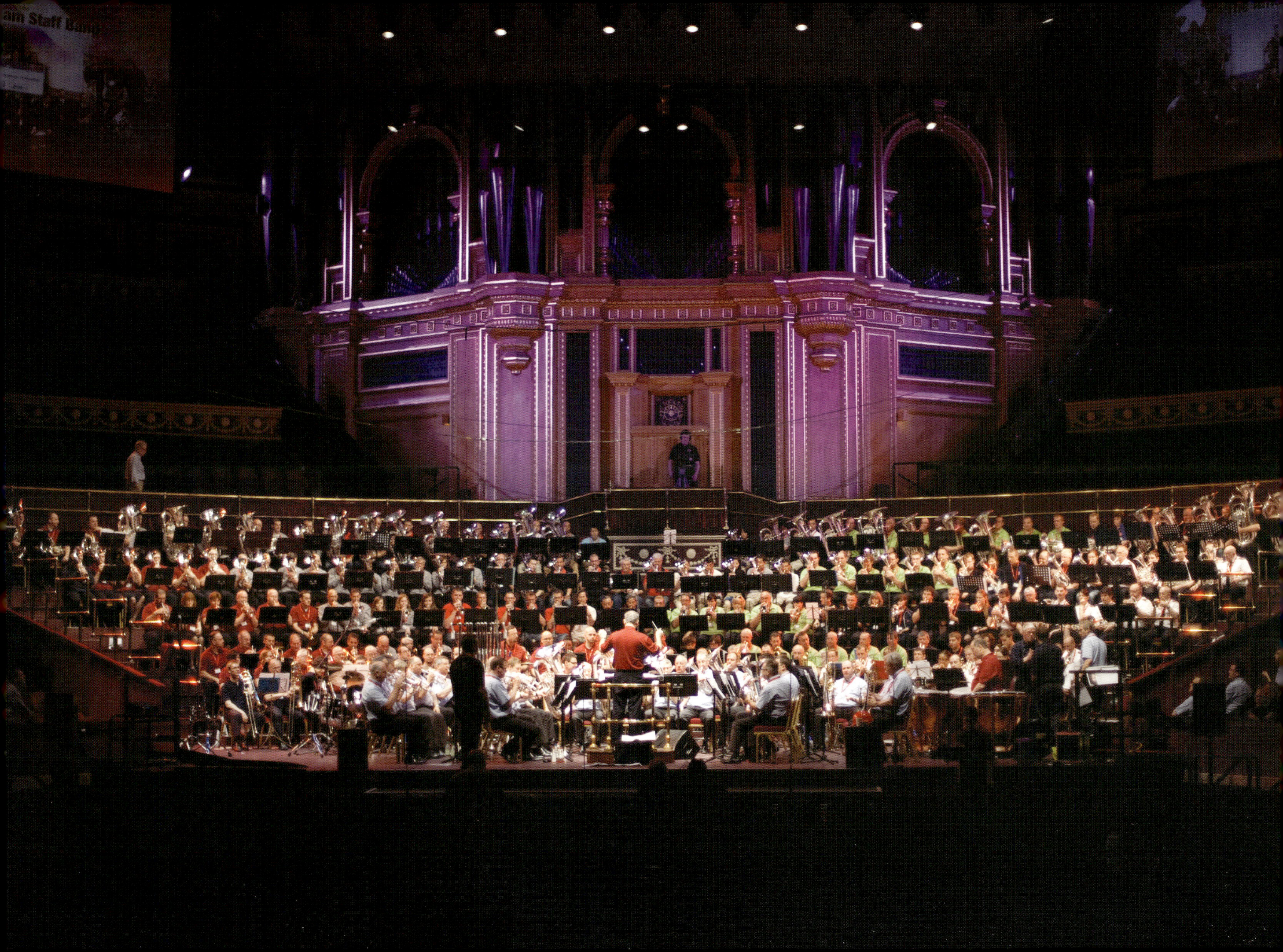
Staff Band

69

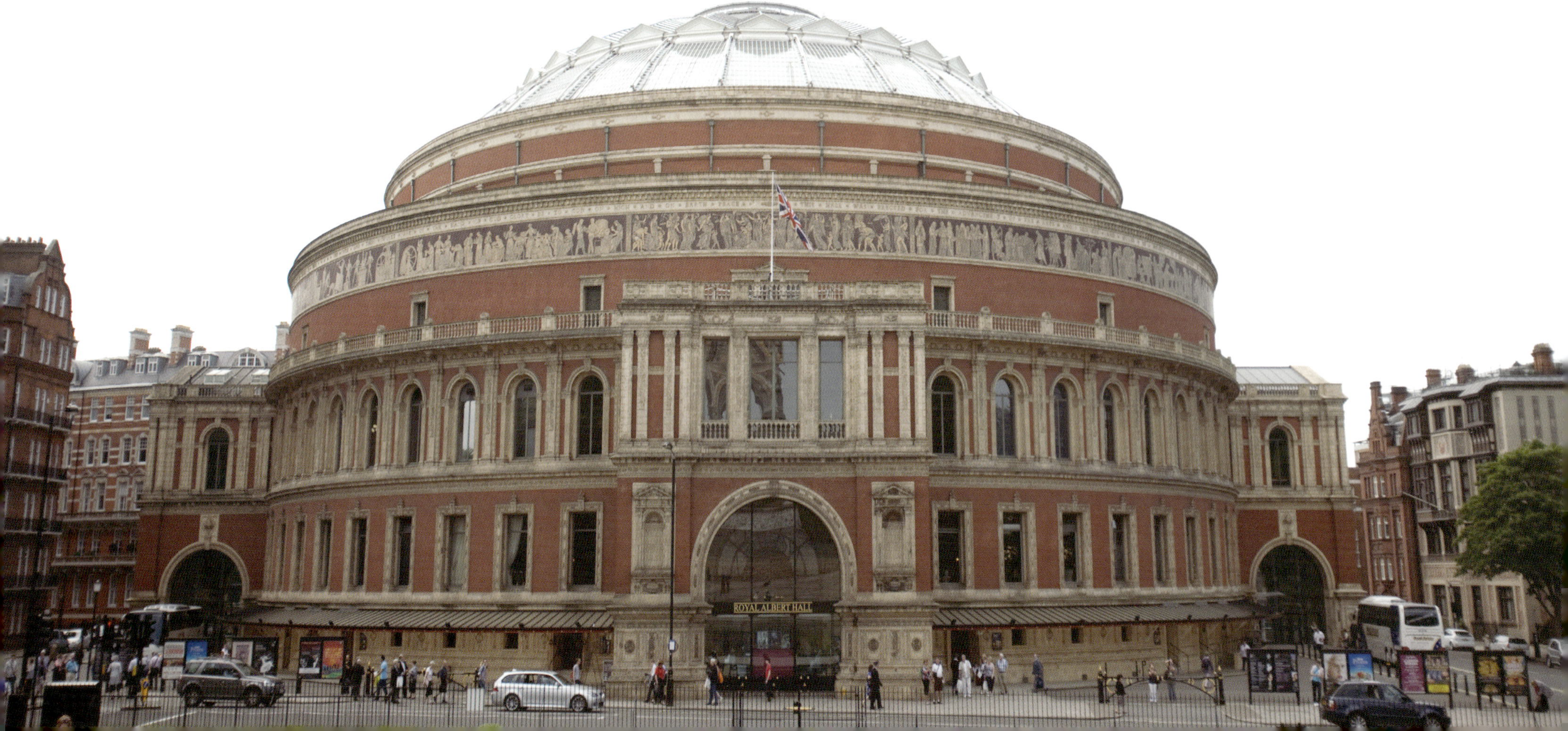
ROYAL ALBERT HALL

Behind the scenes at the Royal Albert Hall

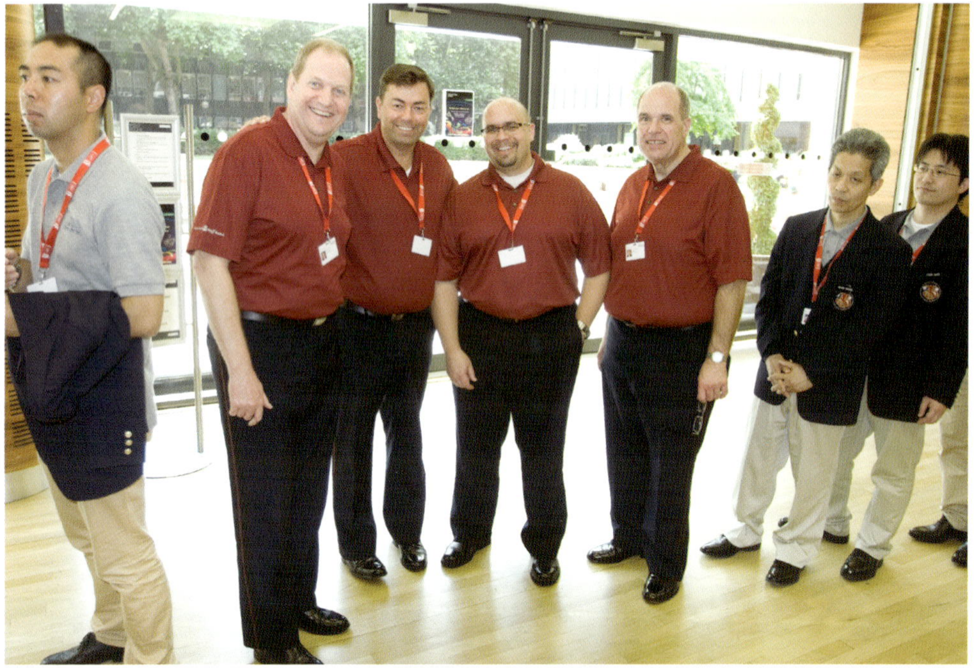

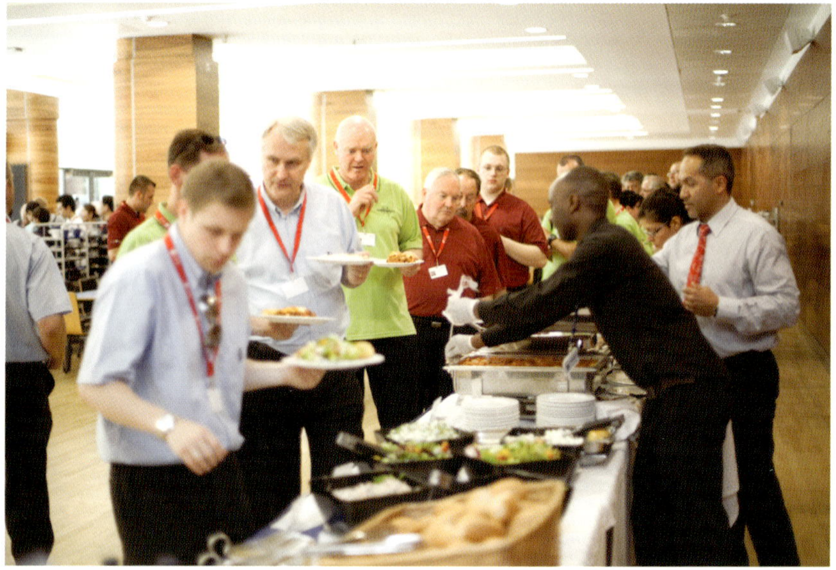

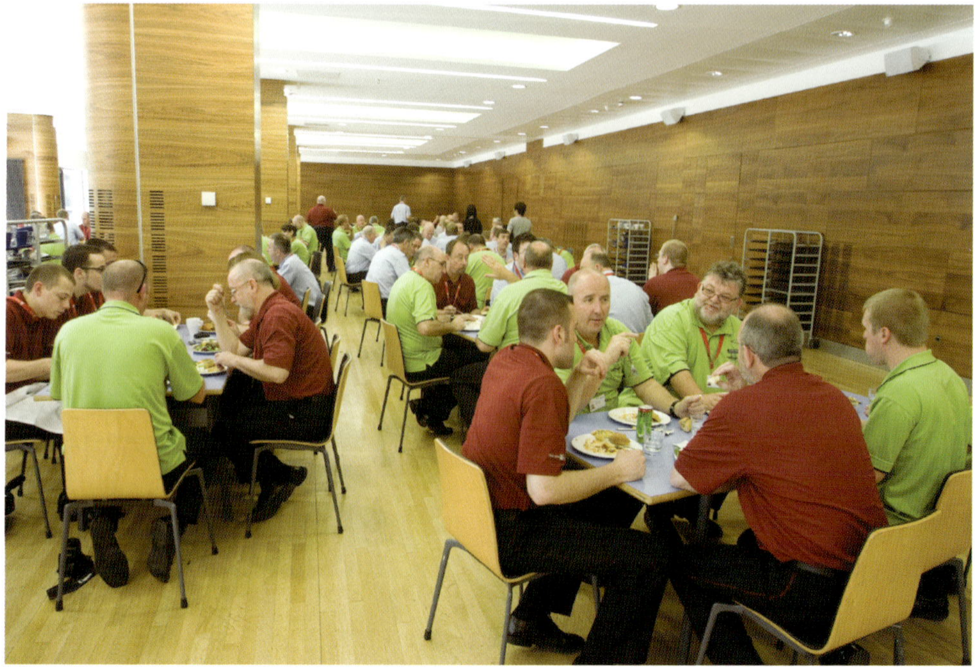

73

74

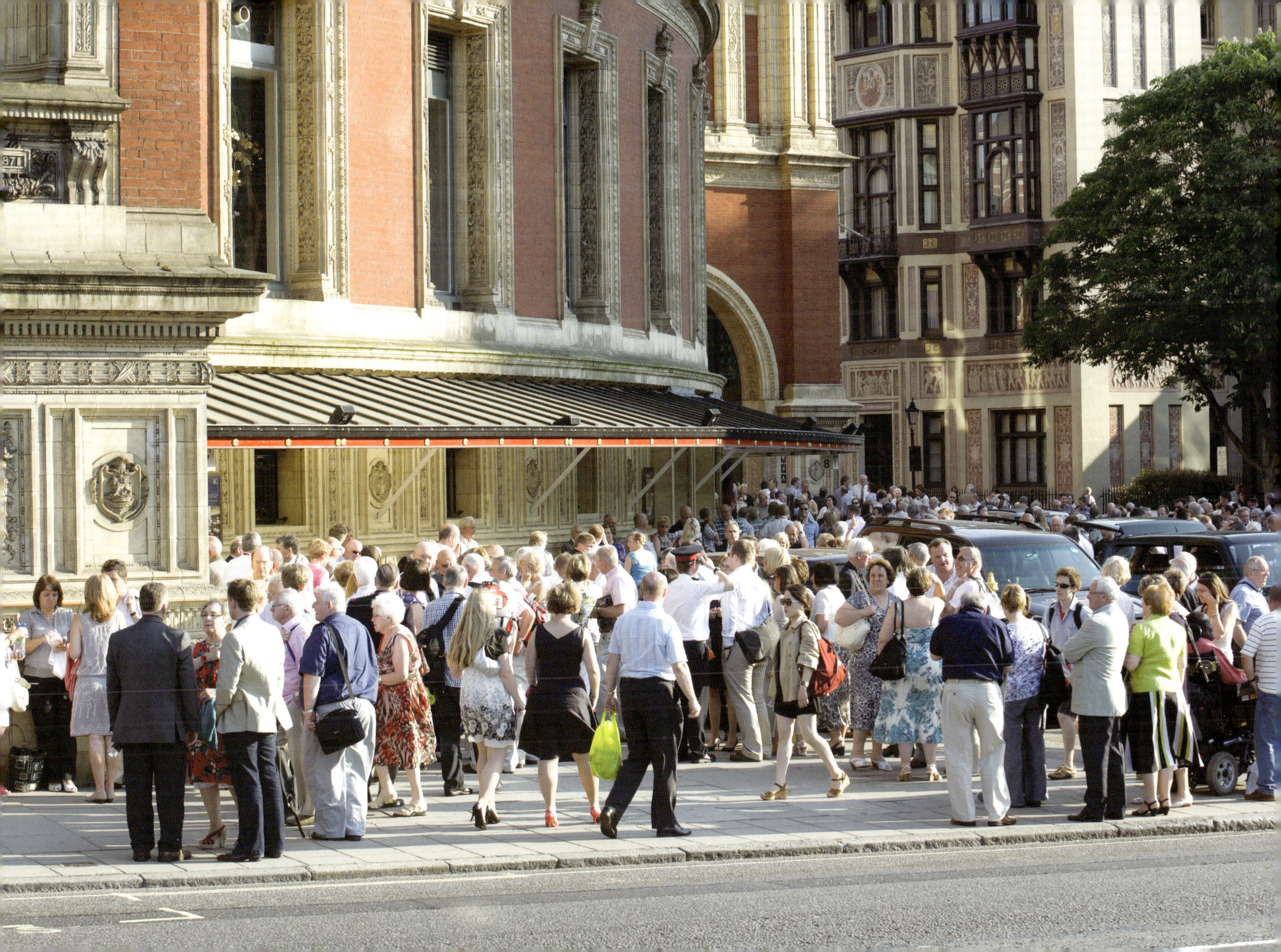

Members of The International Staff Band waiting in 'the wings' for its Saturday afternoon programme

The audience anticipates the commencement of the *Brass Spectacular* concert

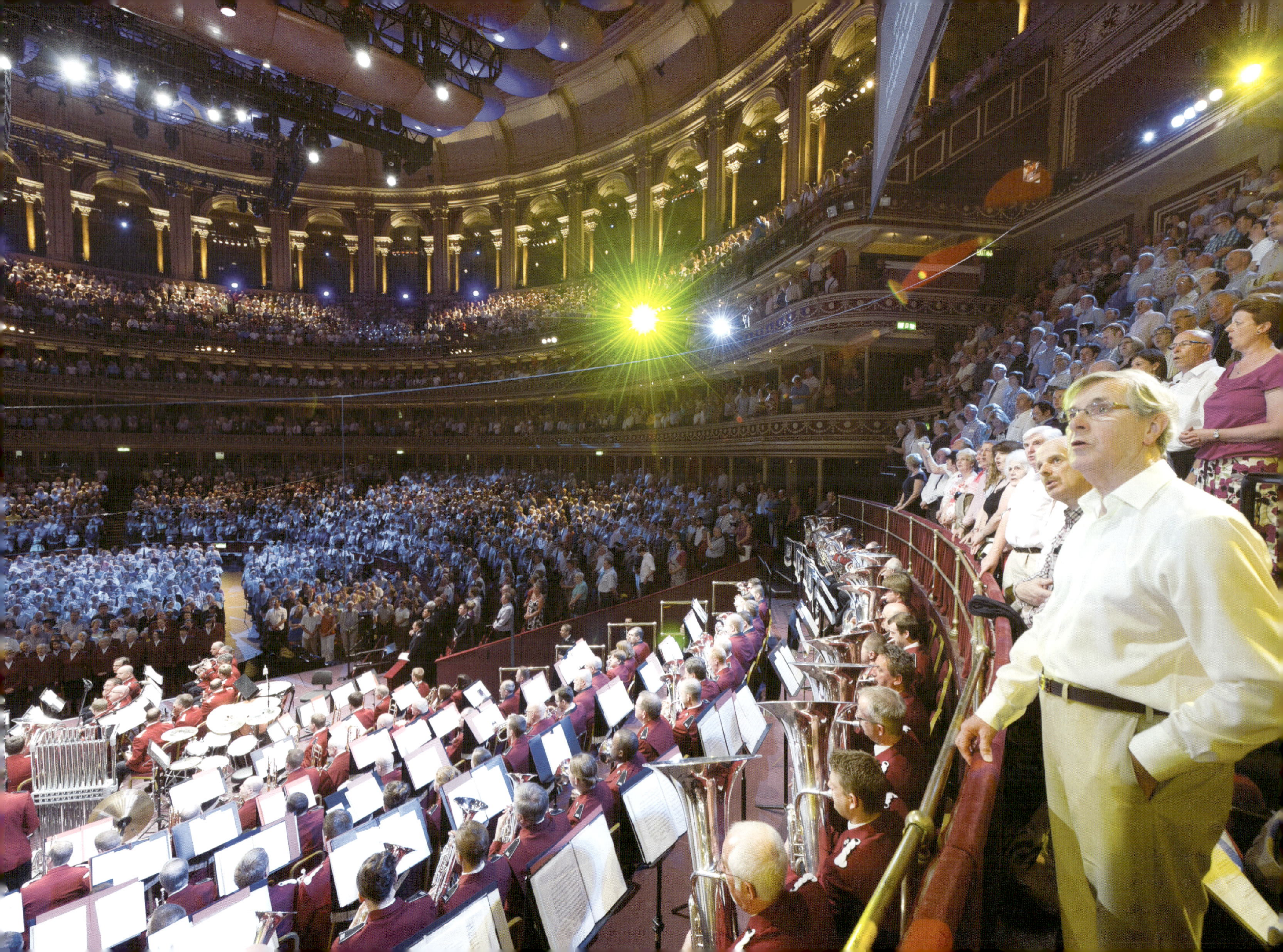

Left: Lt. Col. David Hinton, ISB Executive Officer
Right: William Flinn, voice-over compère, Saturday evening *Brass Spectacular*

80

Top: Colonel Brian Peddle commences the celebrations on Saturday afternoon
Right: Trevor Caffull introduces the individual bands
Far right: Stephen Cobb welcomes and recognises special guests to the *Brass Spectacular*

Entry of the Staff Bands of the world

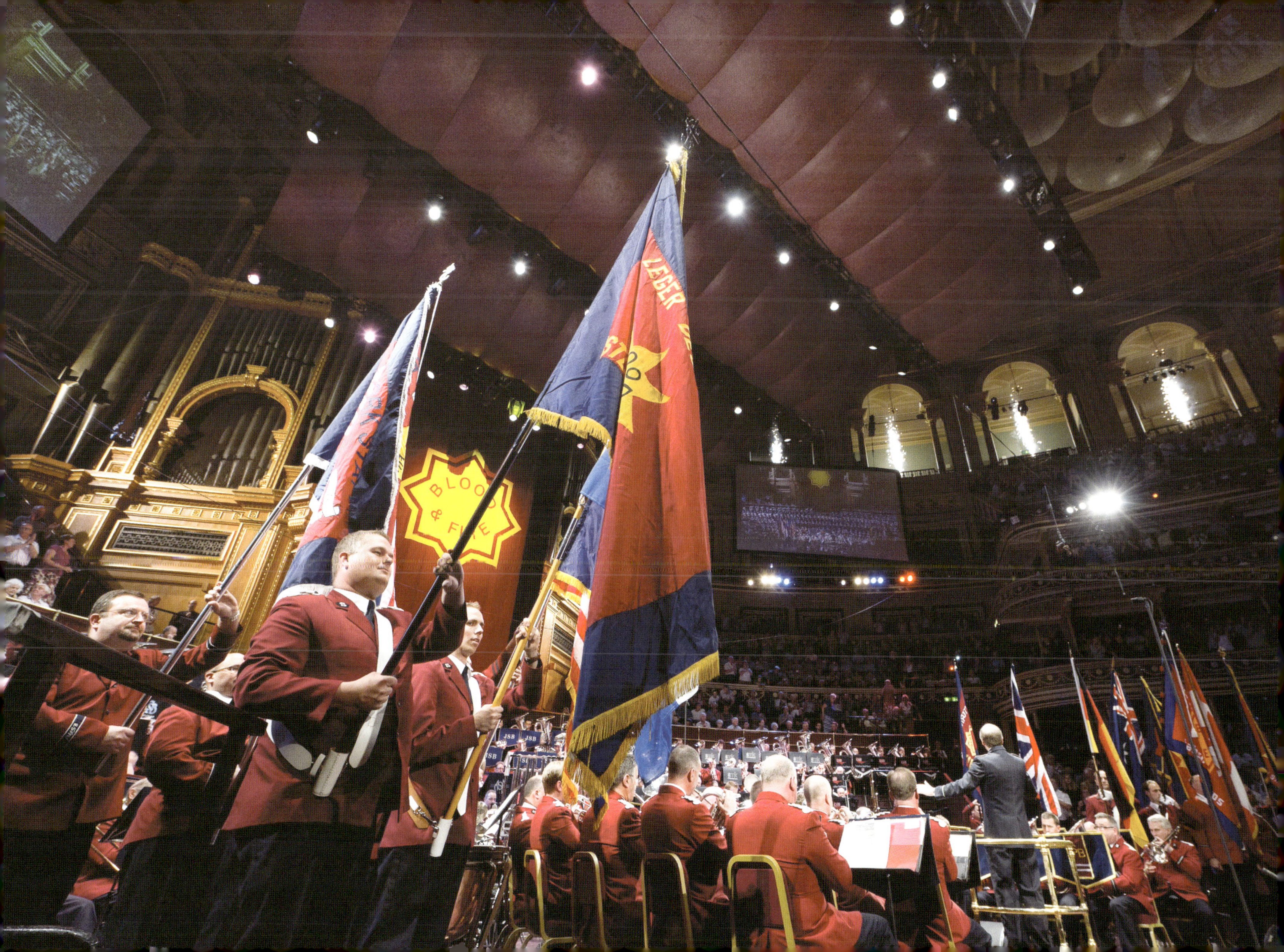
BLOOD & FIRE

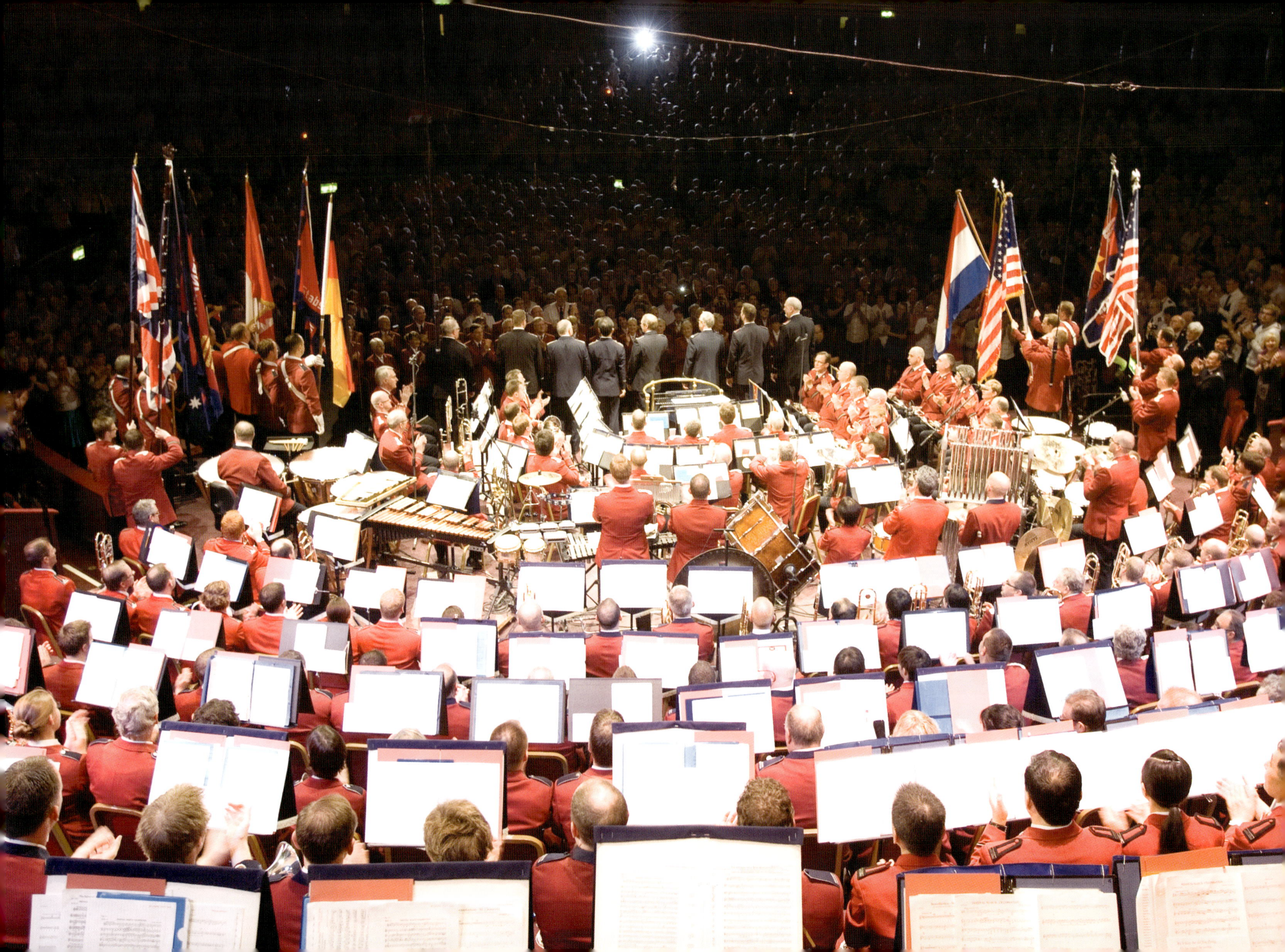

85

THE BANDS

AMSTERDAM STAFF BAND
Steef Klepke

Build up to the weekend
With the decision being made within seconds to go to London and to participate in ISB120, the speculation began during the same rehearsal as to which colleague Staff Bands would be there and which 'well-known' people like composers, star players etc. would also be there. Soon after we got approval from National Headquarters the Staff Bandmaster, Olaf Ritman, explained to us that he would like to showcase the band by highlighting all the sections in the band. This proved to be exactly the right choice. So the band used the format which was to be used in the Royal Albert Hall in all its concerts leading up to the ISB120 weekend.

Initial thoughts
At the outset we had our doubts as to whether or not our playing would be of any significance, but they soon vanished. Of course it would be of significance! Looking back, our brothers and sisters of the Japan Staff Band proved that it is the way you do things that count, and I think that anyone present at ISB120 agrees with me that, of all the bands, the JSB blessed people the most by the way they did what they do. So, filled with excitement and eager to show 'the world' that, even in a small country (we were the smallest participating country) like The Netherlands, Salvation Army music was 'alive and kicking', the band prepared its repertoire, rehearsing, and recording in very good spirits.

Preparation
If you have never been part of a band it is impossible to imagine the preparations needed for such a weekend. Recording a CD is probably one of the easiest tasks, and so that is what most Staff Bands did. The Amsterdam Staff Band invited three world-renowned soloists from the Rotterdam Philharmonic Orchestra (trumpet, bass trombone and tuba) to participate and a distinctive and 'ground-breaking' recording *(Rendez-Vous in Brass)* was the result. Also we prepared to make full use of the time each band was allocated during the *Staff Bands in Concert* on the Saturday afternoon with many rehearsals and concerts working towards this epic event. The most impressive preparation for this amazing weekend in London was on the Thursday before, Ascension Day, namely a concert with our close friends the Canadian Staff Band, who were touring Europe for the third time. With a packed hall and an absolutely unbeatable atmosphere two great bands shared friendship, fellowship and food. This is what Salvation Army banding was all about; praising the Lord in the best way you possibly can with fantastic Salvation Army brass band music.

Arrival
Our arrival in England was also special and we were welcomed by composer and former ISB member Keith Manners, who was our Tour Manager and trouble-shooter for the weekend. The Dutch do not have the same sense of humour as the English as Keith found when he greeted us at the airport with *"my goodness, is that bunch of guys my band for the weekend?"* However, when delivering us to the airport after the weekend he had to admit that this was one of his best ever weekends with a band! Back to the arrival; soon the bus arrived at **Maidstone Citadel** where the band was heartily welcomed by former corps bandmaster Keith Thomas, while former Upper Norwood and Melbourne Staff Bandsman (and composer!) Ian Jones helped the band to set up for a sound check.

Experiences
Although the Amsterdam Staff Band is a band like any other Staff Band, this weekend was certainly unlike any before and probably one that will never happen again! The weekend itself was bigger, greater and better than we could ever have imagined.

> "The weekend itself was bigger, greater and better than we could ever have imagined. It was very important and extremely impressive that everything was managed to perfection down to the smallest detail... everything was extremely well planned and smoothly executed."

It was very important and extremely impressive that everything was managed to perfection down to the smallest detail. Whether it was the coach, tickets, food (to keep band members happy and feed them well) music, hotel (which we shared with our good friends of the German Staff Band), friendliness, or even the distribution of the chairs in the Royal Albert Hall, everything was extremely well planned and smoothly executed.

Apart from all the playing during the weekend it was of particular interest to meet so many friends, fellow band members, composers, musical heroes and many more people. Many knew each other for years without ever having met. What a great Army we have!

Of course, just like all the Bands, the Amsterdam Staff Band was very pleased to see such a large Dutch delegation in the audience. When we played in the afternoon as the first band of the day people started to cheer and wave the Dutch tricolor. Few of the band members were able to hold back tears because of the emotion of playing in this majestic building on this great occasion. One of the former (English) Bandmasters of the Amsterdam Staff Band, who was also in the congregation, said when we were ready to play; "silence please, now MY band is going to play"!

The evening concert was certainly unforgettable. To play in the Royal Albert Hall is amazing; to play with over 250 Staff Band members from around the world on one stage is the next thing to Heaven! You found yourself between people from Japan, Australia, USA, Canada and Germany, and obviously the UK and Ireland. Even if you didn't speak any English, it didn't matter. Music is the only international language, and that was all around. From the beginning with the entry of all the flags, to *Pursuing Horizons*, a brilliant piece for three brass bands, to the flugel horn octet *So Glad!* through to the fireworks during 'We'll keep the old flag flying, flying round the world' in Major Leslie Condon's *Celebration* (he would have loved it!), it was one big God-praising brass feast!

There were many wonderful experiences during the weekend, but there is no doubt that the greatest of all was to play in the march up The Mall to Buckingham Palace. The presence of thousands and thousands of enthusiastic people along The Mall and even on the Queen Victoria statue in front of the Palace was heartwarming and made every Staff Band member, and I am sure also ANY Salvationist, proud to be part of such a great organisation. The International Staff Band playing you through the gate of the Palace is not really an everyday experience either and produced many goose bumps. When we entered Buckingham Palace and all eight Staff Bands played on the forecourt, history, probably never to be surpassed, was made.

Reflections

This was the greatest band weekend ever undertaken in the history of the Amsterdam Staff Band and I am sure in the history of any participating Staff Band. Although there might be a tendency to wonder if, in particular, Staff Bands are still of added value in this era, this weekend proved more than anything else that they still have an important role to play. Too often people forget that in all the exuberance of the concerts and high profile performances the main objective is to tell the good story of Jesus.

The weekend definitely was the 'Encourager of the Century' and will last for long in the memories of all who were present. I really wonder how people like William Booth and Richard Slater would have enjoyed this tremendous occasion. To God be the Glory!

'A once-in-a-lifetime opportunity to meet fellow Staff Band members from around the world and a fantastic way to let the world hear God's wonderful music in this very special way.'
Michel Rosenquist (Principal Euphonium ASB)

'A fantastic historical milestone!'
William Sprokkereef (Timpanist and Archivist ASB)

'A precious moment was the message from General Linda Bond on the Sunday morning. A message straight from the heart, standing in the midst of the Territorial Youth Band.'
Hans van den Hoek (2nd Horn and Band Sergeant ASB)

'It is just great to know that you are part of writing history; moreover it is amazing to share the stage with friends from around the globe who all speak that breathtaking language of Salvation Army band music. Countdown till ISB125!'
Alexander Kruidhof (Eb Bass ASB)

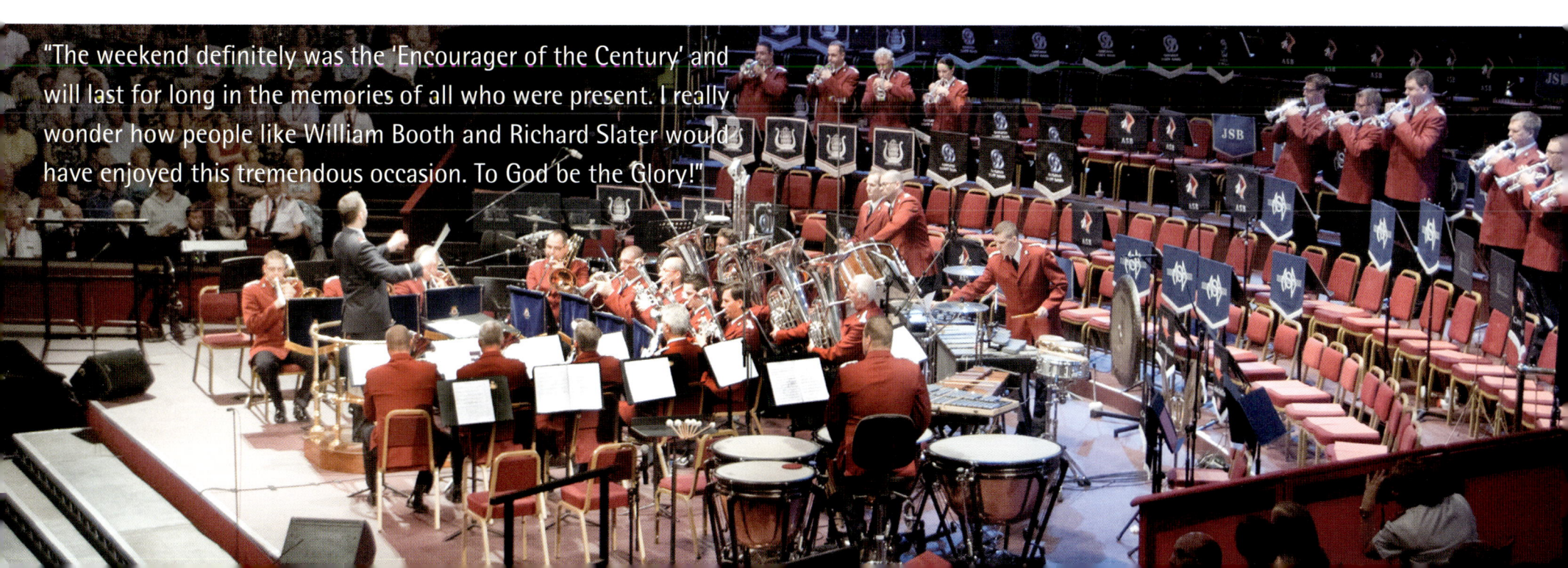

"The weekend definitely was the 'Encourager of the Century' and will last for long in the memories of all who were present. I really wonder how people like William Booth and Richard Slater would have enjoyed this tremendous occasion. To God be the Glory!"

JSB
JSB
JSB

CHICAGO STAFF BAND
CHICAGO STAFF BAND
CHICAGO STAFF BAND
JSB
ASB

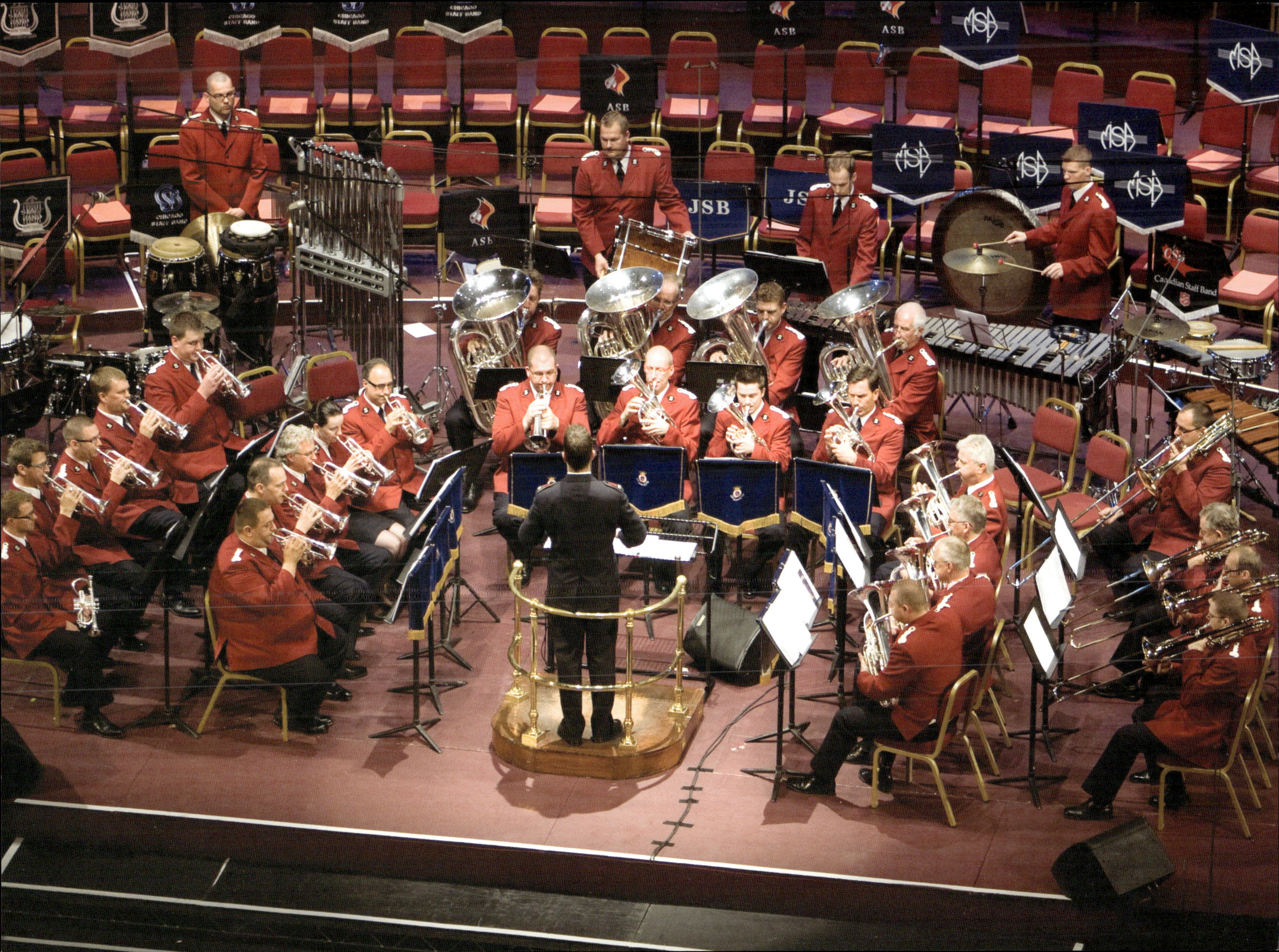
ASB
JSB
Canadian Staff Band

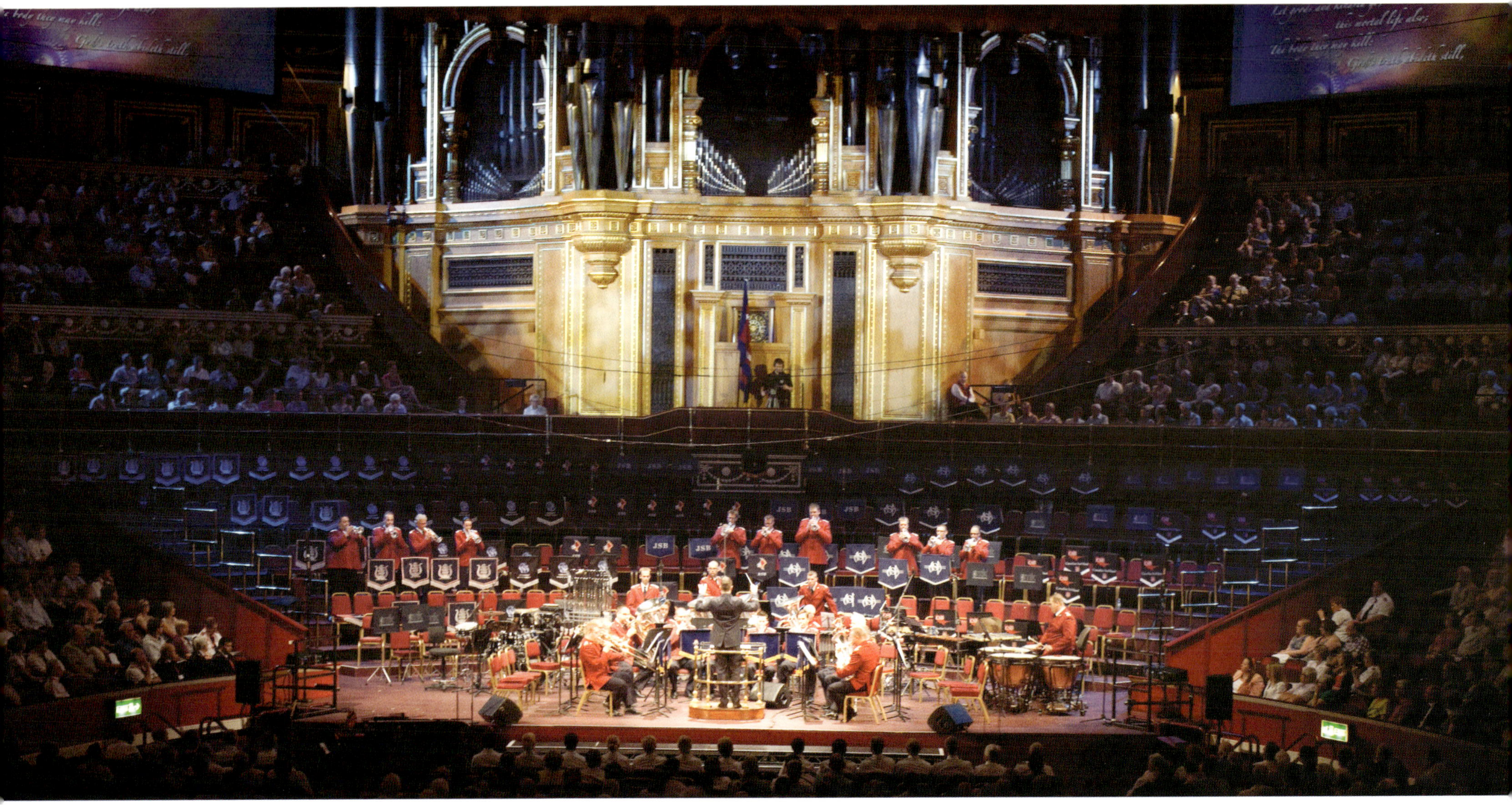

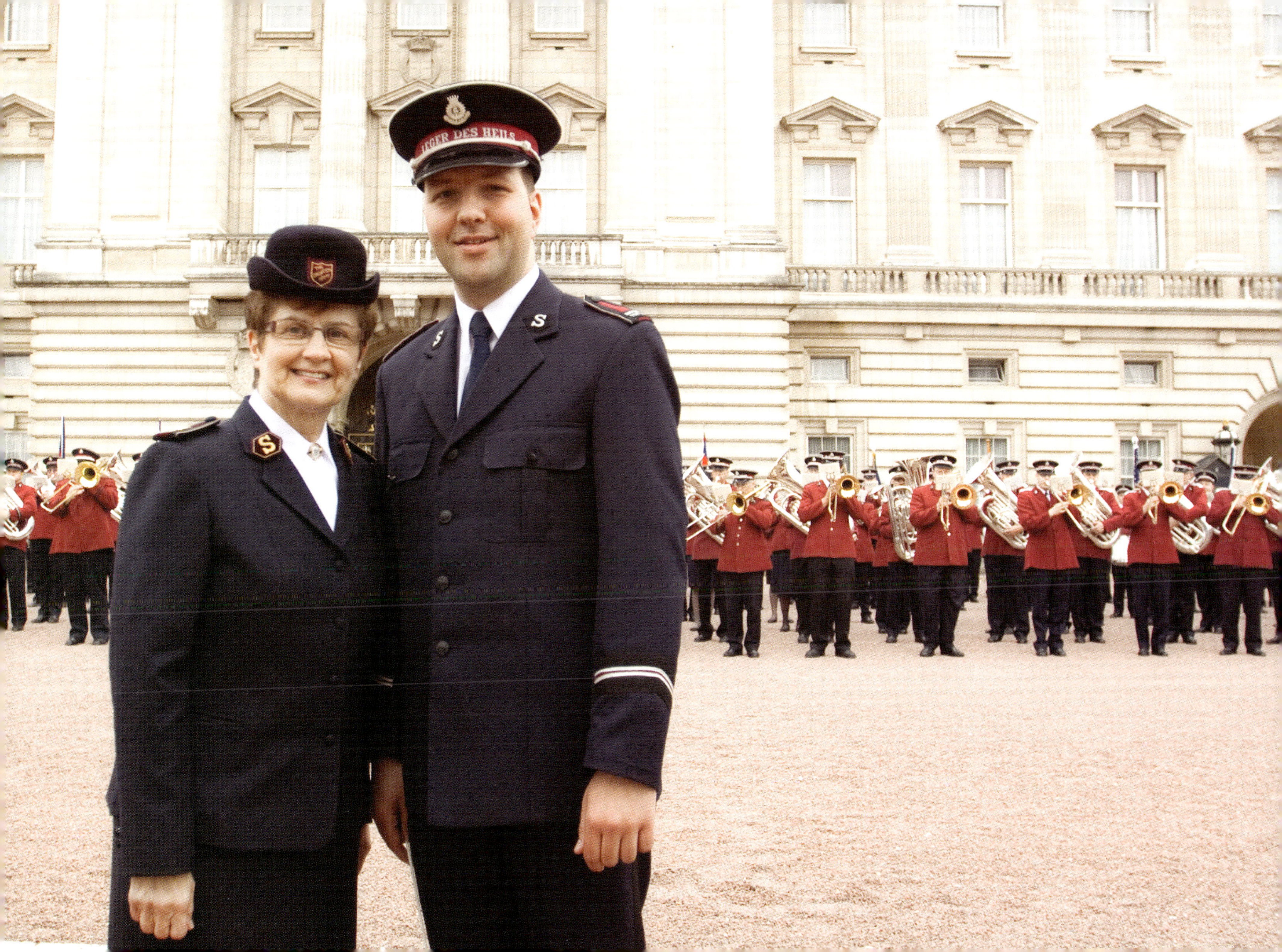
LEGER DES HEILS

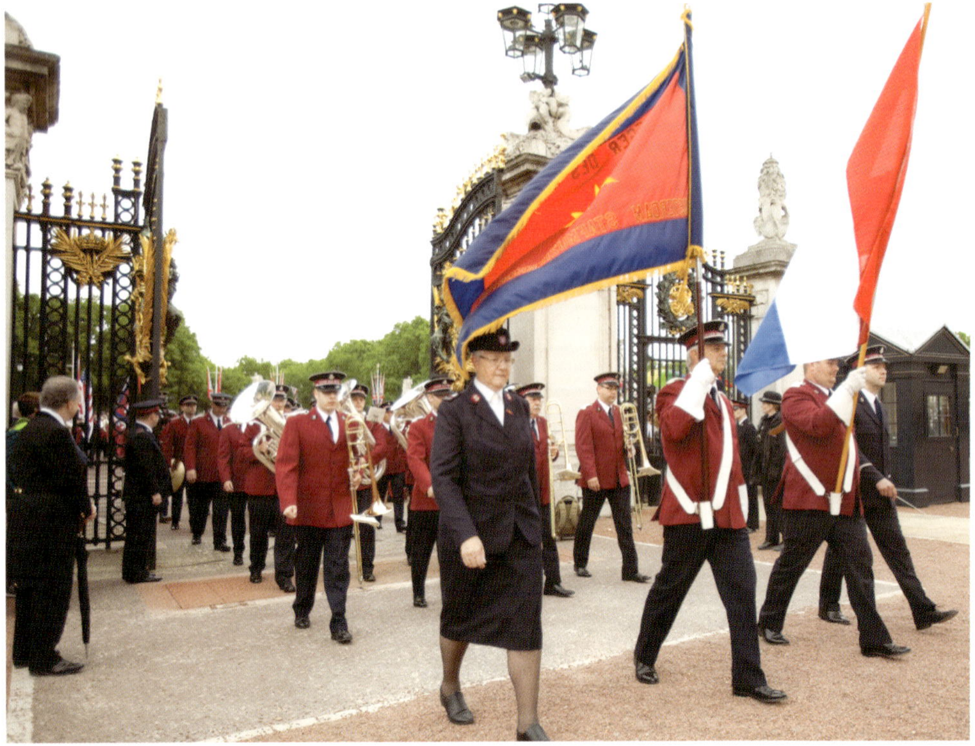

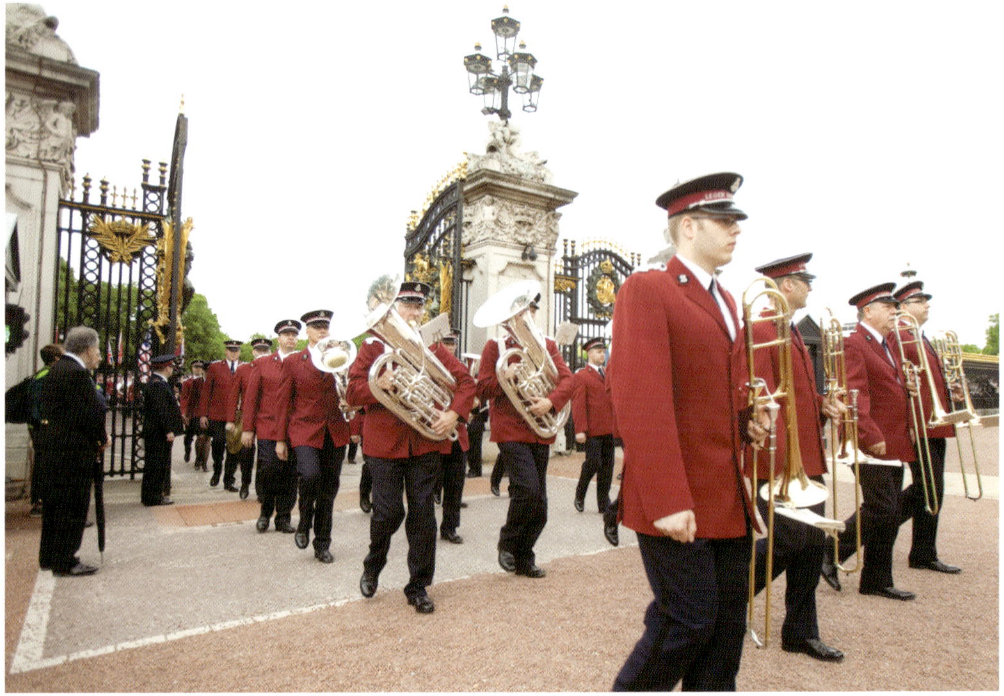

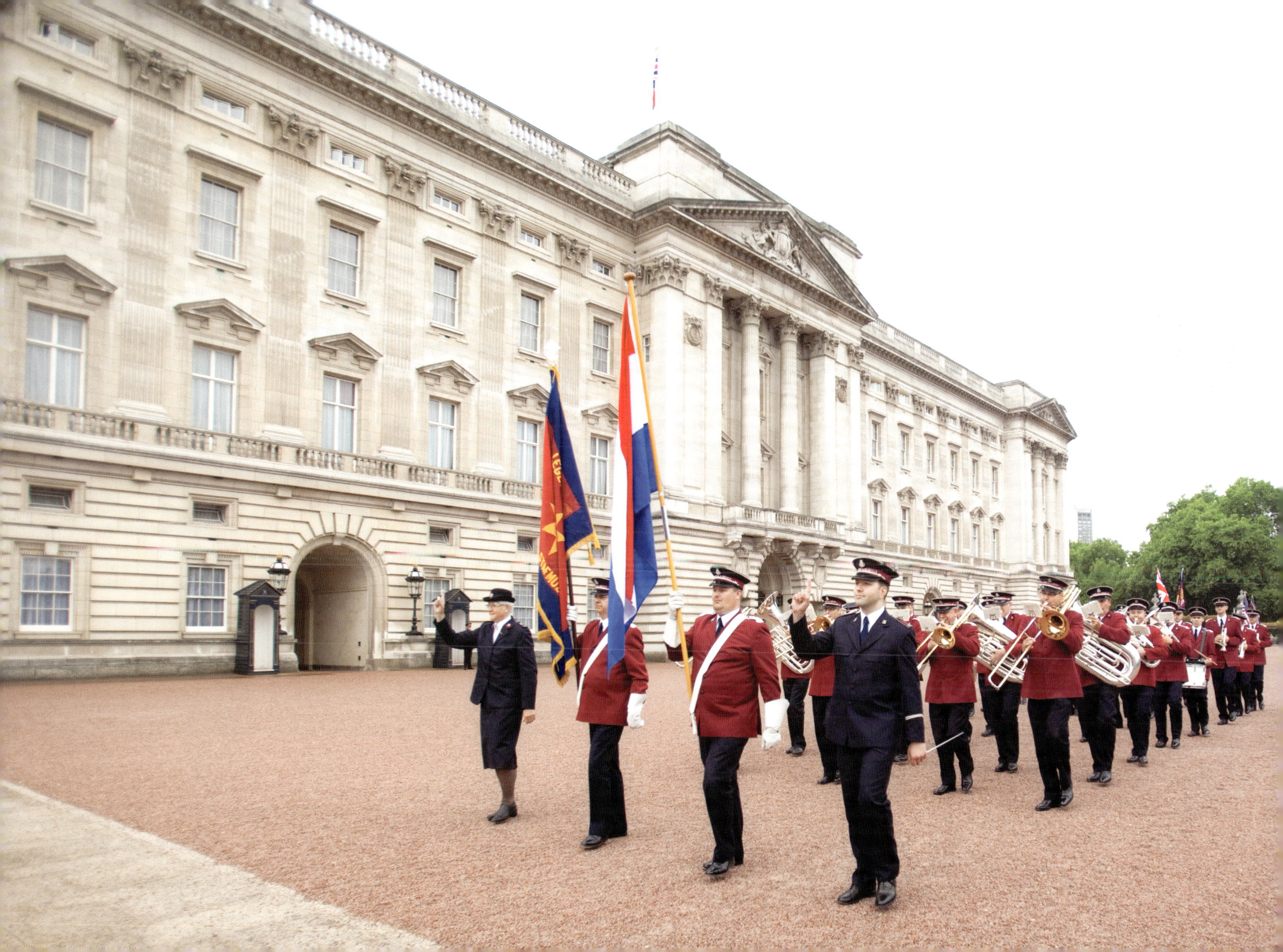

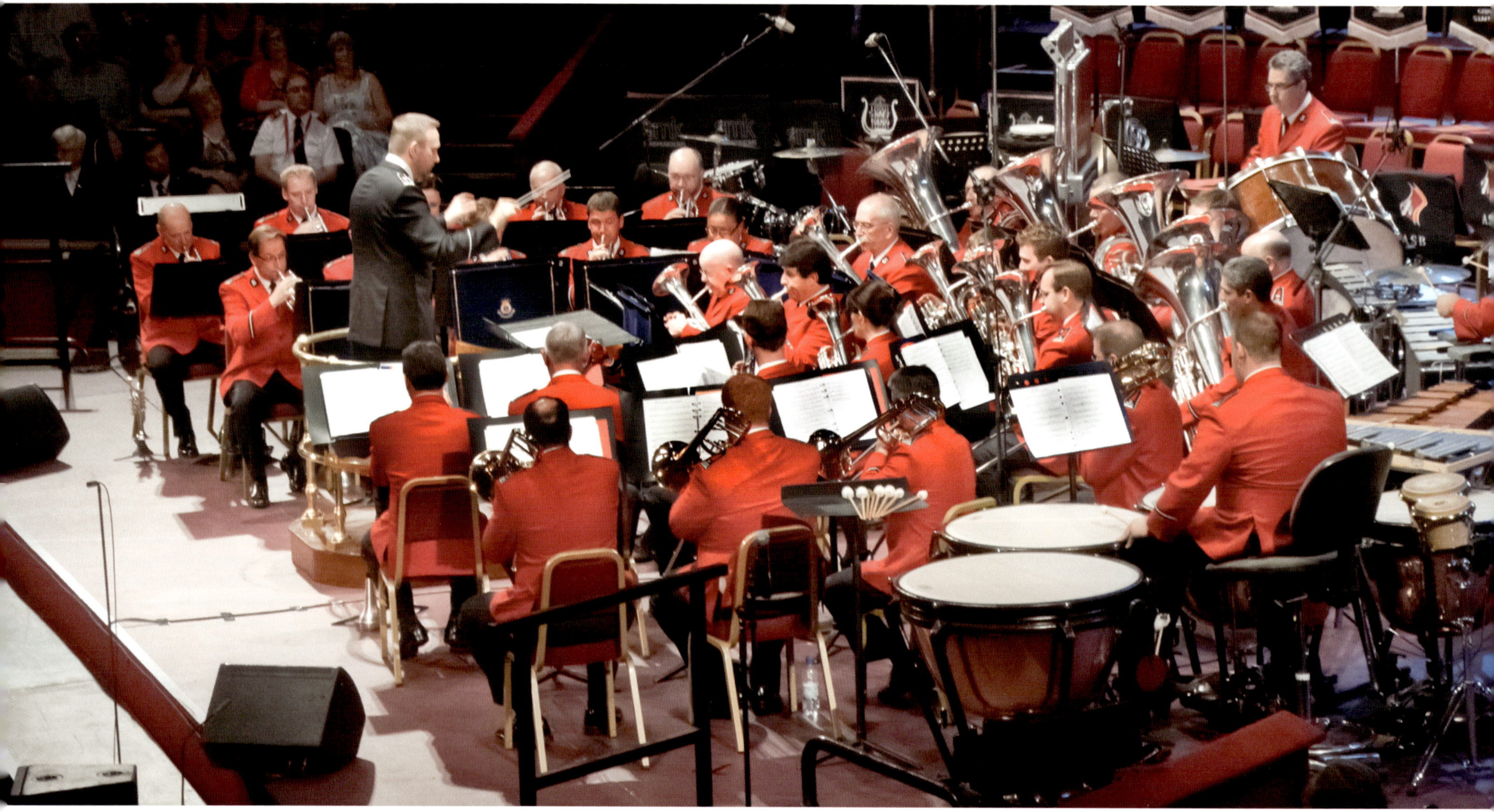

CANADIAN STAFF BAND
Craig S. Lewis

Excitement started building as soon as we received word that the Canadian Staff Band had been invited to participate in The International Staff Band's 120th Anniversary celebrations that would take place in the Royal Albert Hall. For many of us, playing in the RAH had been very high on our personal bucket lists. Months of rehearsals, recordings and a mound of paperwork to be completed were all that stood in our way.

With great anticipation, we met at the airport in Toronto to embark upon our European Tour that would serve as our prelude to the main celebrations in London. Canada has a long and close friendship with the Netherlands and the reception we received there was tremendous. A highlight for many of the staff bandsmen and women was the opportunity to play at the Holten War Cemetery. An extremely moving moment was when each of us was given a single white rose to place on an individual grave, most of the band being older at the time than those who had paid the ultimate sacrifice.

After concerts in Almelo and Leeuwarden, the band crossed into Germany for concerts in Zetel and Essen. It was here at the Folkswang University in Essen, where our partnerships with other staff bands began. German Staff Bandmaster Heinrich Schmidt was our gracious host and the band was able to share music and fellowship with the members of the university's brass band. The German Staff Band was in attendance for our short concert and we all started to feel the excitement of the coming days.

Our last engagement on the continent was a real foretaste of the events of ISB120. In a magnificent old church in Baarn (NL), we joined with the Amsterdam Staff Band to present a night of music that was called *One Heavenly Concert*. The night saw both bands play their own segment and then join together to conclude the night. A highlight of the evening was the ASB joining with us as we presented our 'surround sound' benediction of *God be with you 'til we meet again*. We were now ready to head to England!

Arriving at Heathrow and meeting our hosts from **Stowmarket** for the Friday night, there was a sense that we were on the verge of taking part in something great. Entering the hall for the concert, it was obvious that the audience could also sense that we were starting a weekend of great significance. We were well and truly prepared to play our role in making history.

Saturday brought an early morning call to load the buses and head to the Royal Albert Hall. Faces were flush against the bus windows as we wound our way through London and finally arrived at the mecca of both Salvation Army and brass band events, the Royal Albert Hall. Our eyes were wide open with wonder, disbelief and exhilaration as we made our way to our assigned dressing room in the bowels of this grand hall. The CSB had not been to the UK since the International Congress in 1990, so most of us were experiencing this for the first time together. Then the call came to proceed to the stage for rehearsal. As we walked out onto the stage and saw the size of the hall and the combined staff bands, we finally grasped the enormity of the event. We were in for something very special indeed!

The time for nostalgia was suddenly over – it was time to get to work! Each Staff Bandmaster put us through our paces and we were privileged to have composers Peter Graham and

> "The morning Musician's Councils at Central Hall, Westminster allowed us to step back from duty and allow the Holy Spirit to minister to us. We were very proud to have our Canadian General, Linda Bond, share with us. A musical highlight was the singing of the closing song *Eternal God*. Hundreds of strong, musical voices raised in song: a very powerful moment!"

Dudley Bright on stage to introduce us to their new works. Surprisingly for the number of players on the stage, the rehearsal went smoothly and quickly. As we left the RAH to walk to lunch, we first saw the crowds of people milling about waiting to enter the hall. What an atmosphere. It was electric!

The Amsterdam Staff Band would kick off the afternoon *Staff Bands in Concert* and we waited excitedly in the wings. Then it was our turn. How do you describe the moment when you walk out on the stage of this hallowed hall, when the lights come on and they welcome the Canadian Staff Band? Your heart starts to pound as if it is going to burst through your chest. You turn your attention to the music – and focus on the months of preparation. Principal Eb Bass player, Noel Samuels, describes it as, "Exhilarating on stage to see thousands of supportive onlookers, yet equally terrifying as my individual sound seemed to immediately disappear in the huge hall."

> "A special highlight was the silence as we finished *O Magnum Mysterium*. Despite our nerves and adrenaline, God had been able to use our ministry of music."

Once our segment was over, it was time to relax and enjoy the fantastic music of the other bands. As many will attest, nothing was more emotional than the ovation given to our comrades in the Japan Staff Band. An unbelievable moment!

The feelings of exhilaration and excitement reappeared on Saturday night as we waited in the hallway to enter in the parade of bands for the Brass Spectacular. With the words 'From the Land of the Maple Leaf', we proudly entered from the back of the hall and marched down the steps. Every hair on the back of our necks stood up as we made our way through the throngs of standing, clapping people. History was being made! As the night ended to the triumphant strains of *Celebration*, we left with a renewed sense of unity and internationalism in The Salvation Army.

It is usually the unplanned moments that create great memories and that was the case late on Saturday night. All of the bands were staying in a cluster of hotels by the airport, and after a long and busy day many of us headed out to the closest McDonalds for a late snack. It was an unbelievable scene – Staff Band members from around the world sharing fellowship over fast food. For some of us, the conversation carried on well into the wee hours of the morning.

The morning Musician's Councils at Central Hall, Westminster allowed us to step back from duty and allow the Holy Spirit to minister to us. We were very proud to have our Canadian General, Linda Bond, share with us. A musical highlight was the singing of the closing song *Eternal God.* Hundreds of strong, musical voices raised in song: a very powerful moment!

Finally, we arrived at the concluding event of ISB120: a march of celebration down The Mall to the forecourt of Buckingham Palace. To be part of that great phalanx of Salvationist musicians as it moved down The Mall was an incredible feeling. A road that had been used by conquerors and victors, by royalty and those of international fame was now being used by those proclaiming the Gospel. What a thrill!

The CSB was the first band to pass through the gates. As we heard and felt the change from the smooth pavement to the crushed stone, we knew we had crossed a threshold that we may never cross again. As we took the salute from 'our' General and marched out playing the most Canadian of marches, *Montreal Citadel*, we knew that we had just taken part in something that was not likely to happen again in our lifetime.

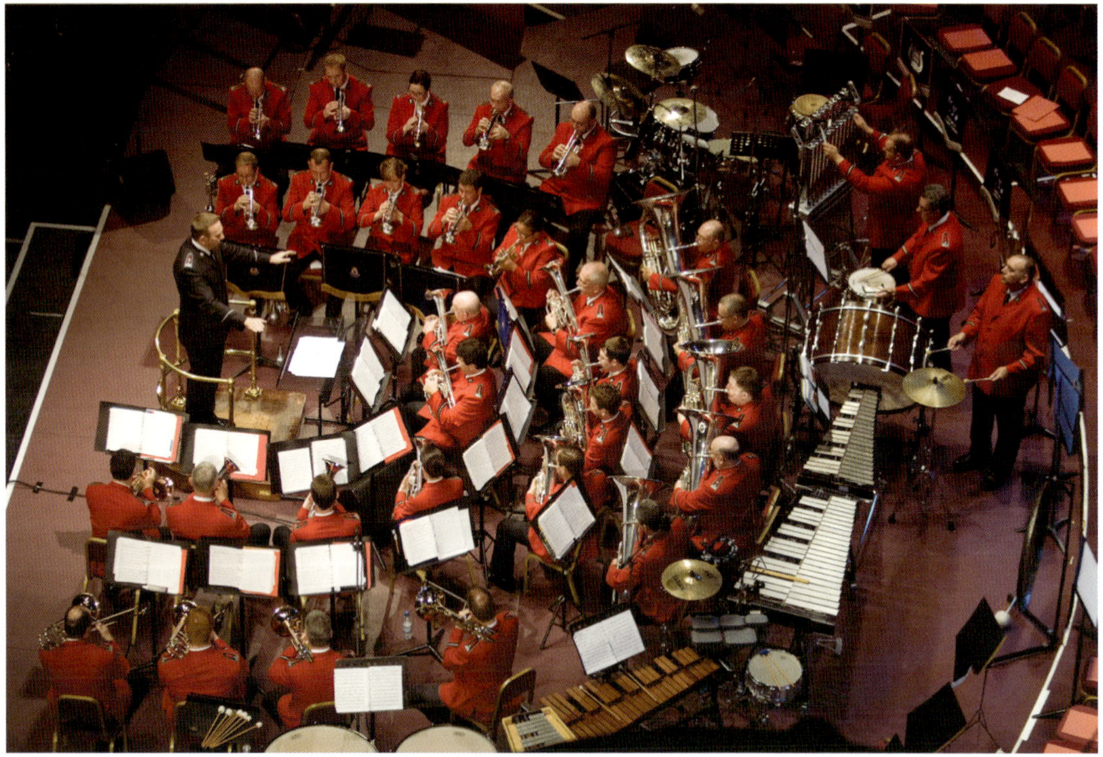

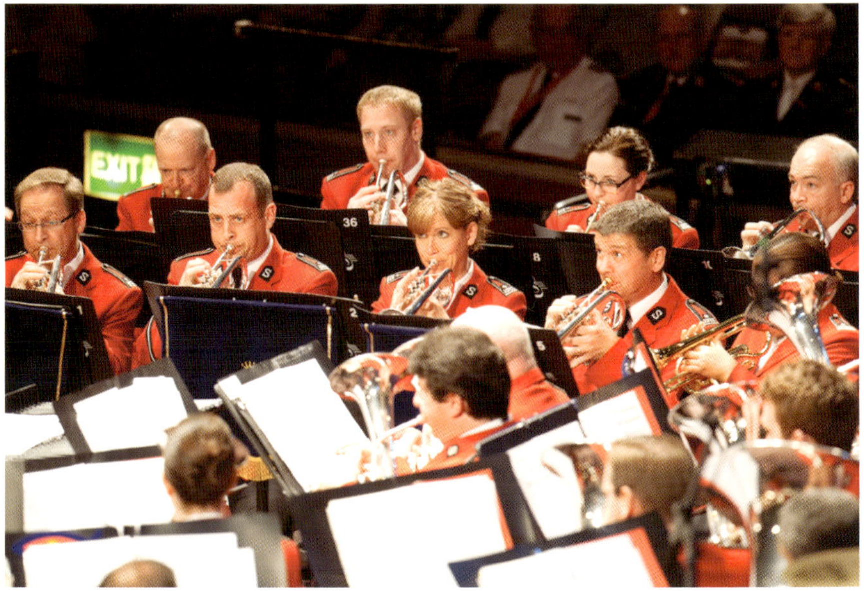

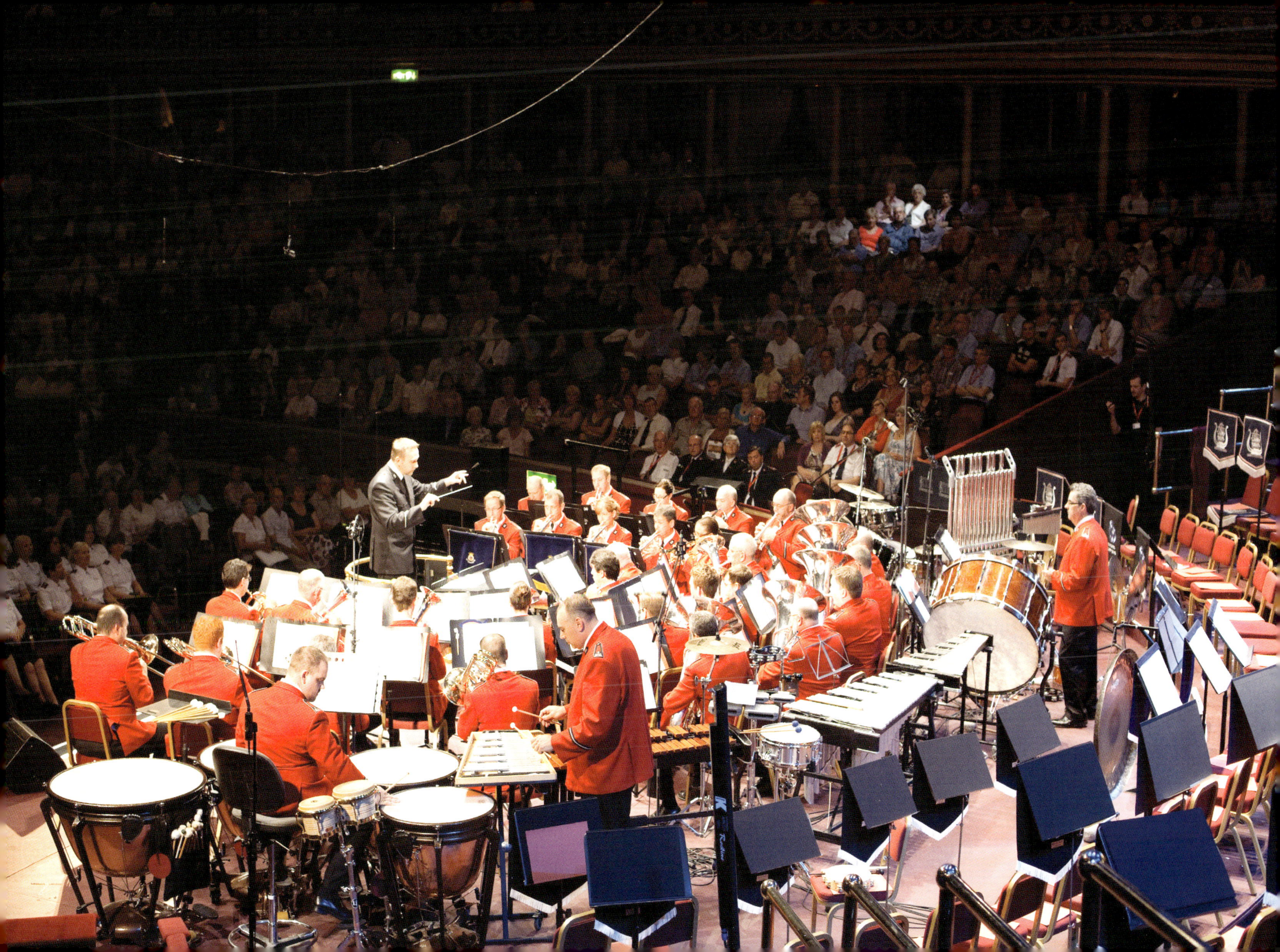

102

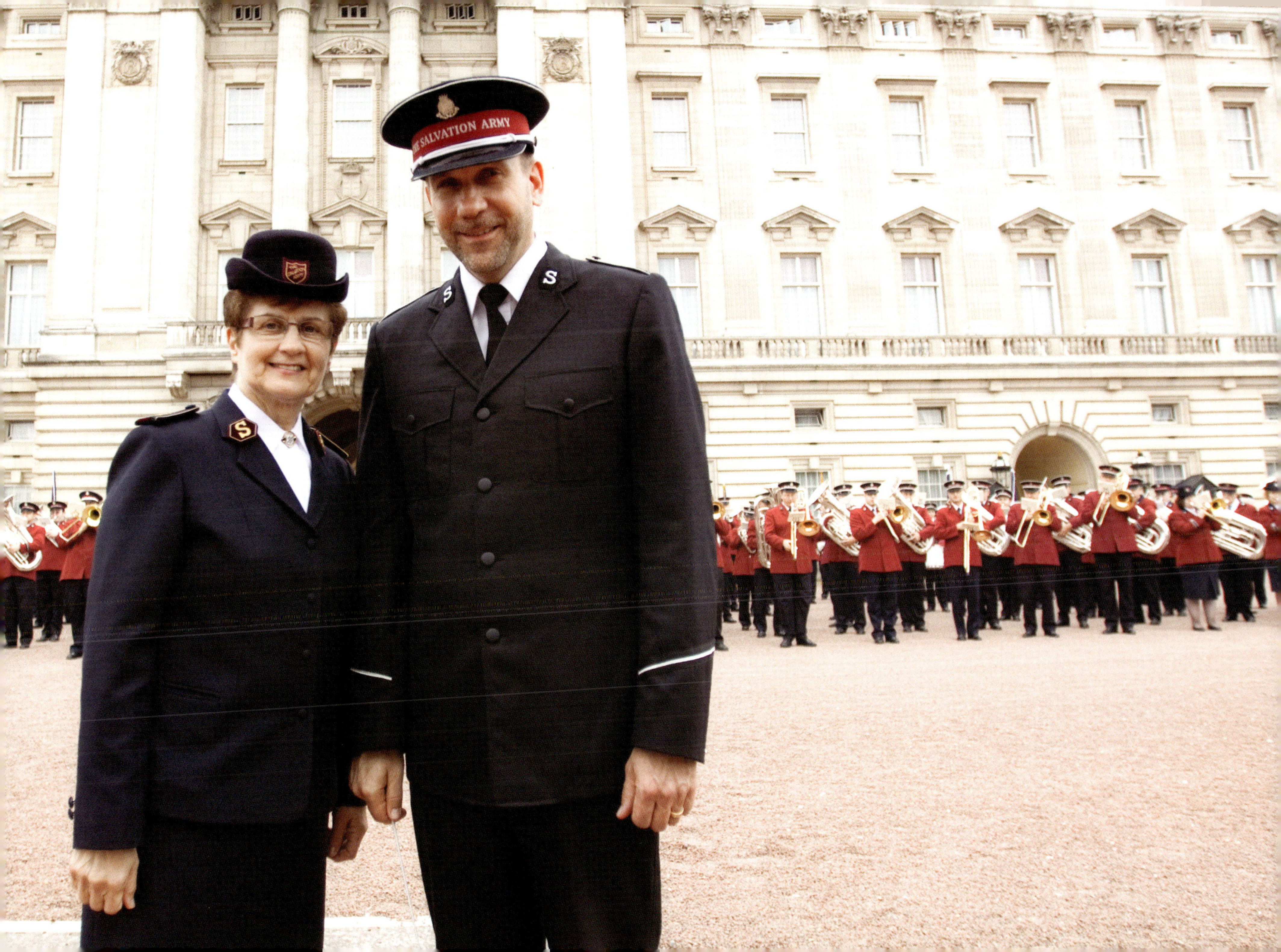
SALVATION ARMY

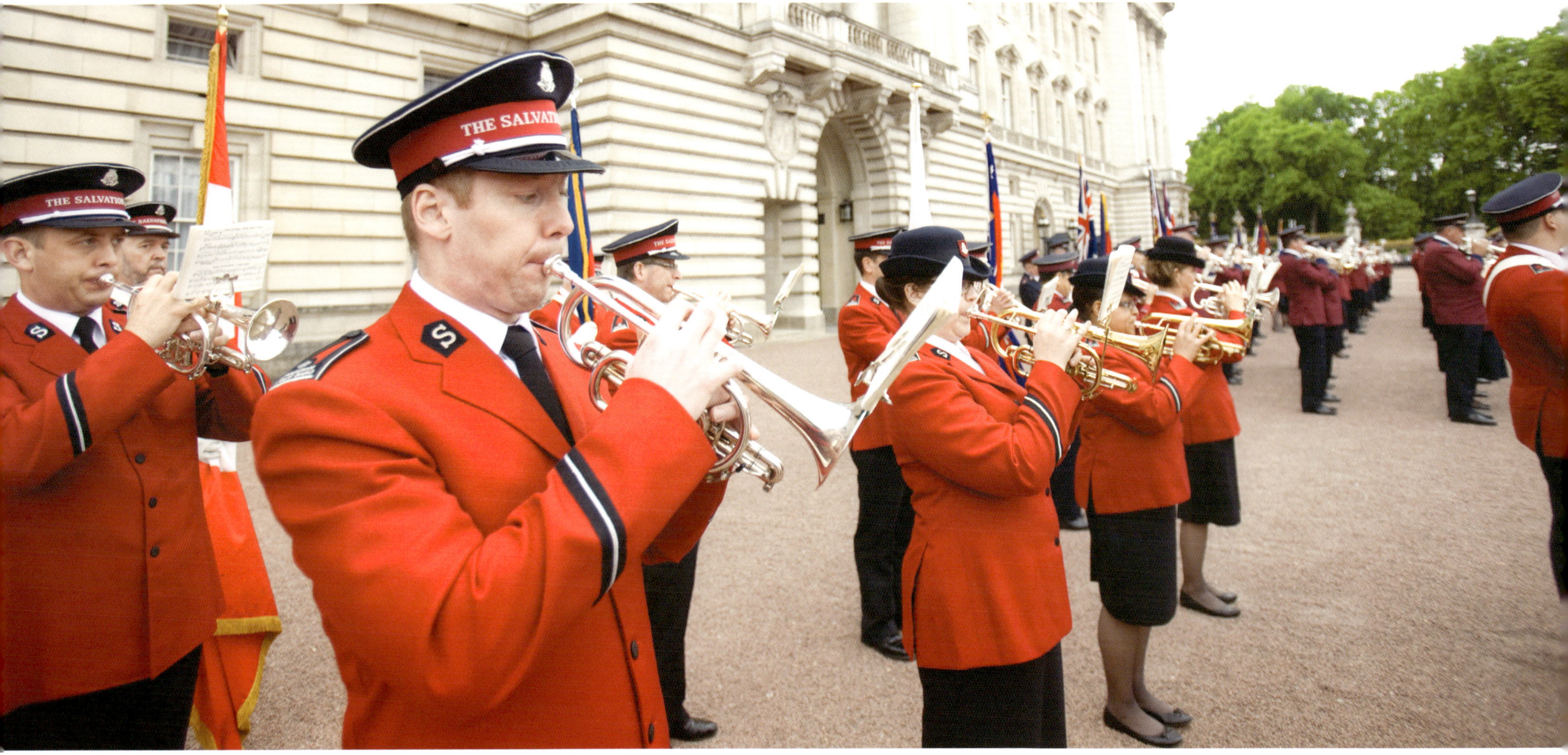
THE SALVATION
THE SALVAT

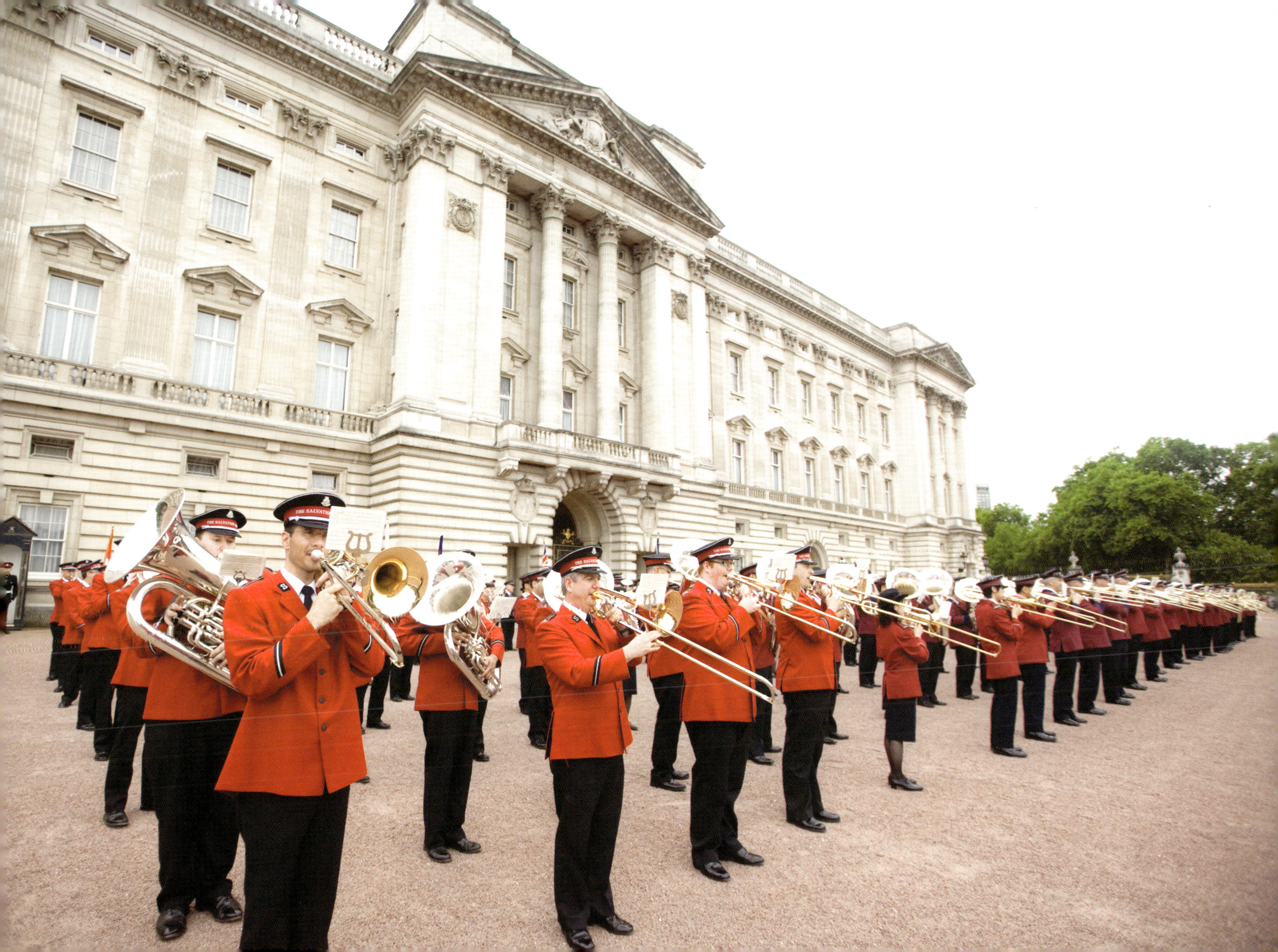
THE SALVATION

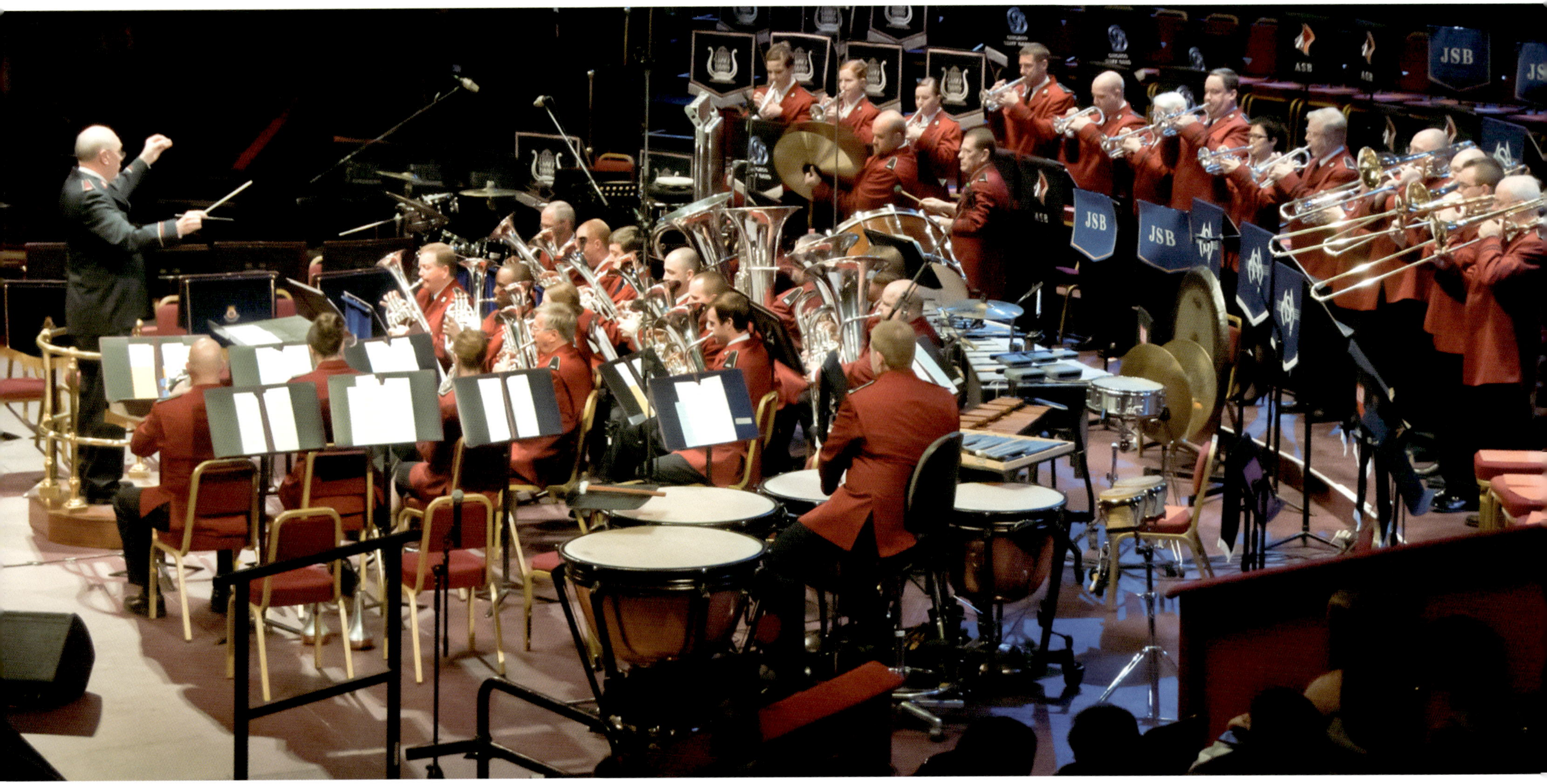
JSB
JSB
JSB
ASB
ASB

CHICAGO STAFF BAND
Martyn Thomas

The nice thing about travelling with the Chicago Staff Band is that each band trip is treated the same. It doesn't matter if the destination is Oak Creek, Wisconsin; South Bend, Indiana; London, Ontario or London, England; the focus is solely on the task at hand. I've seen the same enthusiasm and effort put into local band schools and concerts in high school auditoriums as I've seen in programs with symphony orchestras and concerts at the Winter Olympics. This band always does its best to share the message of Jesus Christ through music to whatever audience is present. And on this trip, the same was true in every location.

Our pre-ISB120 tour of the UK began on the south coast at **Boscombe** Corps in a suburb of Bournemouth. A short rehearsal helped us get settled in, followed by a check in at our hotel and a fellowship dinner of traditional English fish and chips with the Corps Band. The next morning, we had our first concert of the trip at the Pine Walk Bandstand and as the visitors in this southern tourist town passed by, we entertained them with light selections of music.

The concert was followed by a sightseeing trip to Christchurch and a visit to the 900-year-old Christchurch Priory, where the band was delayed as we waited for a wedding to finish. What a surprise for the newlywed bride and groom as they exited the majestic Priory and were greeted by 30-plus people in matching jackets, applauding them.

The day concluded with our first major concert of the trip, followed by the Sunday morning service led by the CSB, including excellent participation from the Boscombe YP Band, Singing Company and Songsters. However, the most impressive part of the service was the singing of the congregation. As we would find out at each stop of our tour, the English Salvationists love to sing, and do it very well. Our Executive officer, Lt. Col. Richard VanderWeele, brought the message *'It's up to us'* based on Matthew 5:1-16, and the Boscombe Songsters sang us the beautiful benediction, *May it Be*.

A quick lunch sent us on our way to **Reading Central** for a combined Salvation meeting of the three corps in the city. The Reading Central Band set the tone by marching the CSB in with the march *Torchbearers*. Again, the local songster brigade participated in the service and there was an extended period of testimonies from the local Salvationists and from the CSB.

Monday started with some sightseeing at Windsor Castle and the town of Eton which is the home of Eton College, described as the most famous public school in the world, with 19 British Prime Ministers and many British royals listed as alumni. Several members of The International Staff Band were in attendance for the evening's concert at Reading Central which featured *Concertino for Flugel and Band* (Beth Cooper), the euphonium solo, *We'll All Shout Hallelujah* (Shaun Thomas), the vocal solo *You Raise Me Up* (Heidi Strand) and *Symphony No. 3, Mvt. 4* by Vittorio Giannini.

The next day, on arriving in the city of **Norwich**, we headed out for a really enjoyable afternoon on a boat tour of the Broads, a series of lakes and rivers joined together into a delightful and beautiful waterway. After dinner at the Carvery at the Oakland Hotel, we headed back to the corps for the evening concert.

And so we travelled north to the city of **Leeds,** where we met with the Lord Mayor of Leeds, who kindly gave us a civic reception. He also joined us for the evening's concert was held at the nearby Morley Town Hall, along with members of the Black Dyke Band, one of the oldest and most famous brass bands in the world.

Thursday was a short trip to the North-East and started with an afternoon concert at Durham Cathedral, built in 1093. About 100 people were expected, but we were more than pleasantly surprised when over 600 showed up. The sounds of the band may still be echoing inside this majestic building, including a work composed by Bandmaster William

> *The evening's concert was far beyond anything we could have imagined. The response of a packed house of Salvationists and brass band enthusiasts to every number and the unified playing of eight Staff Bands brought goose-bumps. A personal highlight was the playing of the march, Celebration, with the Staff Band members singing while an enormous SA flag was unfurled. To God be the glory!*

Himes for this tour, *Soli Deo Gloria*, the prelude *Ein Feste Burg* and the vocal *He Leadeth Me*. The evening concert was held at the Empire Theatre, just down the block from the **Consett** Corps, home of the very first Salvation Army corps band.

Friday brought our earliest departure of the tour, 5:30am and a very quiet bus ride south to **Chelmsford**. A lunchtime concert at the Chelmsford Cathedral, which was also the venue for our evening concert, saw Shaun Thomas celebrating his 25th birthday with a stellar performance of *We'll All Shout Hallelujah*, followed by the entire audience singing 'Happy Birthday' to him!

As great a trip as it had been, everything changed on Saturday morning as the eight staff bands assembled inside the Royal Albert Hall for our united rehearsal. As we sat there crowded on the stage shoulder to shoulder, it became apparent that this would be no ordinary concert. As we greeted each other and got about rehearsing the numbers for the evening, we were joined together by the music on the page and the God that inspired every note – over 250 Staff Band members united in praise.

Walking into that hall will be a memory not easily forgotten. The scope and scale of what we were part of began to sink in as we were reunited with friends from different bands and previous trips. The unique fellowship we have as Salvation Army Staff Band members became apparent as we dutifully set about rehearsing the music for that evening's performance. The intermingling of veteran players and those on their first trips added to the excitement and energy. This collection of men and women from around the world became one band, but the best was yet to come.

The afternoon was filled with spectacular performances by each band with the enthusiastic support of kindred band members, watching and listening from high in the balconies and behind the stage. What a privilege to share in this way.

The evening's concert was far beyond anything we could have imagined. The response of a packed house of Salvationists and brass band enthusiasts to every number and the unified playing of eight Staff Bands brought goose bumps. A personal highlight was the playing of the march, *Celebration*, with the Staff Band members singing while an enormous SA flag was unfurled. To God be the glory!

The celebration continued on Sunday with the march down The Mall to Buckingham Palace. We were amazed at the throngs of onlookers cheering and singing as we marched *en masse*. I kept thinking, 'Who are these people and where did they come from?' Never before have I witnessed such an event, let alone be part of one. And I suppose it will be a long time before I do again.

Even without the final weekend, this was a memorable trip. The Chicago Staff Band truly presented itself as the 'band with a sacred message' at every opportunity and presented the Gospel clearly through its music, words and actions. The impact of this tour will be felt for a long time on both sides of the Atlantic. May Jesus Christ be praised!

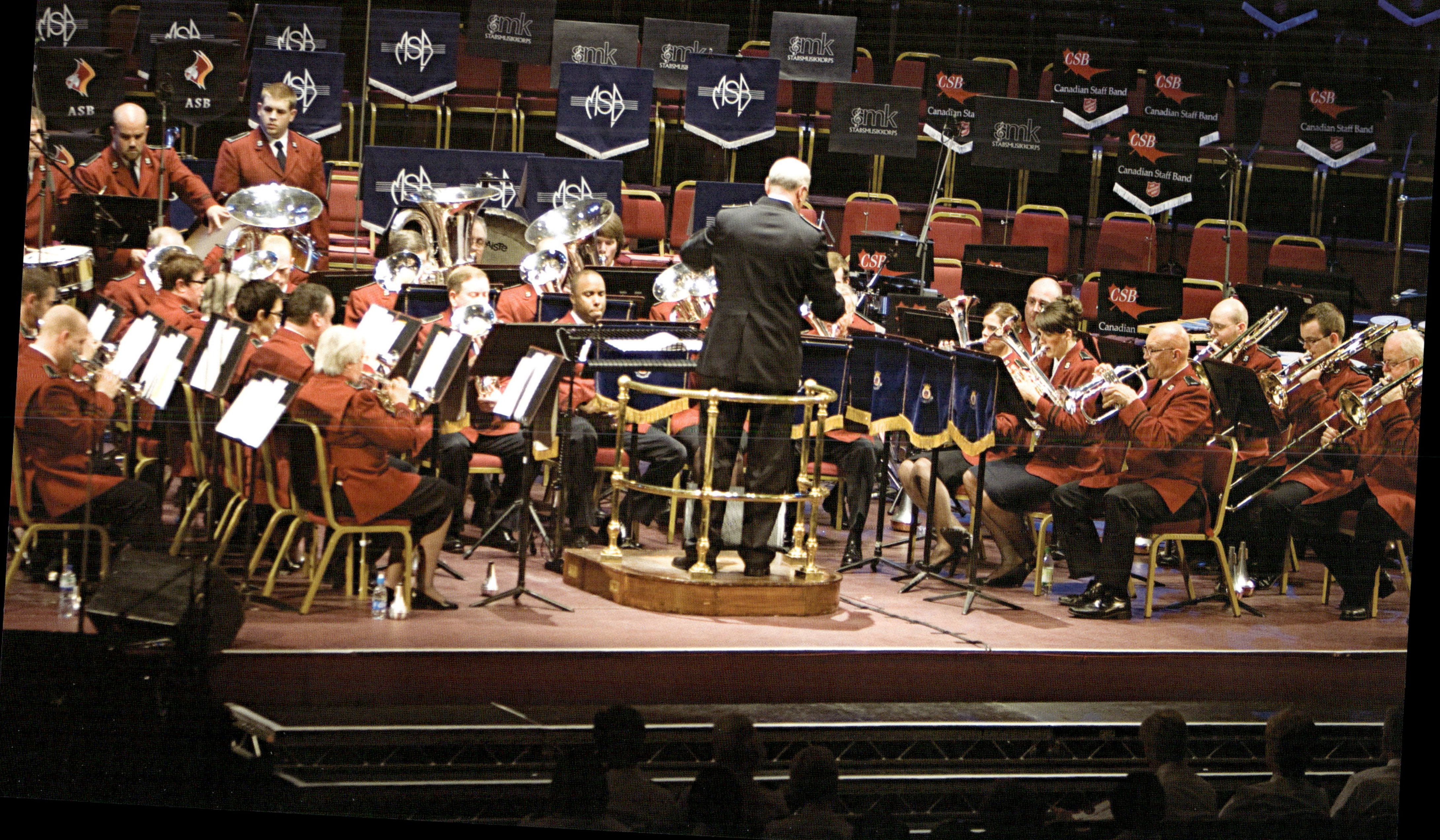
ASB
CSB
Canadian Staff Band

110

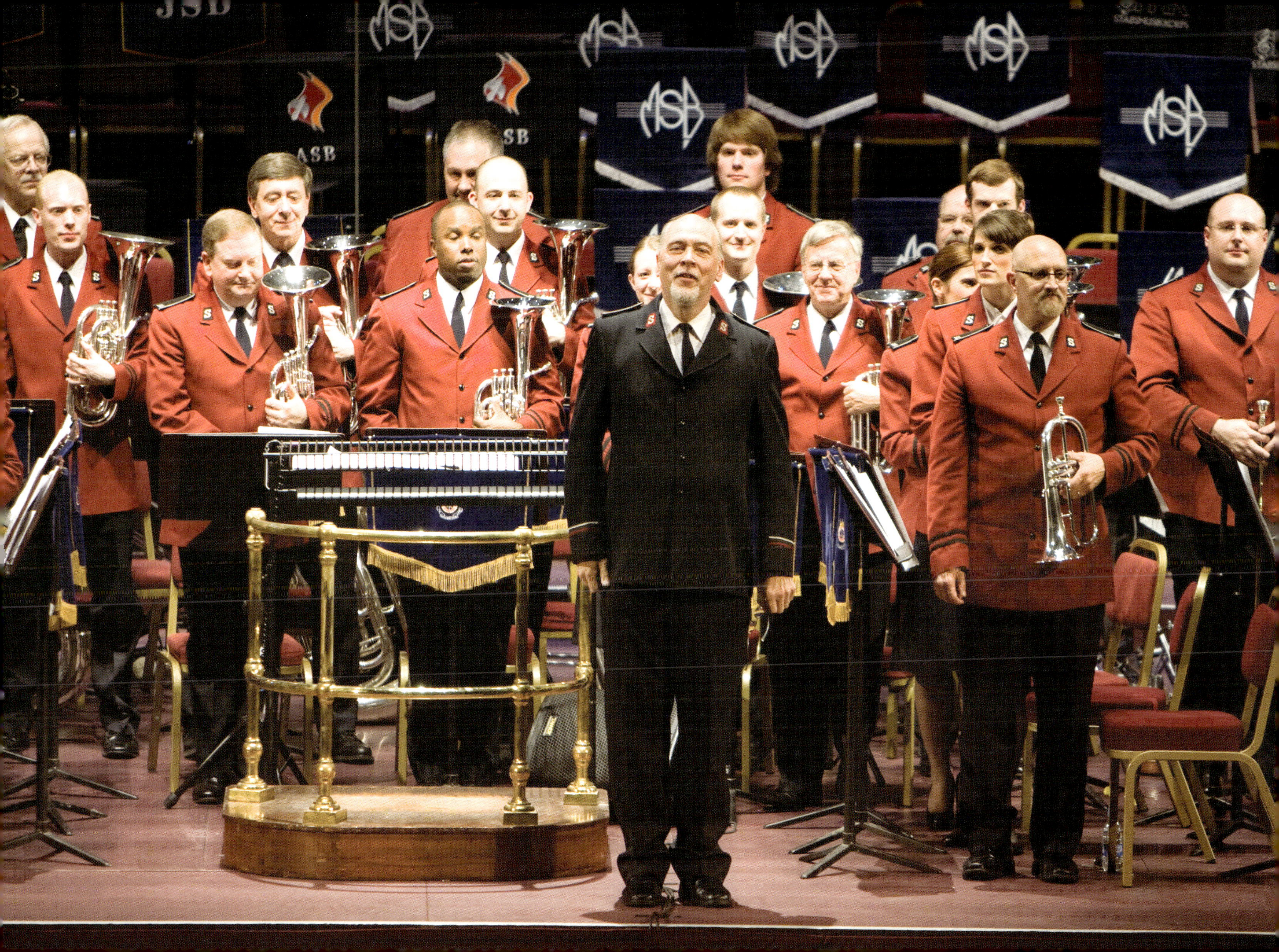
JSB
ASB
MSB

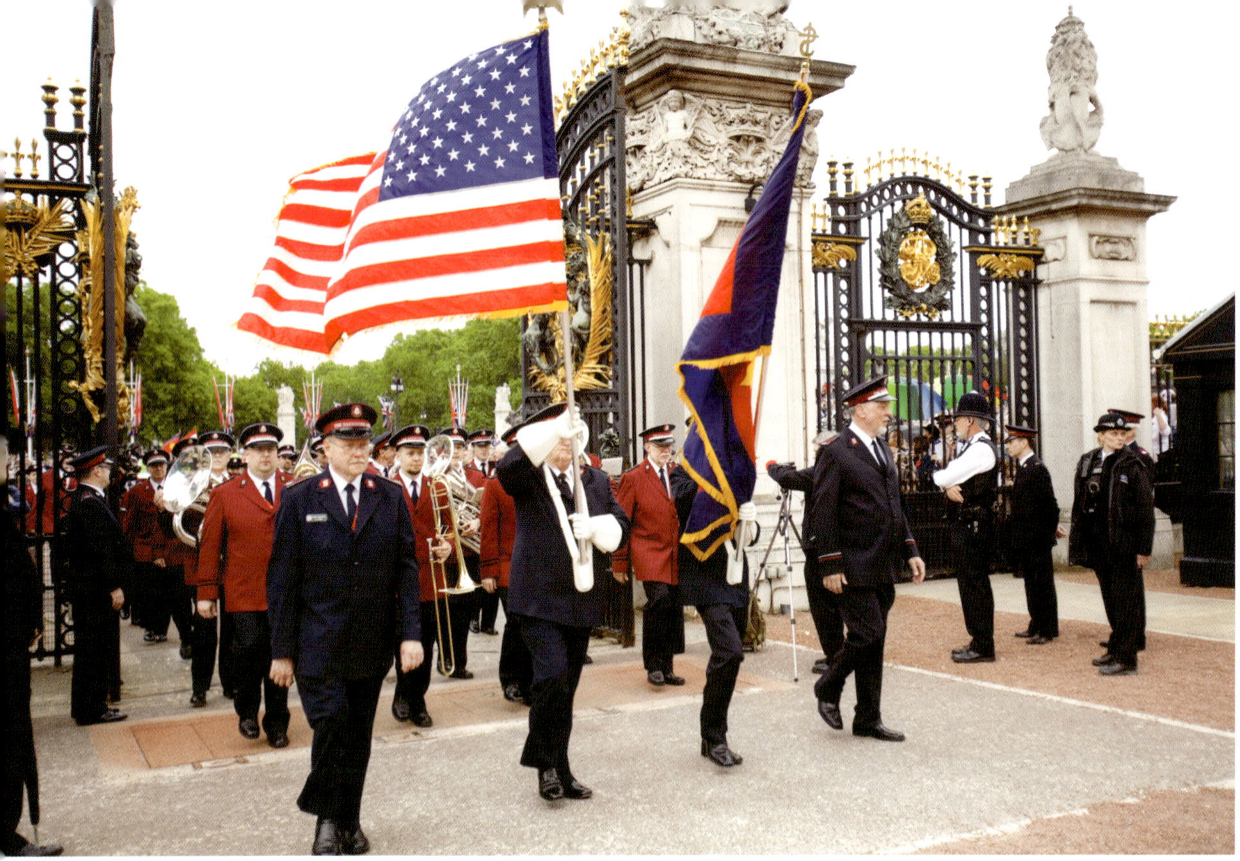

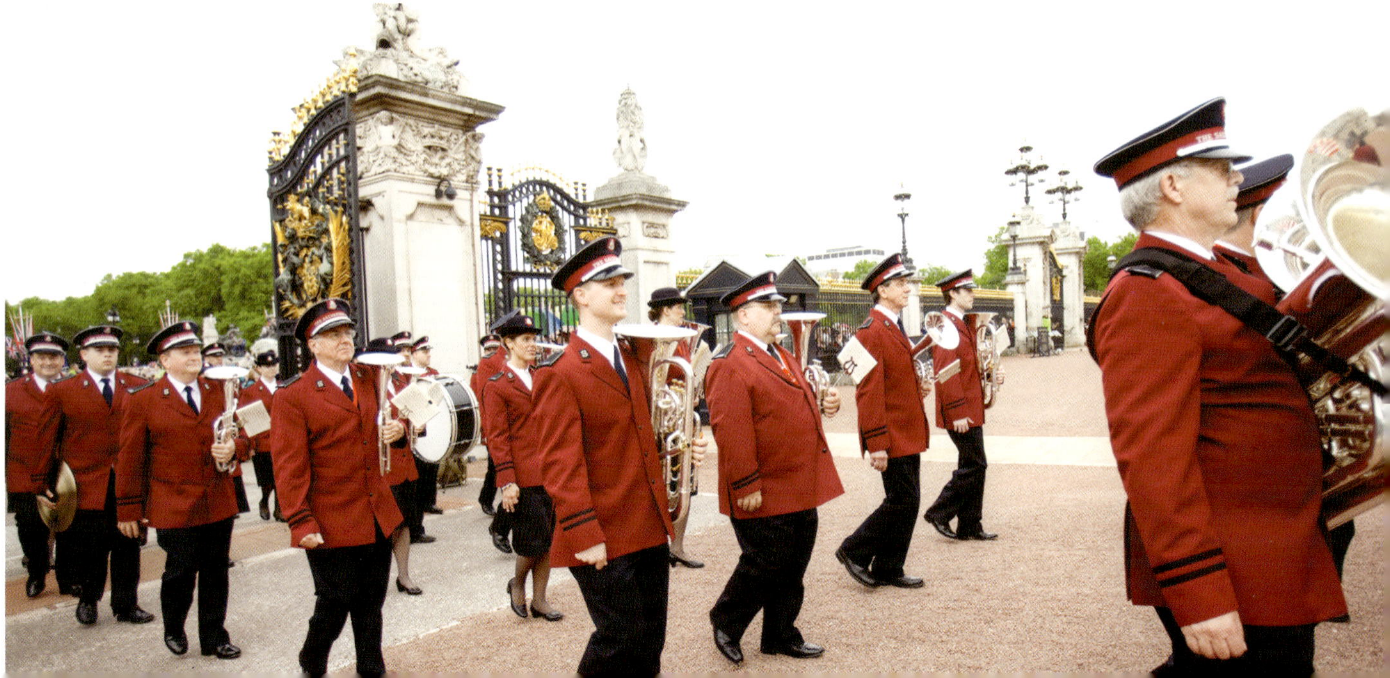

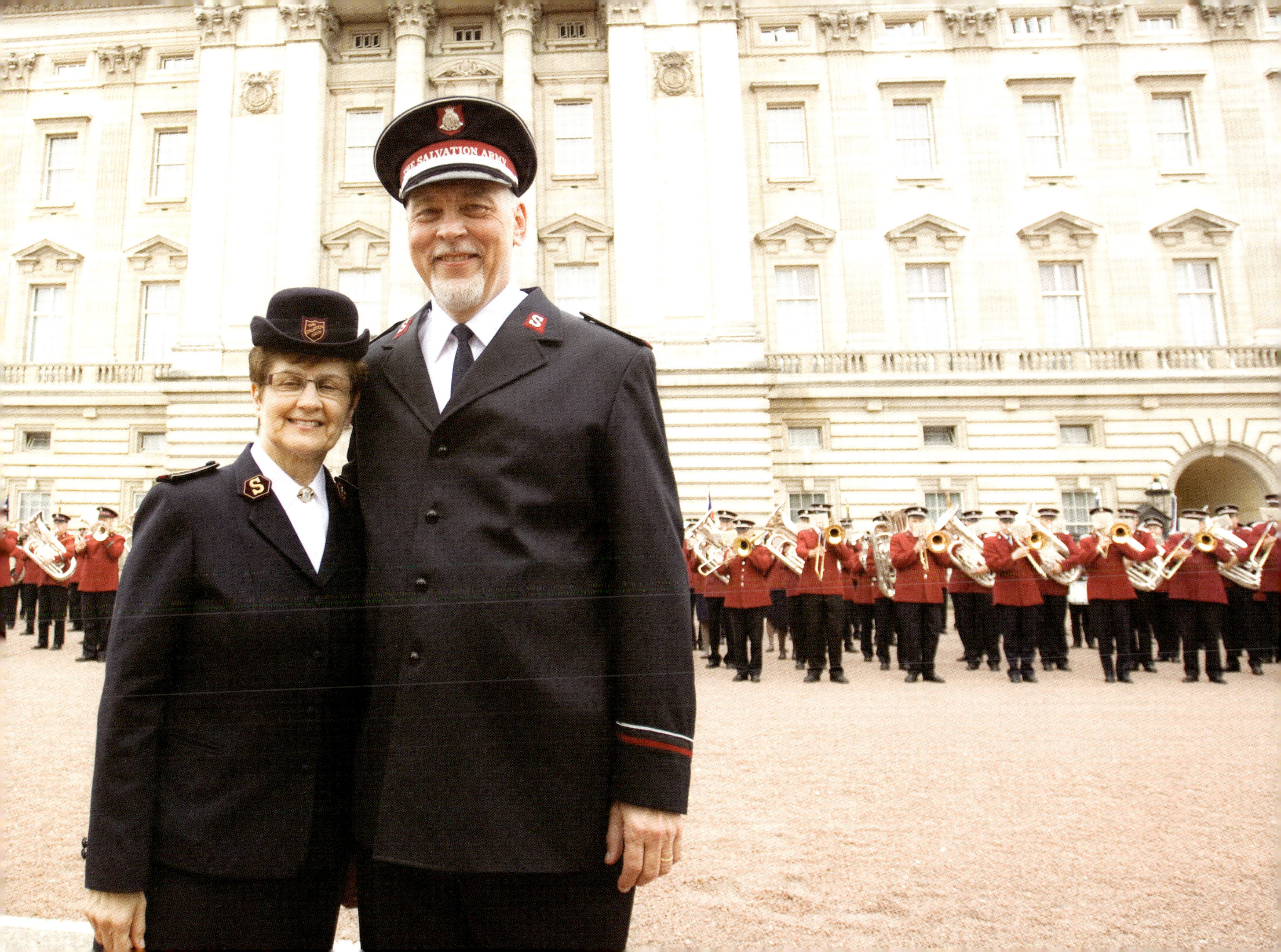
THE SALVATION ARMY

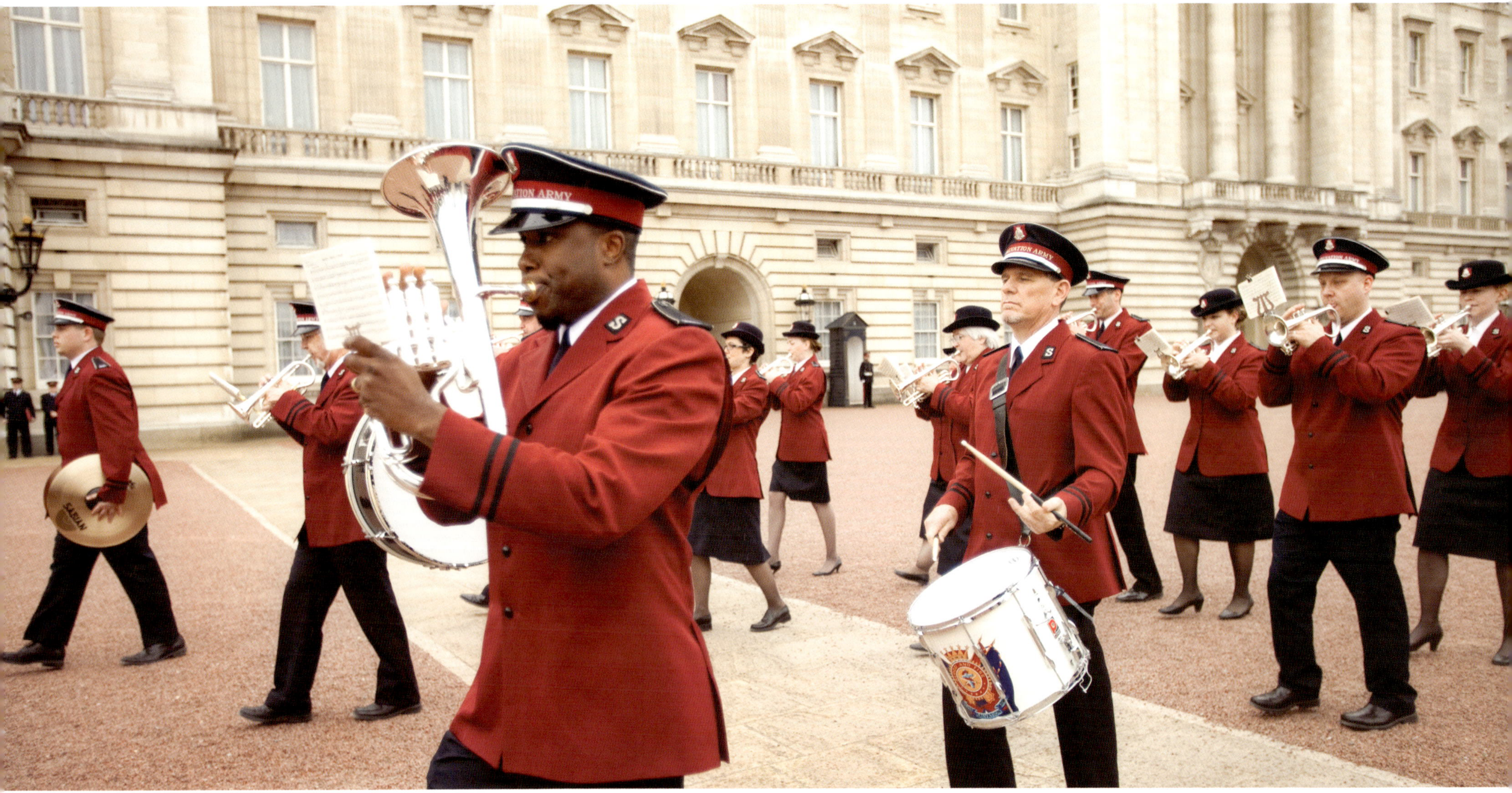

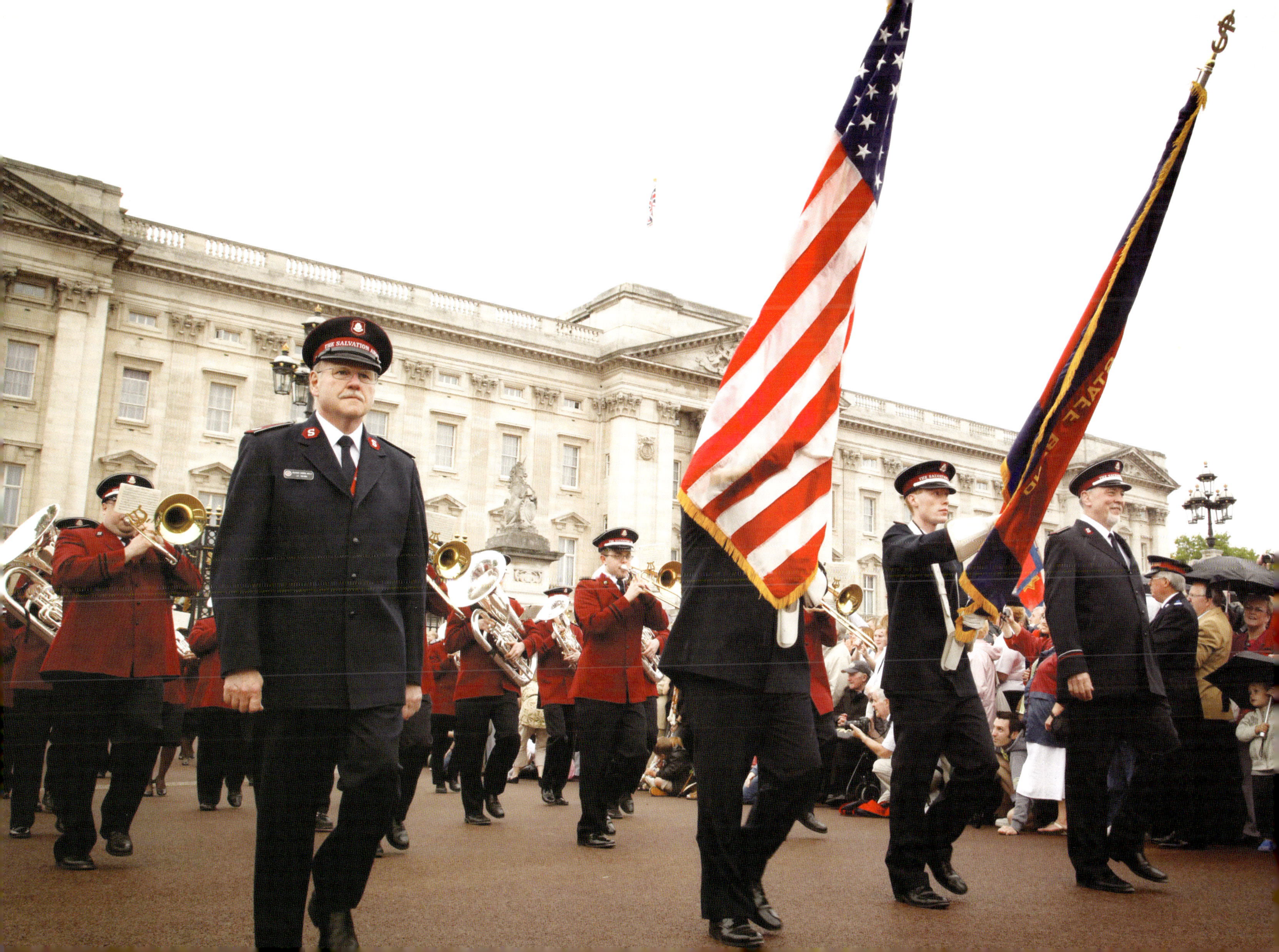

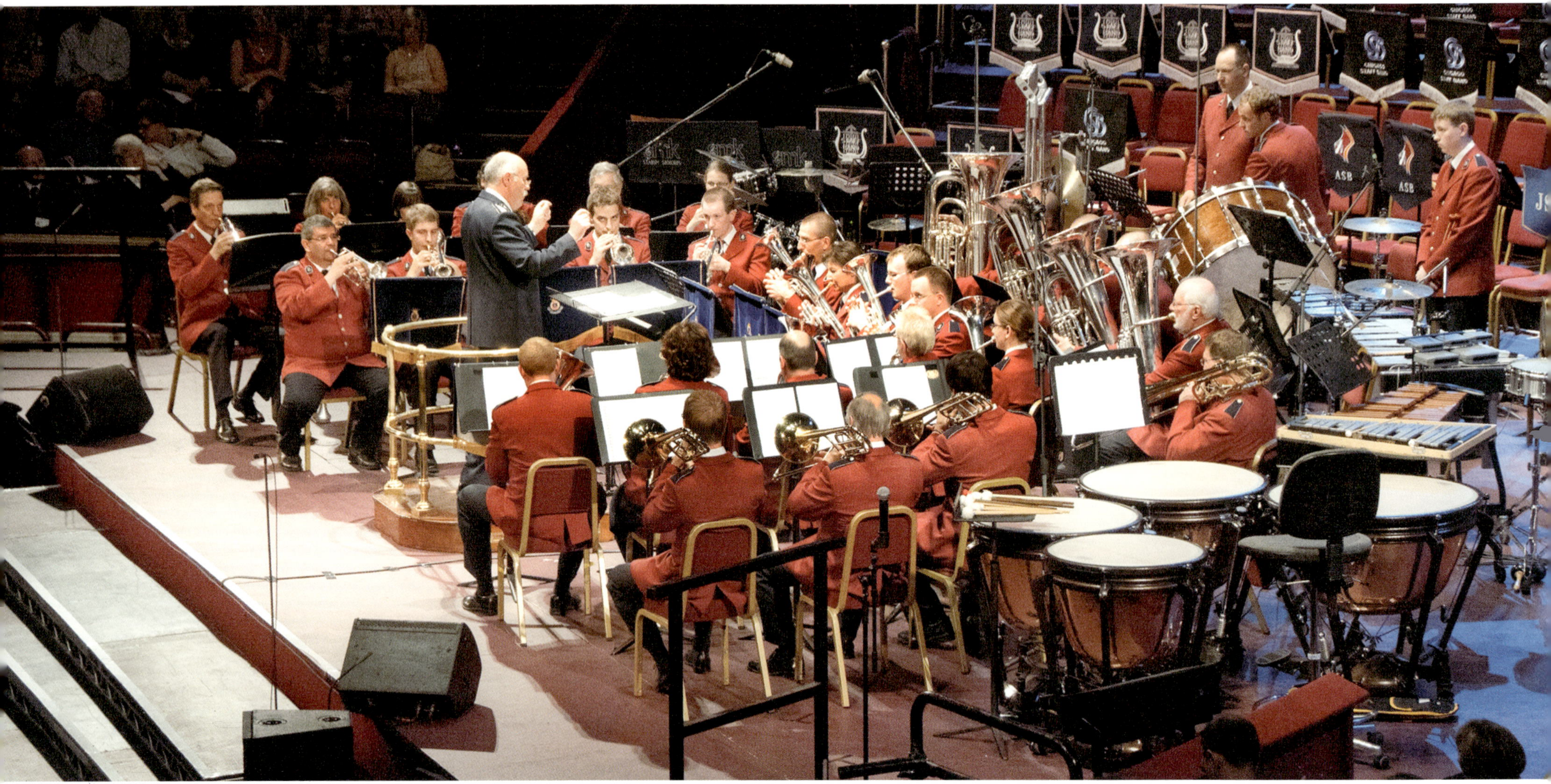
ASB
ASB

GERMAN STAFF BAND

Build up to the weekend - Gernod Kumm

When in one of our practices in 2010 we learned of the invitation to ISB120, we were joyfully surprised but there was a great deal of scepticism as well. Basically, we wanted to be involved but first of all clarification of some aspects was needed. In the following months ISB120 started to get into shape for the German Staff Band (GSB) and for financial reasons we decided not to fly to England, but charter a bus.

During the preparation it became clear that Ruben Schmidt's new piece of music, *A Variation for Jubilee – Lobe den Herren*, would be well suited for the coming event. Because the band members come from all over Germany and many have to drive several hours by car, the GSB can practice only four to five times a year. For that reason each band member has to prepare the music individually.

Besides uniform clothes for leisure time, there were also uniform hats to buy. Then the great event was immediately ahead of us. The last drill was given by practices and section-practices three days just before our journey. On Wednesday the Canadian Staff Band was met in Essen, where first contacts were made. Additionally the band had to practice marching on a sports field and gave our pre-tour concert on Thursday. That night was very short, because the journey to the UK started at 4am on Friday!

On arriving at **Maidenhead,** the home corps of our tour leader, Adam Hall, we had a short sound check before a concert by the GSB was given in the evening. Solos were played by Damian Lingard (trombone) and Stephen Kane (euphonium). Christine Alexander, an accompanying guest soprano singer, gave two vocal items together with the GSB. Again, on Saturday the departure was early (7am) in order to start the united practice with the other Staff Bands at the Royal Albert Hall in due time.

For the members of the GSB it was a special honour to take part in this unique event. There was not only excellent music to listen to but opportunities were availed to get in contact with other staff bands and to meet acquainted or well-known musicians (again).

Happy but tired, and very much richly blessed with lots of good impressions and again overwhelmed by the internationalism of The Salvation Army, we came back to Solingen on Monday evening.

The event ISB120 will occupy us for a long time and the melodies, played to God's honour, still echo in our hearts.

Reflections

Thomas Noack
Reflecting on ISB120, my thoughts first go back to many hours of practice preparing for the great event. My personal tension was high because we were to take part in a unique event with musicians of the highest quality. Spectacular indeed was *Brass Spectacular*, when we made music together with all the other Staff Band members. Seeing all those band members at the Royal Albert Hall was an impressive view for me. The march to Buckingham Palace was a special experience which I will never forget. I greatly admired the whole organisation and staging of the weekend – an enormous task done so well. For me it was a great event with the opportunity to play with the best of Salvation Army brass bands and having the chance to meet with our General. I'm grateful to God that I could be part of all that and I'm a little bit proud of it too!

> "Of course the semi-professionals among us aptly appreciated the performance of those professional musicians, but it was the community we shared and the spiritual unity overcoming all borders of countries and cultures that left the deepest impression on me... However I have been able to see how each instrument through the devotion of each musician became a channel of God's blessing."

Andreas Bargel

In the sphere of professional musicians it is often said "two musicians – one competition." That was what I expected: competition, envy, exhibition in a Christian dress. However, a completely different message was projected at ISB120 by the united playing of the eight Staff Bands.

Of course the semi-professionals among us aptly appreciated the performance of those professional musicians, but it was the community we shared and the spiritual unity overcoming all borders of countries and cultures that left the deepest impression on me. Certainly it is something outstanding when so many well-prepared musicians follow exactly the directions of the conductors and by this, giving the basis for a fantastic musical experience. However, I have been able to see how each instrument through the devotion of each musician became a channel of God's blessing.

For me ISB120 became a fantastic musical occasion, but first of all a human and spiritual experience. I for myself have experienced ISB120 by the slogan: '250 musicians – one spirit!'... and the story continues.

Michael Zalewski

When Bandmaster Heinrich Schmidt first mentioned that there was an idea of bringing all Staff Bands together in London, I didn't think that this could become reality. I knew that two Staff Bands could easily share the Royal Albert Hall's stage like in 1994 when the German Staff Band played there together with the ISB, but I could not imagine how eight Staff Bands could fit on the stage and play together. Considering the financial and personnel challenges GSB was facing at that time, I have to admit I wasn't too optimistic about becoming part of the ambitious idea. Thanks to God, my unbelief was unjustified.

A personal highlight, of course, was to be featured in the flugel horn octet *So Glad!* Playing together with seven other flugel horn players and being accompanied by eight Staff Bands was surely a once-in-a-lifetime situation for all eight of us. Another highlight was the fellowship with the other bands. We met the Canadian Staff Band during its European tour, shared a hotel and RAH's changing room with the Amsterdam Staff Band, had an unofficial coach race with the Japan Staff Band and marched alongside our American friends of the Chicago Staff Band with whom we had played two years before.

As for myself I only realised a few days after the event what we all had become part of – an idea that turned into reality, an idea to bring all the world's Staff Bands together to celebrate and be a witness to each other and to all people who attended ISB120.

Rebekka Freund

When people in Germany ask me about what I do in my free time and I tell them about the GSB and brass music in general, I often get asked 'Oh, like in the movie *Brassed off?!*'

The last time someone asked I had to think about the great event ISB120 again. I probably felt a little bit like the mine workers in that movie when entering the Royal Albert Hall for the first time. I don't even know what was more overwhelming, the building itself with its peerless atmosphere, or the feeling of meeting over 250 Salvation Army musicians for this very special weekend. Even though I was quite nervous before our first performance in the afternoon, afterwards I felt like everyone else in the band and the audience could feel the spirit of the Lord, which clearly filled the Albert Hall with each great performance of the eight staff bands that whole Saturday afternoon.

My personal favourite moment, next to the final piece *Celebration*, with the fireworks and the huge flag behind us, clearly was the congregational singing in the evening when the lights were turned on and we as musicians were able to see everyone in the audience standing and singing *Stand up and bless the Lord*. I am very grateful for this opportunity with the GSB and I am still blessed very much when I recall the weekend and all the great people I was able to meet and befriend.

The FLAG of the German Staff Band shares its experiences and highlights!

Tabea Preuss

Tonight, Saturday 4 June 2011, all bands will march into the Royal Albert Hall with their flags. I myself stay in the dressing room and wait for that moment.

Now, somebody comes and I get ready. My colleague, the German national flag has been sleeping the whole time, while I have been listening to everything that has been going on, especially to the afternoon concert of the GSB and the big applause given to them. After the band members have come back from their meal I get ready for the marching in. Through many corridors, my flag-bearer and I reach the door we will step through into the great RAH. We have to wait while many of the audience are passing by us. I'm very excited and so is my flag-bearer.

Now it starts. One Staff Band after the other is marching in and is greeted by the audience with their shouts and their clapping hands. What a marvellous feeling. The initial phase has been perfect and the evening has all together been wonderful.

Sunday - today is my greatest day: the march down The Mall. All bandsmen and women are wearing their red tunics. There is just enough time for a small 'wink' to the flag of the ASB! Then the Parade Marshall, Band Sergeant Major Ralph Brill of the Band of the Scots Guards, gives his command for us to start marching. It is an inexpressible feeling to march in this big group of flags and bands, while people are cheering and giving applause.

Now we arrive at Victoria Memorial and have to stop and wait. I feel the tension of my flag-bearer, because she has to walk into the forecourt of Buckingham Palace first of everyone in our band. After that, my flag-bearer can put me down for the time of the concert. I touch the ground of Buckingham Palace! It's unbelievable. After the concert, all bands march to Wellington Barracks, where pictures with all flags are made. I'm proud of my flag-bearer, because she is the only woman in this group.

An event like these days I have never had before in the 22 years of my life and I'll never forget it.

> Even though I was quite nervous before our first performance in the afternoon, afterwards I felt like everyone else of the band and the audience could feel the spirit of the Lord which clearly filled the Albert Hall with each great performance of the eight Staff Bands that whole Saturday afternoon. My personal favourite moment, next to the final piece *Celebration*, with the fireworks and the huge flag behind us, clearly was the congregational singing in the evening when the lights were turned on and we as musicians were able to see everyone in the audience standing and singing *Stand up and bless the Lord*.

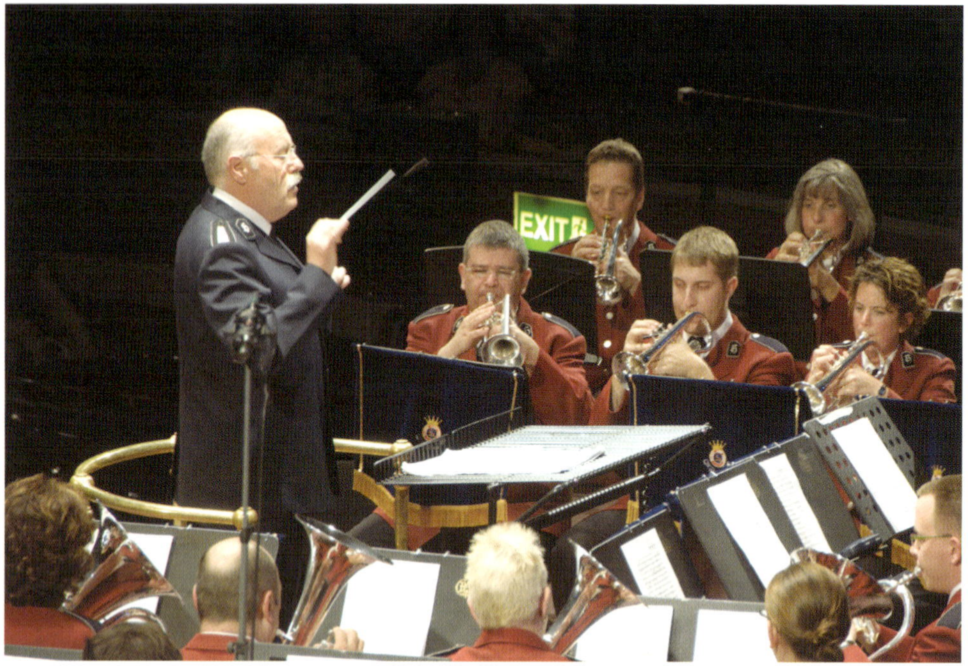
EXIT

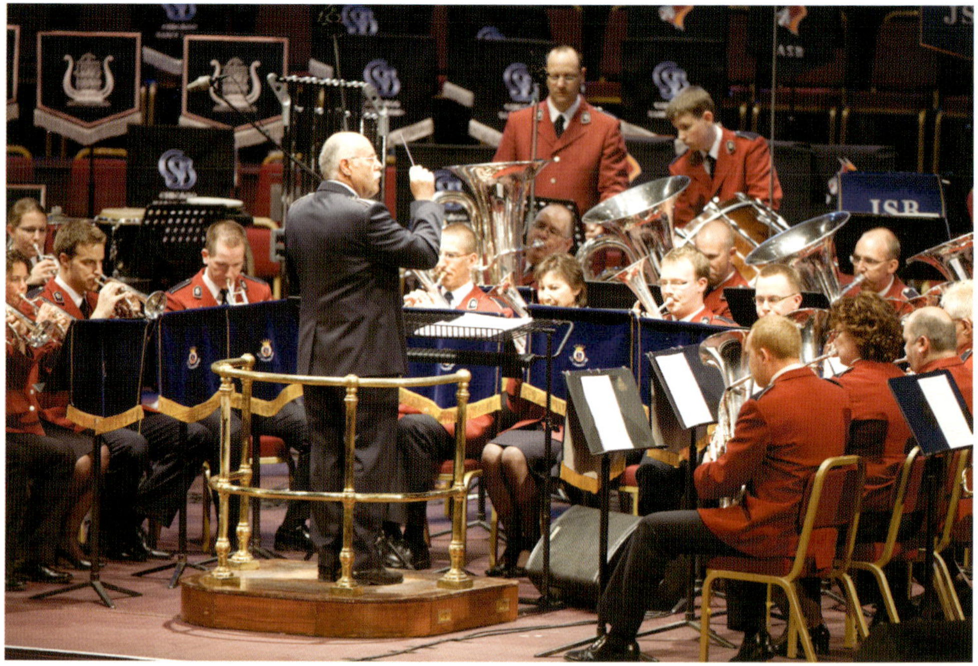
ISB

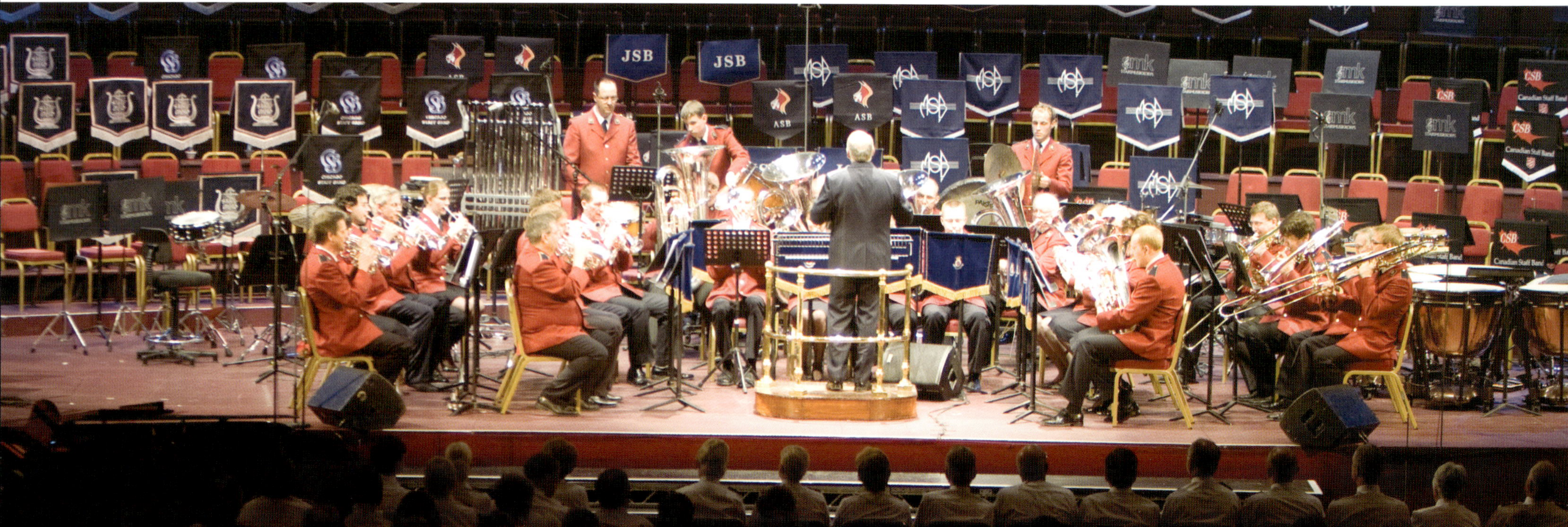
JSB
JSB
ASB
ASB
CSB
Canadian Staff Band

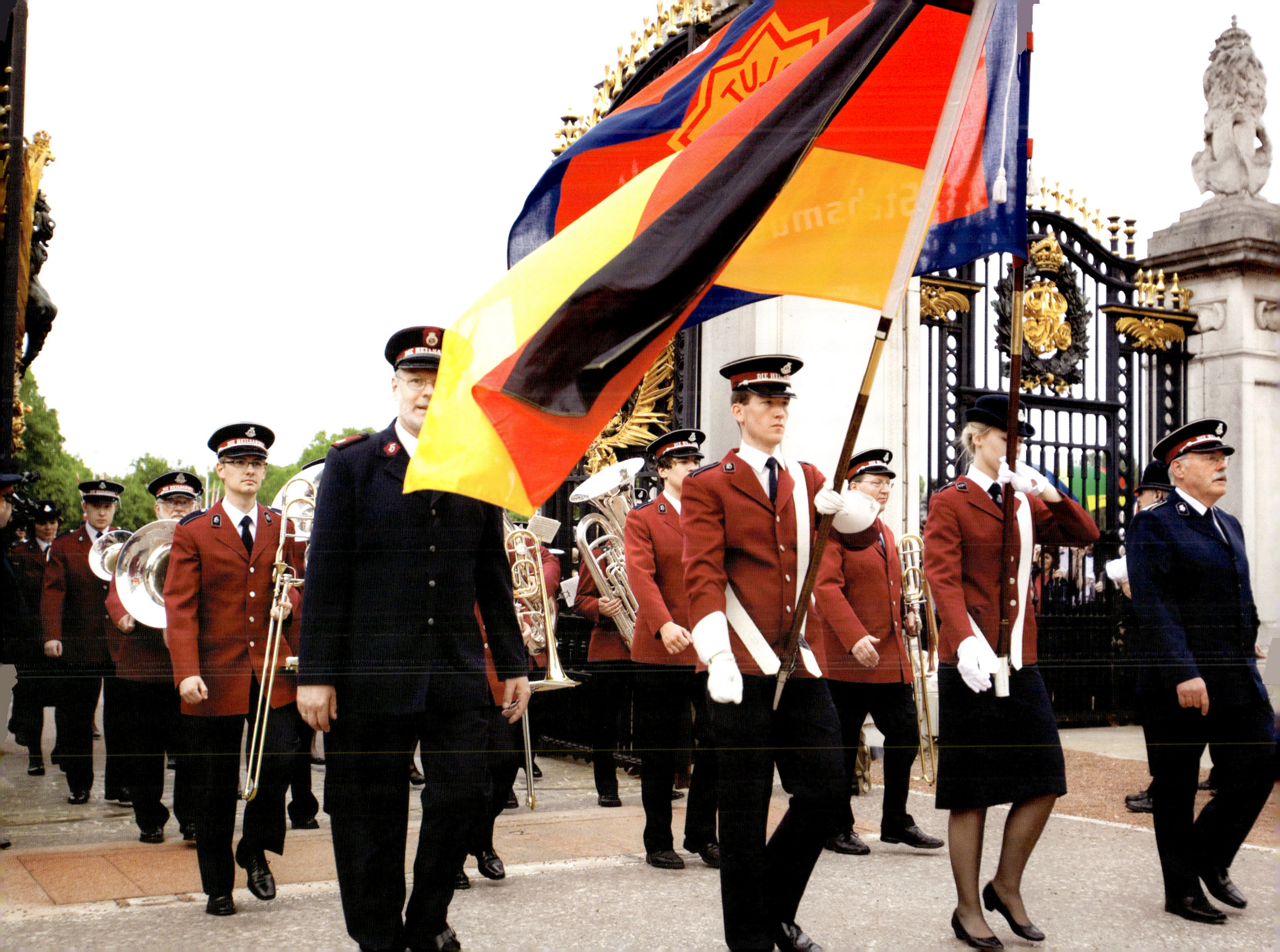

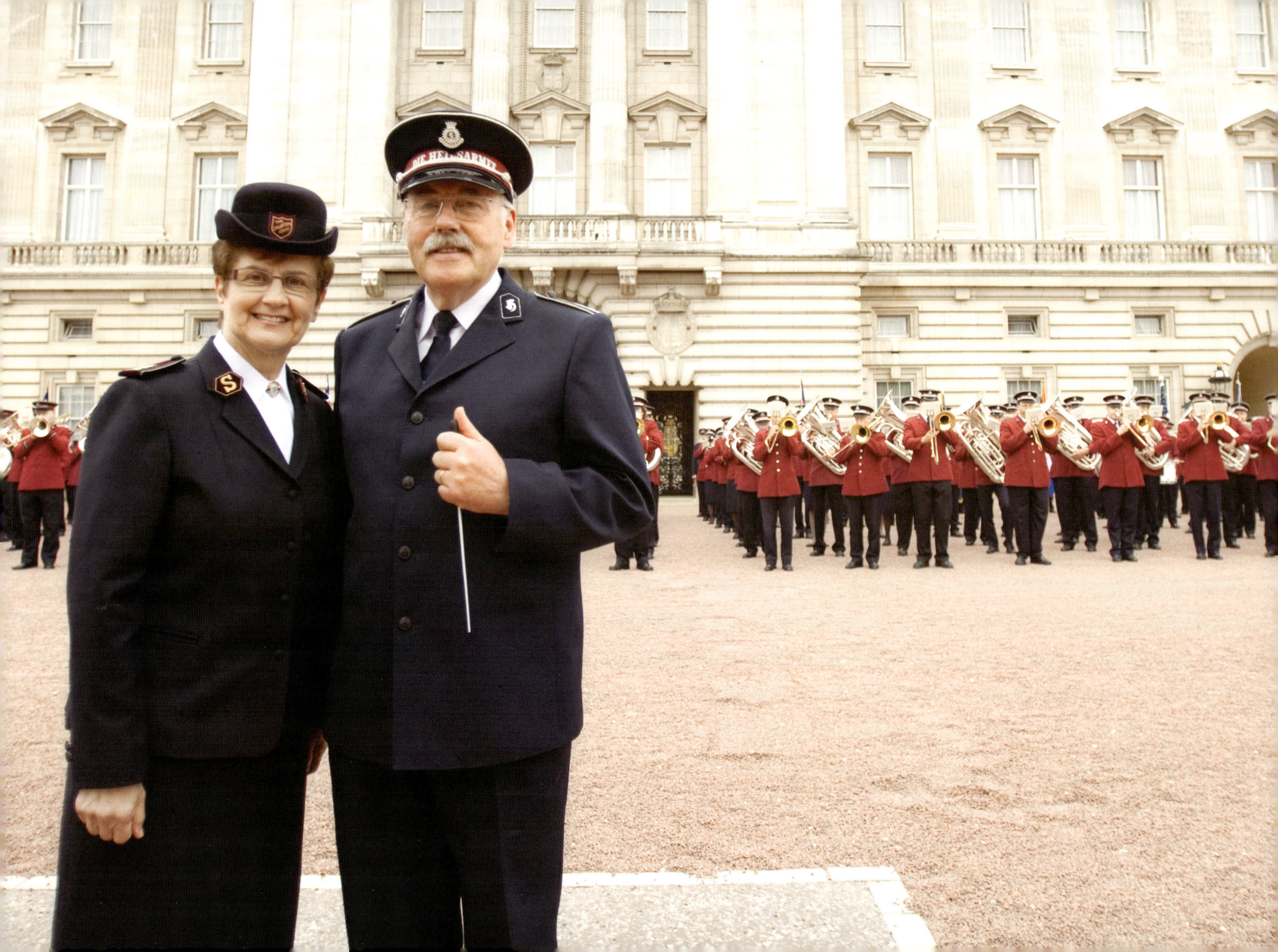

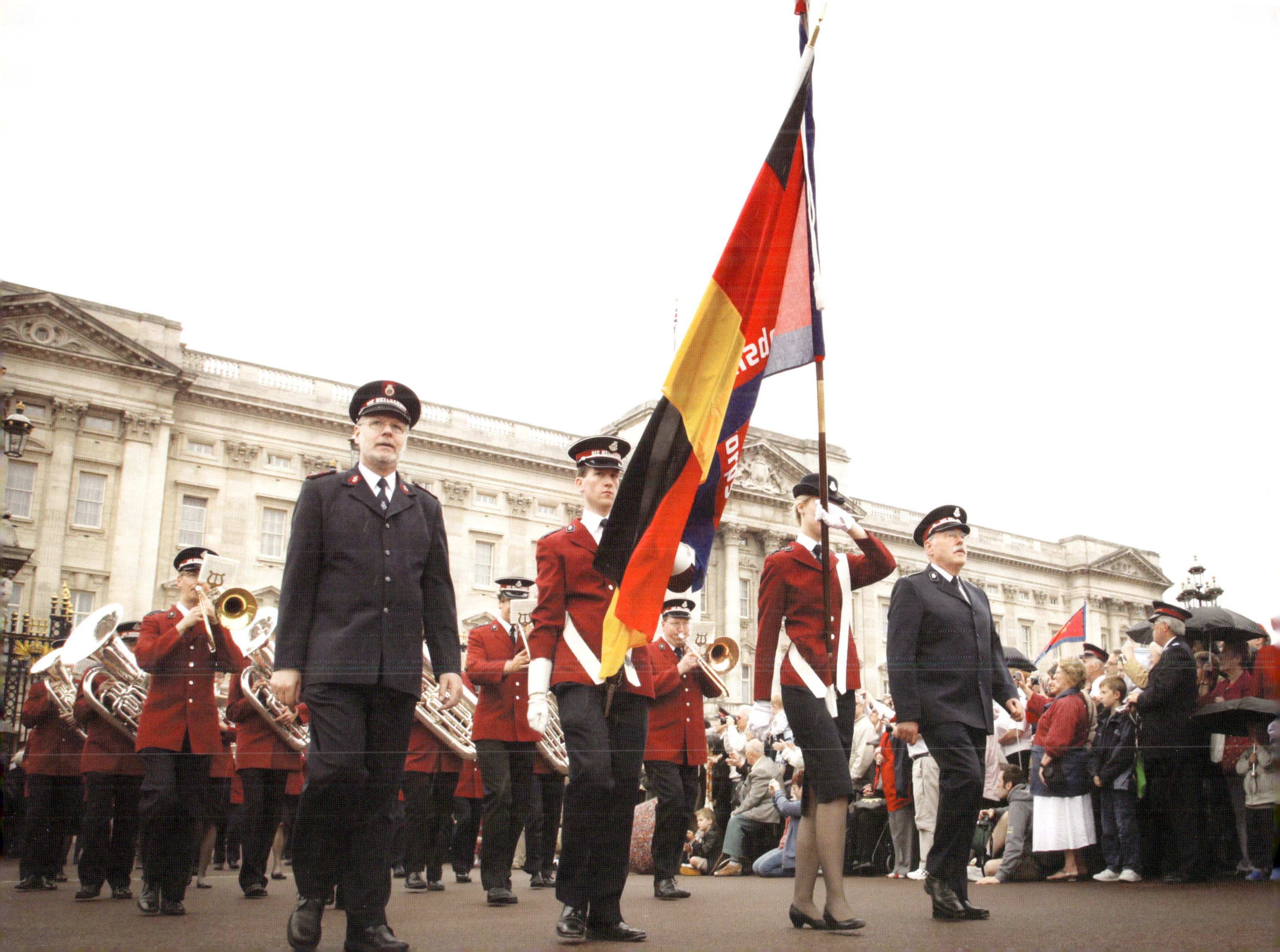

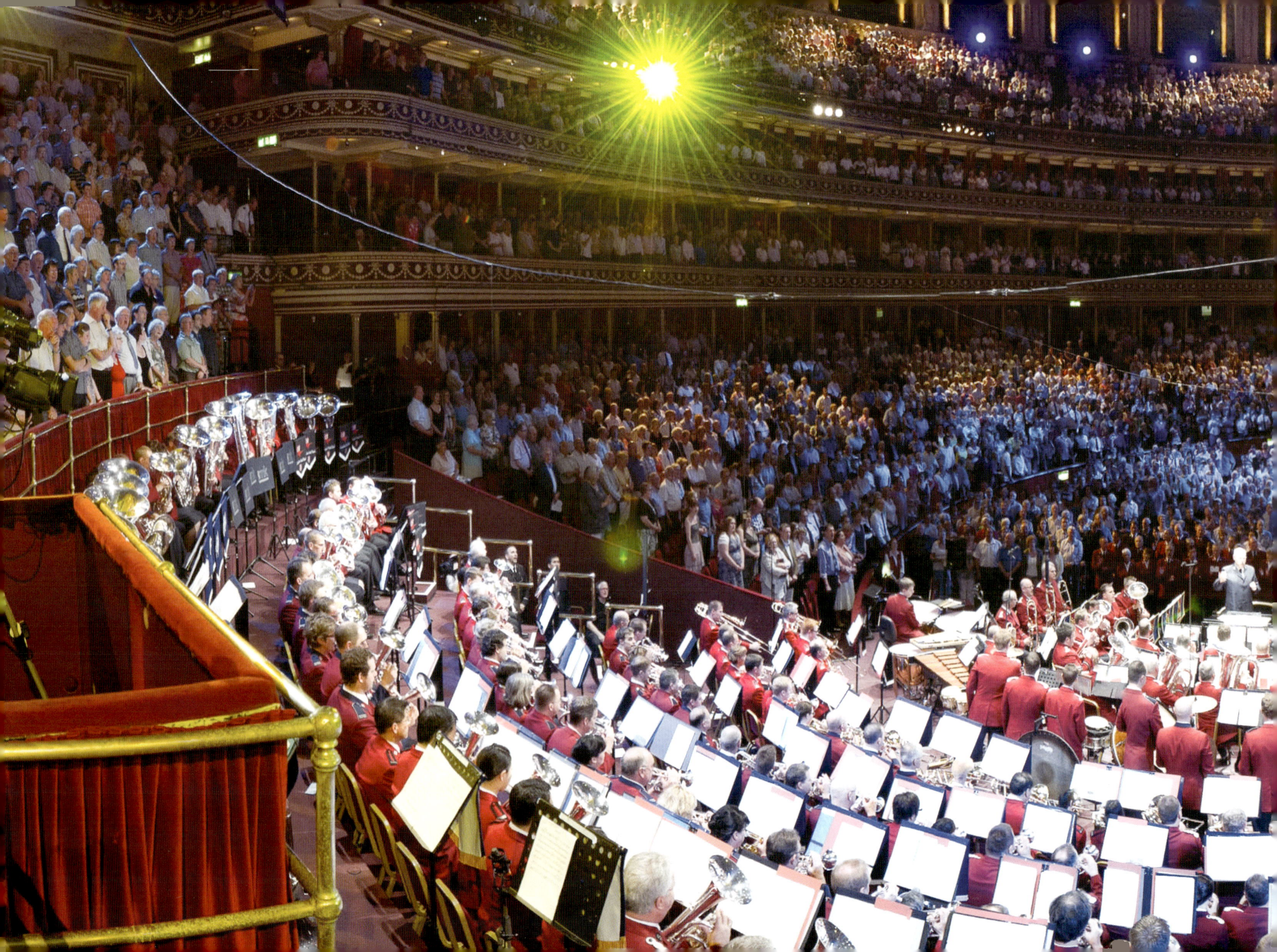

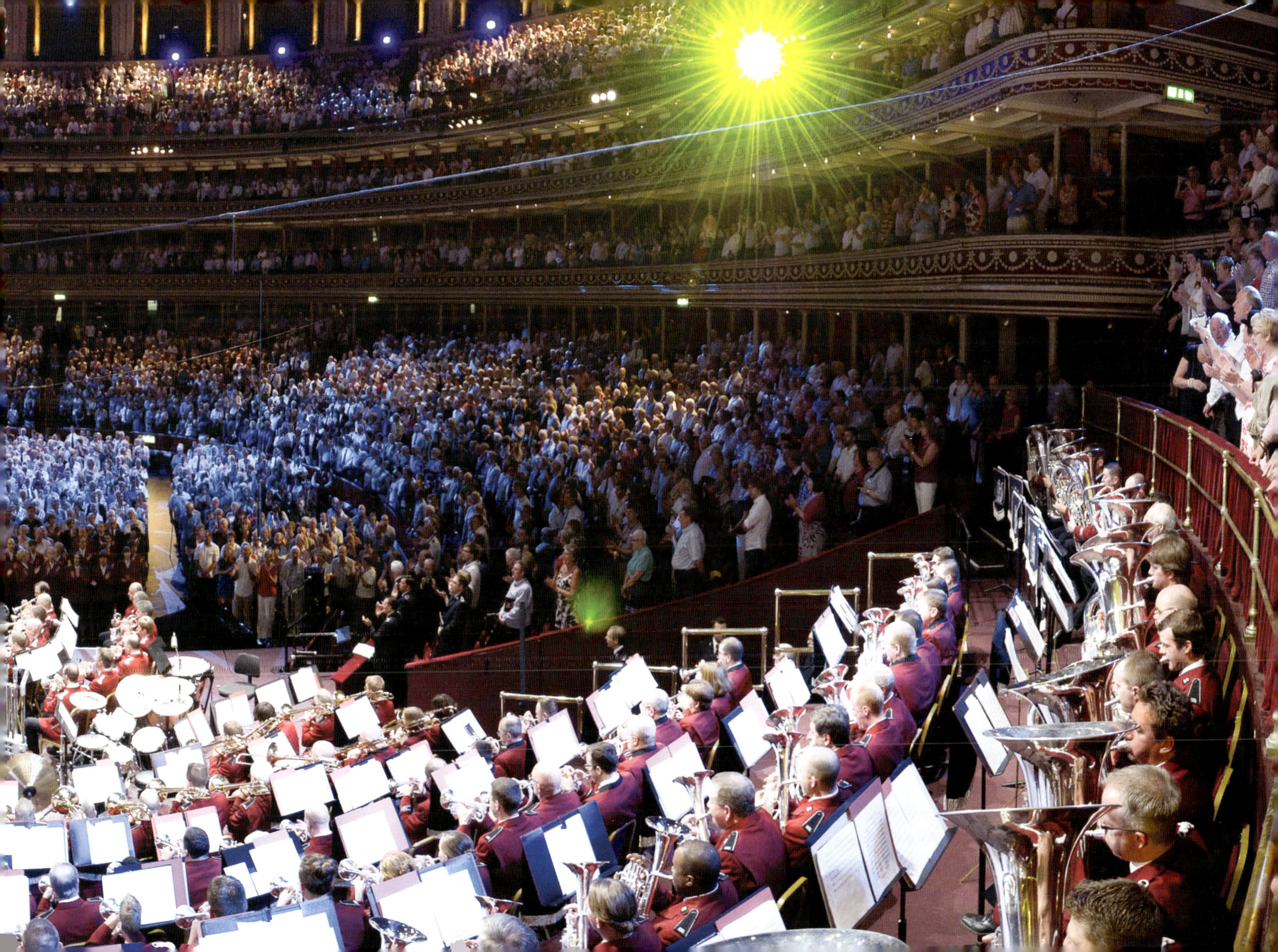

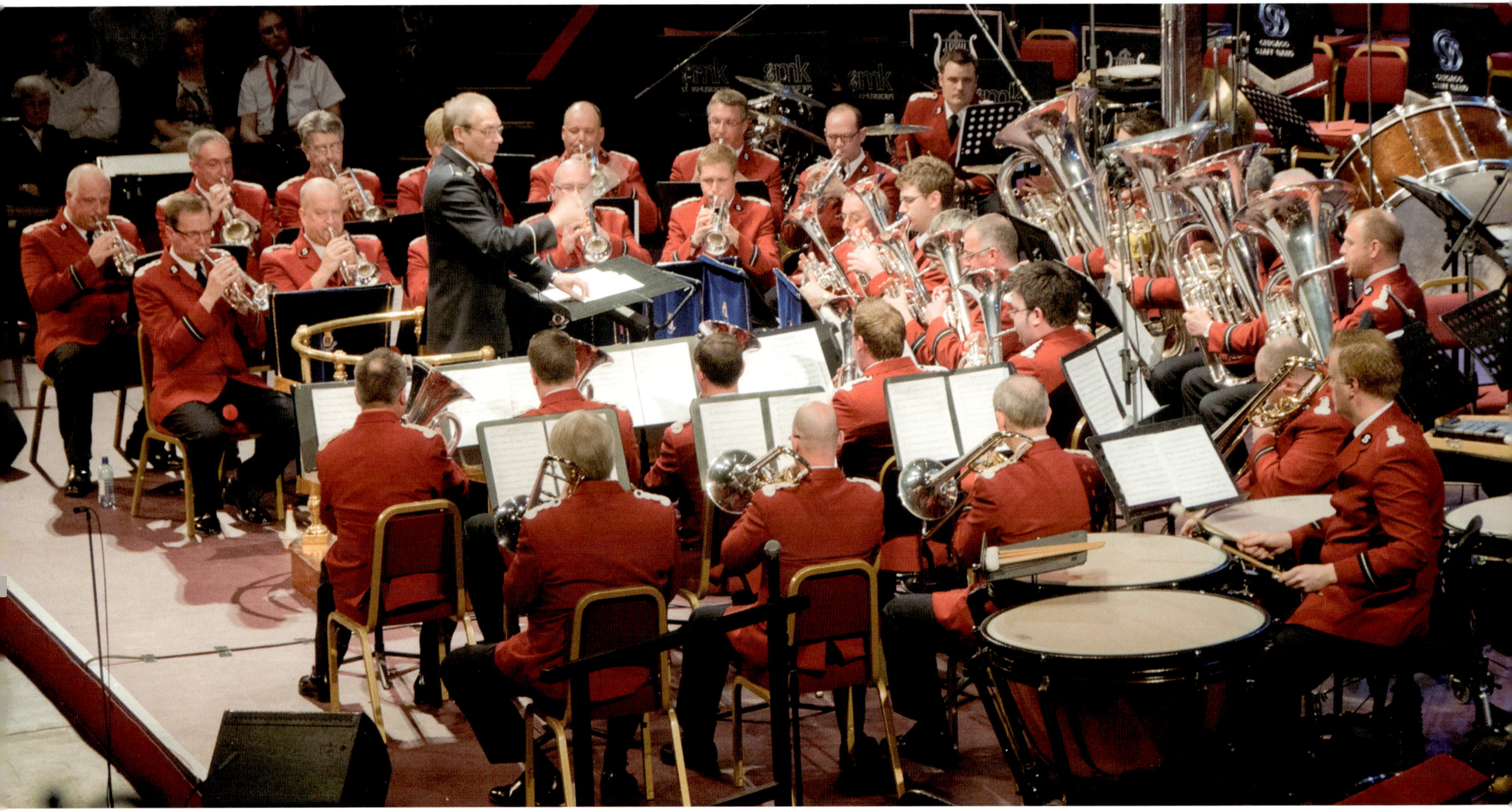

INTERNATIONAL STAFF BAND
Ian Wilson

Being a member of the ISB is a huge privilege and we are afforded many wonderful opportunities to share. On first hearing that seven Staff Bands would be joining us at our 120th birthday party, I thought that this had the potential to be a very special weekend. I have to admit that I didn't realise just how special, and how it would have such a worldwide impact. I grew up in a small town in the North East of England and I still remember Christmas morning, December 1994, receiving the double CD of the four Staff Band Festival in Roy Thomson Hall, Canada. What a wonderful occasion that must have been. I never envisaged that I would ever be part of something such as that, let alone something on an even larger scale.

I have to admit to always being slightly envious of the guys in the ISB who took part in that event in 1994 - a feeling slightly eased by the fact they are all obviously quite old now - but because of ISB120 those feelings can now be laid to rest!

Build-up to the weekend and preparation

As the ISB120 weekend drew closer, the announcements, updates and briefings by Malcolm Quinn at our Wednesday evening rehearsals became more frequent. For me one of the most memorable announcements was learning that Stuart Hall, a member of our trombone section and a key part of the team responsible for organising ISB120 had, just a few days previously, marched along The Mall (on his own) to count the number of steps needed and the time taken. More than this, he then equated that to the number of SA marches needed to ensure the seamless transition of all eight bands into the forecourt of Buckingham Palace. It is still to be confirmed whether or not Stuart was playing his trombone when marching down The Mall on his own, but it's impressive nonetheless! To me this embodies and encapsulates the level of planning that went into making this weekend such a success and the many people involved deserve huge credit.

Following the announcements about the march down The Mall, we were then presented with what I can only describe as a 60-page dossier on how it would work and the role that we as a band were to play in this. In no uncertain terms we were told to study and digest these instructions. An individual much more paranoid than I may have begun to think that the ISB is not known for its marching, but we were completely aware of the role and position of ALL bands on the march!

> " ISB trombonist Stuart Hall... had, just a few days previous, marched along The Mall to count the number of steps needed and the time taken. To me this embodies and encapsulates the level of planning that went into making this weekend such a success and the many people involved deserve huge credit. "

The weekend itself began to feel very real for me when, two weeks before ISB120, the ISB was travelling to the North West of England for our monthly weekend of ministry. Whilst at the Service Station on the M1 (waiting for the coach) we were discussing the Melbourne Staff Band's arrival the day before and how they had gone straight to visit Lord's Cricket Ground, no doubt to re-acquaint themselves with the famous urn! The various staff bands were now beginning to arrive in the country and in two weeks time we would be sharing the stage in the Royal Albert Hall with 250 bandsmen and women from around the world.

> "Many will say of this historic weekend – 'we were there'. Only you will be able to say – 'we were members of the ISB'!"

Experiences

The Friday of our ISB120 weekend finally arrived. We met as a band that morning at THQ to share in a reception with Commissioners John and Betty Matear, the UK's Territorial leaders. It was at this point that the significance of the weekend and what we were about to experience really hit me. I remember the words of Commissioner Matear as he spoke to us that morning:

"Many will say of this historic weekend – we were there. Only you will be able to say – we were members of the ISB!". If any further incentive were needed to seize all of the God-given opportunities that the weekend would afford us, then that was it.

The Friday evening concert at Cadogan Hall, sharing the stage with our friends in the NYSB and with many familiar faces in the audience was a wonderful start to the weekend. Although there was a capacity audience I imagine that for all of the people gathered there were a similar number of people, if not many more, who would have loved to have been there. Thankfully the wonderful DVDs produced by SP&S ensure that all have an opportunity to experience this fantastic occasion.

We didn't want our friends from overseas ever to feel like they were too far from home so in travelling back to our hotels at Heathrow Airport, our base for the weekend, we shared in food and fellowship which was a great end to the day.

Many words have been written about the ISB120 weekend and specifically the Saturday. I am not sure I can adequately sum up all that happened during the day or the range of emotions that we as a band experienced:

- The rehearsal that morning – all bandsmen and women together on the stage where I think it would have been virtually impossible for anything to have gone better.
- The Amsterdam Staff Band starting the afternoon with the beautiful arrangement *We are not Alone*.
- The reception given to the ISB at the end of *Fire in the Blood*, and if that were not emotional enough, the Japan Staff Band taking the stage and receiving the most wonderful ovation. How they managed to play so beautifully following that I will never understand.
- Andrew Garcia's fantastic playing of *Children of Sanchez*, followed by the gorgeous Bill Himes arrangement of *This I Know* – a tribute to the late James Anderson.

I have never known an event strike so many emotions – from excitement, to nervousness, to tears! What also struck me was how almost all of the audience stayed to hear every band and each band brought their own unique personality to the stage that afternoon.

Then to the Saturday evening *Brass Spectacular*. As a member of the ISB it was a wonderful experience to play the other Staff Bands onto the stage and to see the flags making their way through the arena, followed by our wonderful orator for the evening, Bill Flinn, inviting the capacity audience to welcome the eight staff bands of the world.

I never had the privilege of meeting Major Leslie Condon. However, from what I have heard of the great man I am sure he will have been looking down from Heaven with a smile on his face and a tear in his eye as we all played his fantastic march, *Celebration*. I cannot think of a more fitting piece to conclude that evening and playing it in the future will never quite be the same for me.

The Sunday morning meeting at Central Hall, Westminster gave time for the members of the respective Staff Bands to relax and fully appreciate the hour or so spent together. Listening to the members of the Territorial Youth Band, The International Staff Songsters and of course words spoken by the General was an uplifting and special experience.

We then moved onto The Mall for what proved to be something quite extraordinary. To be greeted by what the police told us was over 15,000 people was incredible. Many proud Salvationists stood alongside those people who just happened to be there at that time on that day. Has there been a greater opportunity over any number of years for us to speak into people's lives, to witness and to help build God's Kingdom?

Being a member of the ISB, leading the march with the seven bands following, and behind them thousands of people supporting and cheering provides memories and feelings that I'll not forget.

The final aspect of the weekend was a slightly more intimate occasion, yet just as fitting. A time for members of the respective Staff Bands, along with families of current and past ISB members, to share in food and conversation. The ISB obviously has an illustrious history which has only been made possible because of those previous members of the band and it was lovely to be able to spend time with them. Of course, no member of any staff band, either past or present, would be able to be part of such a group without the unwavering support of their families and so it was also very special to be able to thank them in this way and to offer them the recognition that they so fully deserve.

Reflections

The London 2012 Olympics were secured on the promise of delivering a significant legacy. If ISB120 is to be measured in the same way then this was a tremendous success.

The letters, emails and feedback that we as a band received, and continue to receive, from individuals around the world who speak of having a renewed vigour for The Salvation Army and for Salvation Army music making because of this weekend is quite humbling.

To have been able to contribute towards the expansion of The Salvation Army's work in Burkina Faso, West Africa, with funds delivered through this weekend is a remarkable achievement.

There are many people to thank for this event being the success that it so undoubtedly was. Of course, the ultimate thanks go to God. He was clearly in and through everything that took place prior to the weekend, during it, and now subsequently. He deserves the highest praise.

> " Of course, the ultimate thanks go to God. He was clearly in and through everything that took place prior to the weekend, during it, and now subsequently. He deserves the highest praise. "

132

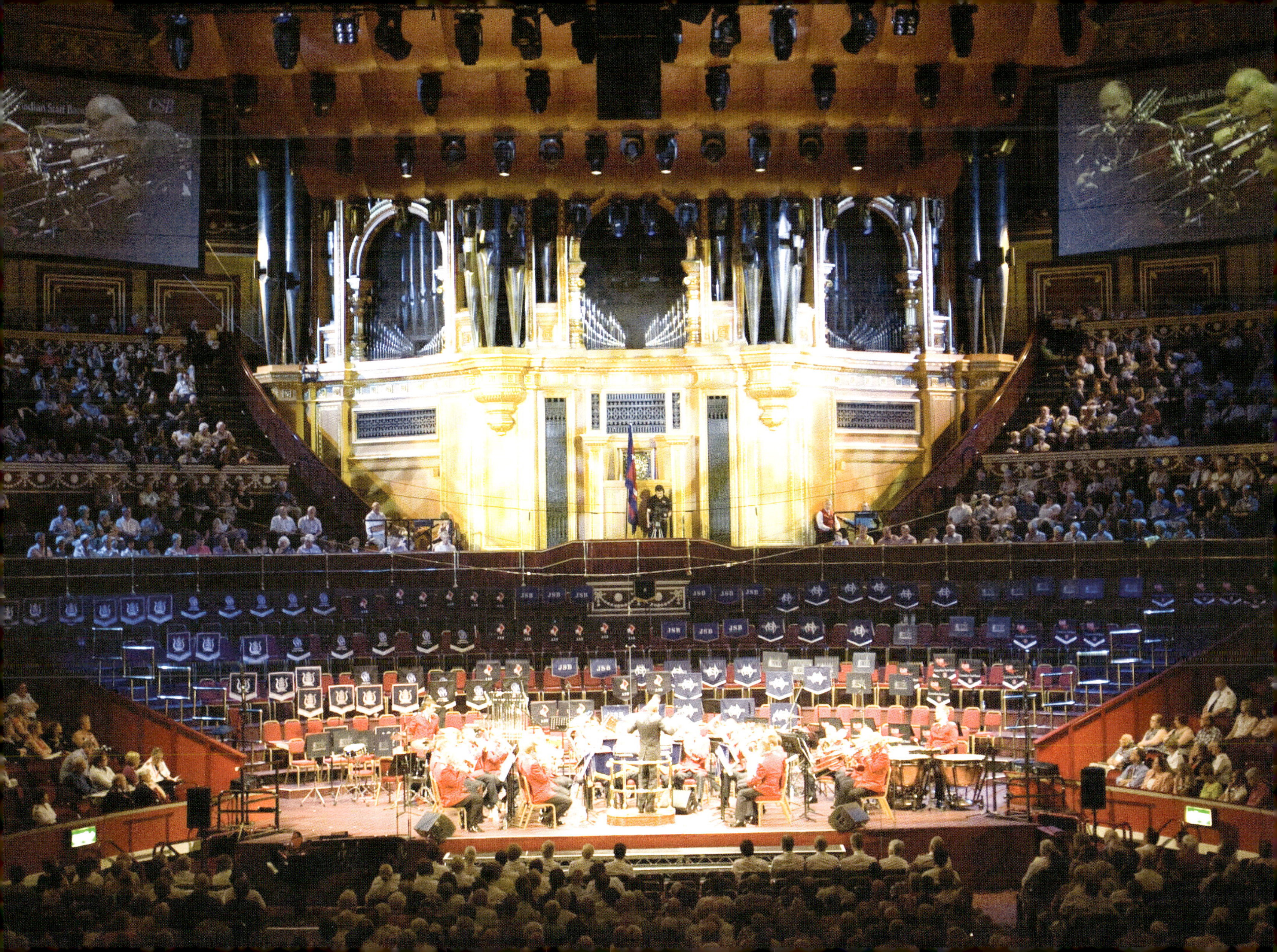
CSB
JSB

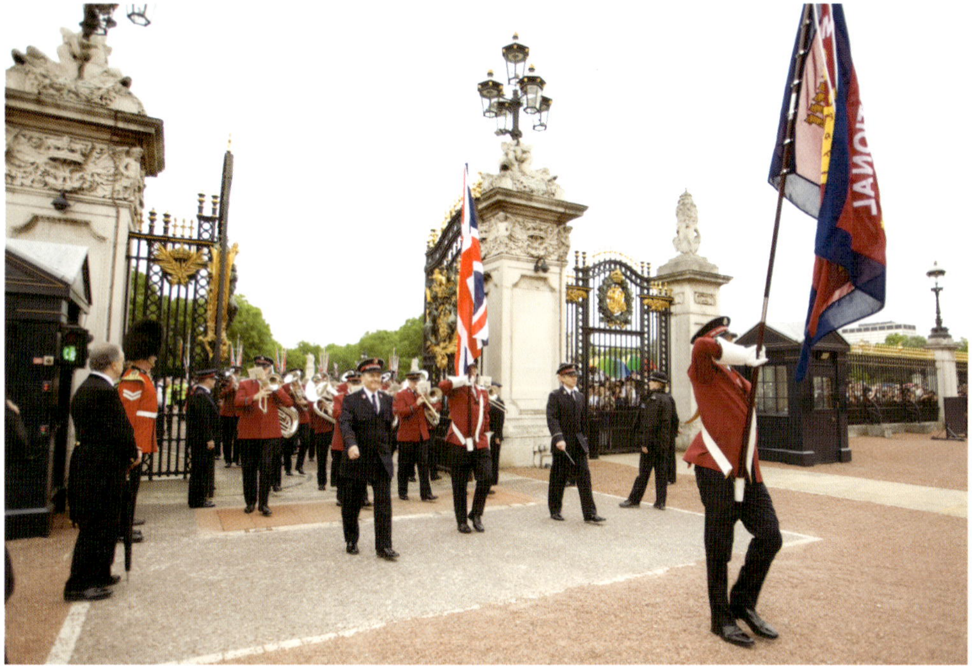

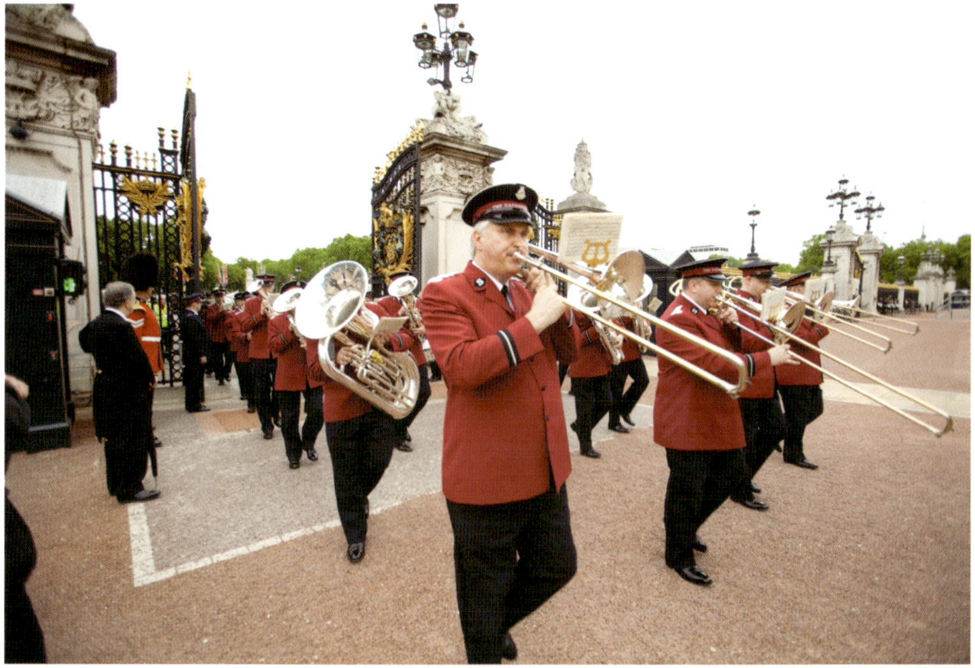

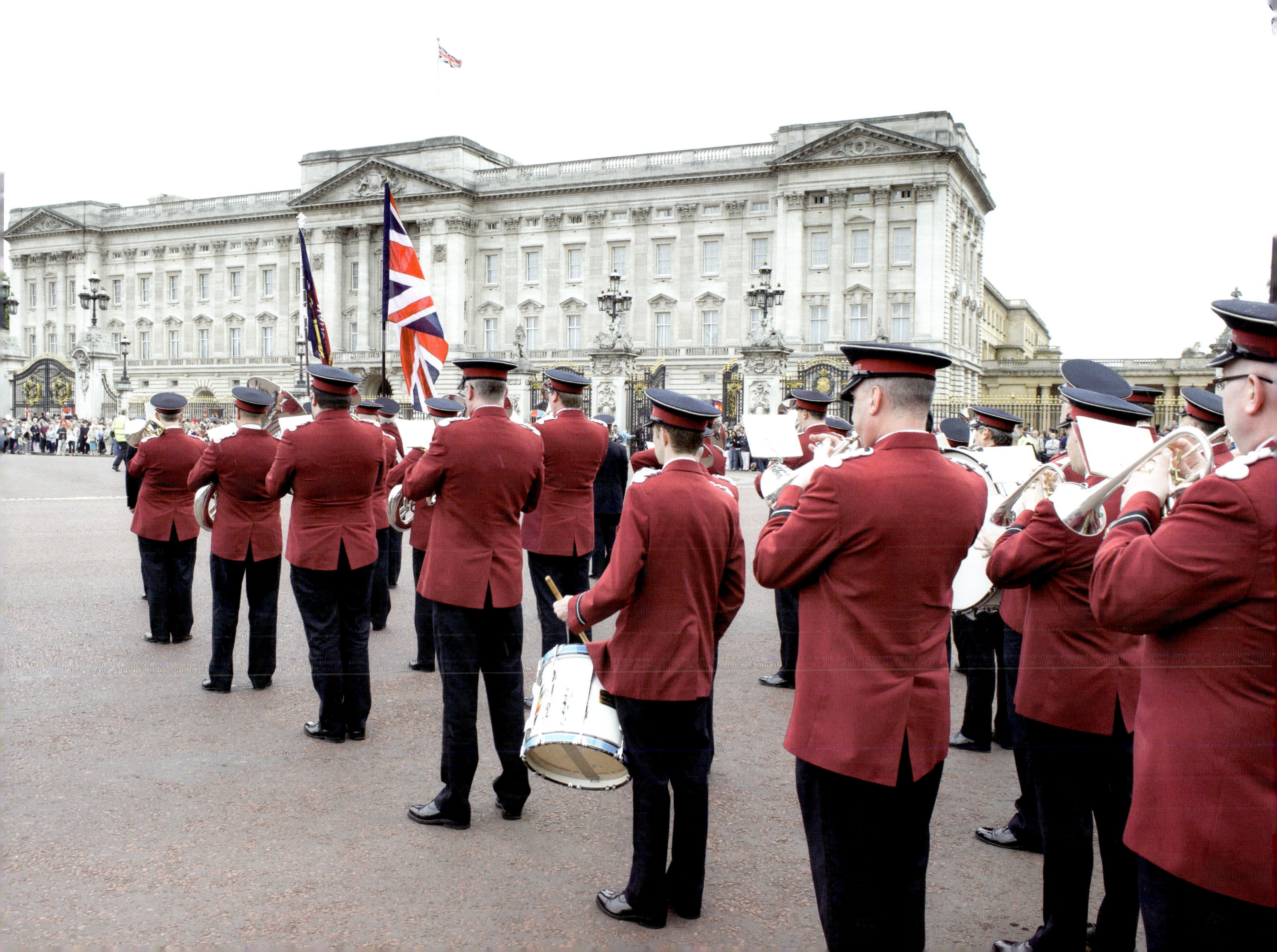

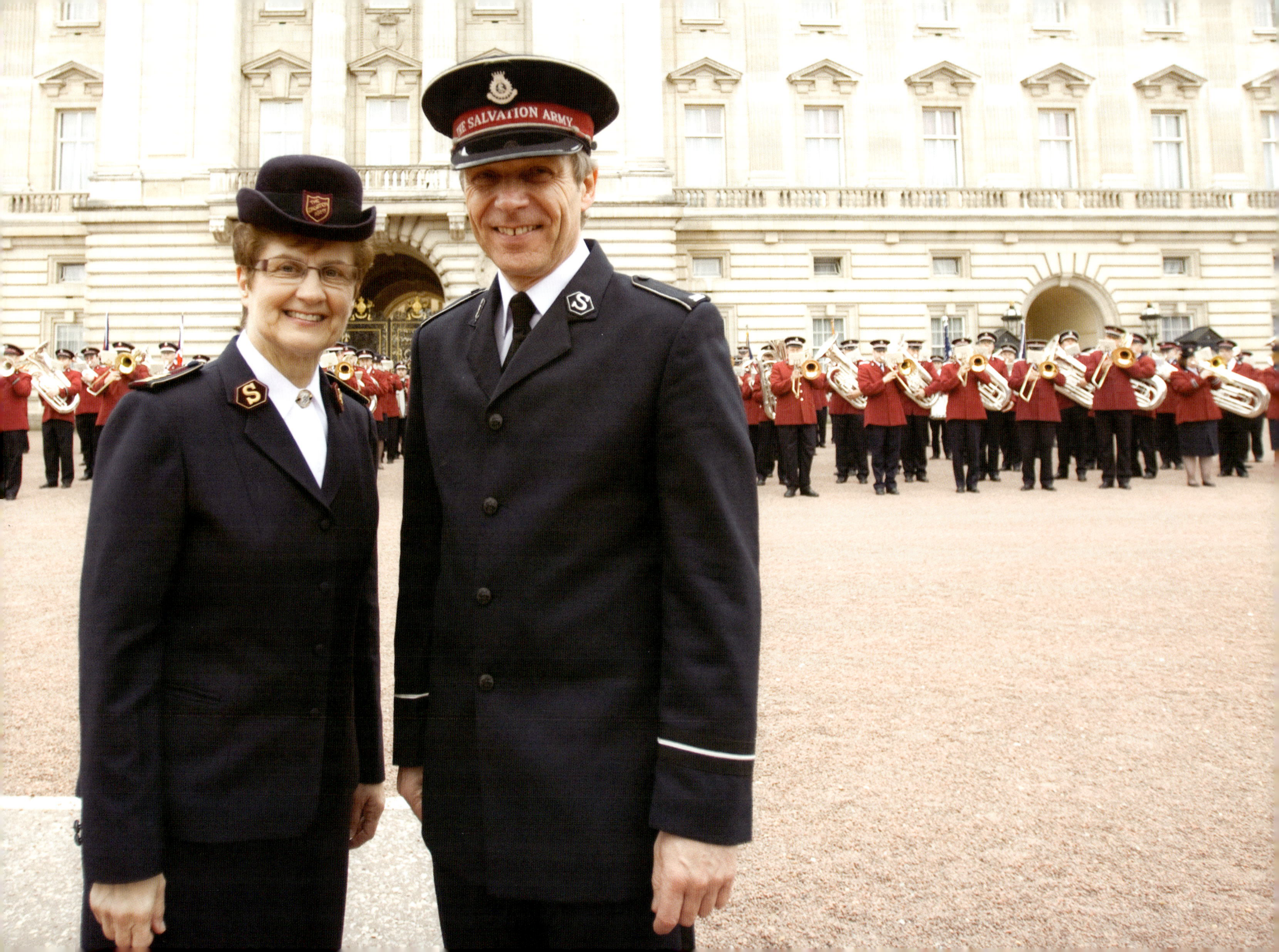
THE SALVATION ARMY

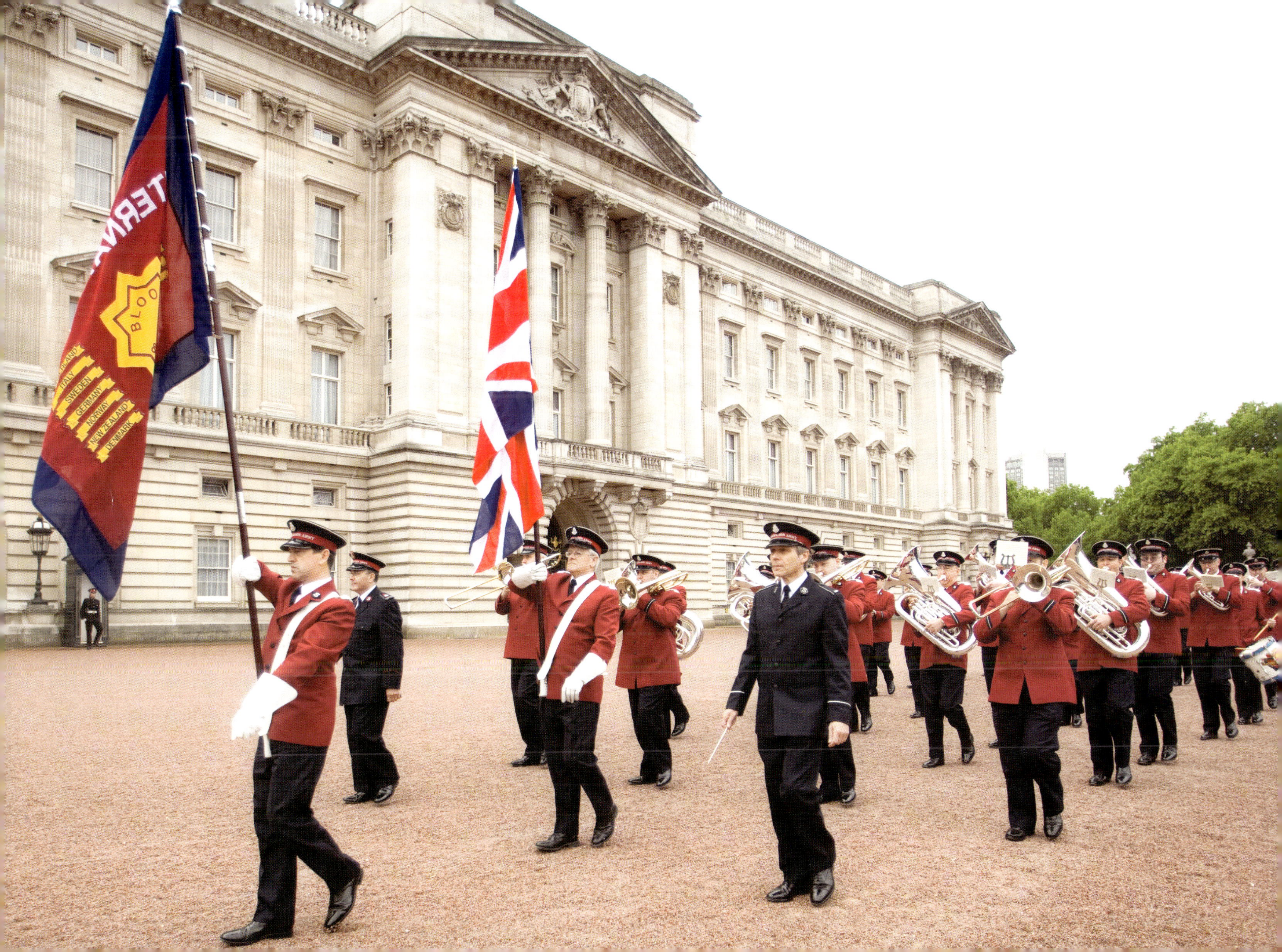

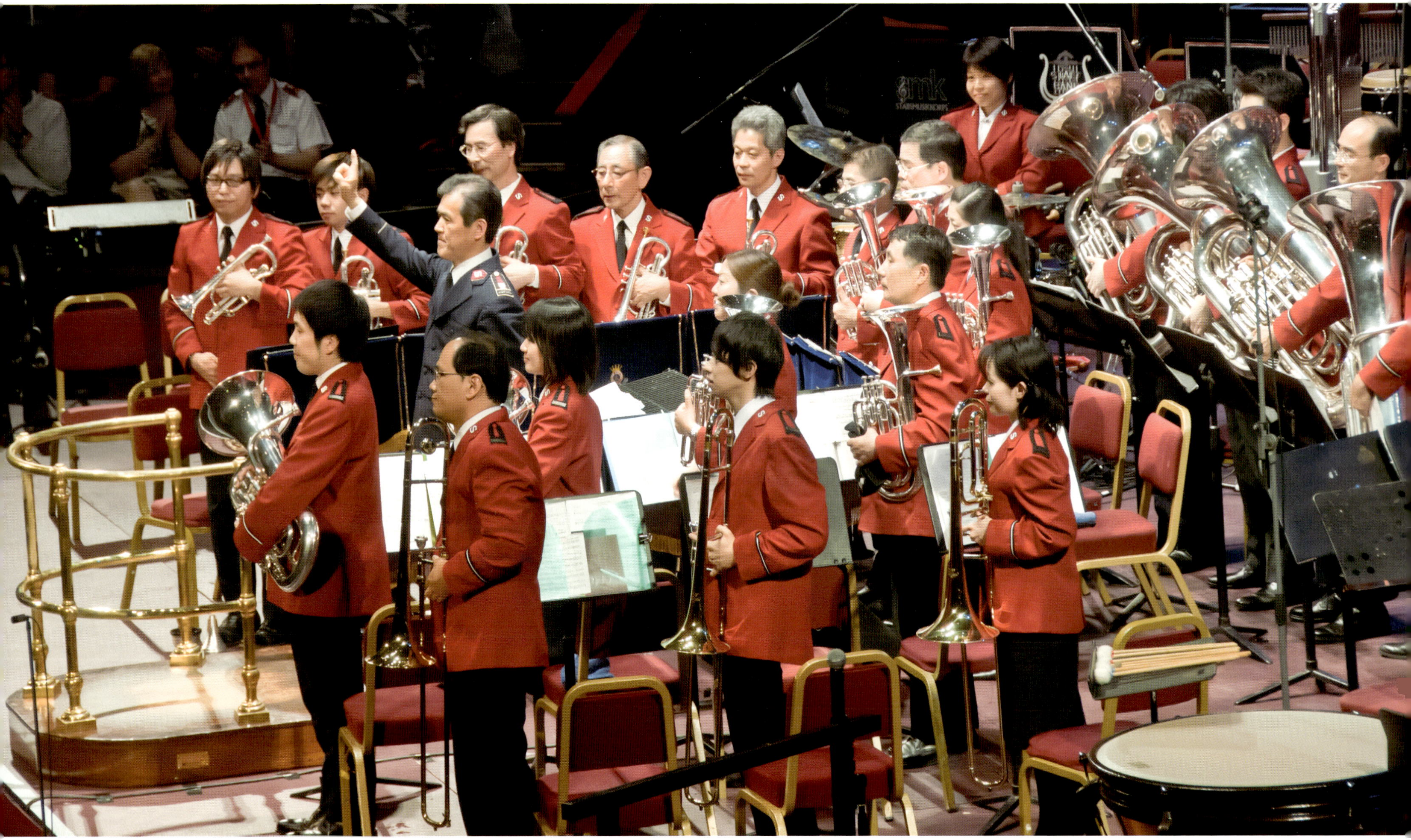

JAPAN STAFF BAND
Major Makoto Yamaya

The prelude to us visiting the United Kingdom started from mournful monotone. 11 March 2011, an earthquake, tsunami and nuclear accident hit Japan. We had never ever witnessed such devastation before and I hope I never see it again. There were repercussions right across Japan, blackouts, no food or water, roads and railway lines just washed away, lack of petrol, and lines of communication smashed. Would we still be able to come to the UK? In a dignified way, Japanese resilience came to the forefront and despite having to cancel practices and recording sessions, and having to help with the emergency relief operation, there was a determination to make sure the visit still took place.

Surely it would and should take place! We, the band smallest in form, are the band earnestly wishing to serve suffering people through the practical love of Christ. The Salvation Army responded to the devastation from its first day by sending a spearhead team, delivering hot meals and life requirements to sheltered people. The relief work is continuing even to this day. Many members of JSB participated in it, and continue to do so.

On 27 May, we arrived at London Heathrow, received by ISB Bandmaster Dr Stephen Cobb and Tour Coordinator Mr Martin Tiplady. We boarded the King's Ferry coach and Colonel Alex 'Sandy' Morris joined as Tour Leader to assist us throughout our time in the UK.

The Japan Staff Band had the privilege of serving music ministry in six UK towns as a prelude to the special ISB120 weekend in London, starting with the old gateway town, **Hythe,** the Cinque Port. The Salvation Army tricolors and flag of the Sun unfurled in high street as we marched past and saluted the Mayor, Mr David Owens, performing in front of the town hall. Saturday evening at SAGA Pavilion was full to capacity in the presence of Mayors and Lord Warden of the Cinque Ports, which was to happen at every corps we visited. The band testified to the power of the Cross that heals suffering humanity. The message was double strengthened by powerful singing of Shepway Community Gospel Choir, a corps music ministry. We saw the first standing ovation there.

JSB led the Sunday Holiness Meeting. Commissioner Nozomi Harita, Band Executive Officer and former Territorial Commander of Japan, delivered the message of Hope in Christ. At the afternoon promenade concert we were joined by ISB Principal Cornet Kevin Ashman, a joyful happening! Sunday evening, Hythe Band and Songsters ministered for JSB members and Corps Officer Captain Phil Layton delivered the message of resurrection and future.

Throughout our visit, Commissioner Harita led devotional time, reading Psalms of Pilgrimage day-to-day on the coach as we travelled to each venue. The imagination caught us in a thought we were on the pilgrimage to Jerusalem. Terumi Ota, Solo Horn, says, "It was precious devotion that made it possible for me to go through the whole journey."

We arrived at **Cradley Heath**. Old Mansion, Hyden Hall was the place of our music for civic dignitaries. That night, the corps was full to capacity and the band witnessed to the living Hope in Christ. We saw the standing ovation again. Major Masakatsu Miyamoto, Band Flag Sergeant, recalled, "I was told a standing ovation was rare here. Tested in Hythe, then in Cradley Heath, I was convinced that our choice of music and programme was right."

Our journey headed to **Doncaster**. Industrial country in the past, it was now converted to a green city around a beautiful lake where the modern corps building was located.

> "Then how were we changed? After coming home, JSB visited the most tsunami devastated towns two times. What kind of music should we play after stepping out from the Royal Albert Hall? Nothing else, but just doing the music for Jesus, music for people. But we performed it in keeping a sense of that oneness, one Salvation Army band. So still we feel you are sitting next to us, laying hands on us, praying blessings for us."

The evening concert was full to capacity and Commissioner Harita put on a 'yukata', a Japanese bathrobe, just as pioneer officers did when they landed their first steps in Japan, to show how they struggled to communicate the Gospel to Japanese hearts.

We moved to **Staines,** where we were thrilled to be introduced to Malcolm Quinn, the ISB120 Project Director, who we got to know very well as a friend as time went on throughout our trip. We had a chance to visit Windsor Castle. At our concert the congregation marked congratulation to retired Bandmaster Maisie Wiggins, who was presented with the MBE by the Queen that morning. Corps youth vocal group, Hallelujah Anyhow!, sang beautiful songs including *May it be*. That was the song for us. People queued in a long line to shake hands with us. Then we were warmly accepted by host families. Satoshi Kojima, 2nd Horn, says, "Though I couldn't communicate well by language, they received me with warm hospitality." The same hospitality we met everywhere in the journey.

We reached Plymouth, visiting the harbour point where Pilgrim Fathers departed to the New World. Lord Mayor Mr Peter Brookshaw received us and Lady Mayoress, a former Salvationist, showed us her tambourine! We sang joyfully and she drilled with it! Then we marched to **Plymouth Congress Hall**. The band shared message of hope through music and word to well attended audience where was presence of Leader of the City Council. The conclusion of the night was enthusiastic singing of *O Happy Day* altogether. Makoto Kobayashi recalled it, "The congregation sang with all their body and soul. I was taught I should sing this song always just as they did."

Finally we moved to **Basingstoke**. Corps Sergeant Major Peter Burrow took on waiter cloth and served us dinner. In him we saw a Servant Leadership. Mayor of Basingstoke Mr David Leeks received us at the Town Hall, then we walked to the United Reformed Church, our venue for the night. A full capacity congregation, with the presence of the Mayor, was challenged by a local testimony which sought help for Japan. It was announced that the sponsor bank had promised to double the amount of donations from the night. A good response followed!

Now we were stepping into the main chapter. Saturday morning was consumed for rehearsal at the Royal Albert Hall. We enjoyed sharing lunch, chatting and photo-shooting with Staff Band members of the world at the café of Imperial College. It felt like being in the Pearly Gate Café in New Jerusalem! Then the moment came. We were all very nervous as appropriate prayers were shared. The stage manager pushed our backs. We stepped in. Royal Albert Hall was filled with hand-clapping and a standing ovation that continued for many minutes. That was the scene 'before' we played. We couldn't stand there without a tear. We all understood that it was the encouragement from the world not only to us, but to all people in Japan. Then we did it as we always did. Doing music for Jesus, music for people. Masaki Hikichi, Euphonium, says, "We Japanese might have felt deep trauma from the disaster. However, in that very moment on the stage, we experienced consolation from people of encouragement, people of faith."

Saturday night, we were amalgamated with eight Staff Bands into one Salvation Army band to celebrate its origin, mission, history, and witness. The celebration was pointing out a glorious future of the one Salvation Army band. Satoshi Ugajin, Bb Bass, recalled it as "The highest moment of my life."

Sunday, as one band, we worshipped at Central Hall, Westminster. Major Miyamoto recalls, "The General challenged us to be holy. I was tearful and sniffing. The person next to me, Bandmaster Ian Dickie of Bellshill, laid his hand on me and prayed for me. I experienced great warm consolation and power."

As one band, we did the March of Witness from The Mall to Buckingham Palace. Tempei Matsui, Bb Bass, says, "I wasn't conscious of the heaviness of my instrument at all. I wished to continue the march more and more, even to eternity." The march ended and we went back to a private reception.

We all came back home on Monday. What is the after-effect? Memory of the journey will become a story. The story will become a legend. The legend will be handed from generation to generation. Is it possible this great journey could happen again? We do not know. But we are assured that we are nothing more than one Salvation Army band, marching everyday towards New Jerusalem. There we will join again for the great music of redeemed mankind.

Then how were we changed? After coming home, JSB visited the most tsunami devastated towns twice. What kind of music should we play after stepping off from the Royal Albert Hall? Nothing else, but just doing the music for Jesus, music for people. But we performed it in keeping a sense of that oneness, one Salvation Army band. So still we feel you are sitting next to us, laying hands on us, praying blessings for us.

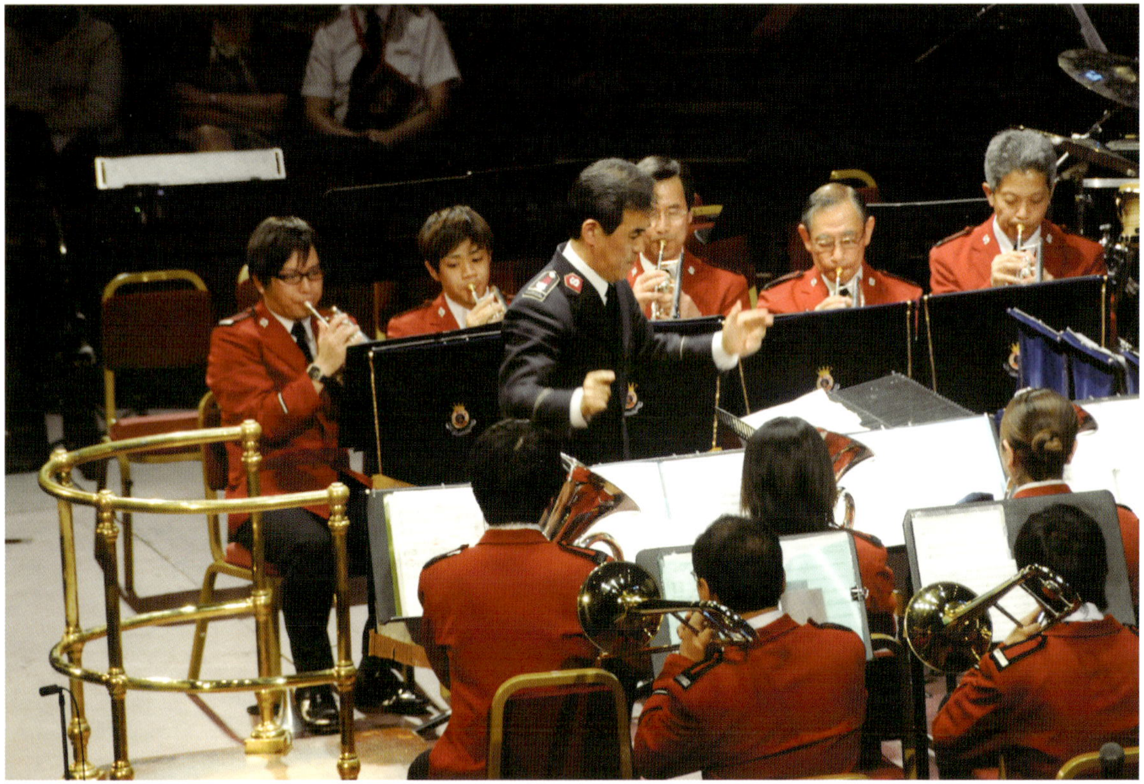

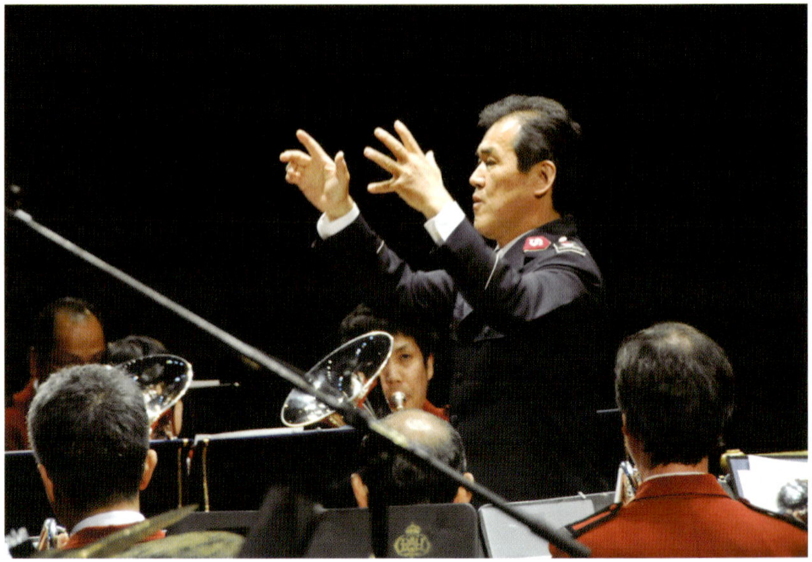

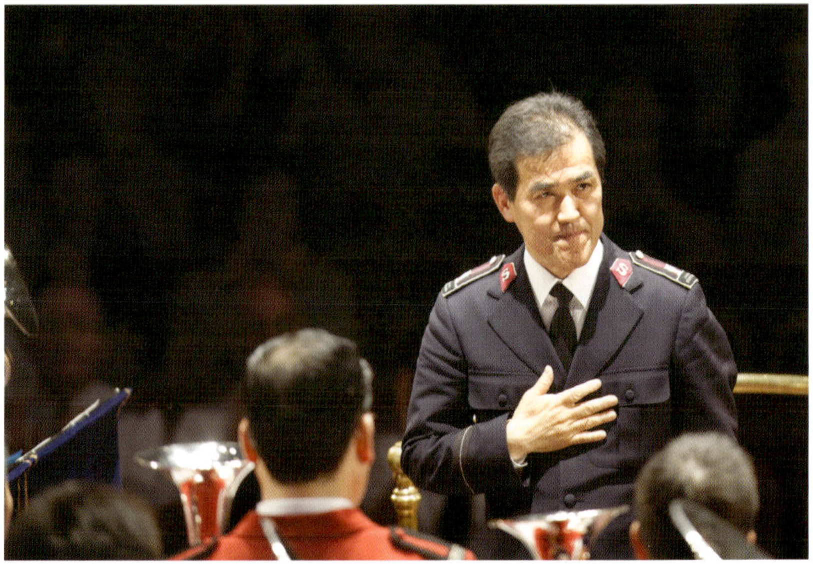

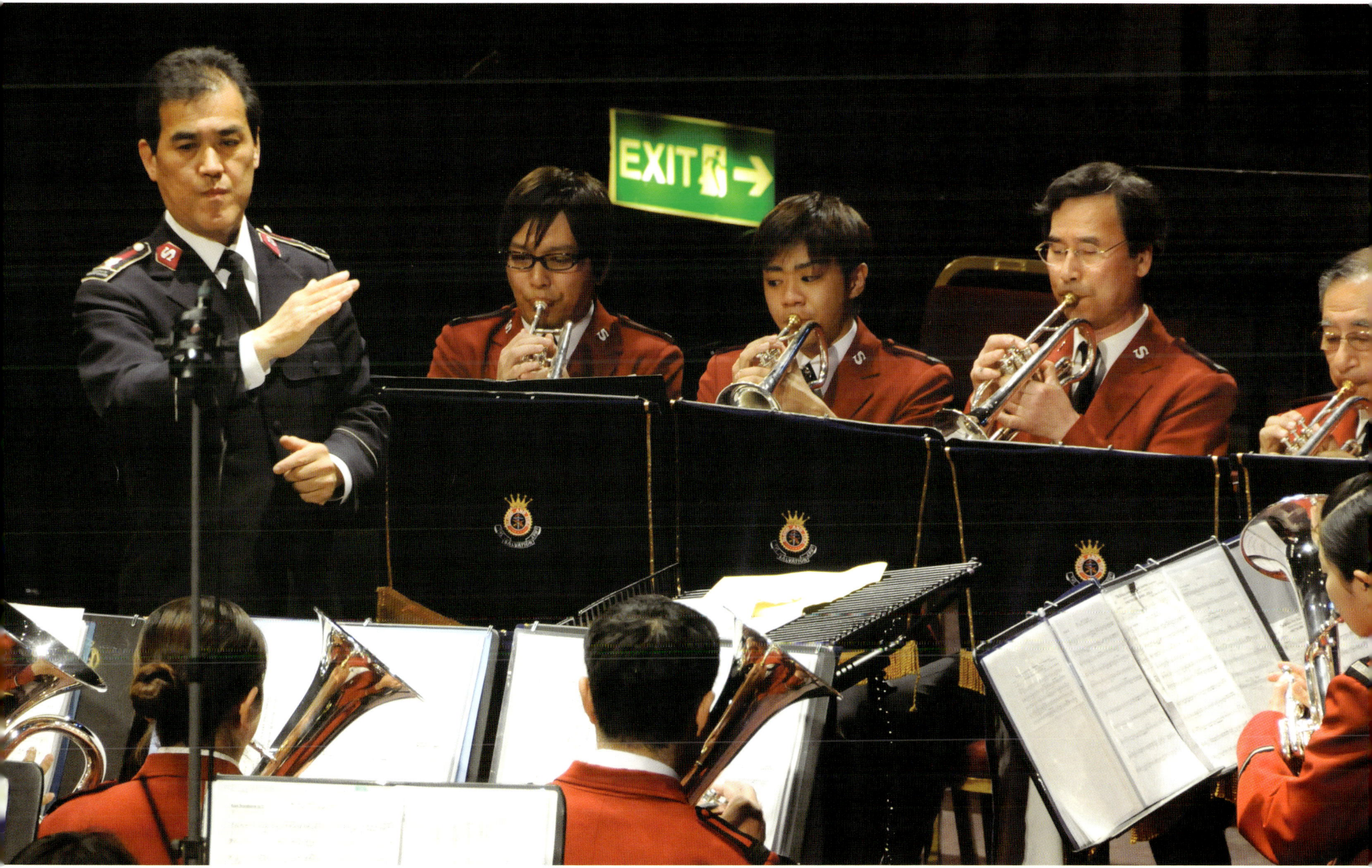
EXIT

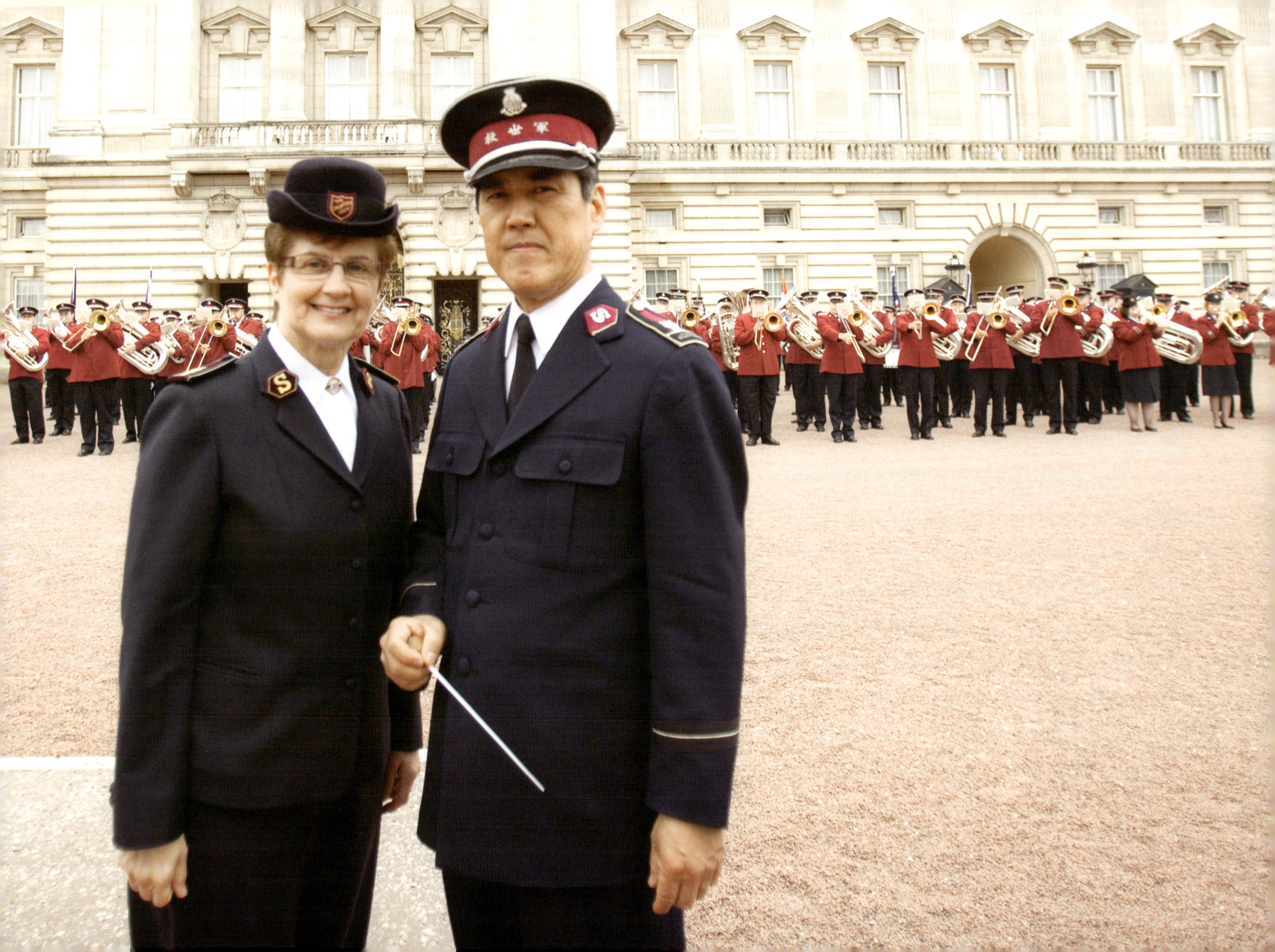
救世軍

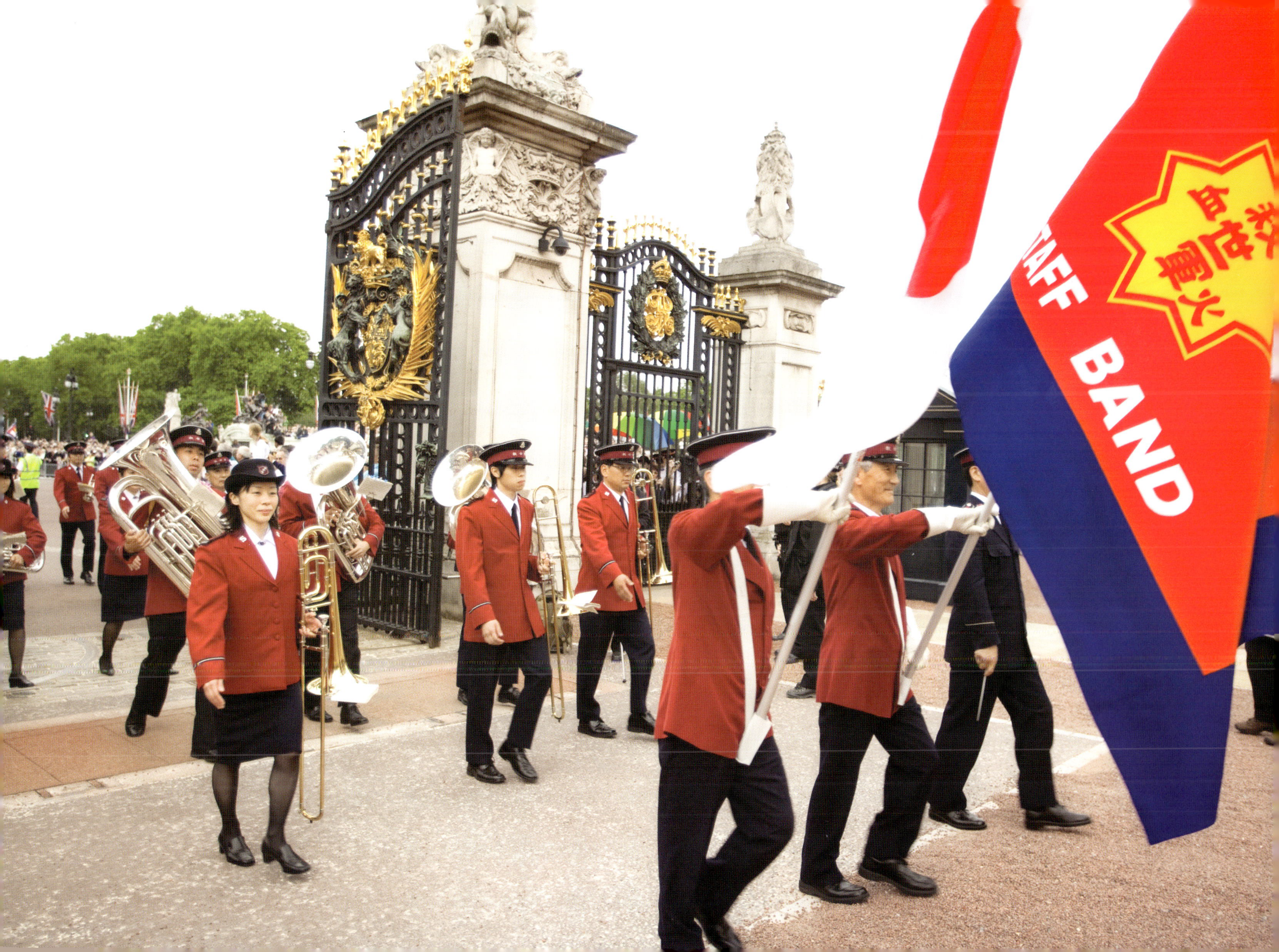
救世軍
血
火
BAND

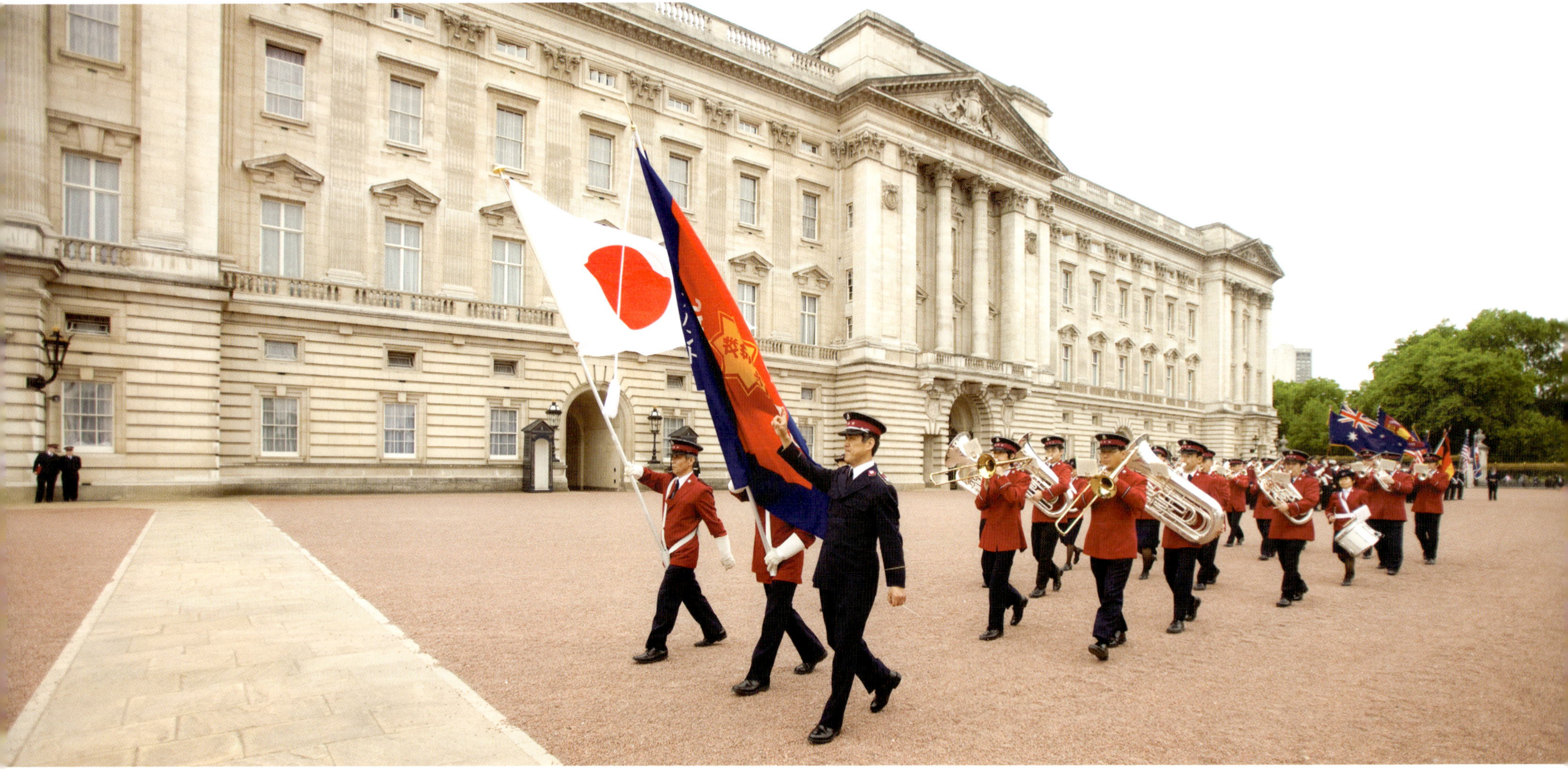

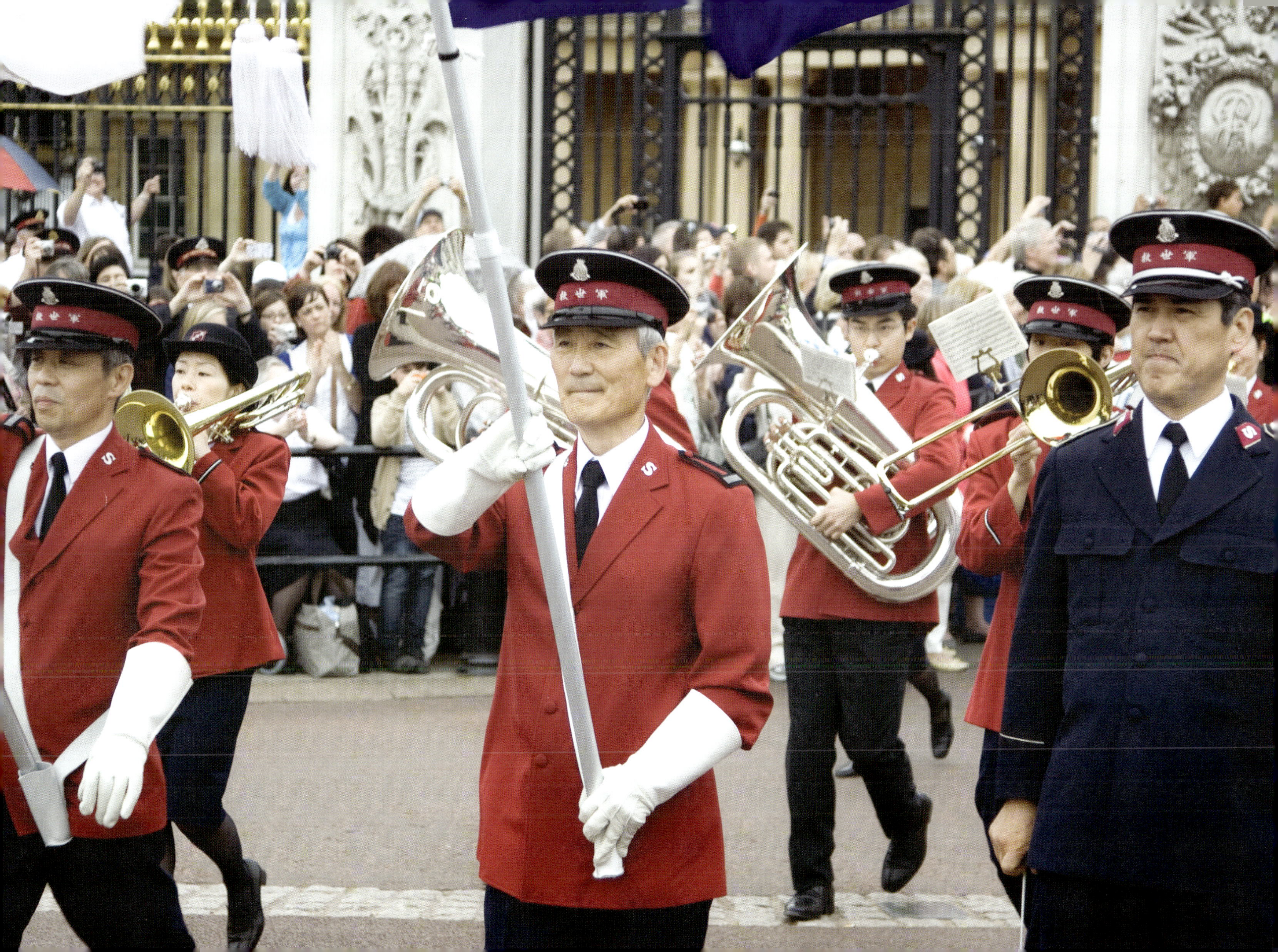
救世軍

Melbourne Staff Band vocal soloist Rebecca Raymond

MELBOURNE STAFF BAND
Stephen Webb

'There was movement at the station, for the word had passed around...'
A.B. 'Banjo' Paterson

The opening line of the poem *The Man from Snowy River*, by celebrated Australian poet A.B. 'Banjo' Paterson mirrors the experience in the Melbourne Staff Band (MSB) rehearsal room when, in May 2009, the MSB members heard that The International Staff Band was planning a celebration of 120 years service with an invitation for the MSB to come to London to join with them and the other Staff Bands of the world. Excitement coupled with apprehension framed the initial thoughts of MSB members with more questions than answers in the early stages of planning.

Very early on Bandmaster Ken Waterworth began considering what music would be suitable to feature on the tour, music that would be musically satisfying but more importantly that would clearly communicate the Gospel message.

New works commissioned included *Tunesmith Overture* (Stephen Bulla), *Synergy* (Martin Cordner), *Atonement* (Roger Trigg) and *I'm In His Hands* (Stanley Ditmer/Phil Laeger arr. Brian Hogg). Music which would showcase a combination of Australian themes and/or composers and would assist the MSB in proclaiming the Gospel through music.

The focal point of the MSB tour was obviously the ISB120 celebration weekend. As well as preparing items for our solo recital at the Royal Albert Hall, there was the massed band music for the *Brass Spectacular*, the march down the Mall and the recital in the forecourt of Buckingham Palace. Prior to the celebration weekend we had the added privilege of undertaking a 10-day of tour around the UK.

A popular inclusion into the MSB's concert format over recent years has been *Brass on the Edge* and it was decided it would be featured during the UK tour. Loosely subtitled *'Music, Movement and Mayhem'*, with the stage cleared of stands and chairs, music committed to memory, the band presents a choreographed 'routine'. Hours of memorising and rehearsing the 40 minute programme of music and accompanying movements was required. These seemingly endless rehearsals were designed to ensure that on tour the MSB would present effortlessly and communicate the Gospel in an entertaining and effective way.

To commemorate the tour and to provide a lasting memory, the MSB recorded a new CD, entitled *Chronicles*, which featured a selection of the tour repertoire. The high work rate of the MSB with additional rehearsals, recordings and pre-tour concert programmes was excellent preparation for the tour.

On Tuesday 24 May 2011, after travelling for almost 24 hours, we arrived at London's Heathrow Airport to be met by The Salvation Army's Heathrow Chaplain, Major Melvyn Ackroyd, who used his influence to arrange for the band to be fast-tracked through Passport Control. ISB120 Project Director Malcolm Quinn, ISB Bandmaster Dr Stephen Cobb, and Martin Tiplady also met and greeted the band. A coach ride to the Home of Cricket for a guided tour of Lord's Cricket Ground was a real treat, followed by the long and very quiet journey up the M1 to **Sheffield**.

> " A real connection was made with folk in the North East which was evident at the march up The Mall in London on the ISB120 celebration weekend with banners prepared and waved by Sunderland Millfield friends in support of the MSB. "

The MSB first visited **Sheffield** during its 1978 UK tour and it was an ideal place to commence the 2012 tour. The band was kept busy with a civic reception given by the Lord Mayor of Sheffield followed by an outdoor lunchtime performance at the Peace Gardens. With people arriving as early as 90 minutes before commencement of the evening concert, the hall was packed with only standing room available. The band responded to an enthusiastic audience and set a good standard of performance at the first concert of the tour.

Moving on to **Warrington,** and prior to a civic reception, the band formed up in front of the impressive gates of the town hall for a photo opportunity before a march. The Mayor of Warrington, Michael Biggins, was so new to the role that the painter was just finishing adding his name to the mayoral honour board. A second consecutive standing ovation greeted the conclusion of *William Tell* and many warm comments were received as we mingled with the audience.

On our way to **Kettering**, Corby Business Academy in Northants was our first destination for the day, playing to an audience of over 300 Year 7 pupils and their teachers, who demonstrated their enjoyment with enthusiastic appreciation and a standing ovation. The MSB marched down the centre corridor of the school in front of the whole school population of over 1,000 pupils and staff. It was a special time for the year 11 students as this was their last day at school. A crowd in excess of 250 people including the Mayor, at her first official engagement since taking office, councillors, Salvationists and friends came to the concert with eager anticipation.

Saturday morning had arrived and the band was on its way to Sunderland. The MSB gave a short recital in the magnificent Durham Cathedral. Hymn tune arrangements such as *Colne, Praise My Soul, French* and *Bethany* resounded around the Cathedral. A concert was held at Durham Johnston School in front of a packed hall once more. The MSB felt right at home spending Sunday at **Sunderland Millfield** Corps. During the morning meeting many were moved, and decisions were made for the Lord. An afternoon Festival followed with participation of Sunderland Millfield's Songster Brigade. A real connection was made with the folk at Sunderland Millfield which was evident at the march up The Mall in London on the ISB120 celebration weekend with banners prepared and waved by Sunderland Millfield folk in support of the MSB.

A large group of corps folk from Sunderland Millfield Corps waved the visitors off, as the touring party headed for Scotland. The MSB received a warm welcome from the folk of **Clydebank** Corps, the West Scotland Divisional staff and Provost Denis Agnew of West Dumbartonshire Council. Close to 300 people enjoyed an evening of fine music. Notably, cornet soloists Garry Todd and Neil Roper performed the cornet duet *Synergy* in the presence of Captain Martin Cordner, the composer of the piece.

After the coach trip from Glasgow to **Blackpool,** MSB members were given about an hour's free time to wander the streets of Blackpool on arrival. The MSB presented another well received concert which included the classic, *The Call of the Righteous,* and the new work *Atonement.*

The trip to **Coventry** was certainly the quietest of the tour as fatigue was starting to kick in and was taking its toll. We visited the Transport Museum followed by a short walk to Coventry Cathedral. The MSB sang a couple of verses of *When I survey the wondrous cross* inside the Cathedral. A camera crew from World of Brass, who were capturing footage for the ISB120 weekend DVD, joined us. The concert venue for the evening was the United Reformed Church. The MSB routine had some extra degrees of difficulty with a slope akin to Lord's Cricket Ground and audience members surrounding the band. A rousing response was received from the audience.

After morning devotions we were on the road to **Bristol Easton**. The first stop was Bristol Cathedral with tour guide Professor Philip Wilby, followed by an outdoor recital at Cabot Circus. Clifton Suspension Bridge provided a photo opportunity prior to arriving at the Clifton Cathedral for a sound check and measuring of the space for 'the routine'. With a good crowd in at the Clifton Cathedral the audience was blessed and entertained with resonant sounds ringing off the concrete walls in the relatively modern building.

Excitement was palpable in the coach as MSB members recognised that this was the last touring day and the ISB120 celebration weekend was only one day away. The MSB arrived at the Hadleigh Farm and Training Centre where the staff were preparing celebrations for the 120-year anniversary of William Booth opening the Farm Colony. Members of the MSB were given a whistle-stop tour of the facility and the various classes held for special needs kids and adults.

There was an international flavour for the final concert of the 2011 UK Tour at **Hadleigh Corps**. There were a good number from 'the Continent' and it was also great to meet up with former MSB member Roger Trigg, who was able to hear his composition *Atonement* performed live for the first time. The audience sent us on our way with huge applause and an even larger sense of achievement for the whole two weeks of the tour.

ISB120, Royal Albert Hall, London – 4 June 2011

Leaving Hadleigh at 6.00am, we headed to London to be part of creating history! Arriving at the Royal Albert Hall around 7.30am, the scene certainly resembled a bus-man's picnic as eight coaches full of Staff Band members encircled the RAH stage door. Preparation and rehearsal for the *Brass Spectacular* scheduled that night were in full swing. The Staff Bands were directed into place and remarkably almost 250 players were organised and ready for the rehearsal without fuss. The essential rehearsal time ensured that the evening *Brass Spectacular* would be a highly polished performance.

A delicious buffet meal was served at the Imperial College and gave a welcome opportunity for all MSB band members to mix with fellow Staff Band members from around the world.

Although the afternoon was a full four hours of brass band music, there was certainly plenty of variation in the music presented by each staff band. Those in attendance will never forget the emotional ovation given to the Japan Staff Band as they arrived on the Royal Albert Hall stage.

The evening *Brass Spectacular* was a fabulous event of God-honouring music. What a mighty throng of God-honouring musicians. What a privilege to be part of such an event.

Methodist Central Hall, Westminster/The Mall/Buckingham Palace – 5 June 2011

Spirits were high on the morning of the final official day of the tour. It was a delight for us to attend the Musicians' Councils held in conjunction with a normal Sunday worship service

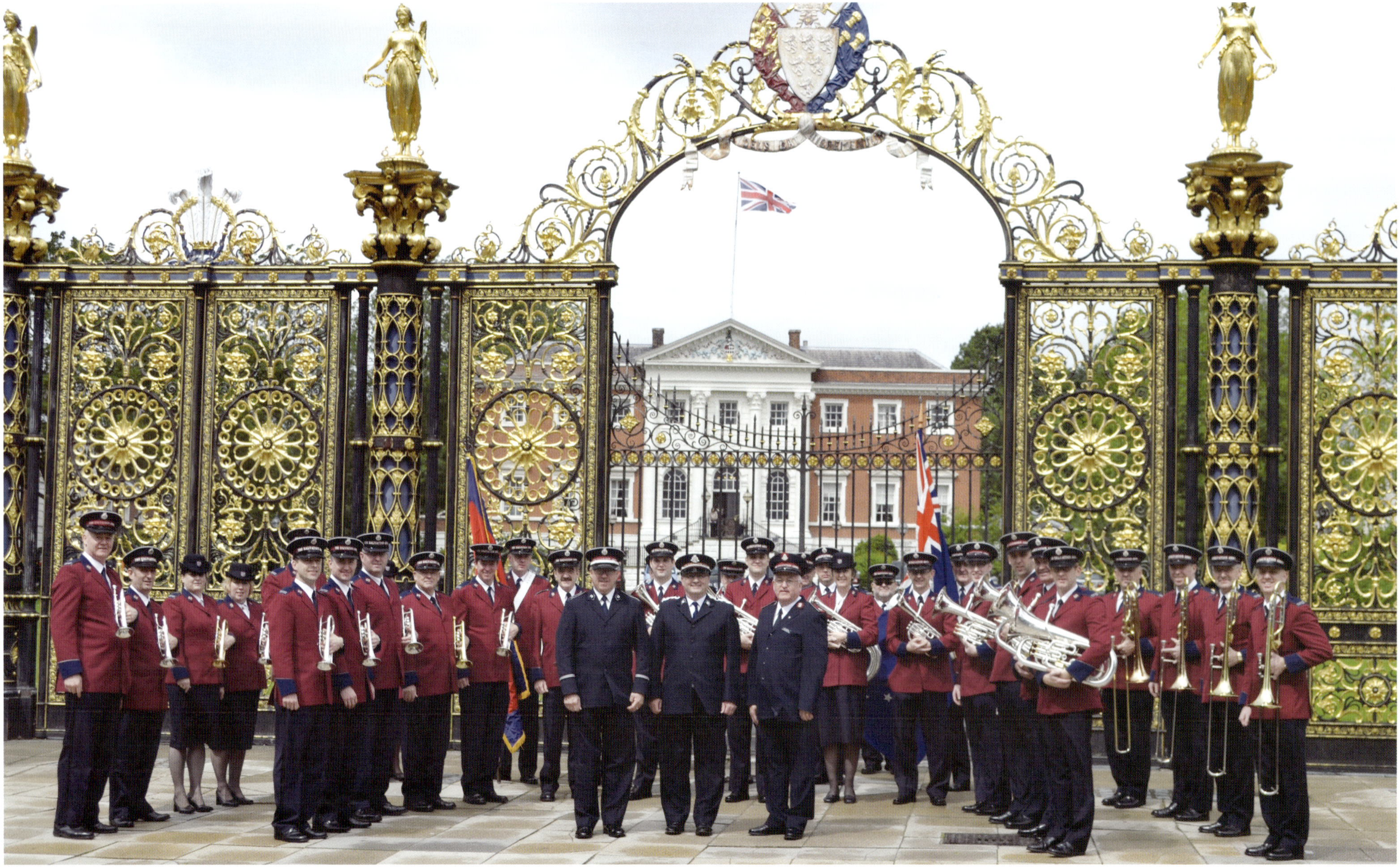

at the Methodist Central Hall. General Linda Bond told of the privilege of being invited to speak to musicians, and relished the company of musical giants like Ray Steadman-Allen, Kenneth Downie, Bill Himes and others. The General expressed her desire for every Salvationist to know what it is to have a clean heart using Psalm 51:1-13 as the basis for her message.

Following the buffet lunch and a short walk, the Staff Bands formed up in The Mall. The eight Staff Bands made an impressive display as they marched, played and entered into the forecourt of Buckingham Palace. Flags and much cheering from around 80 people from Sunderland Millfield Corps gave the MSB added encouragement. The crowd of thousands filled the pavement and approach roads to view this historic spectacle with the combined Staff Bands presenting a concert in the forecourt of Buckingham Palace. The Bands marched past a saluting base which included General Linda Bond, Commissioners Barry and Sue Swanson, Commissioners John and Betty Matear and Colonels Brian and Rosalie Peddle. Appropriately the MSB played Arthur Gullidge's *Emblem of the Army* as it marched out of the Palace.

Endnote

We are indebted to Bandmaster Andrew Blyth, who accompanied the band throughout the tour. We appreciated Andrew's encouragement, guidance and his good knowledge of coffee shops! We were amazed by the skills of our coach driver Adam Croucher, who skilfully drove us on the tour. Adam was a great audience member at our concerts and was often the first on his feet, encouraging others to join him and give a standing ovation.

To the many Salvationists and friends who hosted the MSB in your corps and homes, and who enjoyed and were blessed by our ministry, we sincerely thank you. God Bless The Salvation Army. God Bless the Staff Bands of the world. Give to Jesus Glory!

154

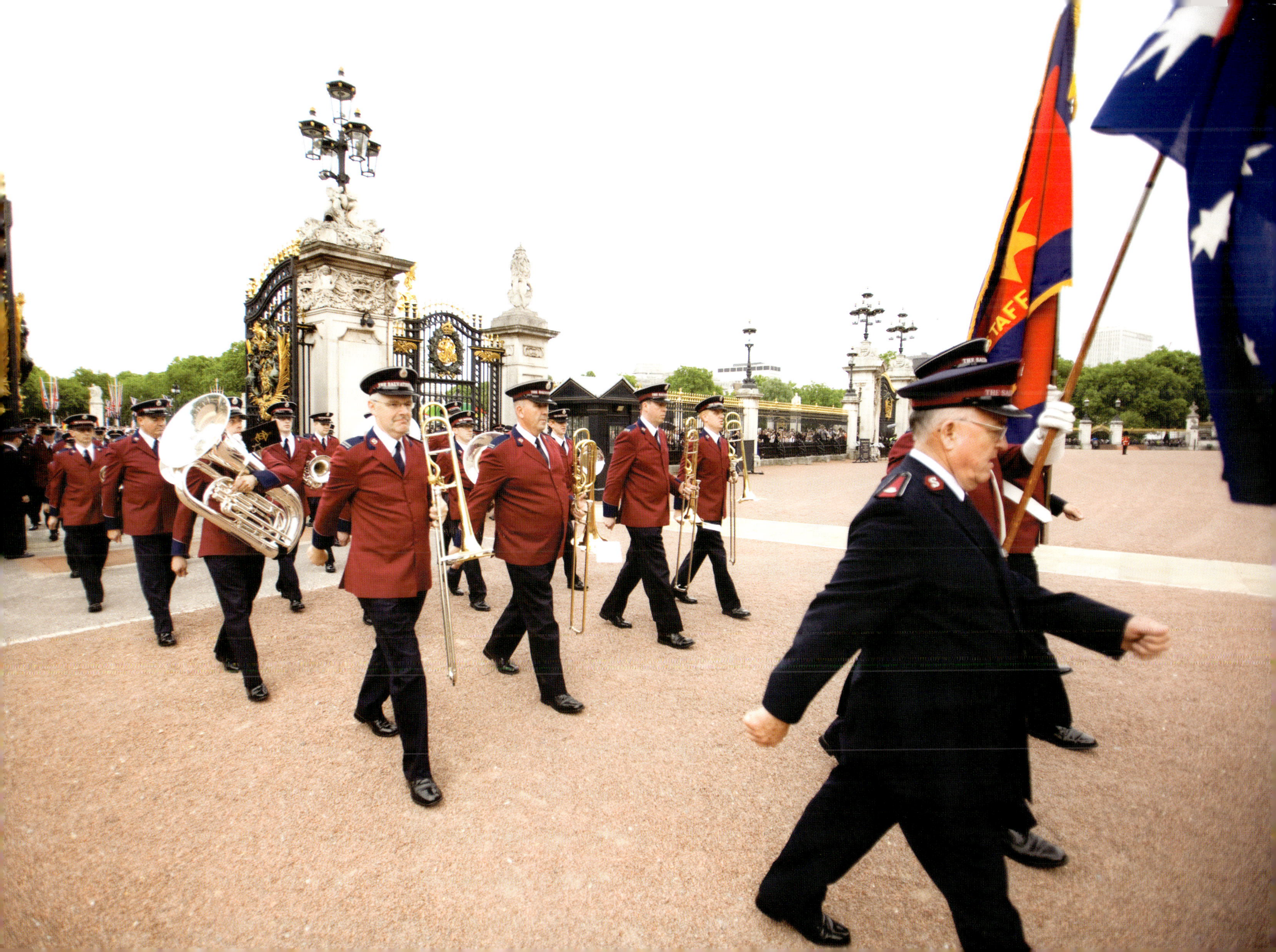

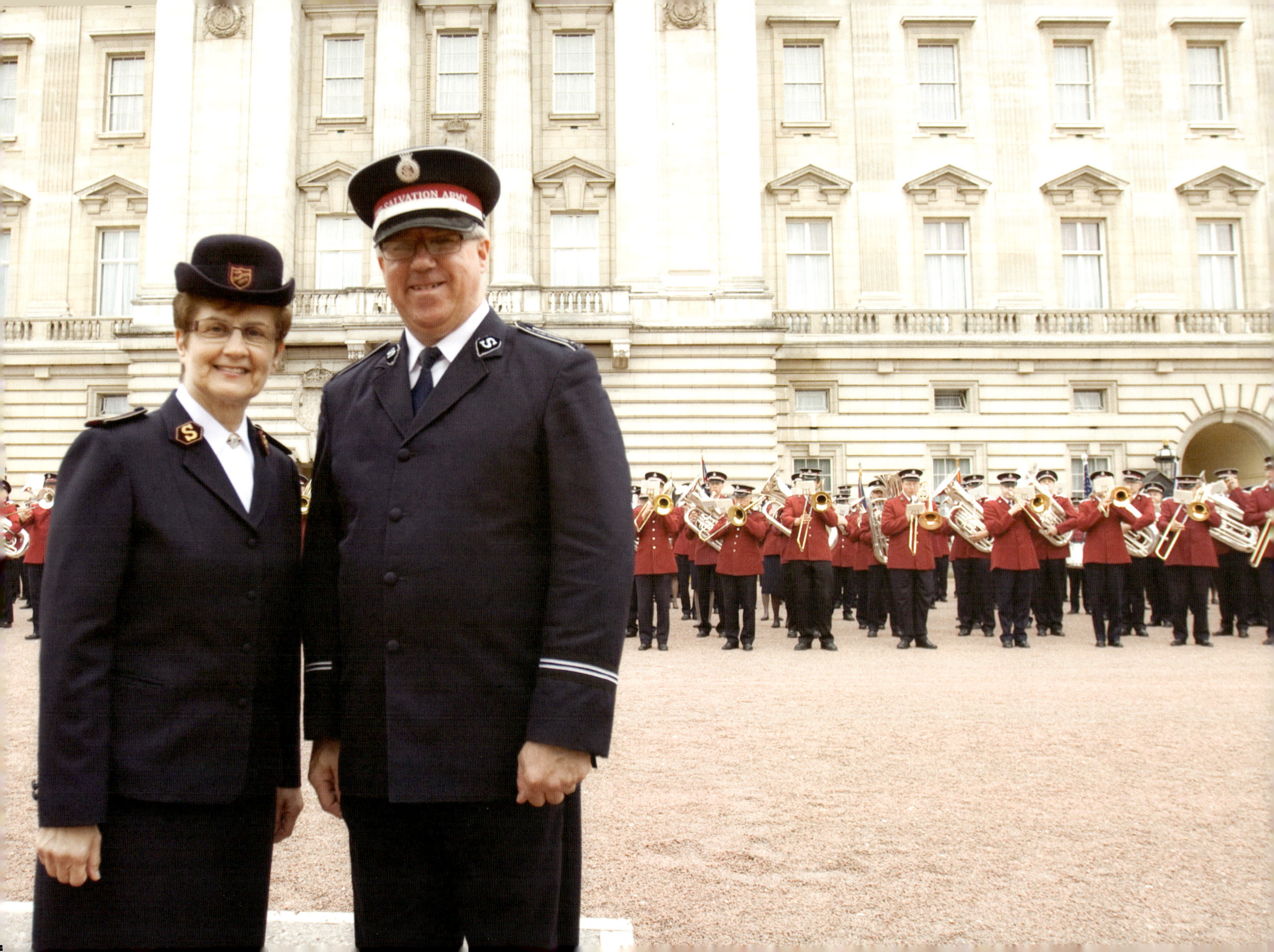
SALVATION ARMY

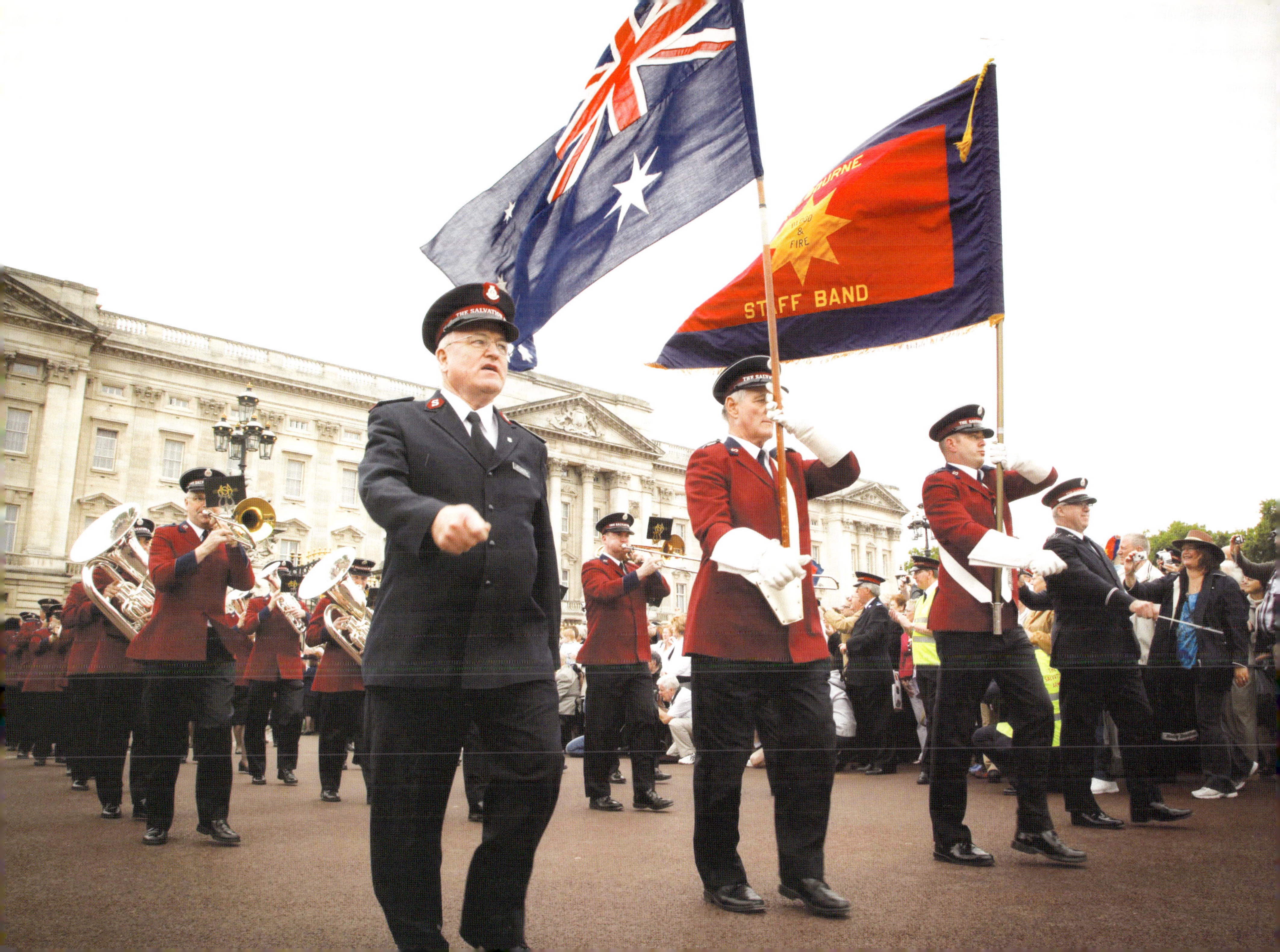
BLOOD
&
FIRE
STAFF BAND

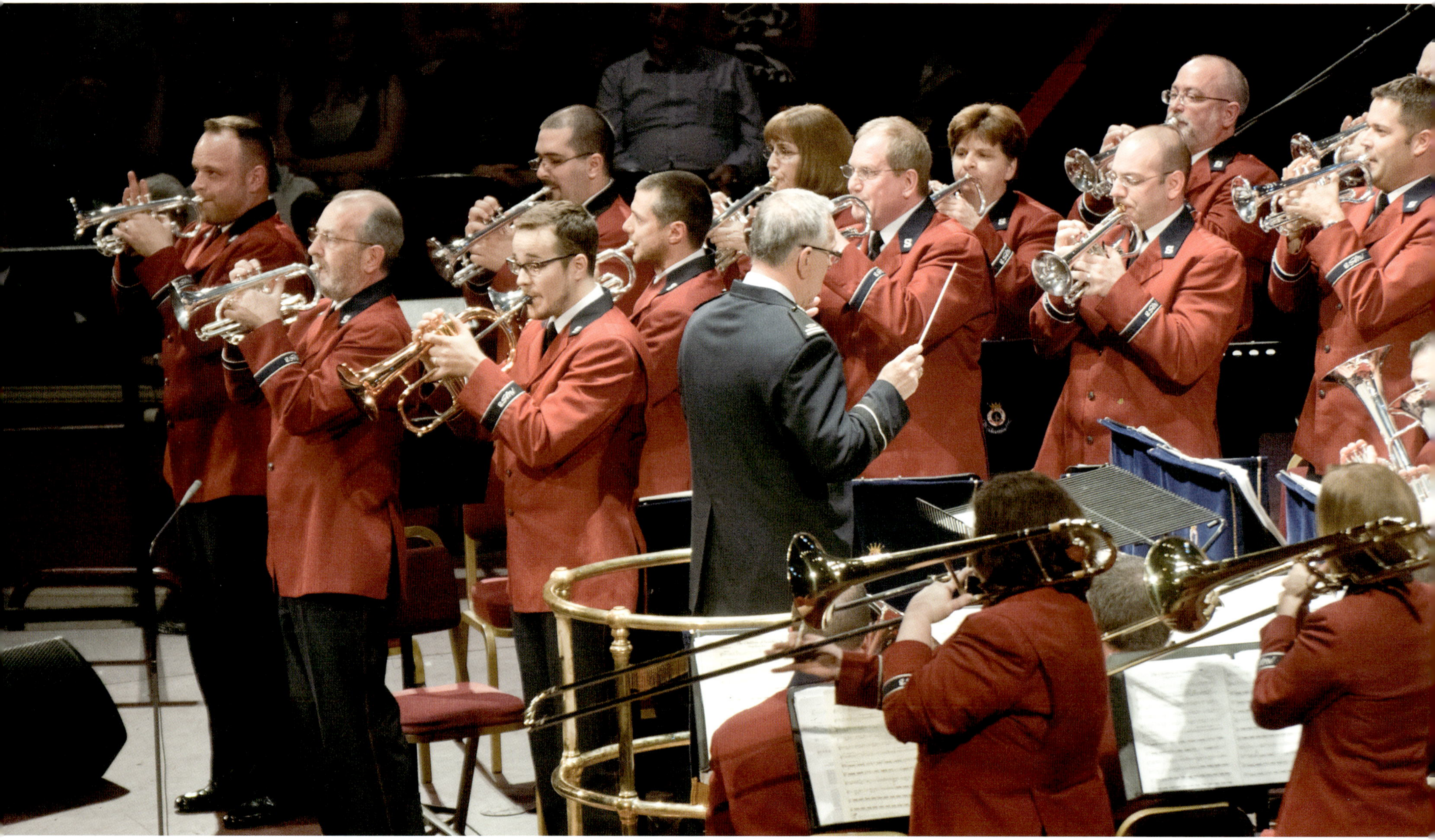

NEW YORK STAFF BAND
Lindsay R. Evans

When I first heard about the New York Staff Band (NYSB) being part of the special events to commemorate The International Staff Band's (ISB) 120th anniversary, I was mildly excited about the prospect of reuniting with ISB band members I've met during my 30 years with the band. I learned soon after that not only would the NYSB be participating but also that all eight Staff Bands from around the world would be as well.

Initially I formed my own speculations about what the celebrations might include, but soon enough we heard details: there would be a concert at the Royal Albert Hall, a march down The Mall, and a concert in the forecourt of Buckingham Palace. Very quickly, the excitement began to build within the NYSB.

For those like me who had been in the band for a number of years, we recalled our participation in the historic gathering of four Staff Bands at Roy Thomson Hall in Toronto 17 years previously. The event was held in celebration of the Canadian Staff Band's 25th anniversary, and the NYSB was privileged to join with the ISB, Chicago, and Canadian Staff Bands for this *International Brass Spectacular*. Because that event had been so extraordinary, we believed that ISB120 would also truly be a once-in-a-lifetime experience for Salvation Army Staff Band members.

As plans were finalised, the NYSB was afforded the opportunity to make several appearances in Ireland prior to our arrival in London, thanks to Dorothy Gates, our Principal Trombone and resident composer, who had emigrated from Belfast some years earlier.

As with any overseas tour, special pieces of music were written specifically for the band, and it was both a privilege and a pleasure for us to premier several pieces during our engagements in Ireland as well as in England.

In the months leading up to ISB120, we also learned that the NYSB, being the oldest Staff Band in continuous existence, would have the distinct privilege of sharing the concert stage with the ISB at a Friday night concert in London's Cadogan Hall. Over the time I've been in the NYSB, we have got to know many of the ISB members, but this would be the first time in decades that the two bands would share the same stage. Now the excitement was really building!

As with all the overseas tours the band has embarked on, the band members began special preparations to make sure they would be fully prepared musically, physically, and spiritually for the tour. For this tour, we had an especially strong desire to be at our very best because we would be sharing the platform with other Staff Band members from around the world.

Once we left our shores, we headed to Belfast, Northern Ireland, where Salvationists greeted us warmly. Major Alan Watters, the Divisional Commander, said that not many Salvation Army bands visit Northern Ireland, so hosting the NYSB was a rare opportunity for them. This was not the first time the NYSB had visited Northern Ireland, as we also visited in the early 1990s. We experienced warmth and hospitality from our gracious hosts at each venue in Ireland. One of the highlights for the band was to participate in a divisional

> "Sunday morning was a time for all the Staff Band members to worship in Central Hall, Westminster. General Linda Bond challenged and inspired the Staff Band members to dedicated service through their God-given gifts. The UK Territorial Youth Band was an enhancement to our worship together."

congress weekend. As Salvationists from across Ireland gathered in Belfast for this special commemoration, the band was ready to witness in word and music to the power of God's love. During our short stay in Ireland, we played to hundreds of people in many venues, but we also had the opportunity to see some of the sights, such as Stormont, the legislative home for Northern Ireland; Belfast City Hall; and Áras an Uachtarain, the president's official residence in Dublin. That turned out to be a very special visit. President Mary McAleese herself offered a warm welcome; she took time to greet each band member individually. In her remarks to us, she mentioned that in the very room we were meeting, she had hosted both the Pope and the US President within the past three weeks. Her warm personality and sincere appreciation for Salvationists made a deep impression on us all and we were given a private tour around the gorgeous mansion. In one room a beautiful grand piano was a focal point. Staff Bandsman Arthur Henry was invited to sit at the piano and 'tickle the ivories'. As Art played an impromptu arrangement of *Danny Boy*, Americans and Irish together enjoyed a poignant moment in this beautiful Dublin setting.

After what seemed like a whirlwind few days in Ireland and Northern Ireland, the band took a short flight to Heathrow Airport in London. It would be the culmination of all we had been preparing for. You could tell that the excitement among the band was increasing; though we are quiet on many flights, there was a lot of conversation and anticipation on this one. It was rather late in the afternoon when we arrived. In typical fashion, we quickly gathered all of our equipment and personal baggage and made our way to the front of the airport terminal, where a hired coach would be taking us to our first venue, an evening rehearsal with a number of invited guests. Standing at the curb, we waited and waited and waited and waited. What had happened to the coach? After a few frantic phone calls by our ISB hosts, it became apparent that the coach would not be coming. The question now was: How do you transport 38 band personnel with luggage and equipment to St George's College, Weybridge for a rehearsal? The answer: 10 or 12 London cabs! It was an unusual sight to see: three to four band members in each London cab, with instruments piled in the back and even the front. The cabbies were most accommodating, and we were able to get everyone to the school. I shared a cab with Dorothy Gates and Phil Ferreira, who brought along his Bb tuba. It's a good thing we're all friends!

On Friday morning the band members awoke to prepare for our visit to The Salvation Army's International Headquarters where we were privileged to be hosted by our new General, Linda Bond, for lunch. Warm words of welcome included her strong affirmation of support and the importance to her, being a former bandswoman herself, of Salvation Army bands in the ministry of the gospel.

Moving on to a rehearsal at London's Cadogan Hall, we had a chance to get re-acquainted with members of the ISB. Several weeks earlier we were told that all tickets for Cadogan

Hall had been sold - in fact, there were rumours of ticket sales taking place on eBay - so we expected a full house for the Friday evening concert.

The combined concert at Cadogan Hall was a highlight for me. Members of the ISB and NYSB enjoyed fellowship around the supper table, but more importantly, joined together to present some outstanding music. What a blessing to have several of the Army's premier composers present and to have the opportunity to perform under the leadership of current Bandmasters Stephen Cobb and Ronald Waiksnoris! But that wasn't all. Luminaries such as Brian Bowen, Peter Graham and Derek Smith also led the combined bands. The packed concert hall was enthusiastic about the music but more so about the interaction of the various personalities.

Saturday was the high point that all eight Staff Bands had been focusing on for many months. Each band presented a short concert in the afternoon at Royal Albert Hall. While there was a lot of coming and going among the large audience, everyone paid rapt attention as each band performed for the world

This is not an understatement; people from across the globe were in the audience to witness this concert. Who could forget the moment when the Japan Staff Band took the stage to what seemed like a five or six-minute ovation? There were not many dry eyes in the place as Salvationists and band enthusiasts paid tribute to the band members who had endured so much hardship in the previous few months following a devastating earthquake and tsunami and who had worked so hard to be present in London.

It's safe to say that none of the Staff Band members had ever been on the stage of the Royal Albert Hall with 250 other Staff Band members before. What a sight to see: 250 musicians in their red 'festival' tunics filling every square inch of the stage. As one of those 250, I can confirm that it was a full house, especially on stage!

Sunday morning was a time for all the Staff Band members to worship in Central Hall, Westminster. General Linda Bond challenged and inspired us all to dedicated service through our God-given gifts. The UK Territorial Youth Band was an enhancement to our worship together.

It seemed that the events of the weekend were moving along quickly, and suddenly we found ourselves lining up on The Mall for the march to Buckingham Palace. A tremendous amount of organisation was required to pull together all the details for the march.

This was another highlight of the weekend for me. As we marched down The Mall to the cheers of the crowd estimated at more than 15,000 people, I found it difficult to play with a lump in my throat.

All eight Staff Bands formed into one large ensemble in the forecourt of Buckingham Palace and inspired the enthusiastic crowd with the best of Salvation Army music. I suppose we could be forgiven for having a feeling of pride as Salvation Army band members. Later that afternoon all eight Staff Bands gathered at the Central Hall, Westminster for a final reception before departing for all parts of the earth to resume our individual ministries.

Andrew Garcia thrilling the audience with his flugel horn solo *Children of Sanchez*

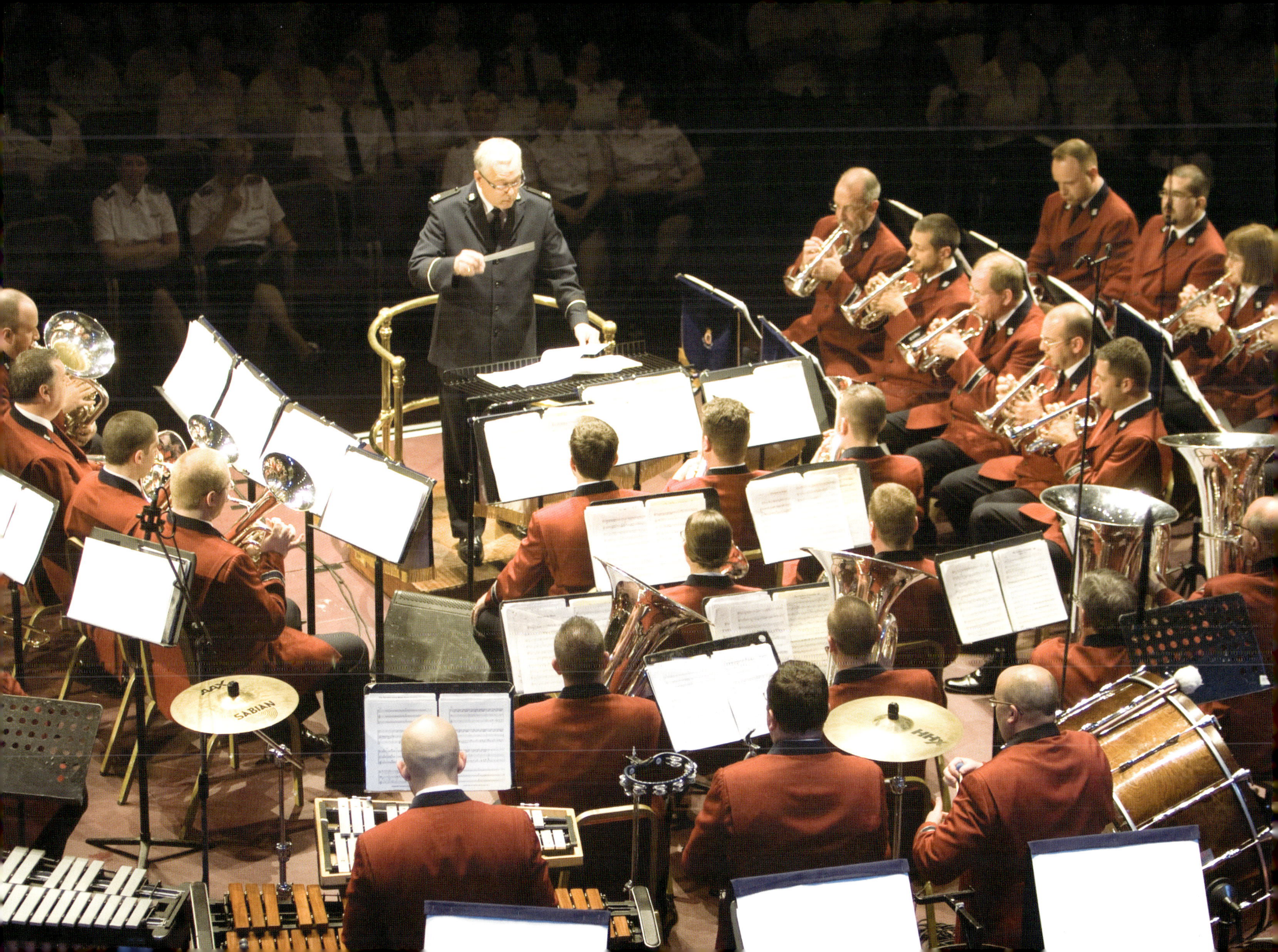
AAX
SABIAN
HHX

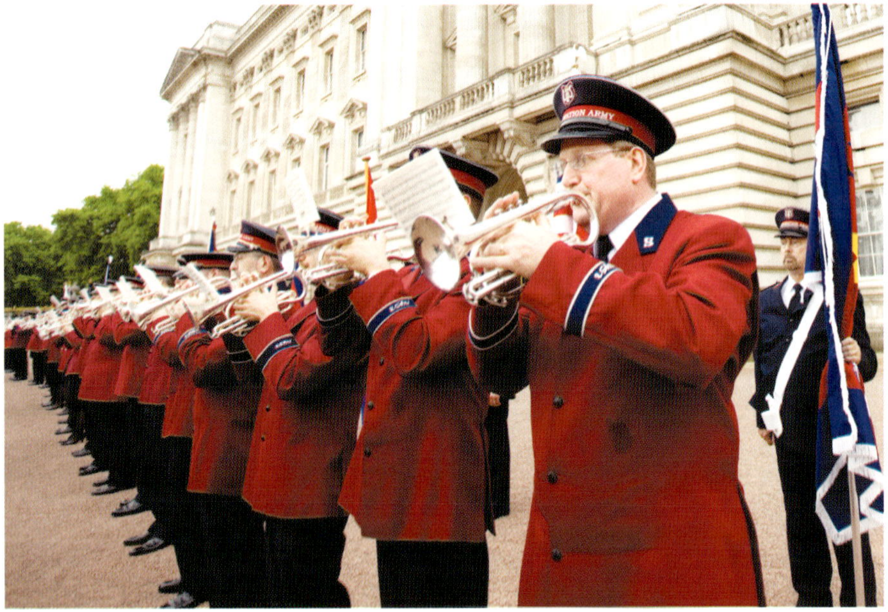

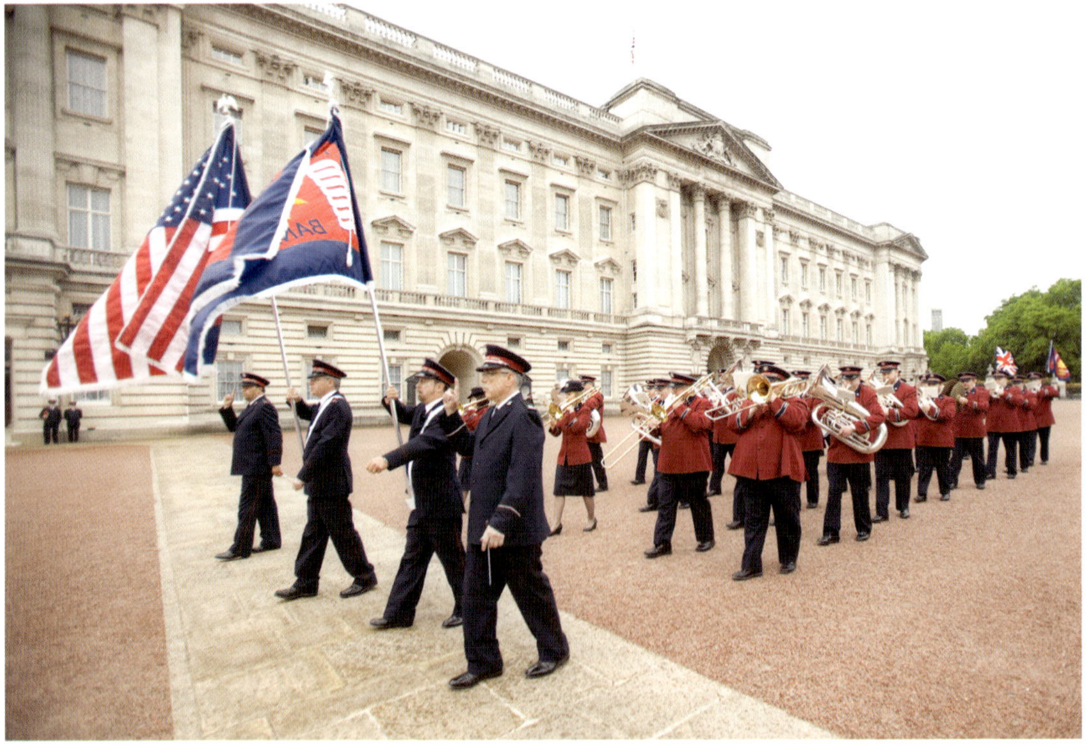

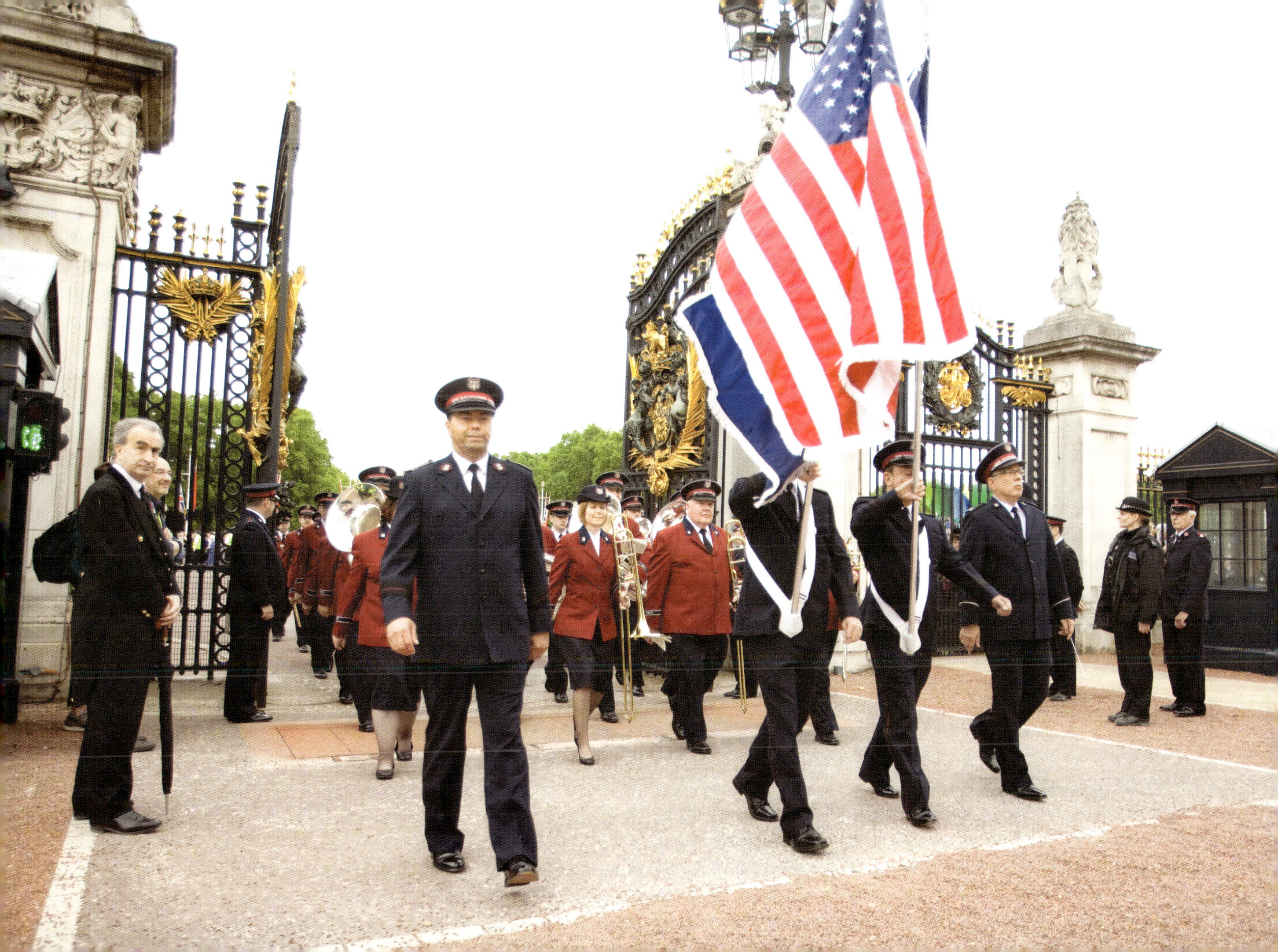

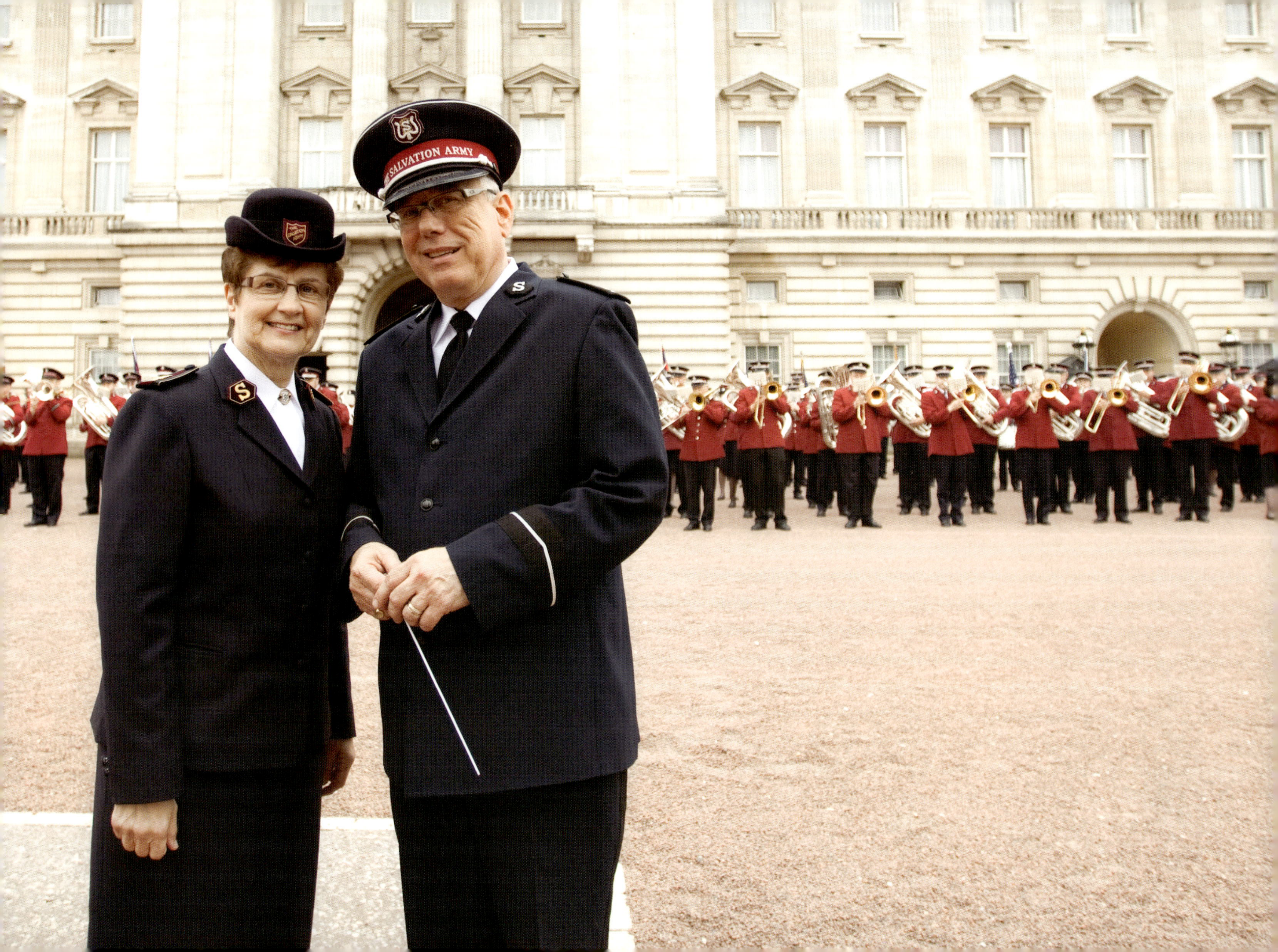
SALVATION ARMY

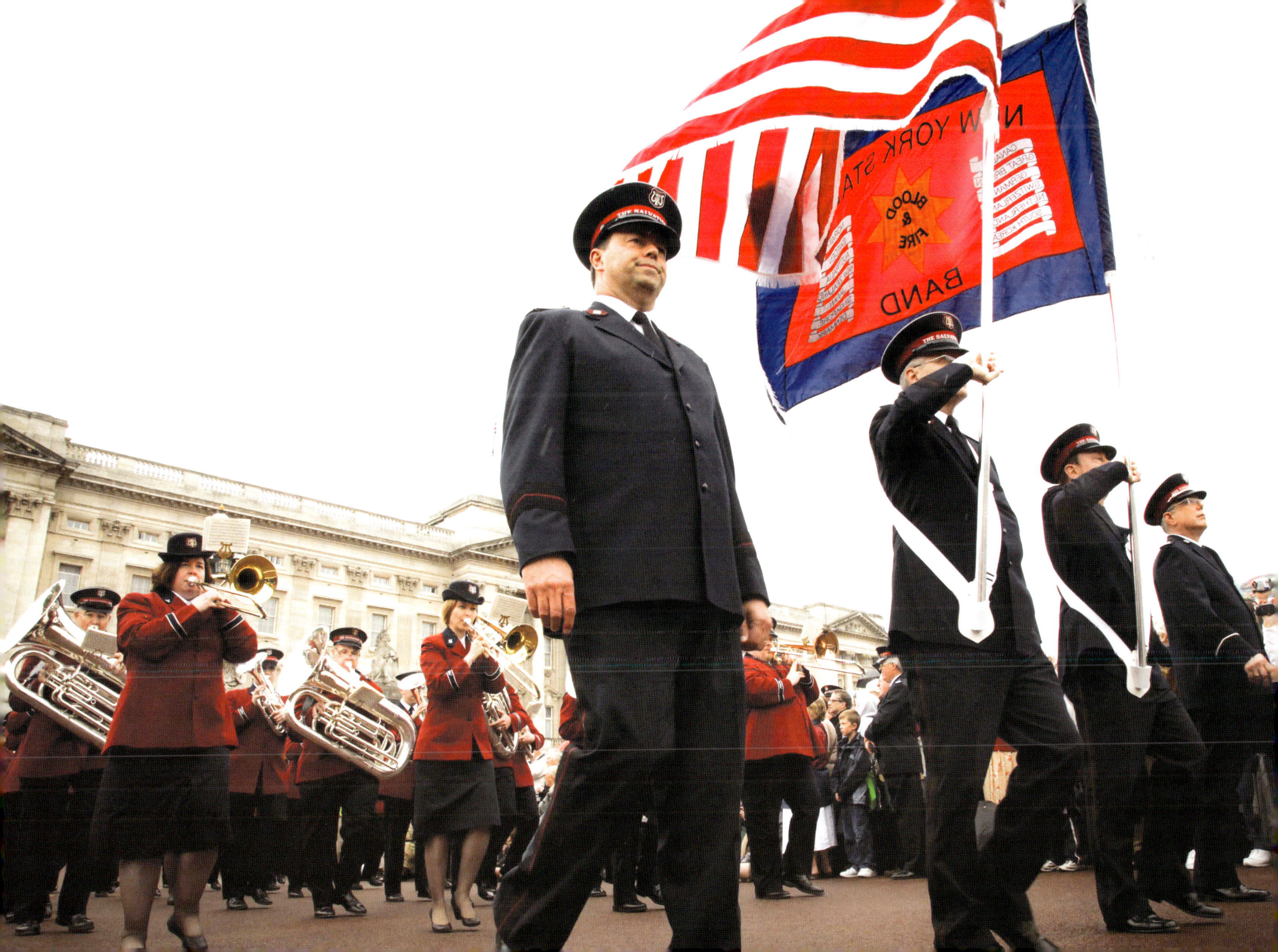
BLOOD & FIRE
BAND

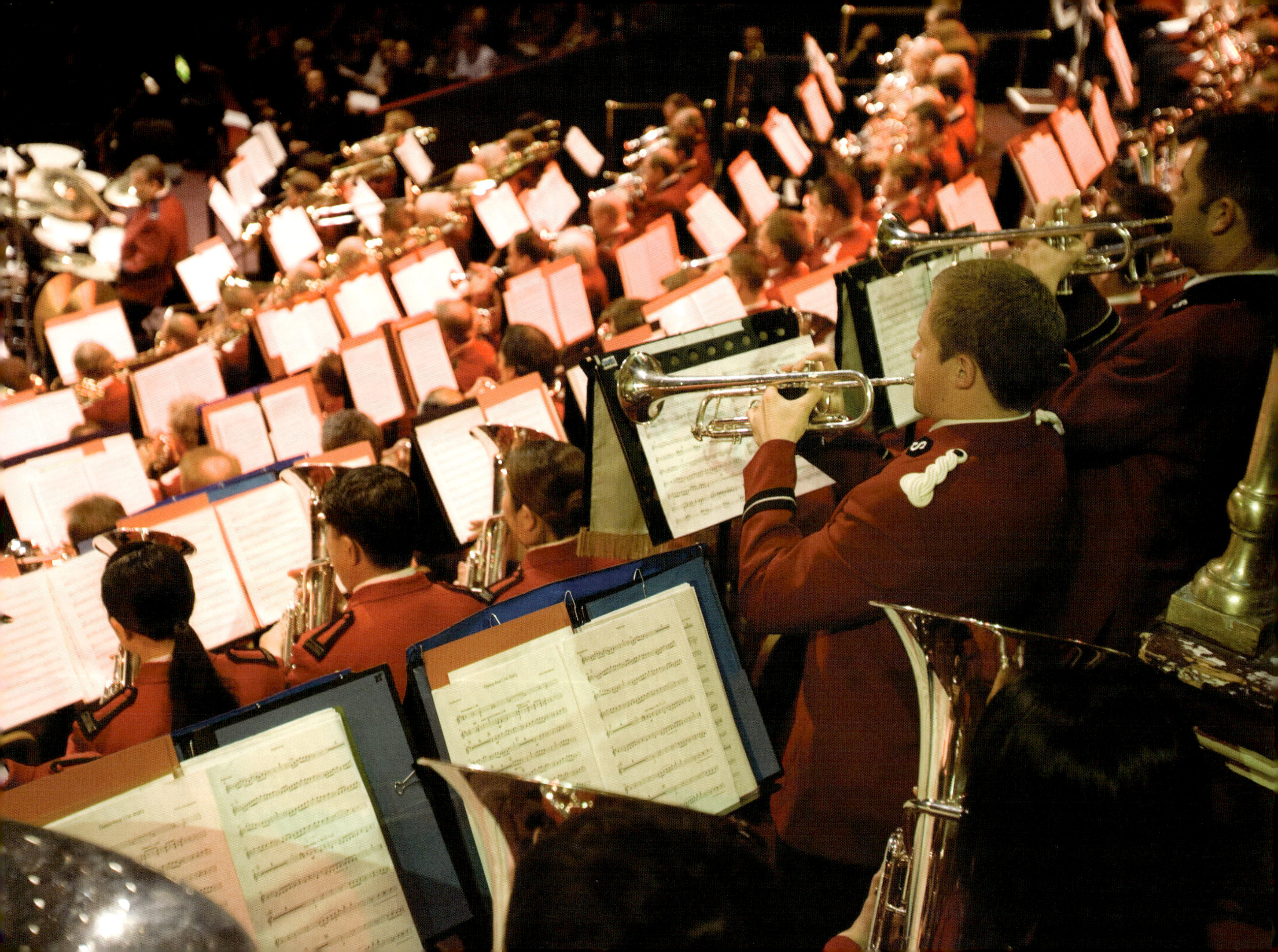

COMPOSER
Dudley Bright

Looking back on ISB120, one cannot but marvel at the huge feast of music heard that day. That *Pursuing Horizons* was just a small part of that diet was for me a privilege and an honour. Ever since The International Staff Bandmaster had heard a recording he had expressed interest in it being adapted for band. Composed in 2004 for The London Symphony Orchestra's Brass Academy, under the title of *Pursuing the Horizon*, it was scored for 40 individual orchestral brass players divided into three separate ensembles. I had little appetite for multiple doublings but wanted to make the best use of all the players. Although the hymn tune *St Luke* appeared near the end, the piece had no specific programme and I subsequently provided the ISB with an alternative, *The Cost of Freedom* premièred in 2008 at Epic Brass II in The Sage Gateshead. The intention was to paint a work with an expressly spiritual message but with a similar musical pallet to the LSO piece.

> Closer to the event I began to consider what words might be used to introduce the work *Pursuing Horizons*. Casting the mind back to its initial conception, I was struck by how the idea of attainment was reflected in St Paul's words to the Phillipians (Chapter 3): 'Now I long to know Christ and the power shown by his resurrection… I do not consider to have arrived… But keep going… to whatever lies ahead!'

However, two years later Dr Cobb yet again broached the subject of adapting *Pursuing the Horizon*, this time as part of his vision for the ISB120 celebrations. I was sceptical but Steve assured me its scale and antiphonal effects were ideally suited to the huge spaces of the Royal Albert Hall and eight Staff Bands. The plan was first to create a version for the ISB alone and then consider how best to expand it. Initially I virtually re-composed the whole piece adding: a reflective verse near the beginning, appearances of motifs derived from *St Luke* and some more idiomatically brass band type gestures. Once the ISB had run the piece, I was still apprehensive and gave the Bandmaster the chance to change his mind. He was so encouraging that I agreed to set about working out how best to fit the music to the splendid forces of eight Staff Bands. The final form was to feature the ISB as a central concertante group with the remaining bands seated behind and divided into two equal groups. Due to the shortness of rehearsal time on the day I restricted the most complex parts to the ISB with the largest forces joining for the climaxes. My colleague at the LSO, Philip Cobb, was earmarked to play the ethereal off-stage trumpet solo and the whole thing was renamed *Pursuing Horizons*.

A score with 54 staves was prepared and the parts given generous helpings of cues (small notation of music played by someone else) to aid individual band rehearsals. With the invaluable aid of Apple computers, Sibelius music software and email, the music was served up to Staff Band rooms around the world.

Closer to the event I began to consider what words might be used to introduce the work *Pursuing Horizons*. Casting the mind back to its initial conception, I was struck by how the idea of attainment was reflected in St Paul's words to the Phillipians (Chapter 3): 'Now I long to know Christ and the power shown by his resurrection… I do not consider to have arrived… But keep going… to whatever lies ahead!'

For me that seemed to describe the sacred mission of the ISB and I pray it may have been of some encouragement to someone hearing the music.

MUSIKKORPS · BLUT UND FEUER · DIE HEILSARMEE · HANN

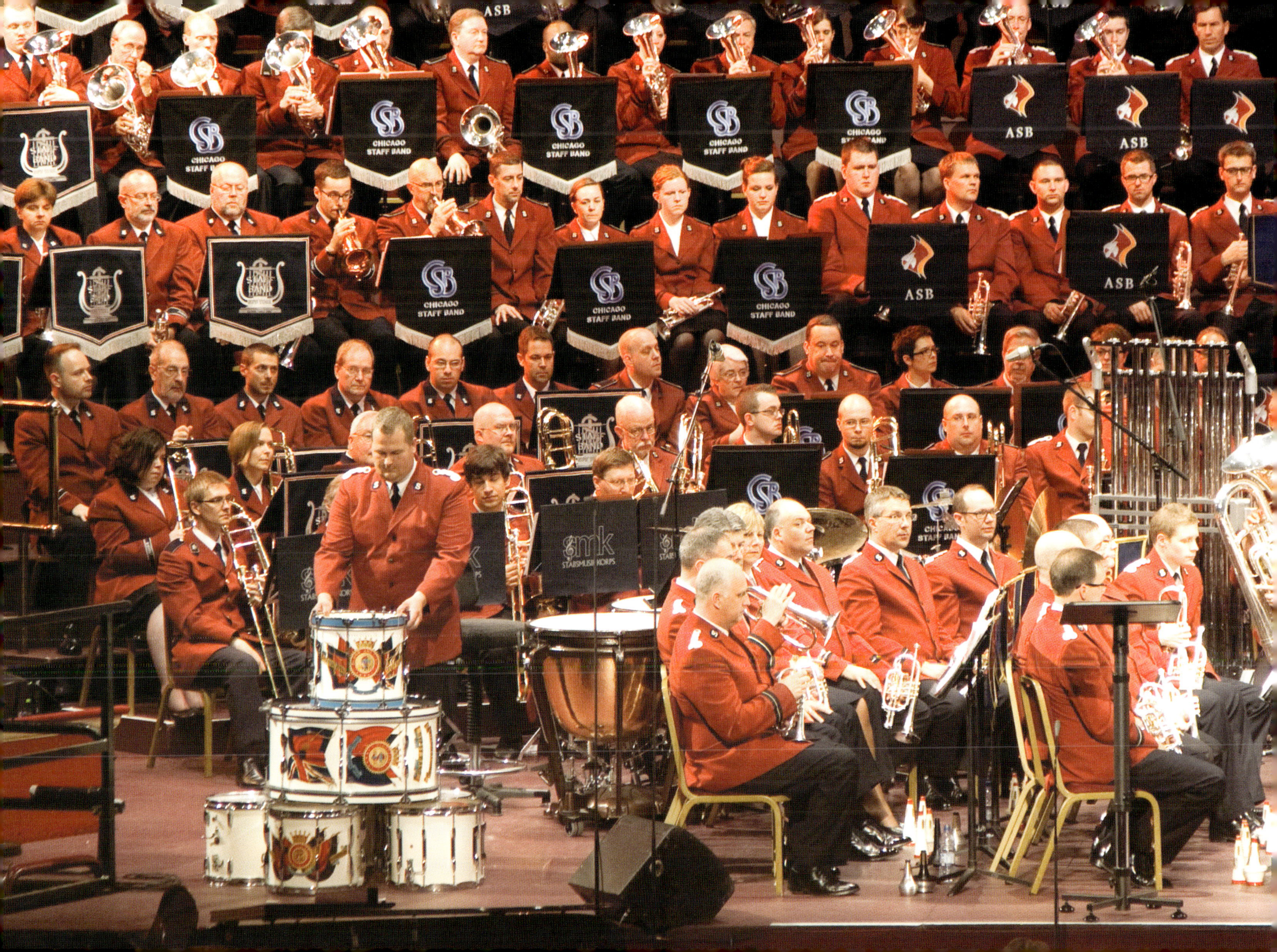
CHICAGO STAFF BAND
ASB
smk
STABSMUSIKKORPS

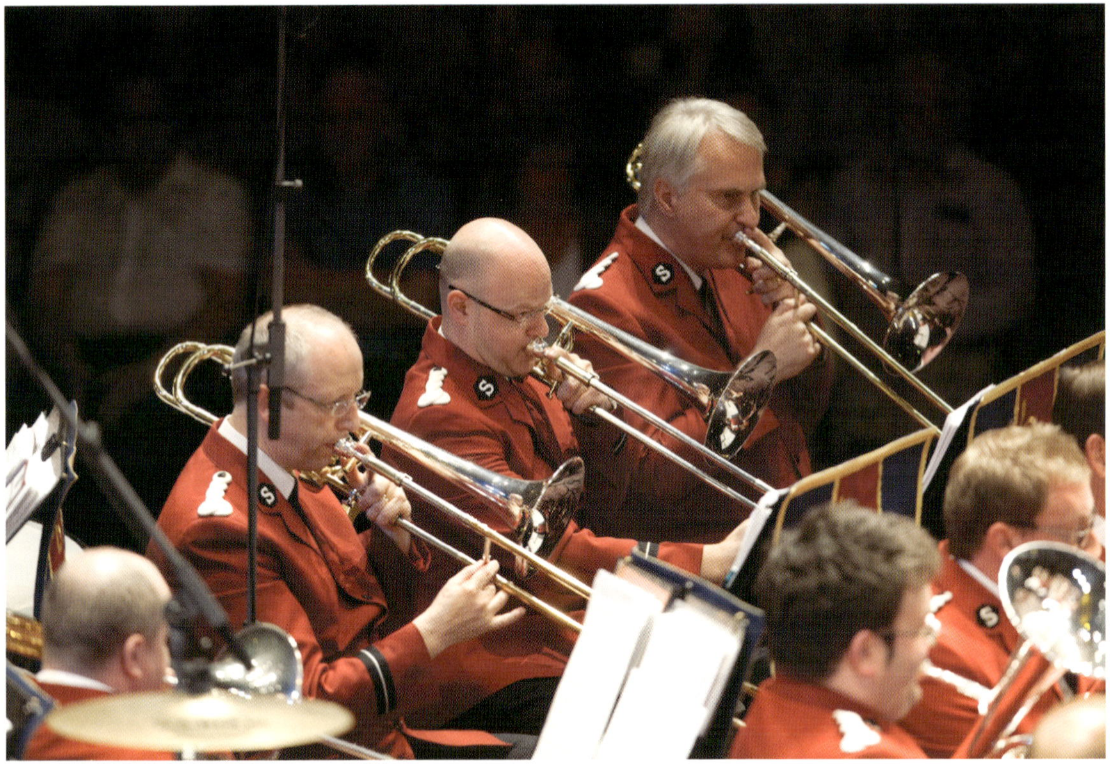

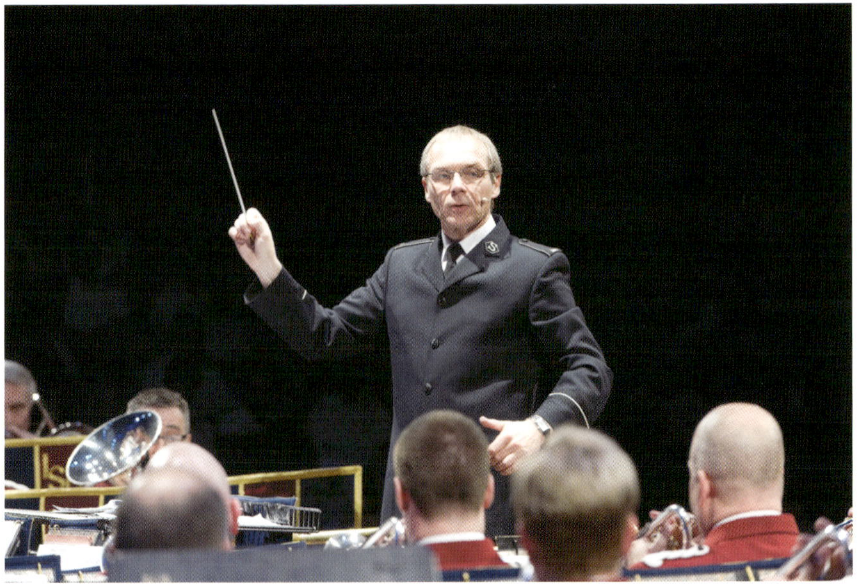

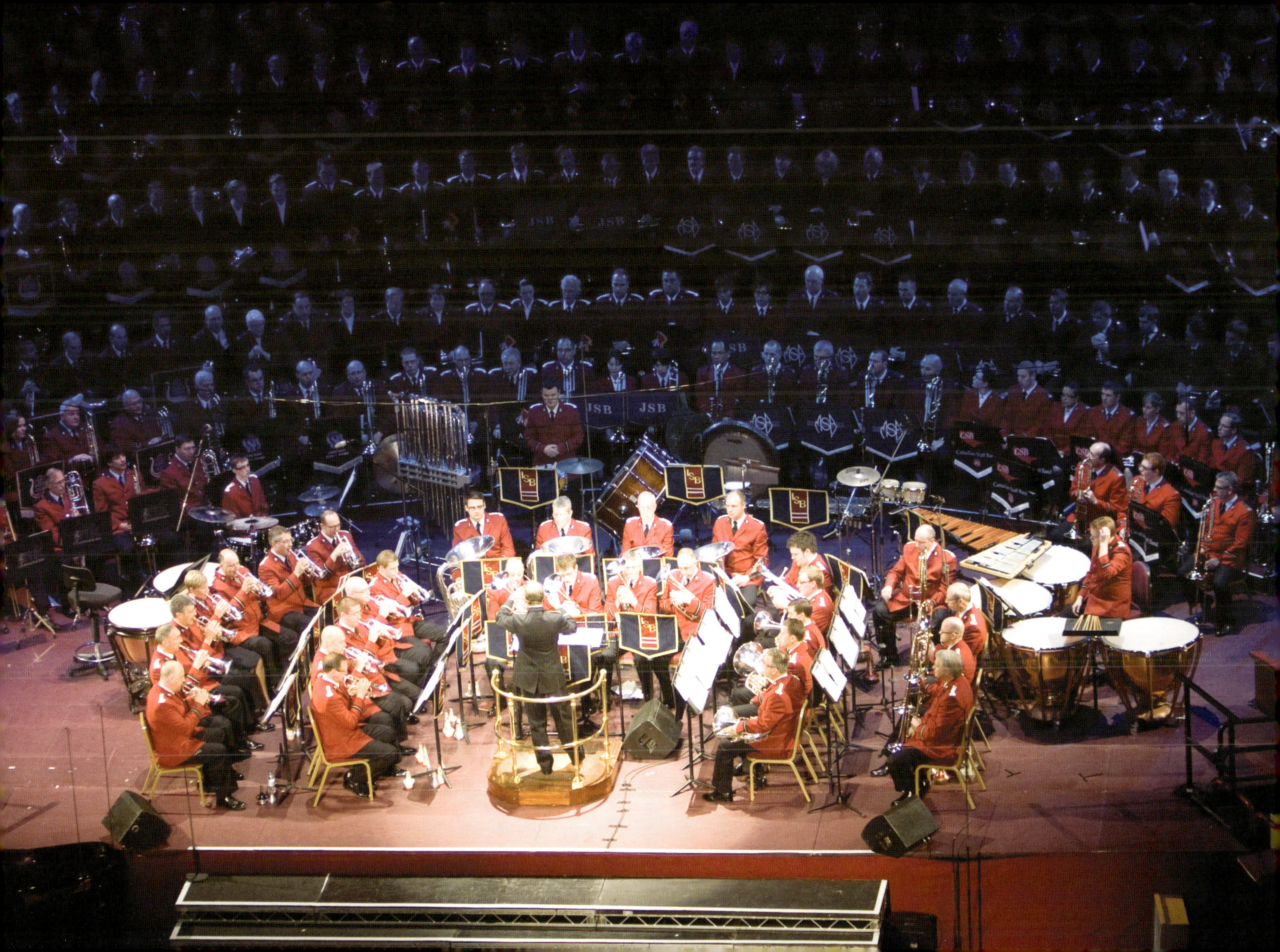
JSB
JSB
ISB
ISB
ISB

Soloist Derick Kane thrilling the audience with *Scottish Folk Variants* (Stephen Bulla), especially commissioned for the *Brass Spectacular*

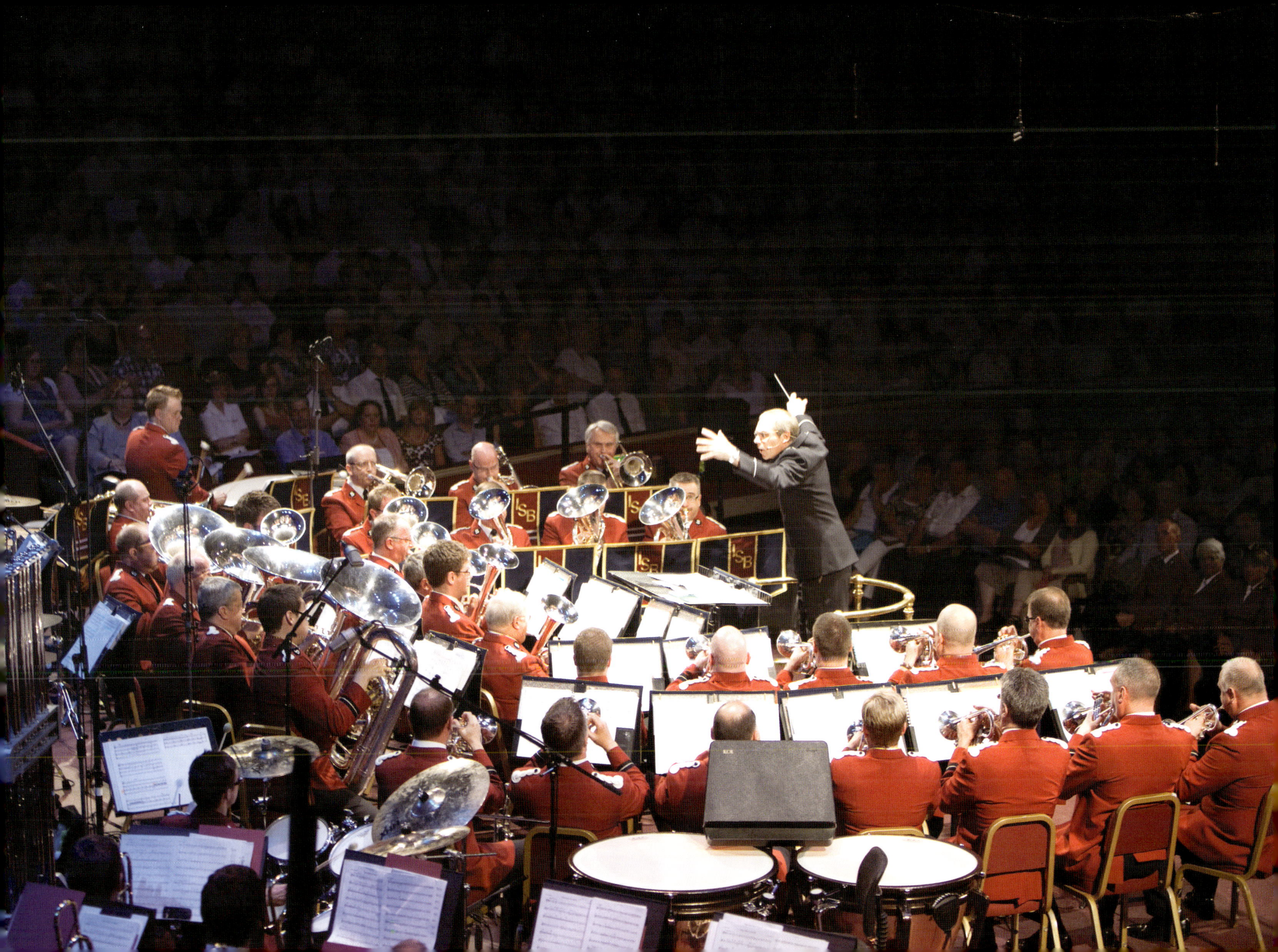
ISB

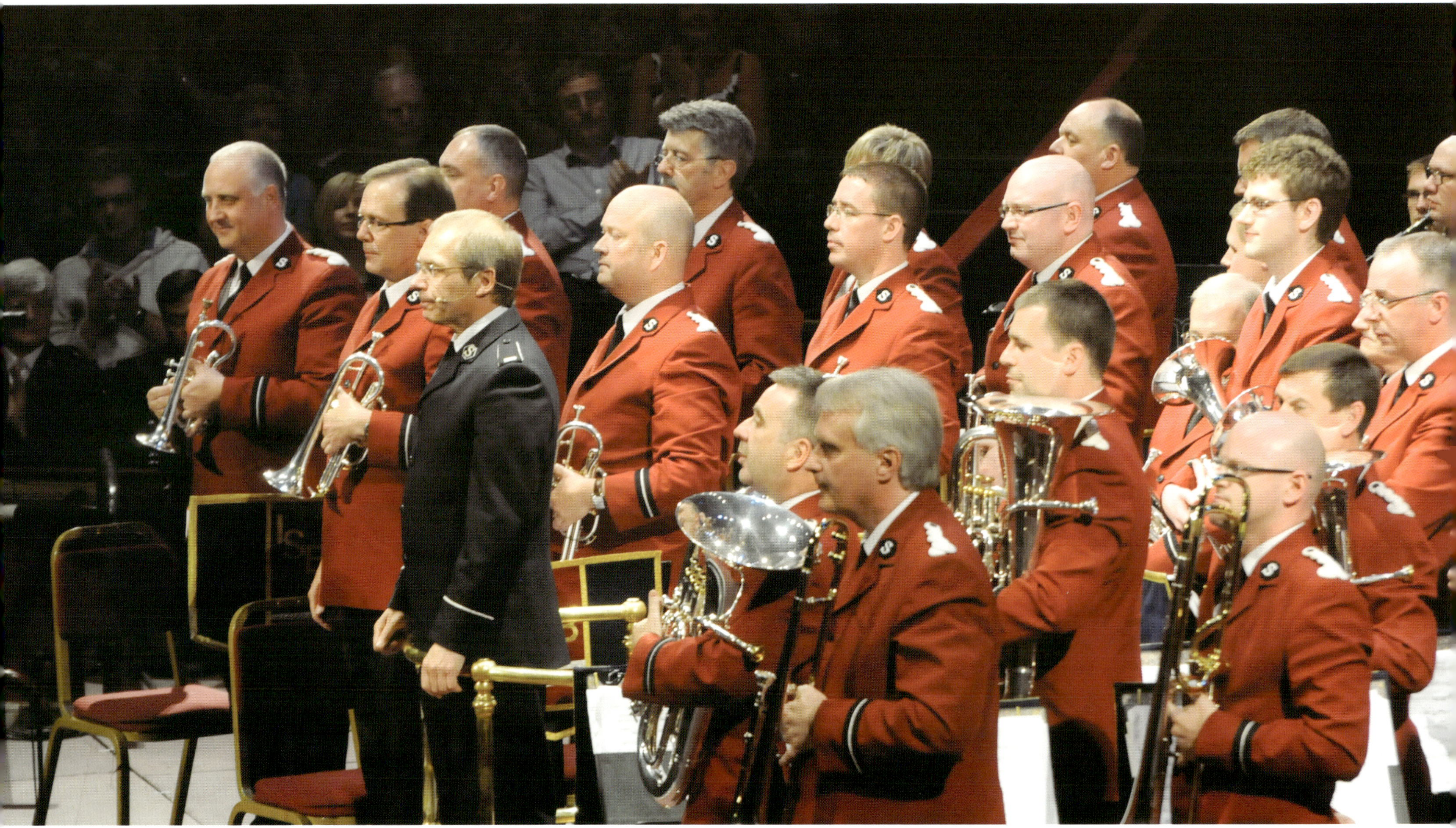

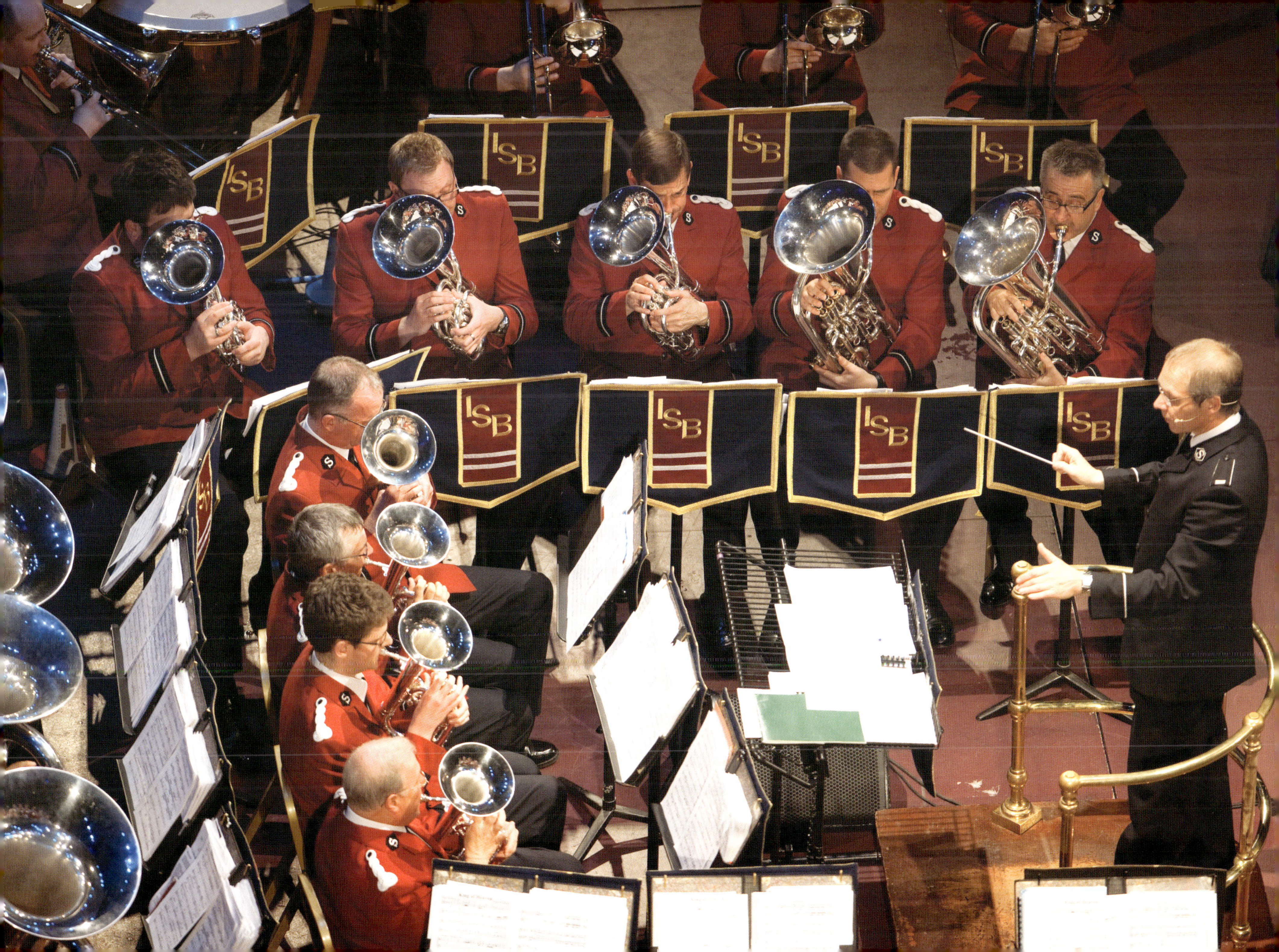
ISB

The congregation 'lifts the roof' singing *Stand up and Bless the Lord* as ISB percussionists are amazed by the 'wall of sound' that surrounds them!

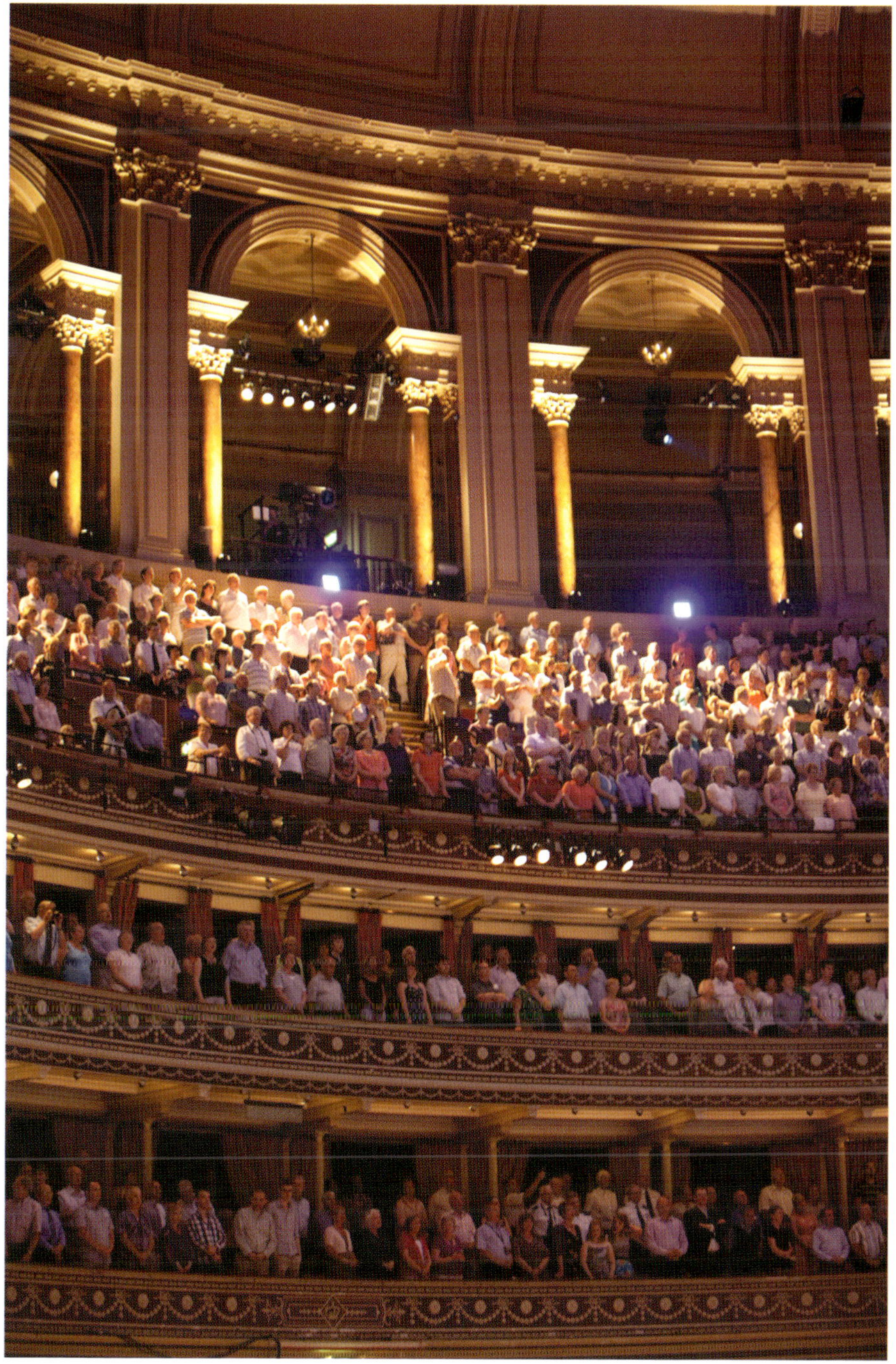

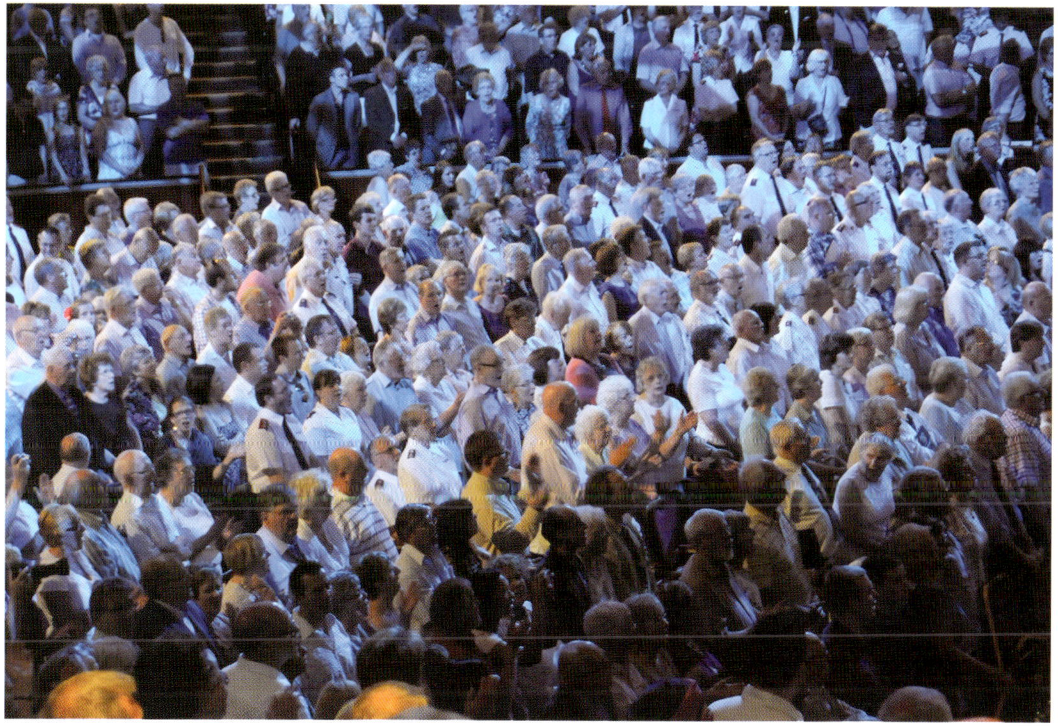

The International Staff Songsters, Leader Dorothy Nancekievill

181

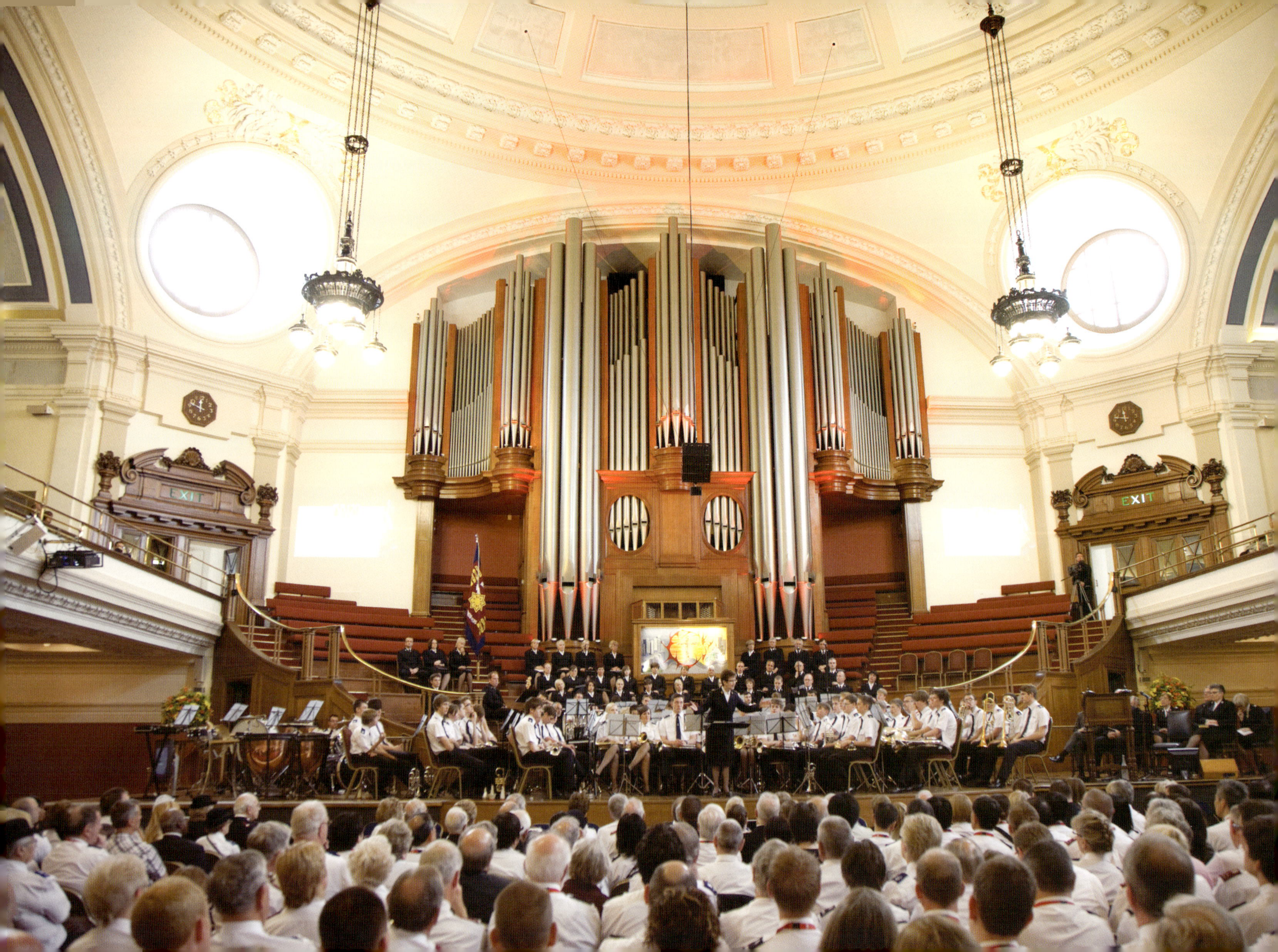
EXIT
EXIT

CENTRAL HALL, WESTMINSTER
Music Leader – Sue Blyth

Walking through London on a beautiful Sunday morning I had an extra spring in my step. Not only was I on my way to worship with other music leaders at Central Hall, Westminster but as my husband, Andrew, had been on tour with the Melbourne Staff Band for 10 days, this was the day I would get him home and we would be reunited!

I was struck by how many Salvation Army uniforms there were on the streets of London that morning - usually we Bandmasters and Songster Leaders are safely tucked away within the walls of the Training College, but not today. As I approached Westminster I was stopped by a curious passing tourist enquiring as to the event and this set the tone for the rest of the day preparing me, along with many other Salvationists, for the questions from people from all points of the globe.

Outside the Central Hall there was a tangible buzz of excitement as coaches dropped off members of the Staff Bands, and music leaders who had not seen each other since the previous year chatted animatedly. I was anxious to get inside and quickly made my way into the hall to be met by a bunch of very friendly Australian band members eager to share some amusing story they had about my husband. Even though we were, at that point, complete strangers, there was an immediate sense of fellowship that I have only ever experienced in The Salvation Army.

Inside the hall, the Territorial Youth Band was preparing to play. We are regular attendees at their annual festival in February and I am always moved by the tremendous musicality of this group but today, more than that, I felt incredibly aware that these young people, who could have chosen to be somewhere else on that Sunday morning, were freely giving of their talents in ministry and helping to draw us into a deeper sense of worship.

We quickly found where we should be sitting and after a briefing about our schedule for the day, and for me a quick catch up with my parents, we settled down to soak in the atmosphere of this very unique occasion.

General Linda Bond took her place right in the middle of the TYB to deliver, without notes, her message to the eager congregation. This was what many of us had waited for and she held each person spellbound creating meaningful moments of reflection with opportunity for renewing promises made.

> " I was struck by how many Salvation Army uniforms there were on the streets of London that morning... As I approached Westminster I was stopped by a curious passing tourist enquiring as to the event and this set the tone for the rest of the day preparing me, along with many other Salvationists, for the questions from people from all points of the globe. "

The sound of singing at Sunday Council's meeting could warm even the coldest heart but join that usual sound to the extra hundreds of Staff Bandsmen and women who sang with us and you have an incredible memory that will live with me for a long time. Heaven will be like that I'm sure! Joining in prayer in different languages was also a special moment and a reminder of the very special fellowship that exists in our global church, serving together one God, under one flag.

Top left: Lord Derek Foster and Lady Anne Foster of Bishop Auckland
Top right: Derick, Hazel and Stephen Kane enjoy lunch at Central Hall, Westminster

Gathering before the Sunday morning meeting

METHODIST CENTRAL HALL
METHODIST
CENTRAL HALL
WESTMINSTER
METHODIST CENTRAL HALL

Staff Band members and families relaxing over lunch

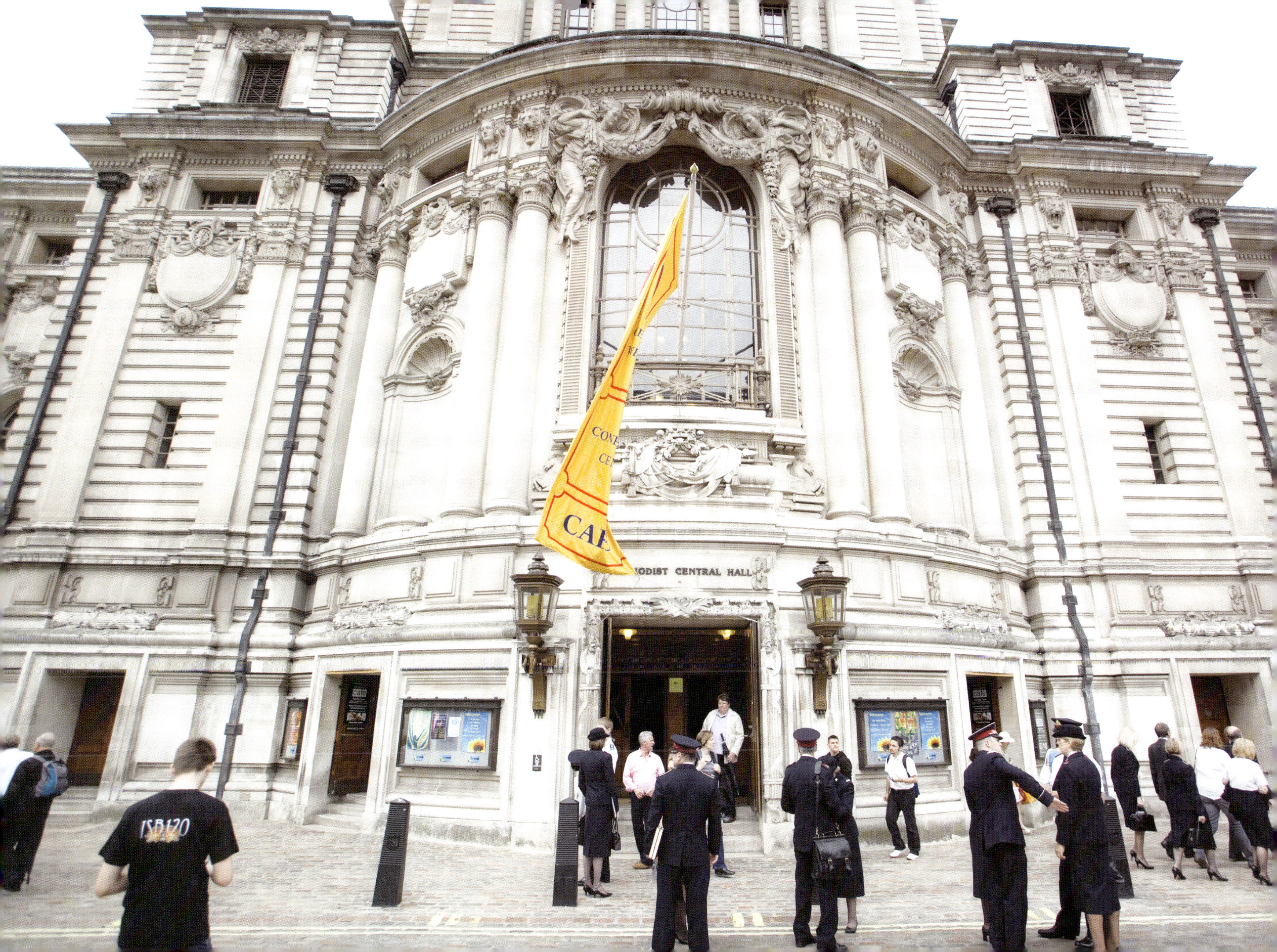
CENTRAL HALL
ISB120

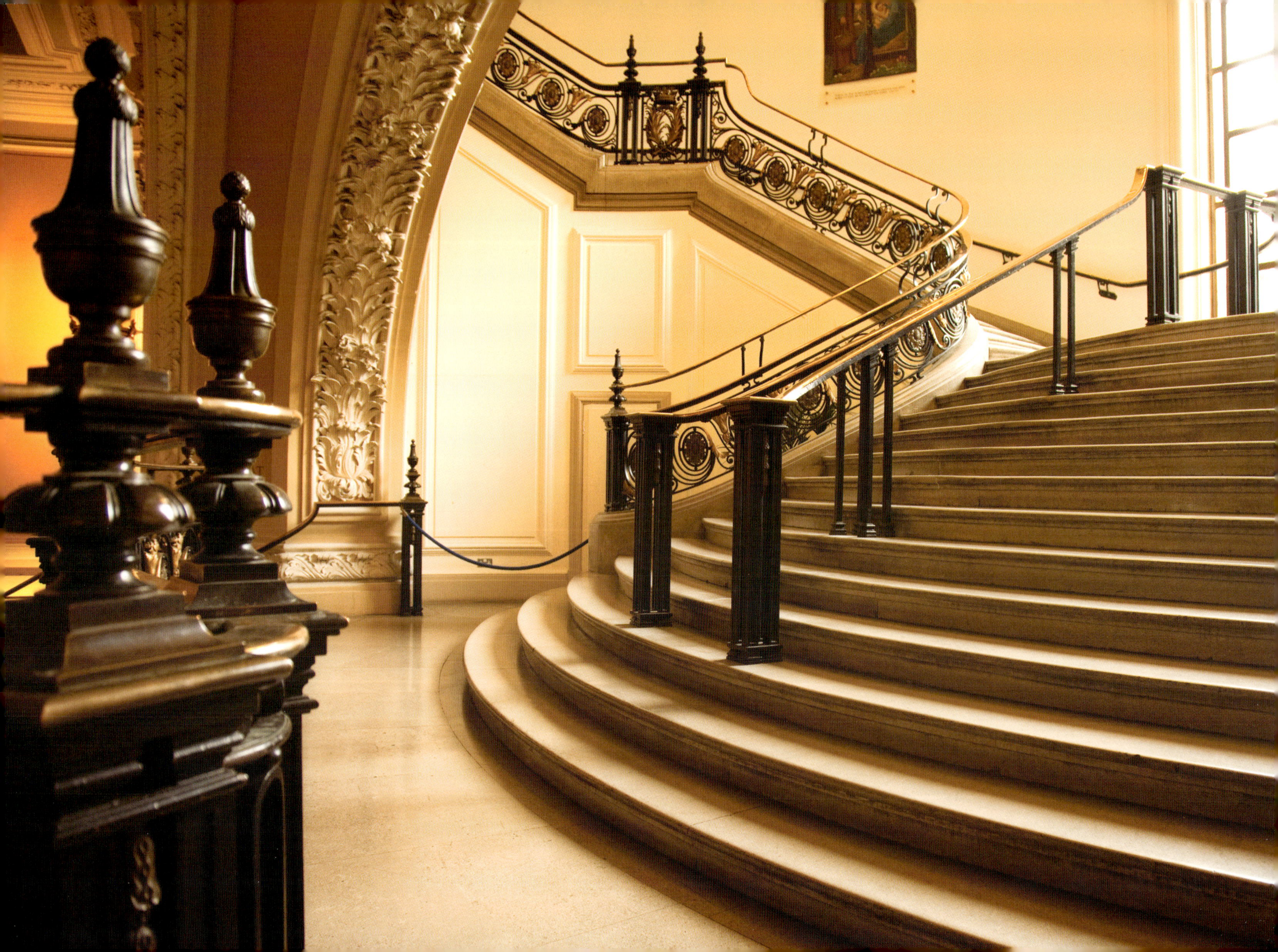

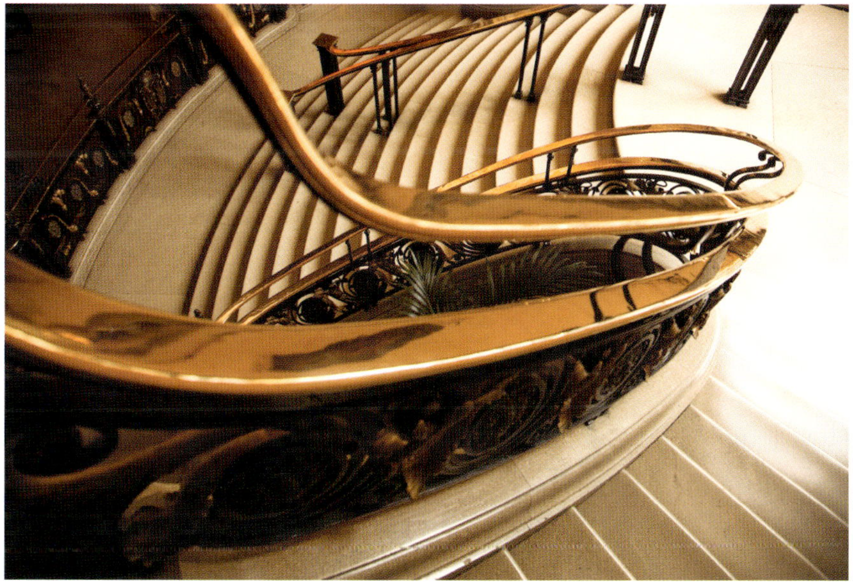

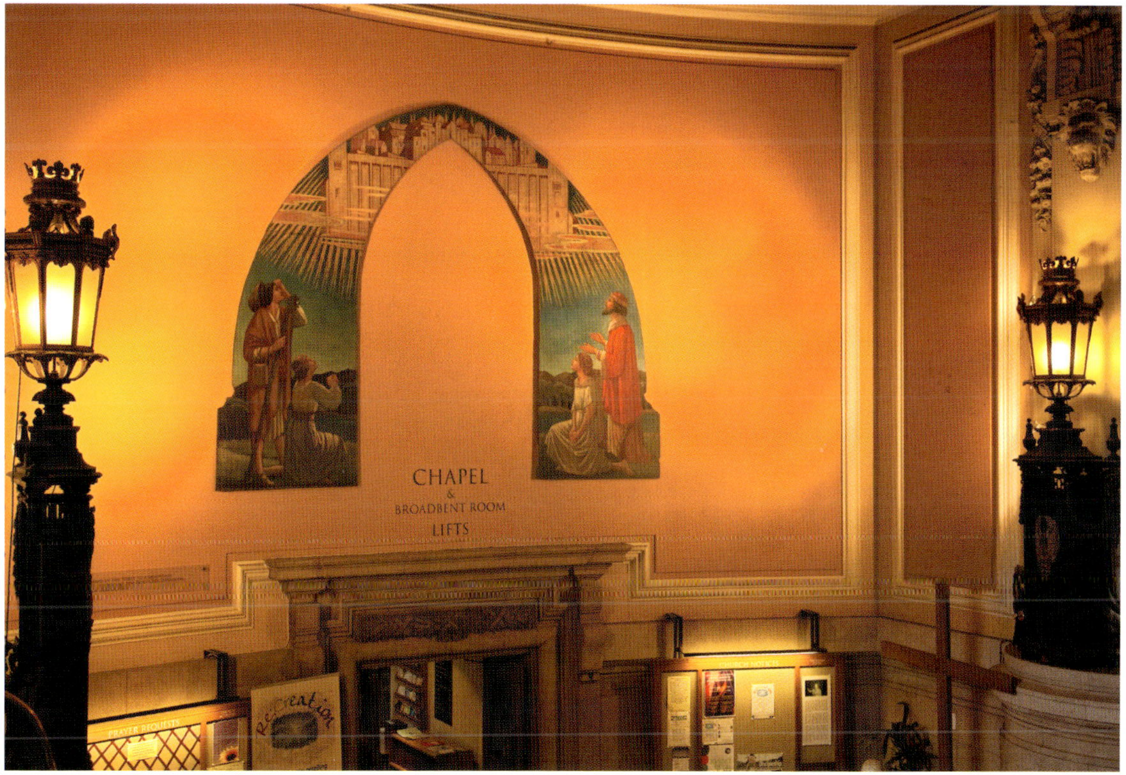
CHAPEL
&
BROADBENT ROOM
LIFTS

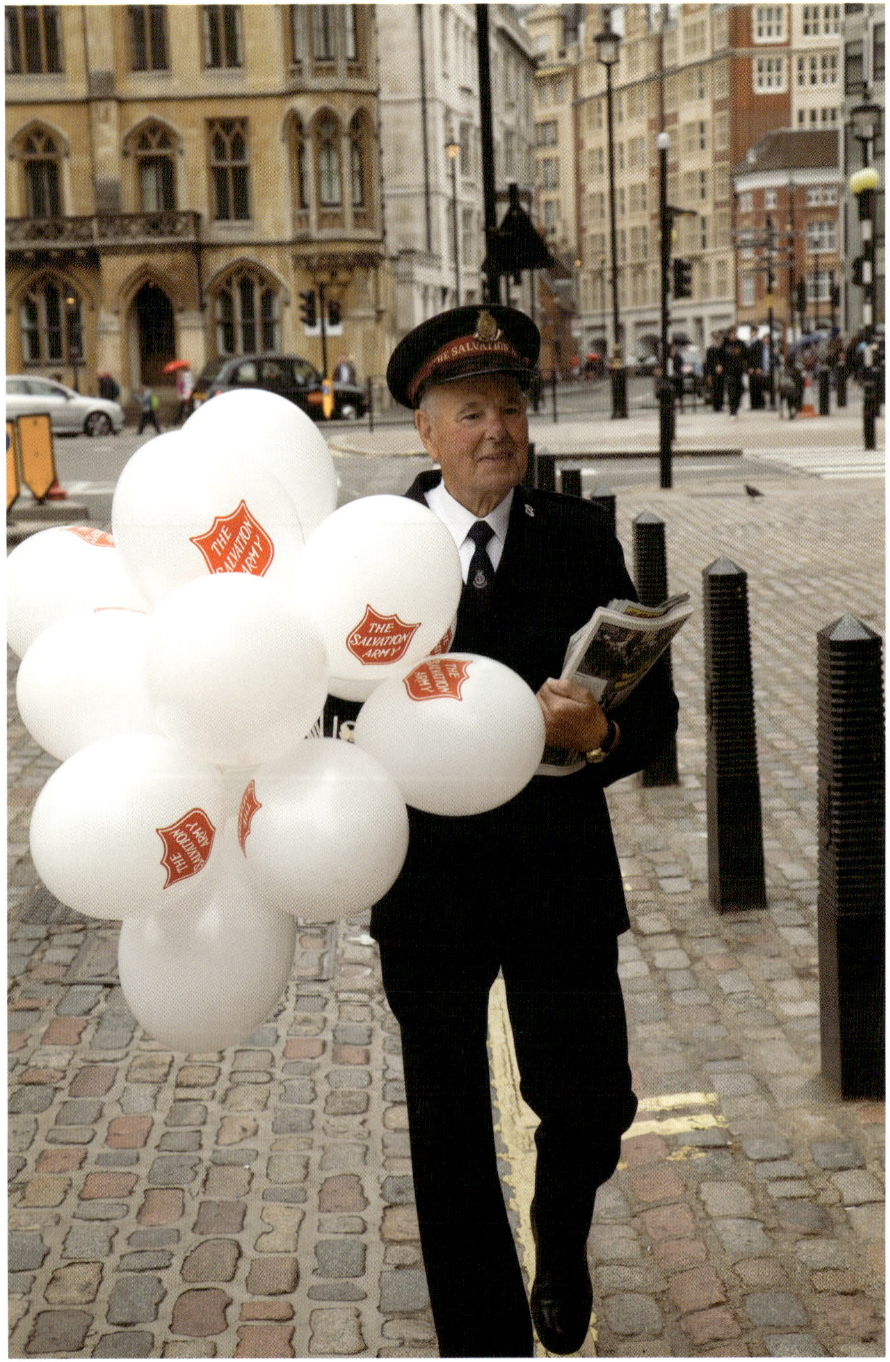
THE SALVATION
THE SALVATION ARMY
THE SALVATION ARMY

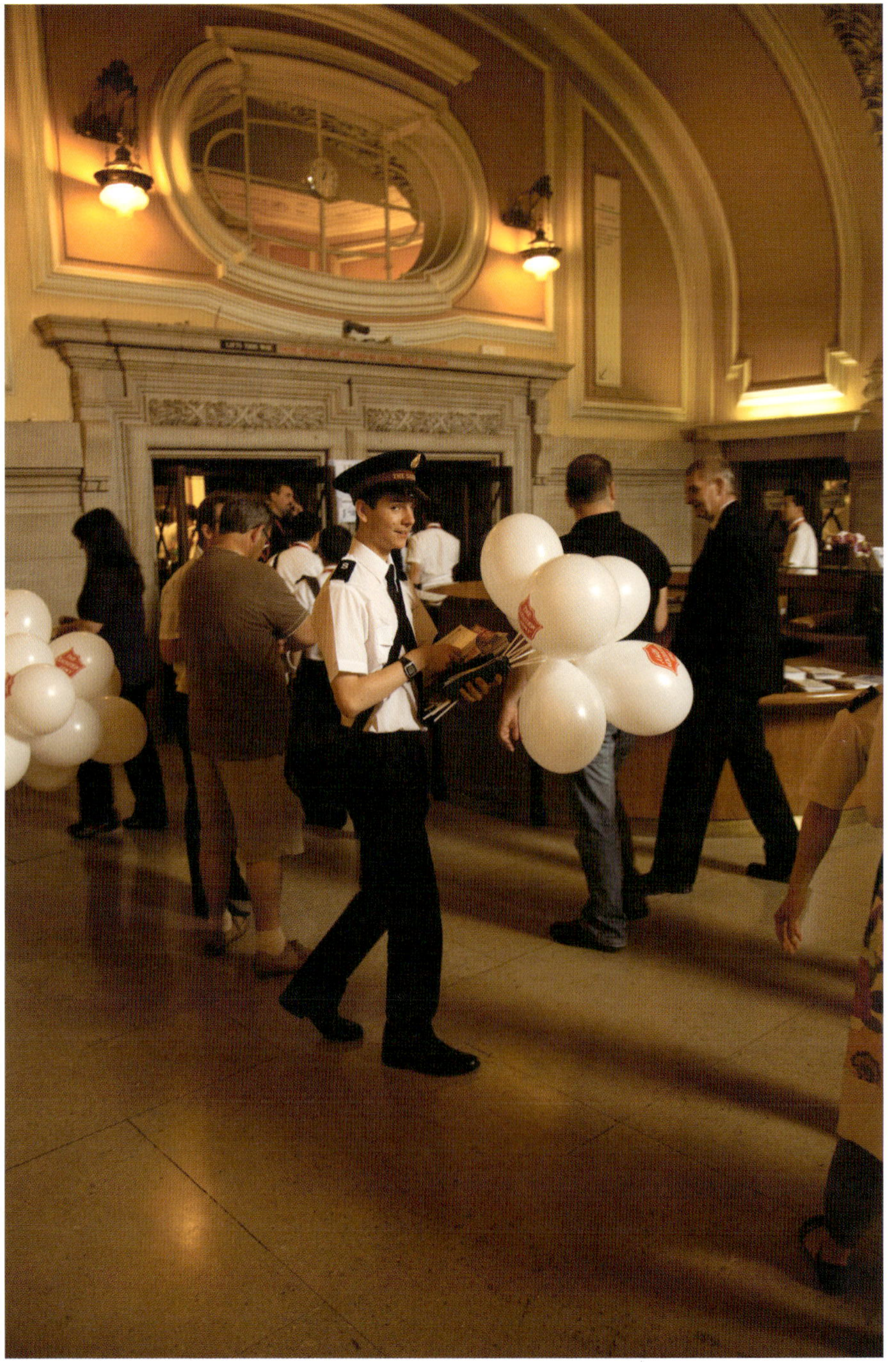

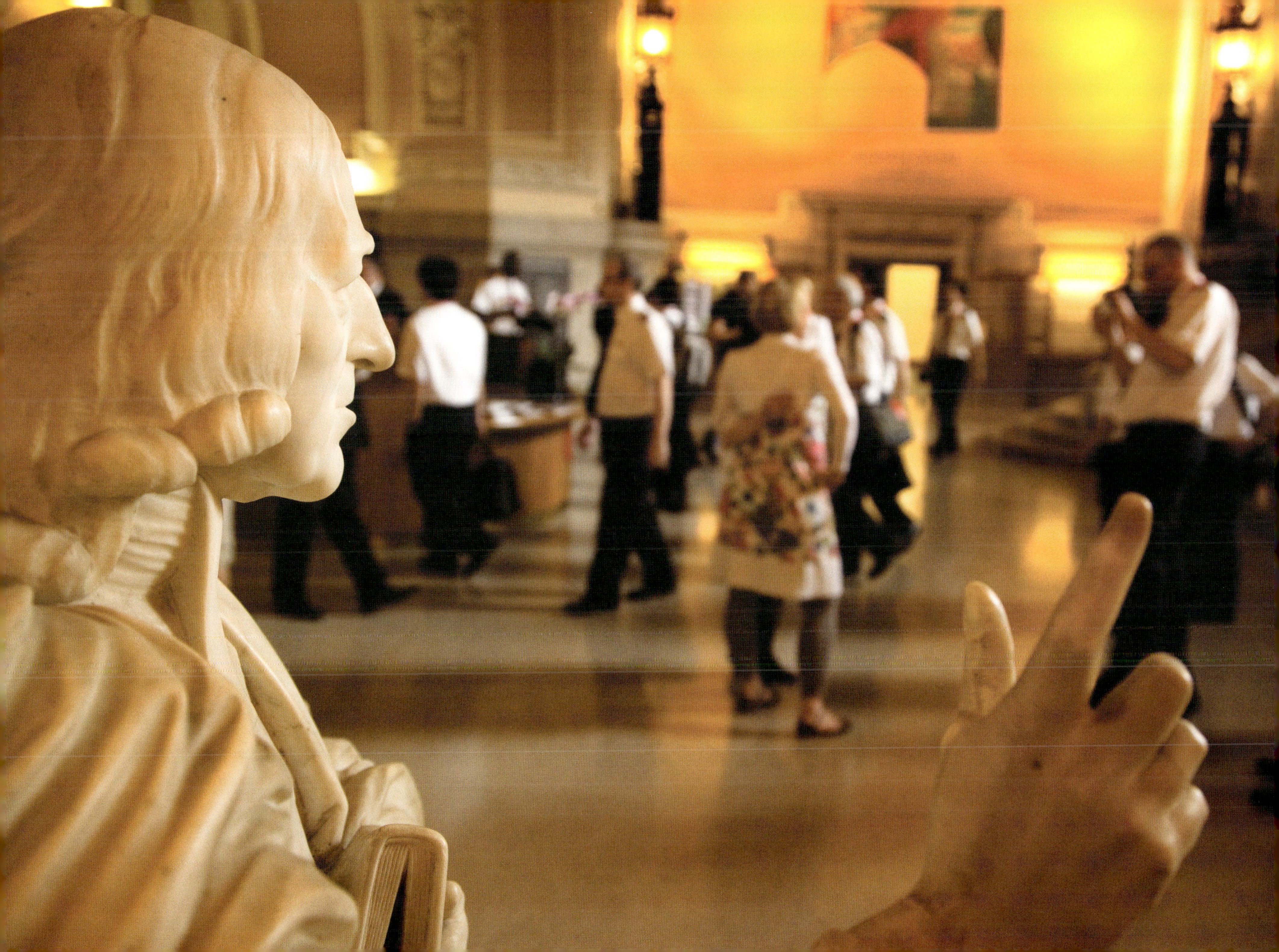

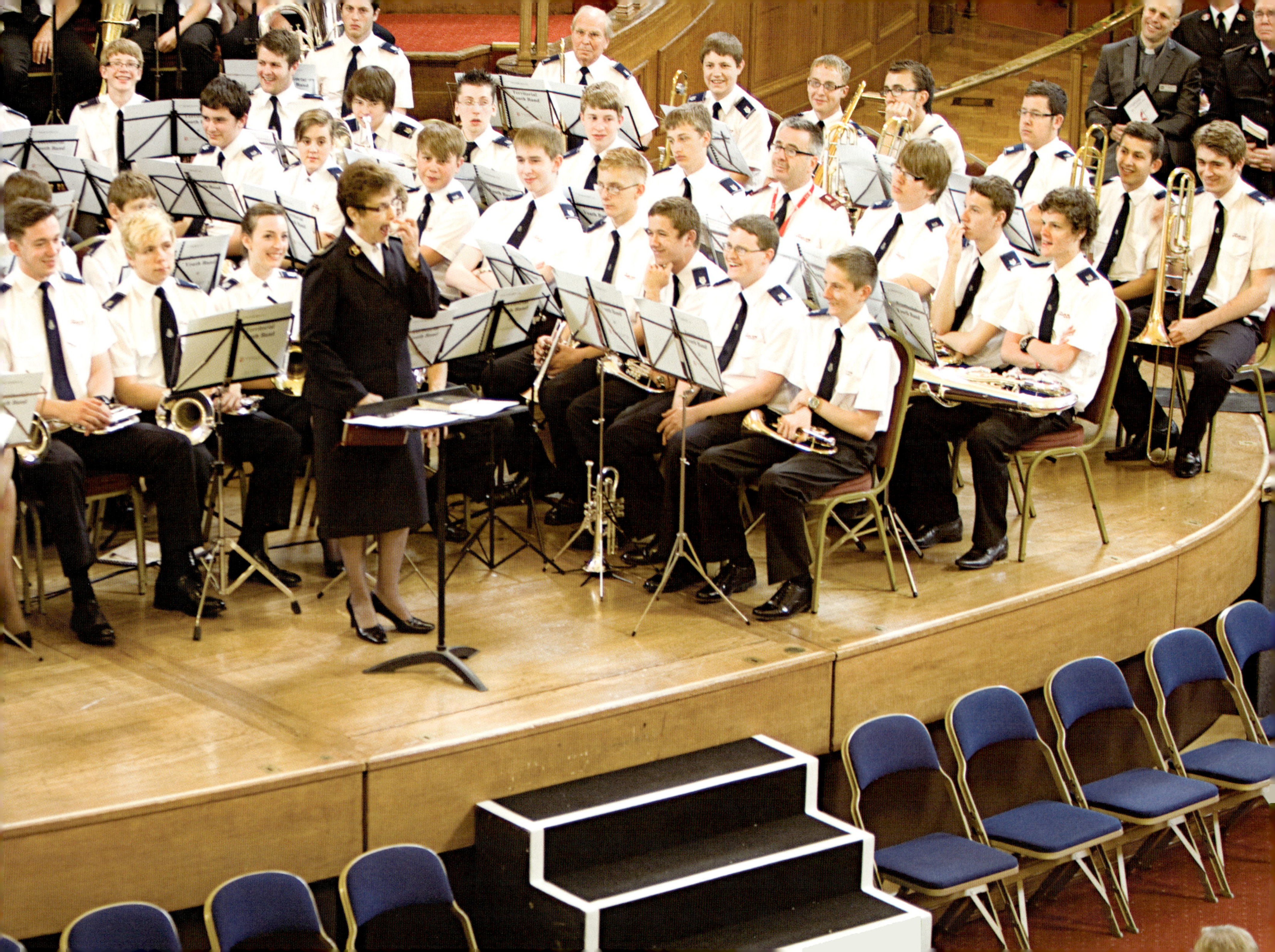

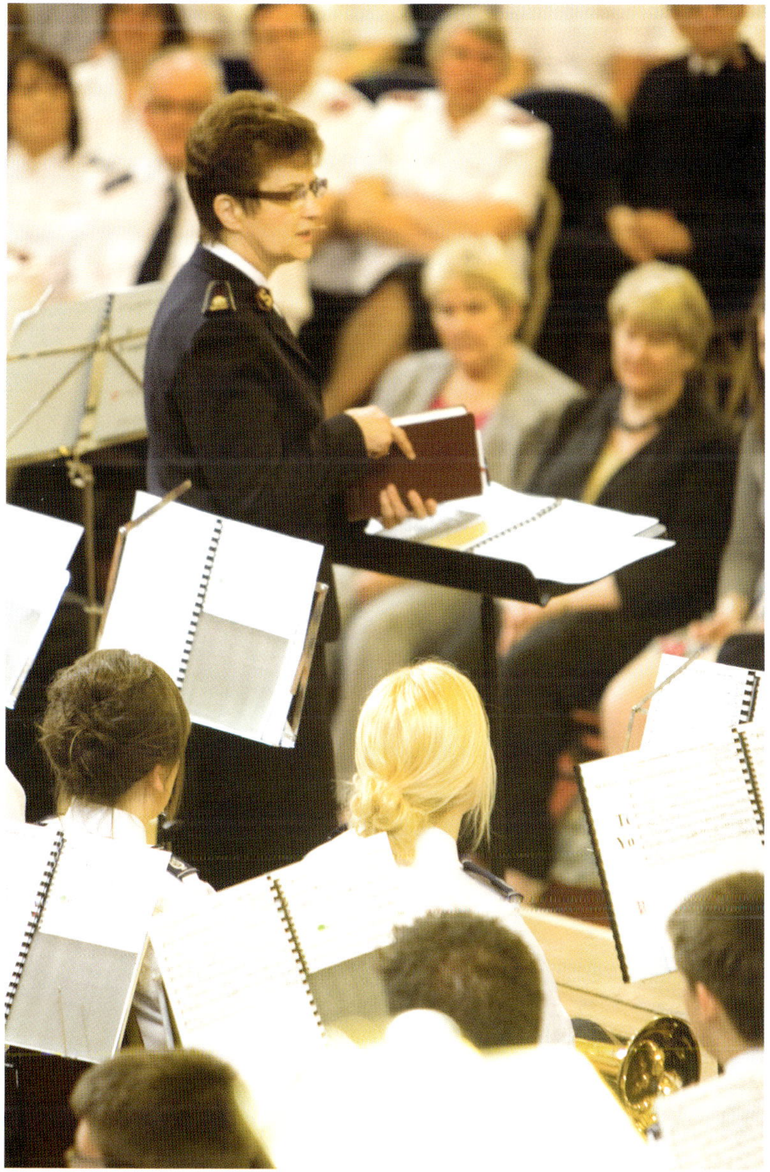

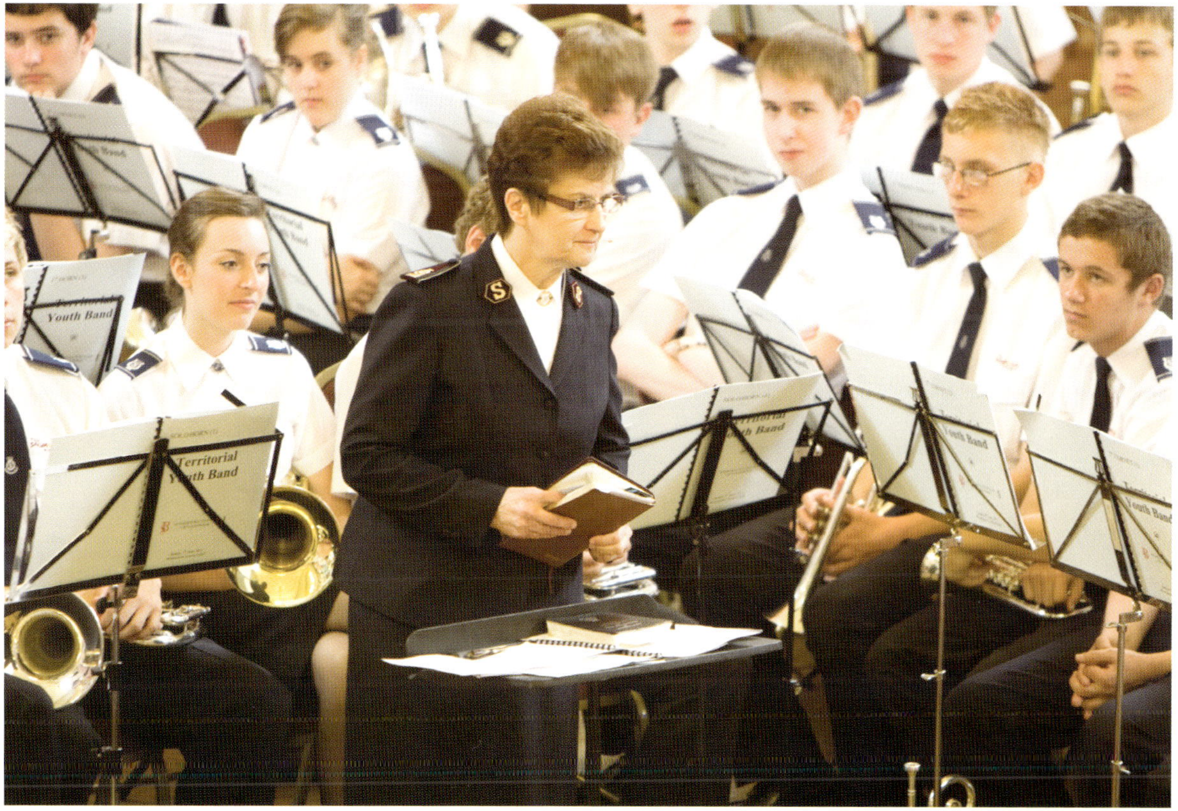
Youth Band
Territorial
Youth Band

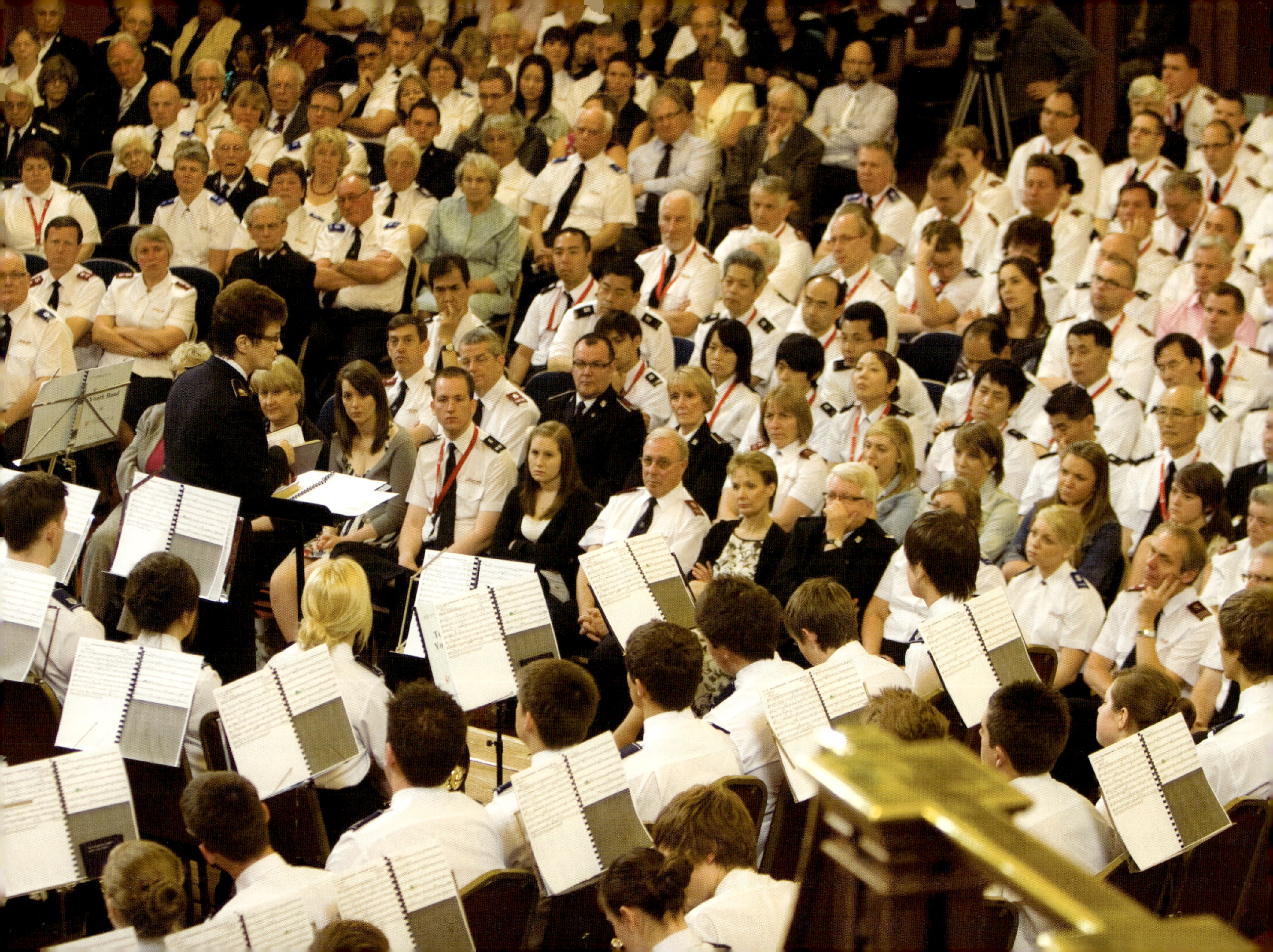
Youth Band

195

196

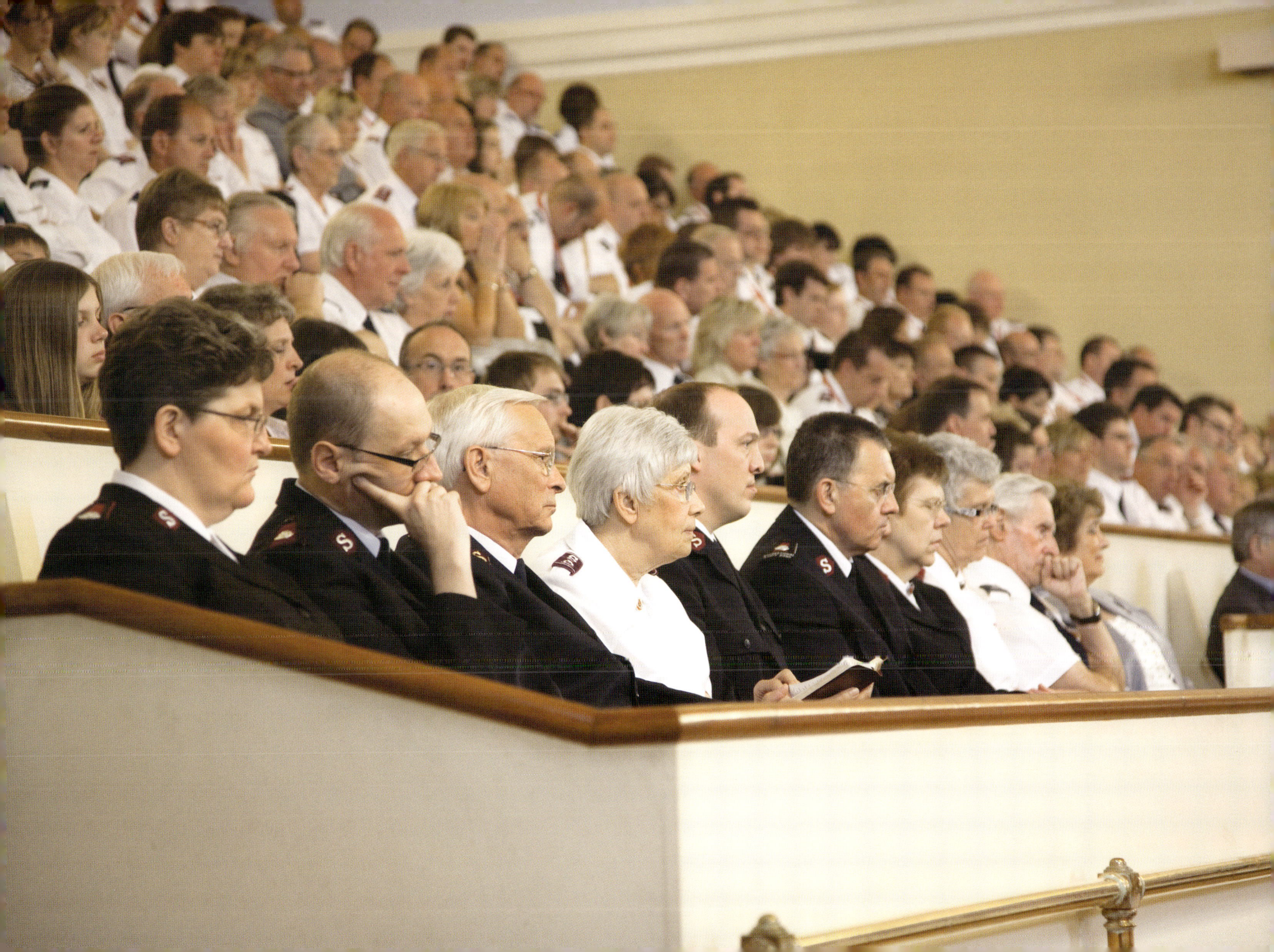

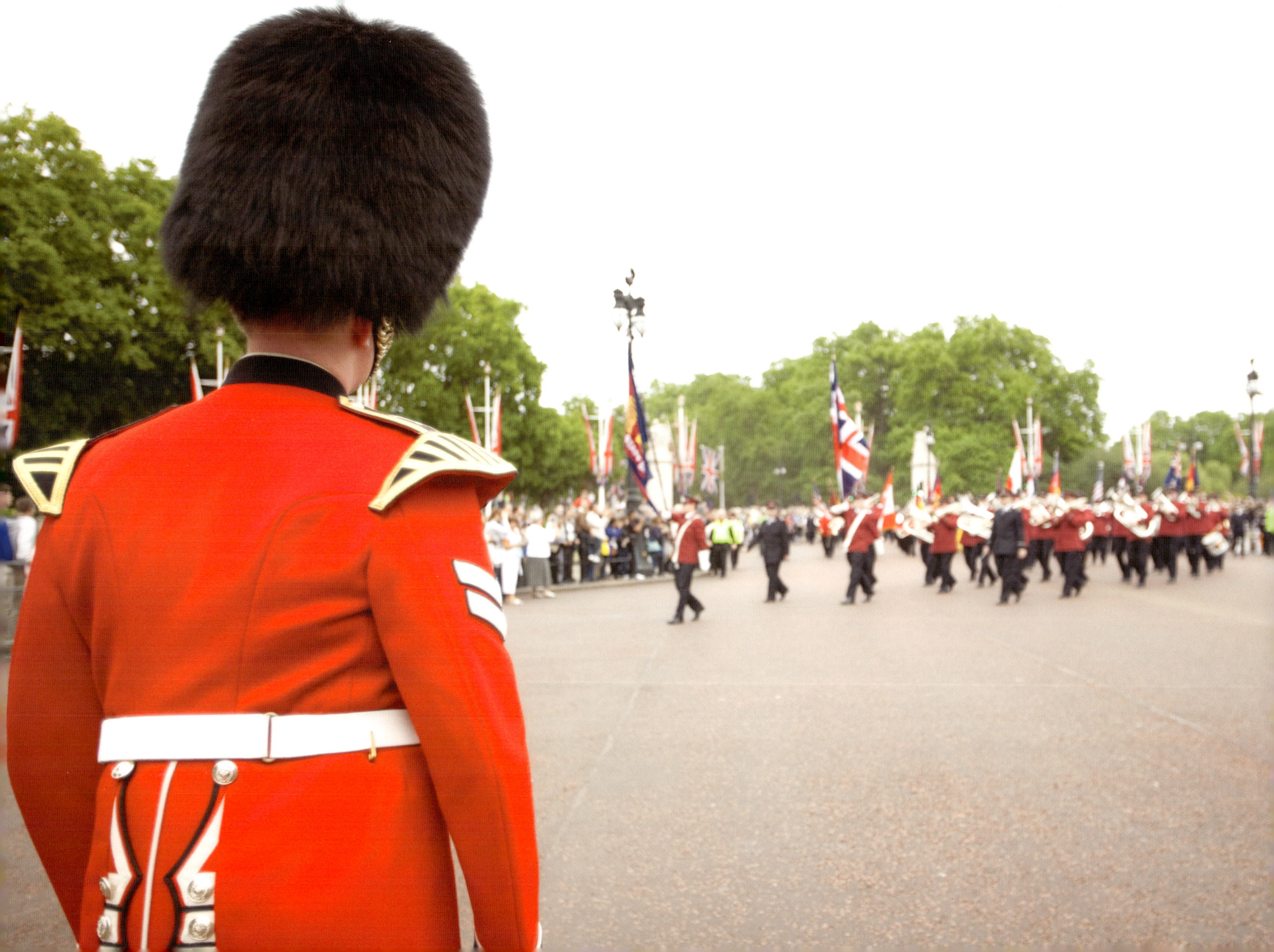

BUCKINGHAM PALACE
Salvationist LCpl Glen Little – Band of the Scots Guards

A normal working day for me in my role as a military musician usually includes marching into the forecourt of Buckingham Palace with the Band of Her Majesty's Scots Guards for various ceremonial occasions. However, Sunday 5 June 2011 was a completely different day for me.

After playing with my corps band, Regent Hall, in St James's Park, I hurried across to Wellington Barracks to change into my military ceremonial uniform. From there I made my way over to Buckingham Palace to prepare for the arrival of the eight Staff Bands into the palace forecourt. On my way over, I could sense a great atmosphere was building with the obvious presence of thousands of Salvationists beginning to line the streets.

> I am proud to be a member of the Armed Forces but, after an event such as this, I am even more proud to be a member of a Christian Church and organisation that is continuing the work begun by William Booth and which has such a strong emphasis on music within its worship.

My role in the palace forecourt was to escort the bands into place as they arrived through the palace gates. Although from here I could not see much of the march down The Mall, it was obvious that they were approaching by the sound of the massed Staff Bands and the increase in volume from the crowds.

Once all the bands were in place and the ISB had joined them, I probably had one of the best views of the massed bands concert from within the forecourt. Normally I would be playing secular music in a military wind band, so it was great to hear a massed brass band playing Salvation Army marches and hymn tune arrangements - especially *Holy, Holy, Holy*, which is one of my favourite hymn tune arrangements and was particularly moving for me.

After General Linda Bond reviewed the marchpast we escorted the bands back to Wellington Barracks. Here it was humbling to be asked by many visiting Staff Band members about our jobs in the military and to have photos taken with them. It was also a privilege for me to be able to witness to non-Christian colleagues living in the barracks who came out to see what was happening.

I am proud to be a member of the Armed Forces but, after an event such as this, I am even more proud to be a member of a Christian Church and organisation that is continuing the work begun by William Booth and which has such a strong emphasis on music within its worship.

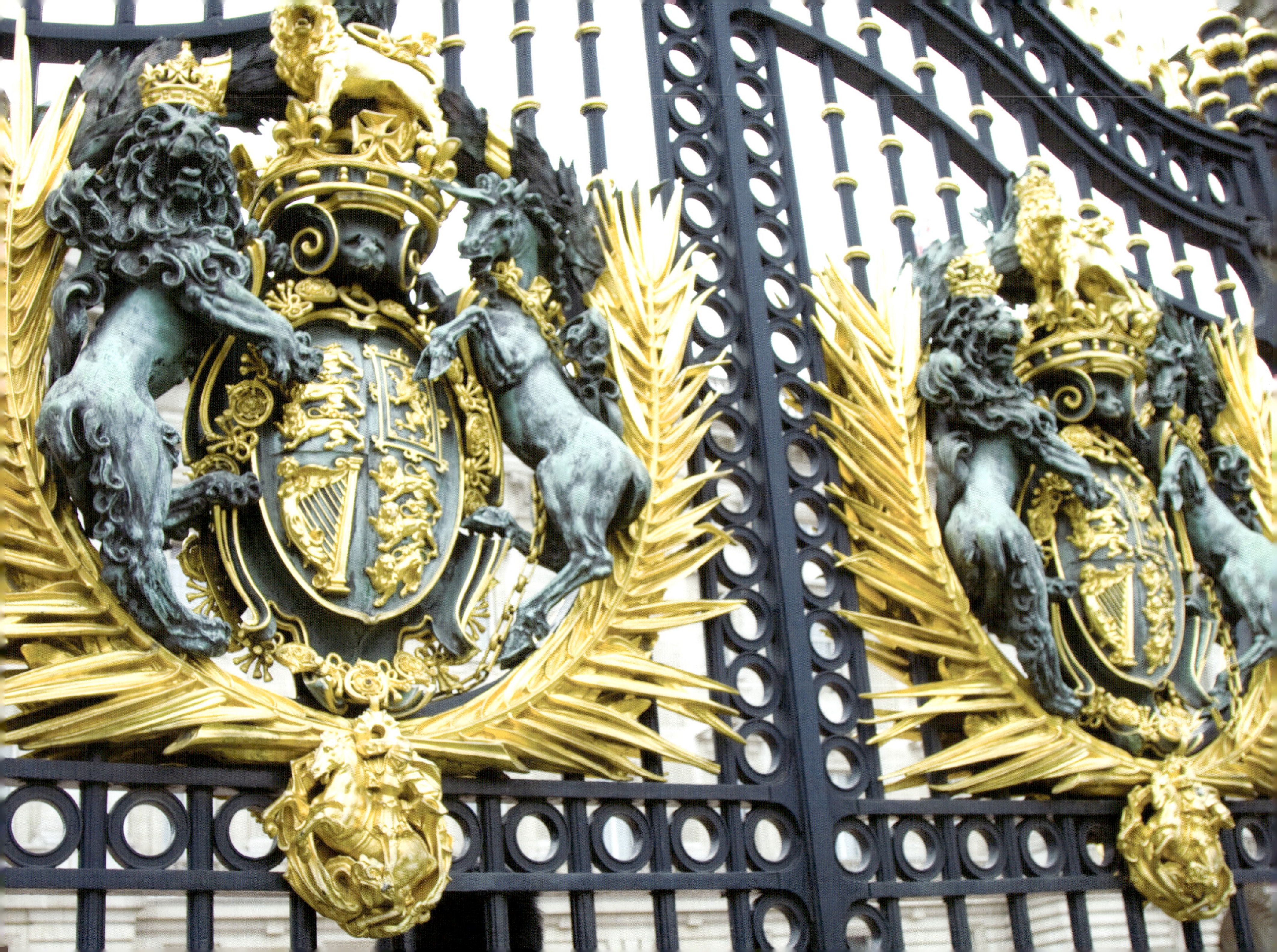

Parade Marshall WO2 Band Sergeant Major Ralph K Brill, Band of the Scots Guards, leads the march down The Mall

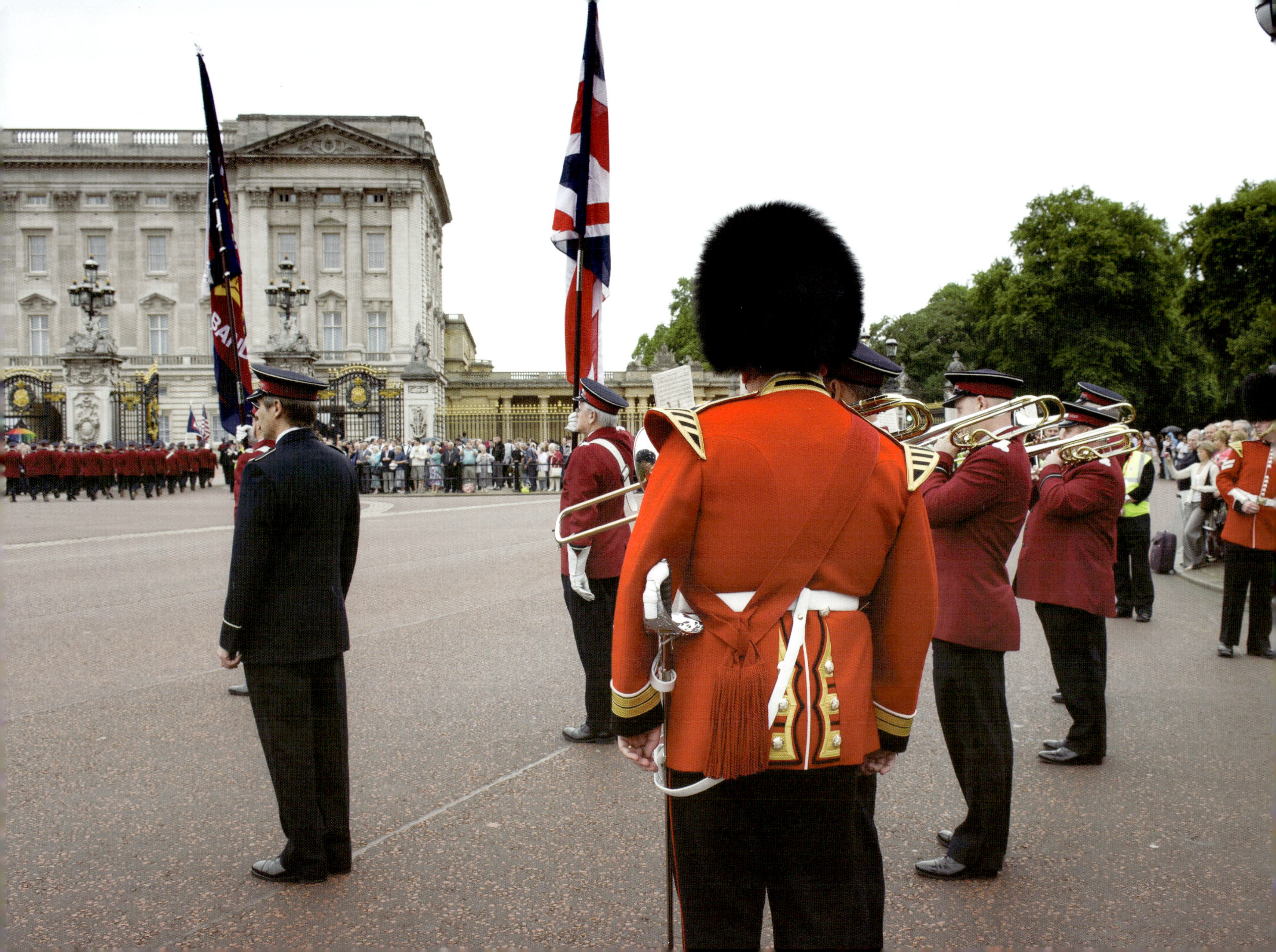

Left: LCpl Glen Little and LCpl Rob Howe, Band of the Scots Guards
Right: LCpl David Lockwood Band of the Welsh Guards – all Salvationists!

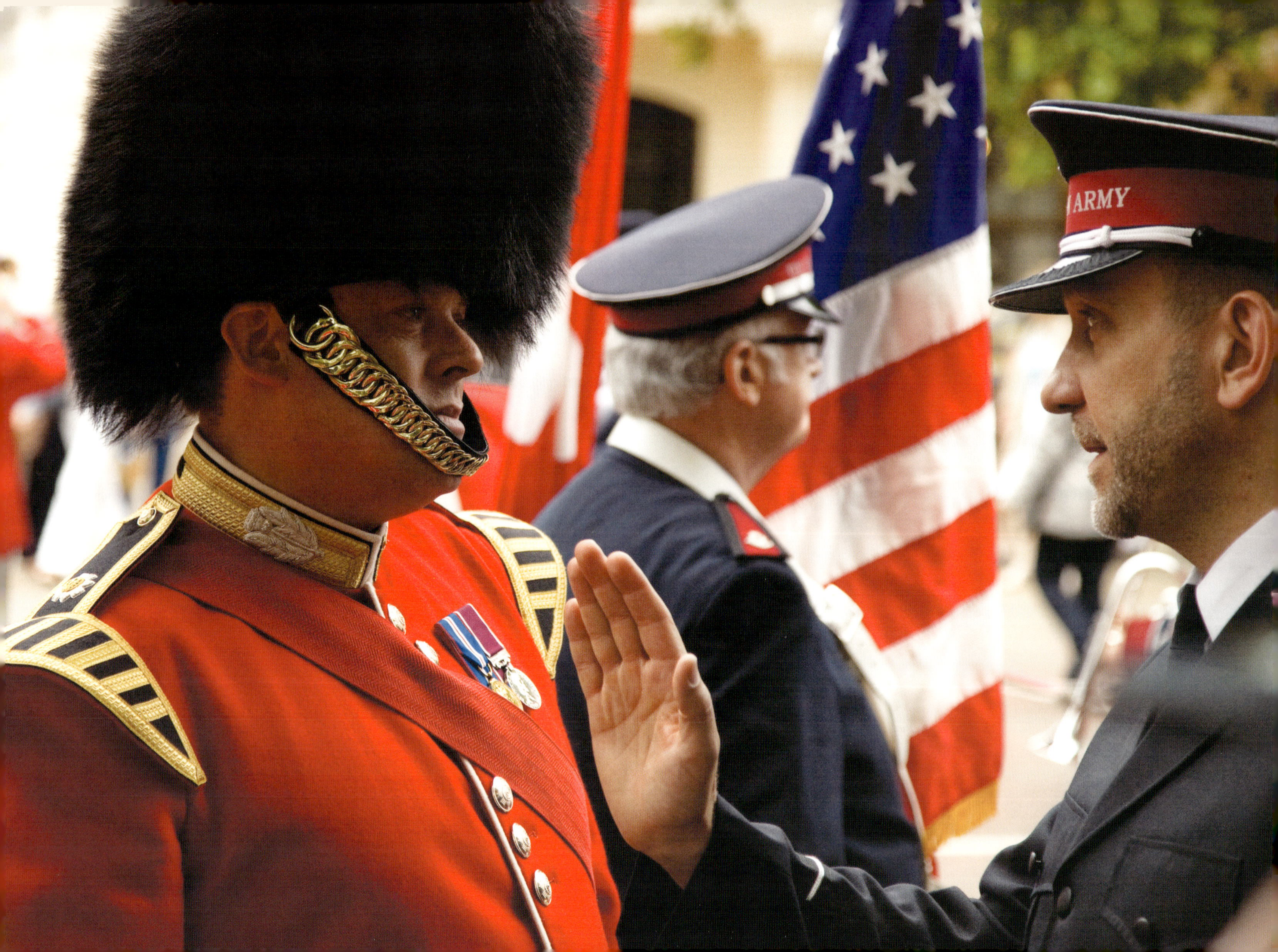
ARMY

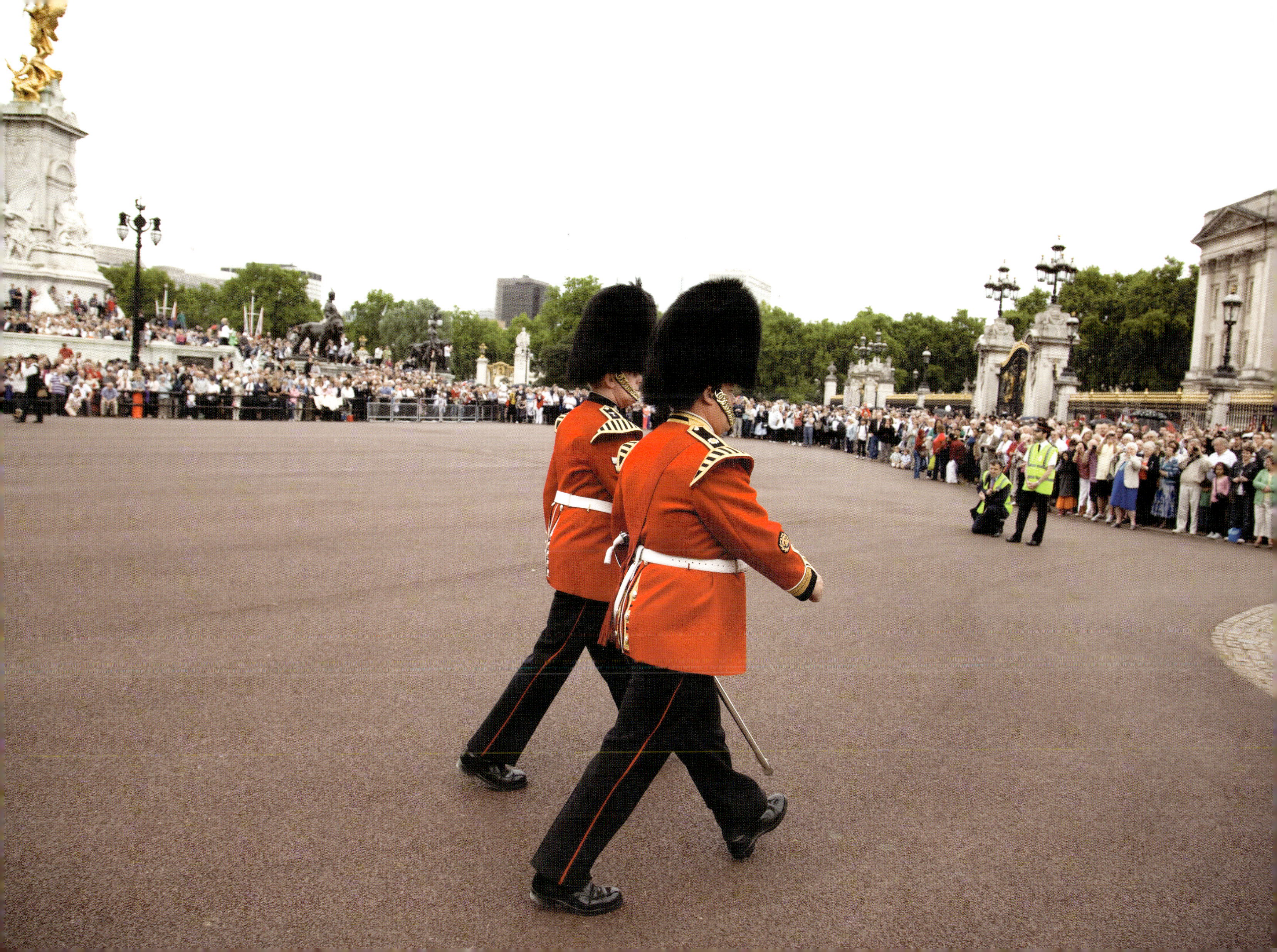

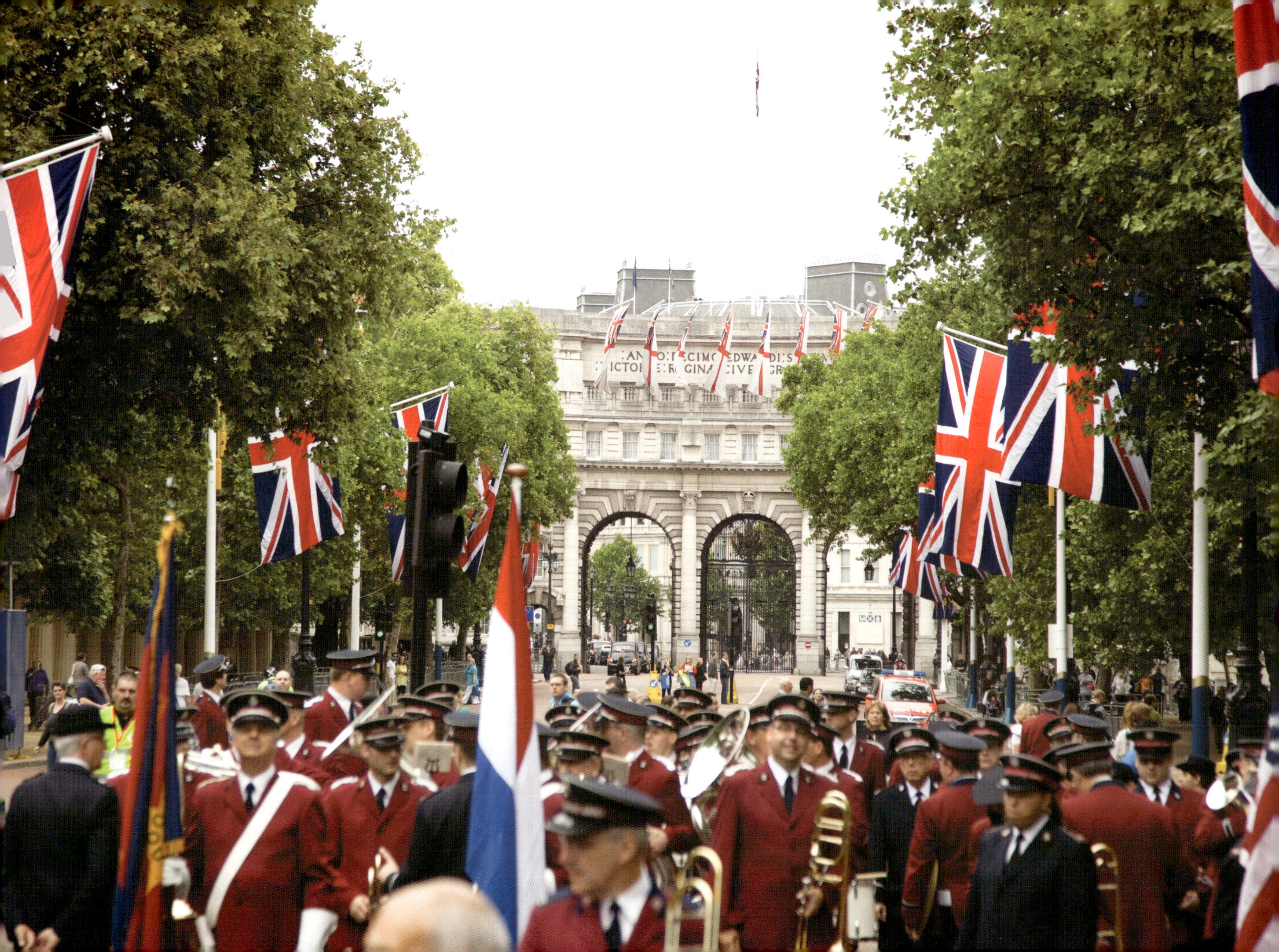

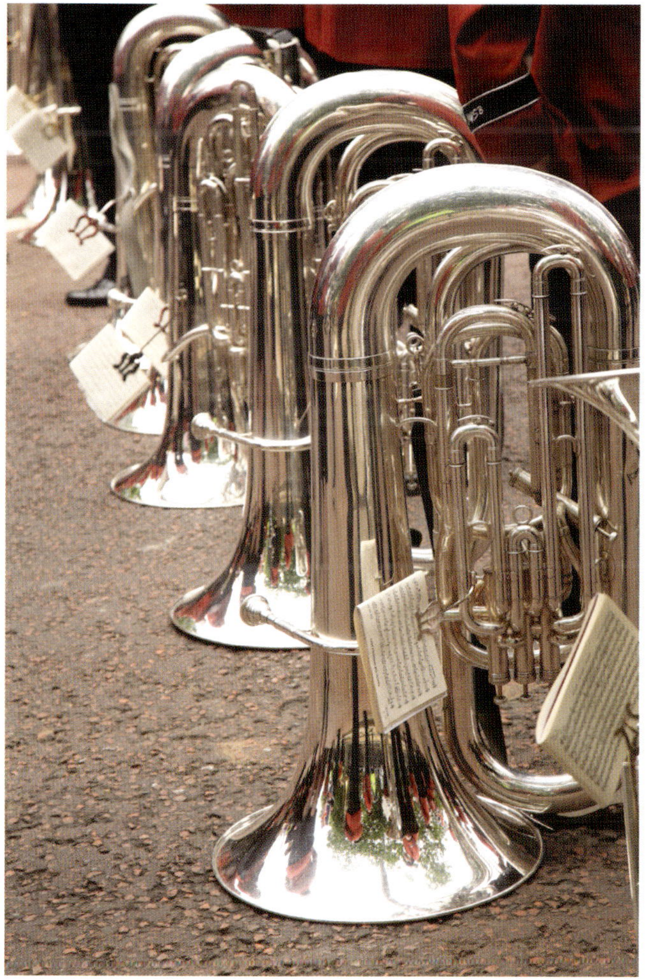

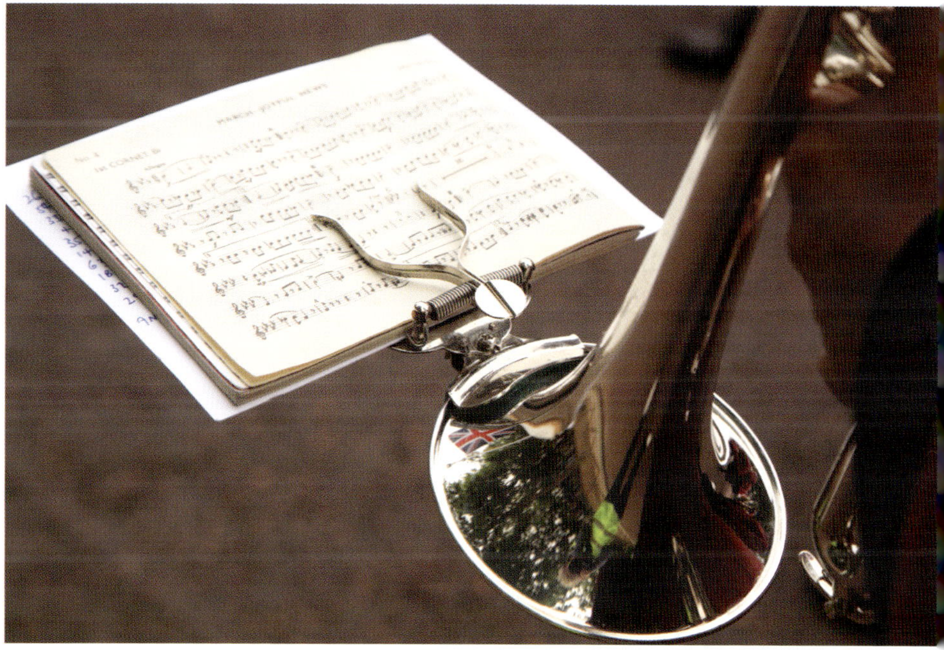

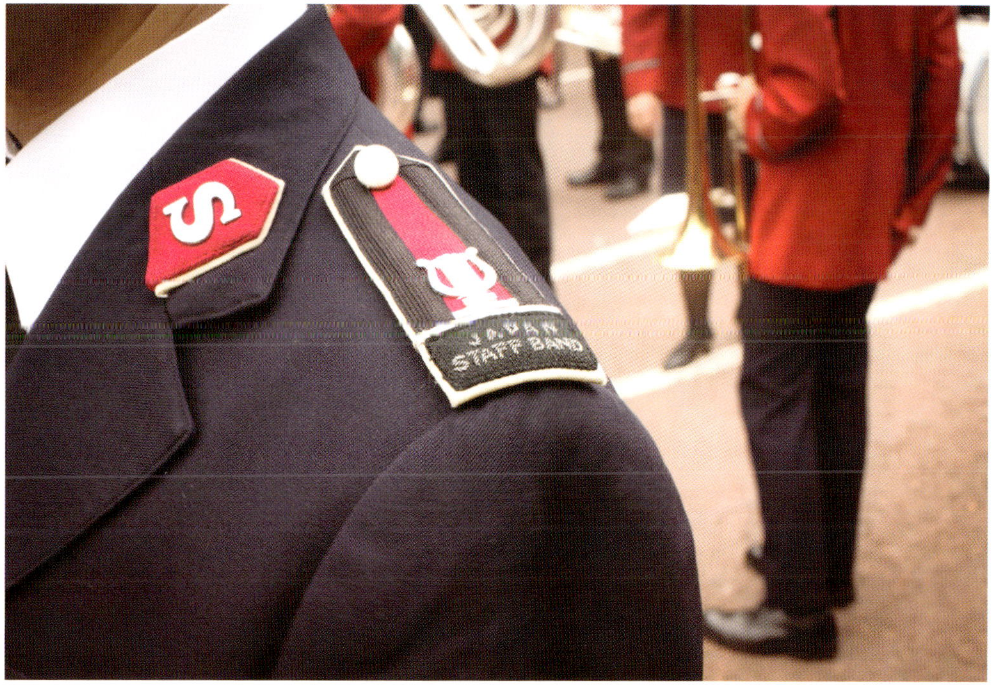
S
JAPAN
STAFF BAND

208

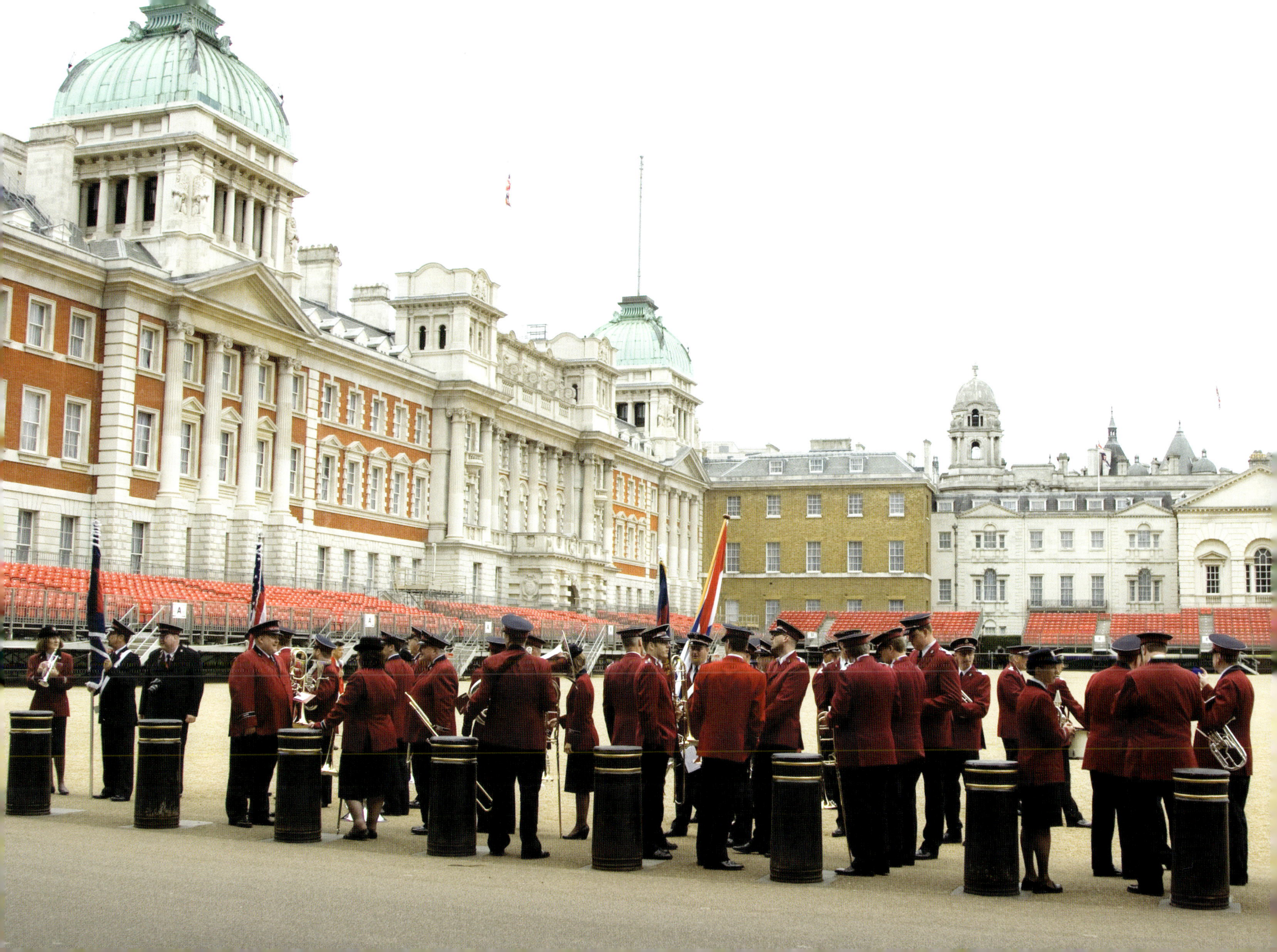

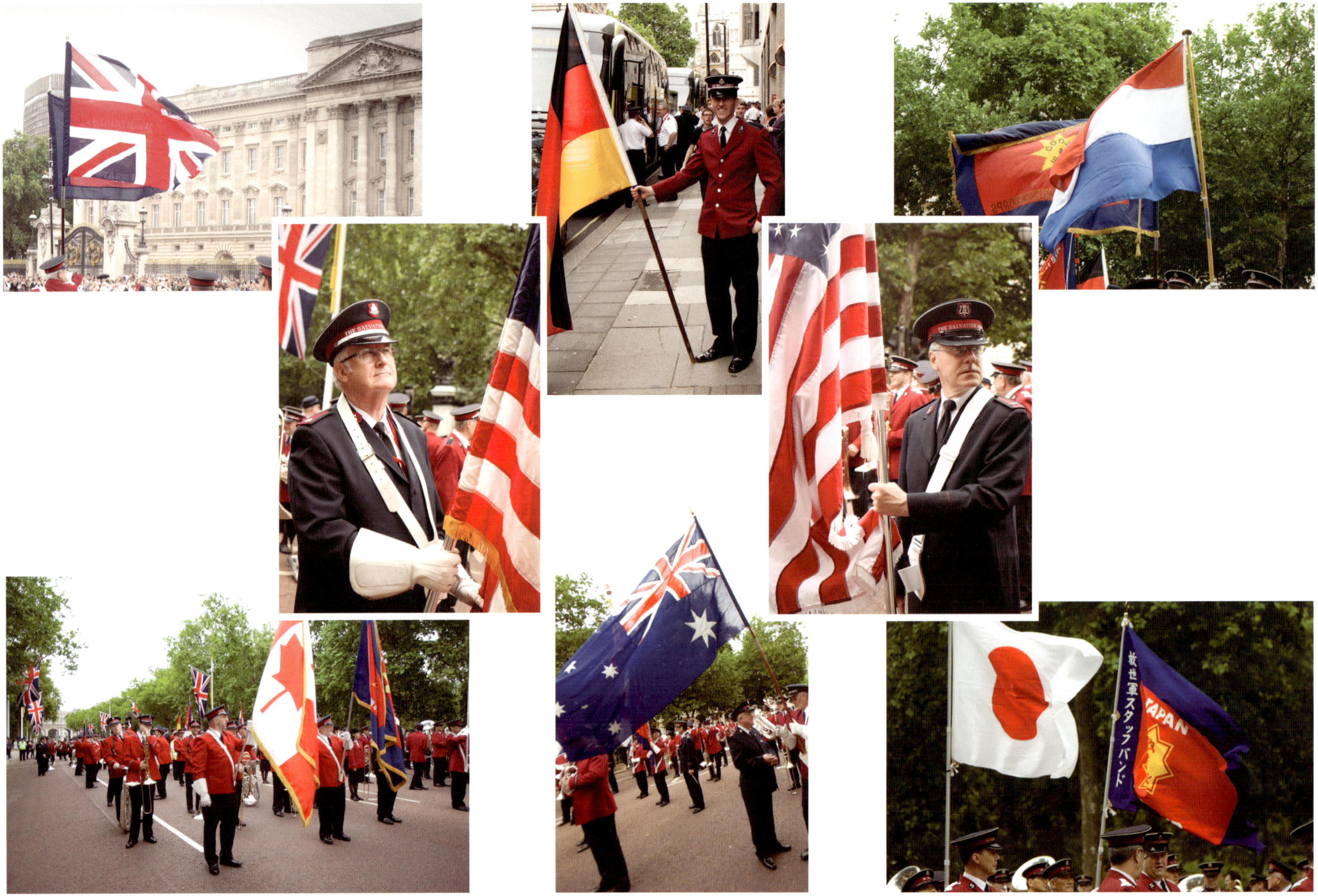
救世軍スタッフバンド
JAPAN

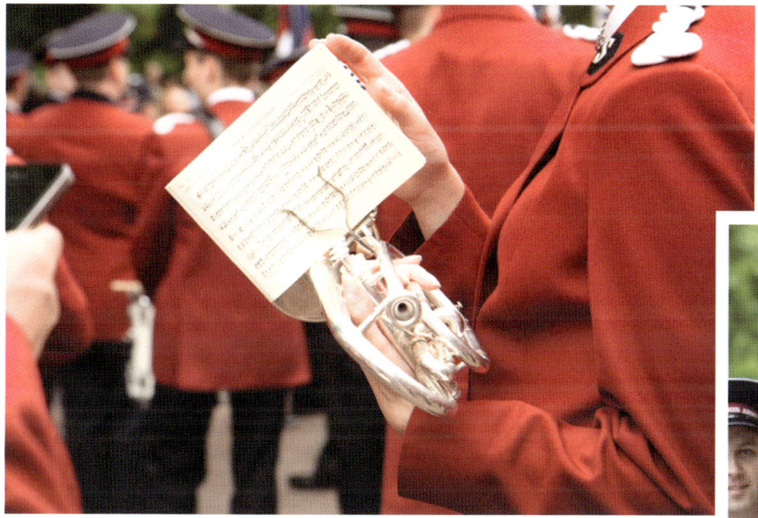

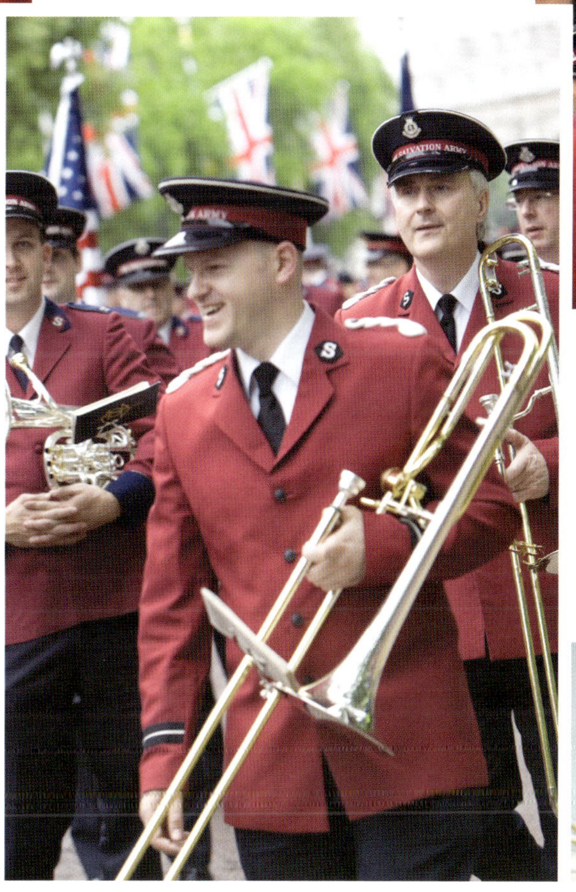

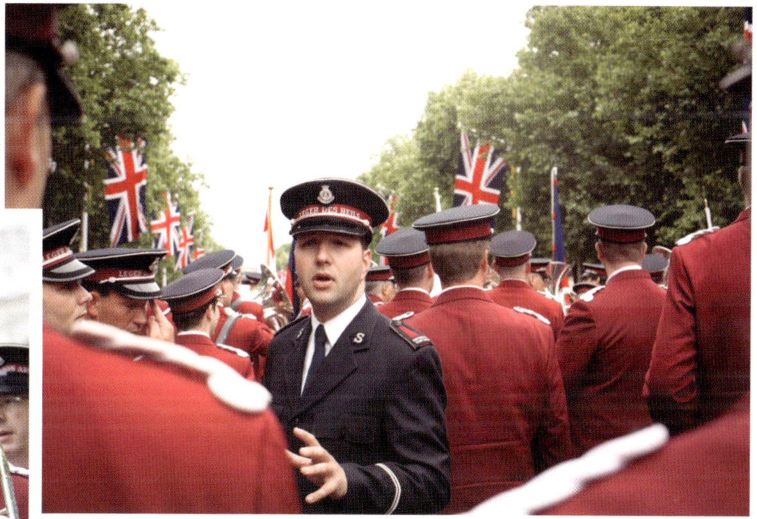

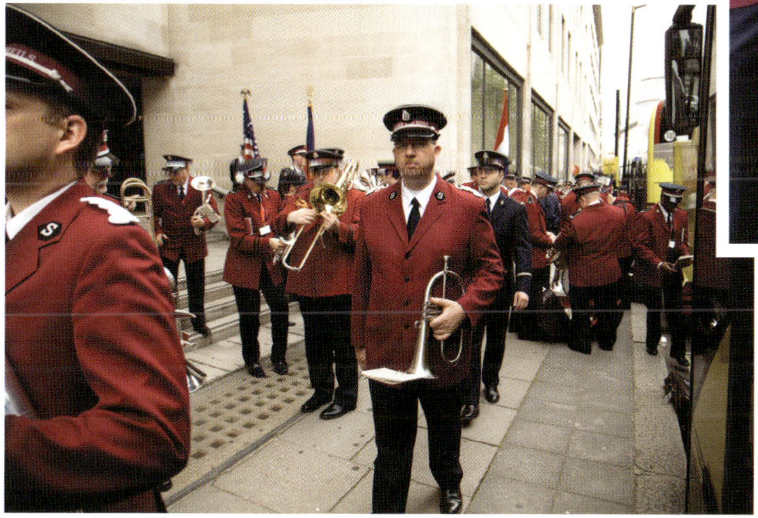

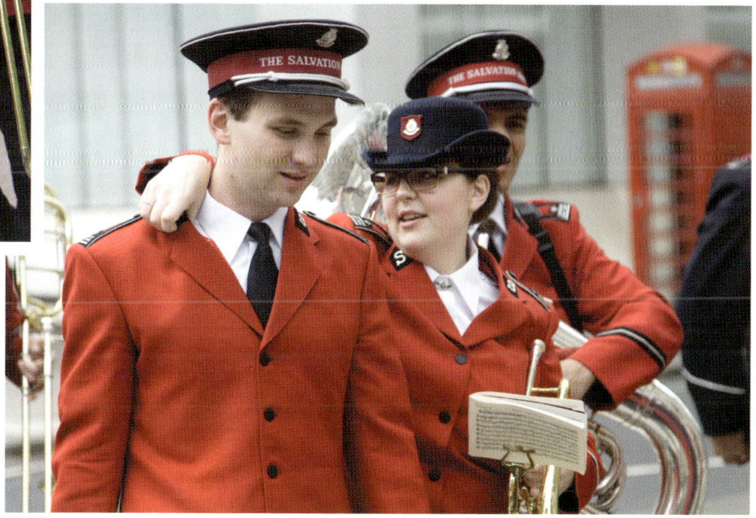
THE SALVATION

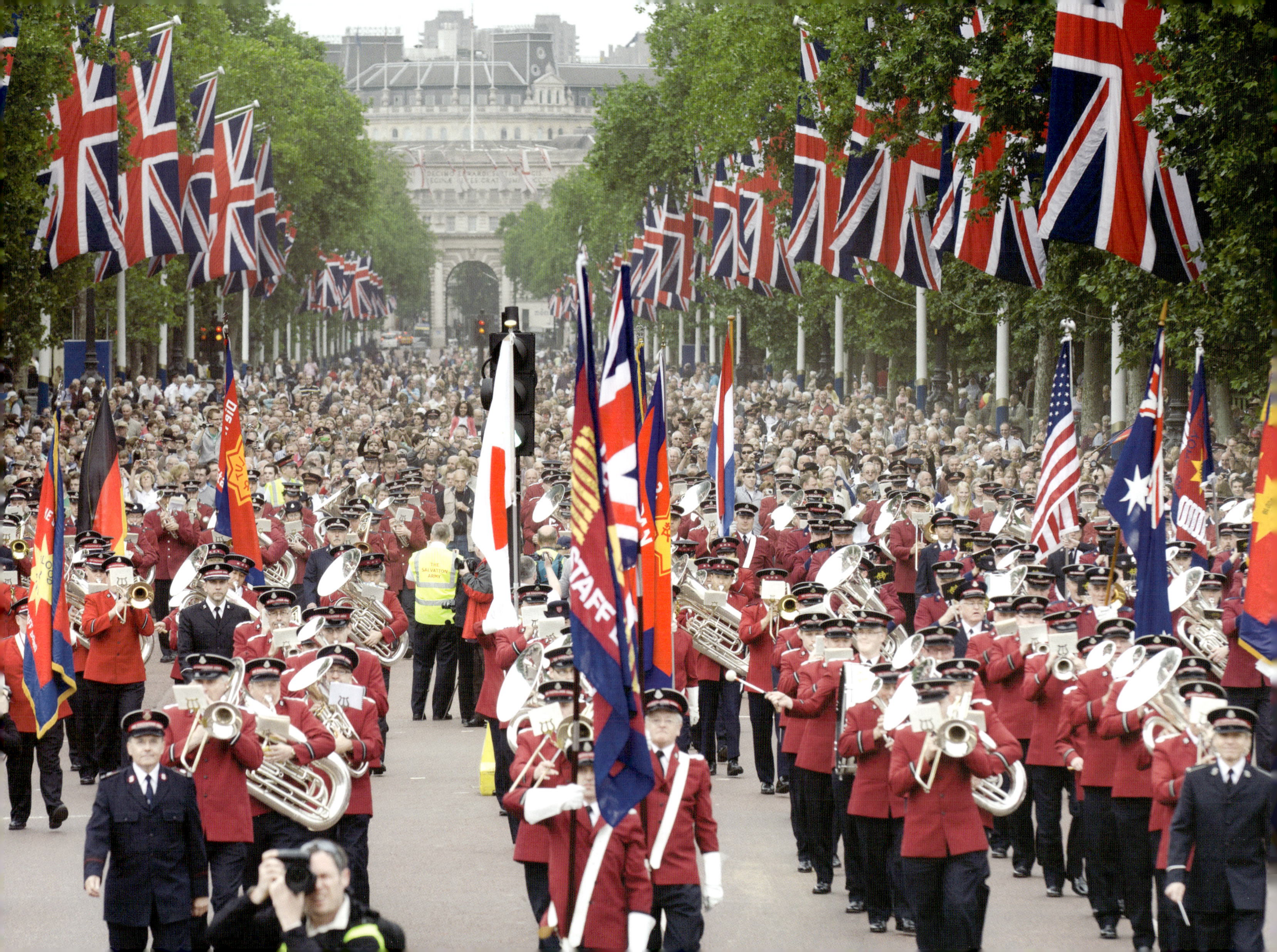
STAFF

THE MALL
Major Paul Johnson

The Mall has been the scene of some wonderful displays of pageantry and has seen history being made down the years including Coronations, Royal Weddings and Jubilees. Although not exactly a Royal occasion, the 120th Anniversary celebrations of The International Staff Band created a real stir as the eight Staff Bands of the world, headed by the ISB, made their way down the world-famous thoroughfare to the beat of drums and the sound of brass proclaiming their allegiance to the King of Kings.

People lined the route to get a glimpse of the Staff Bands, resplendent in red and united in purpose, witnessing to theirs and the Army's faith in the Lord who had called them and the Army into being, to sound out the proclamation of a risen Saviour. Many of those eager to see and hear the spectacle and witness history being made (never before had all the world's Staff Bands gathered in one place before the weekend) were, of course, Salvationists and friends of the Army. There were also many people who were in London for the weekend, or on holiday, who happened upon the scene with questions like 'What's going on?', 'What's happening?', 'What's it all about?' giving those of us who answered them an opportunity to tell them and explain the reason why The Salvation Army exists. 'I never knew the Army was so big!' and 'The TV cameras should be here!' were just a few of the comments made by those not in our ranks.

Earlier in the afternoon, the waiting crowds had been both entertained and blessed by a quartet of songsters from Staines Corps in full uniform who stood in various spots to engage in conversation and sing *a cappella* to the people. They received warm applause for their uplifting singing.

As the Staff Bands approached Buckingham Palace a great cheer went up from those of us fortunate enough to be near its gates as each band entered the forecourt and stood in massed formation. There they presented a programme of marches, selections and devotional pieces conducted by each Staff Bandmaster in turn. For those of us who knew the words behind the music, there was a sense of being on holy ground as the devotional music was received with appreciative and heartfelt silence. We were in the presence of the King.

All too soon, the programme was over and the bands formed up in their groups to move off for General Linda Bond to receive the salute in the marchpast at the exit gate of the Palace. It was only when all the eight bands had marched away that the rain arrived. This sent us all dashing for cover or reaching for our umbrellas!

> As the Staff Bands approached Buckingham Palace a great cheer went up from those of us fortunate enough to be near its gates as each band entered the forecourt and stood in massed formation. There they presented a programme of marches, selections and devotional pieces conducted by each Staff Bandmaster in turn. For those of us who knew the words behind the music, there was a sense being on holy ground as the devotional music was received with appreciative and heartfelt silence. We were in the presence of the King...

When William Booth was interviewed by Raymond Blathwayt, who reserved his time for princes of the pulpit, poets and authors, Blathwayt suggested that some of the Army's methods 'sometimes to the uninitiated perilously approached the blasphemous'. Booth replied, 'don't you think that the dilettante Intonation has failed to touch the heart of the great seething masses surging around us? They don't respond as they are expected to respond. Now I come along with my drums and my trumpets, and at once I get a large and increased following'.

Booth was a clear thinker and straight talker and, in his reply, summed up the main purpose of any Salvation Army band. This was eminently shown on a memorable Sunday afternoon in June 2011 when eight of the best SA bands in the world conducted what was in essence, an open air meeting outside a large house at one end of a London street... and I was there!

Helen Johnson, Susanne Dymott, Simon Turner and Tim Hopkin engage the waiting crowds in conversation and entertain with their *a cappella* singing

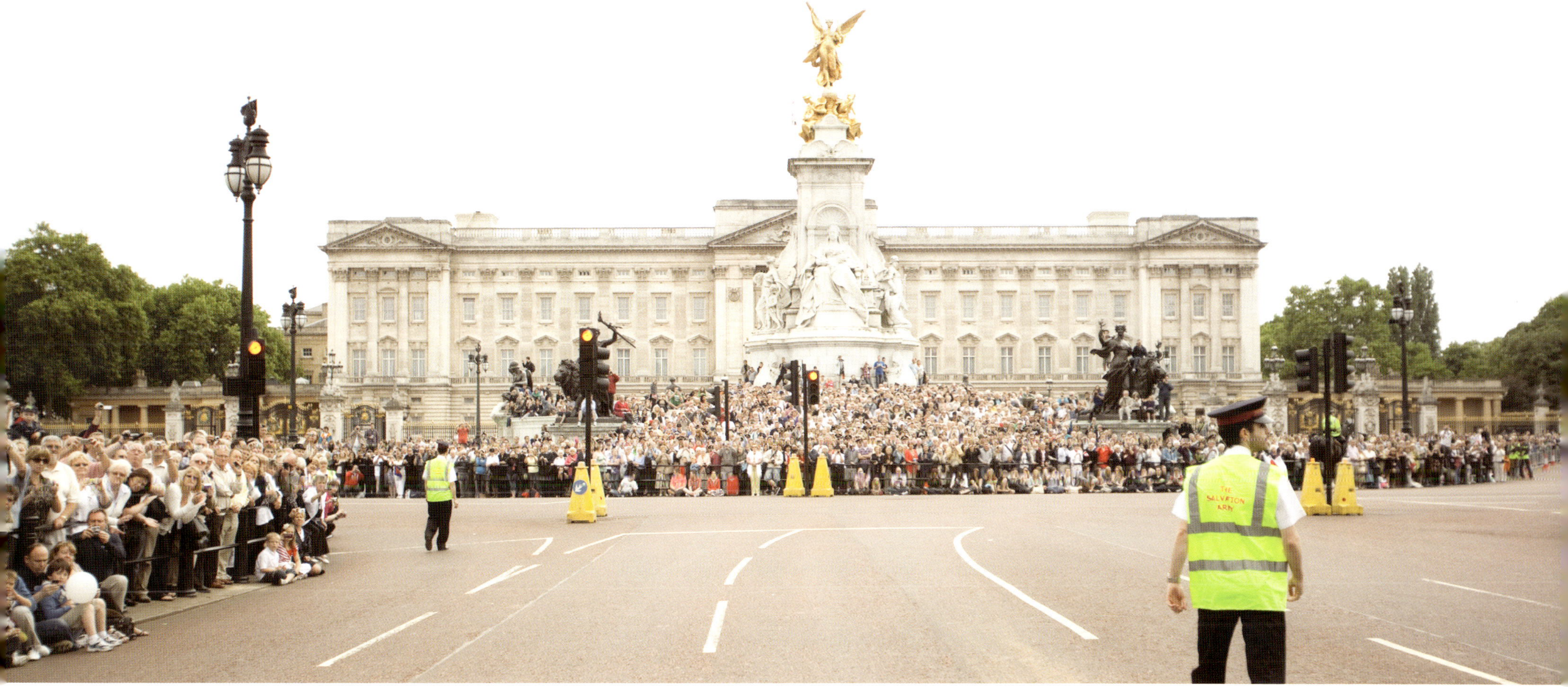

THE SALVATION ARMY
THE SALVATION ARMY
SALVATION ARMY
THE SALVATION ARMY
THE SALVATION ARMY
SALVATION ARMY
SALVATION ARMY
S

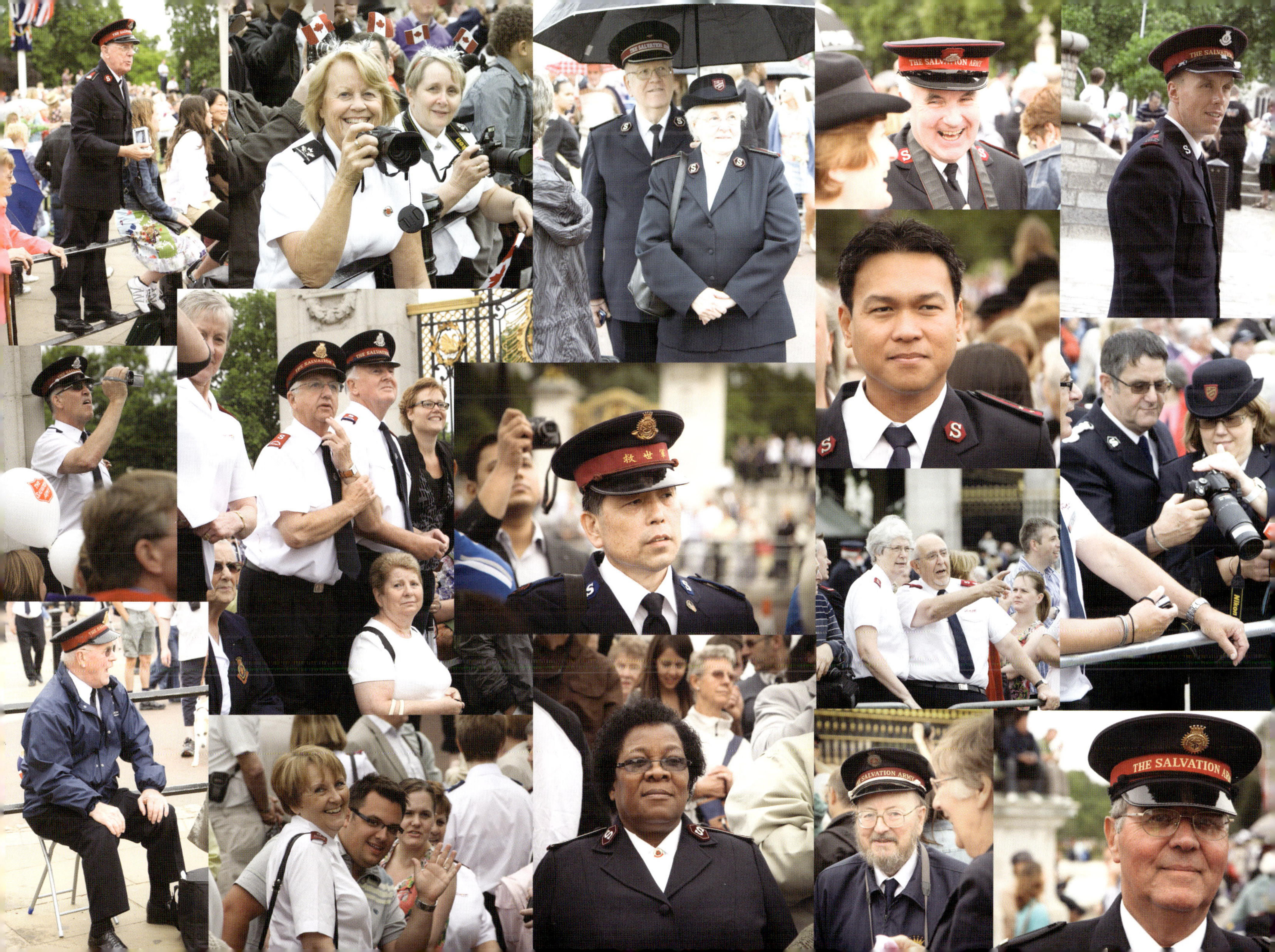
THE SALVATION ARMY

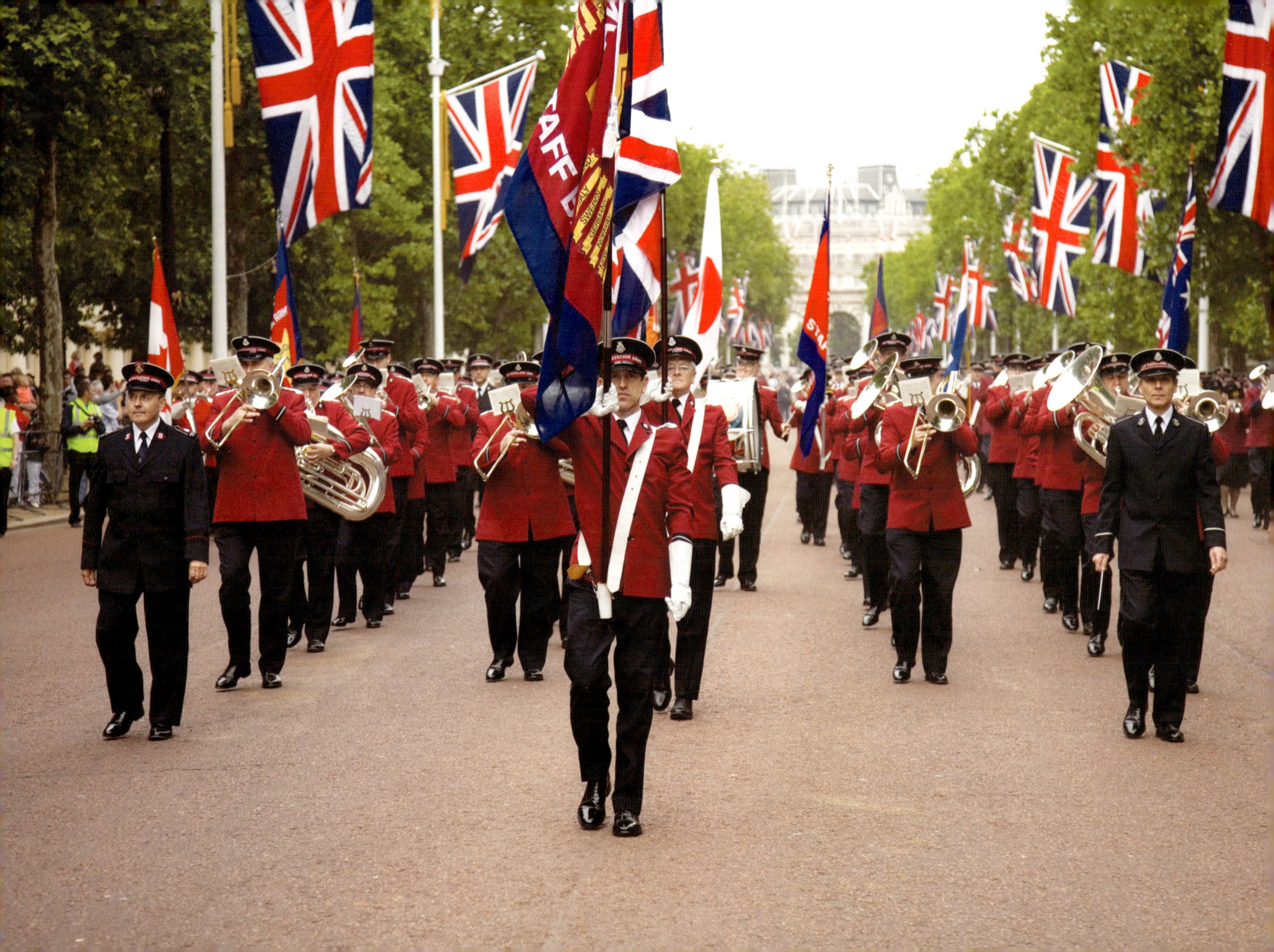
STAFF

219

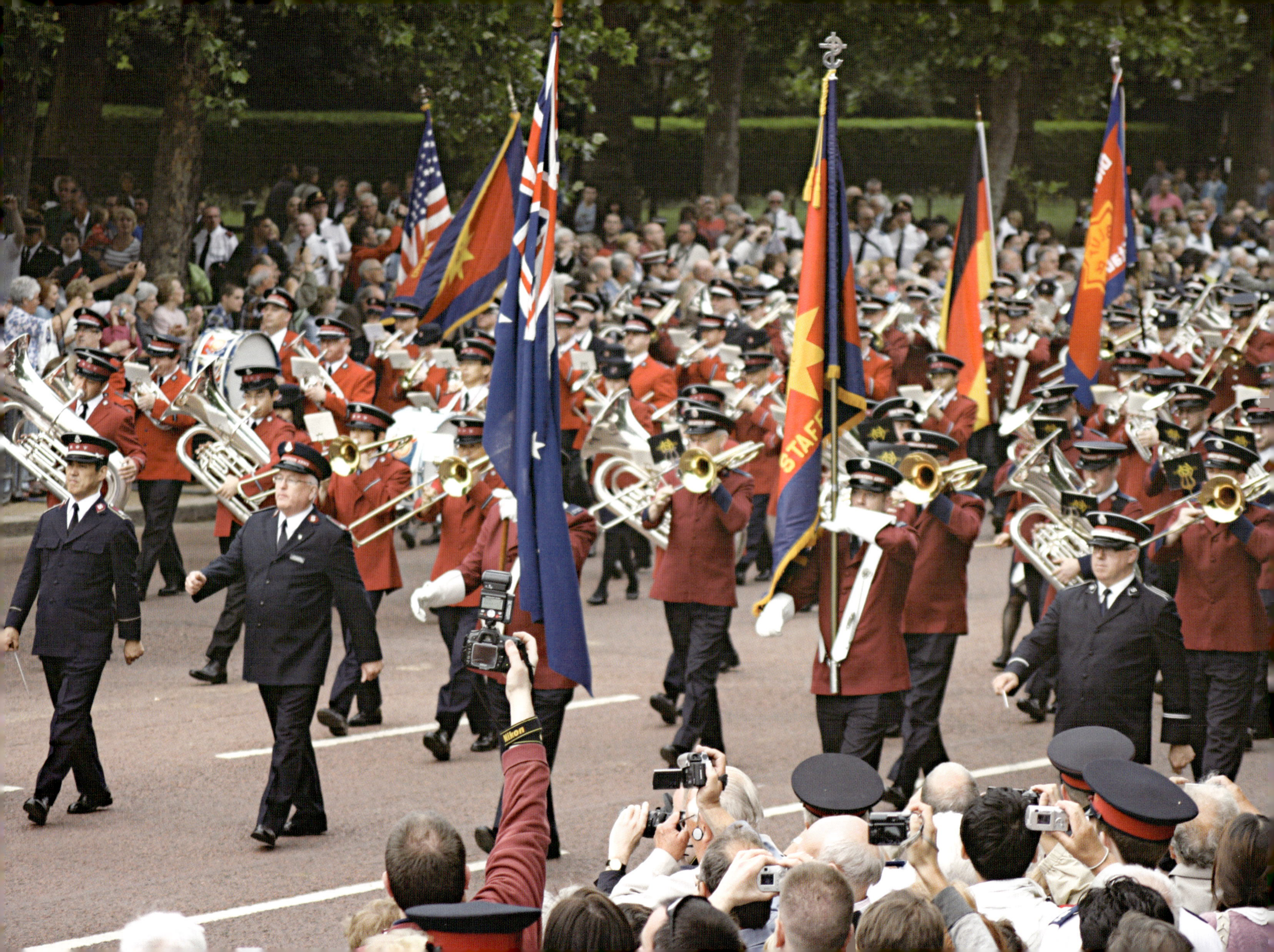
STAFF
Nikon

221

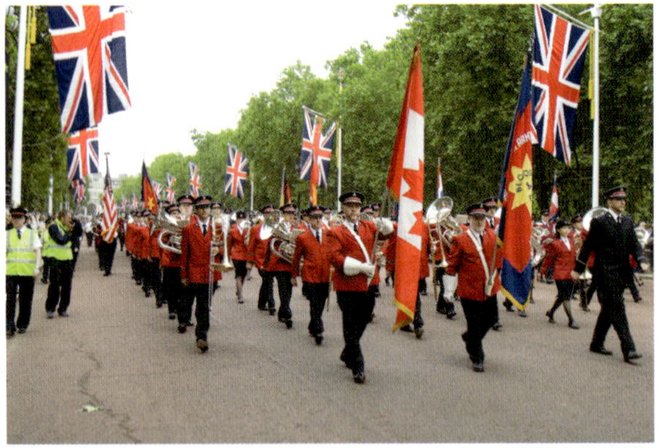
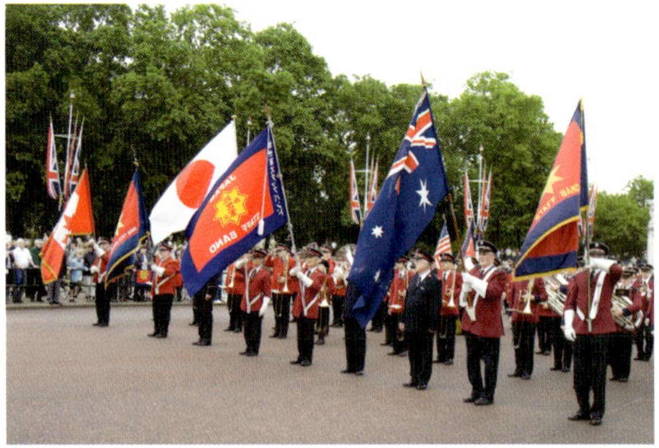
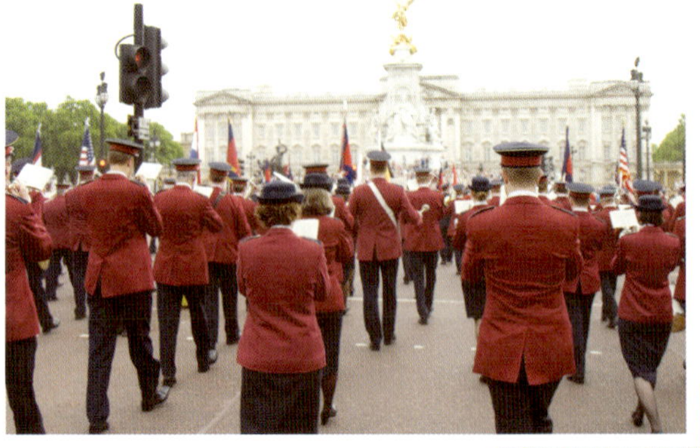
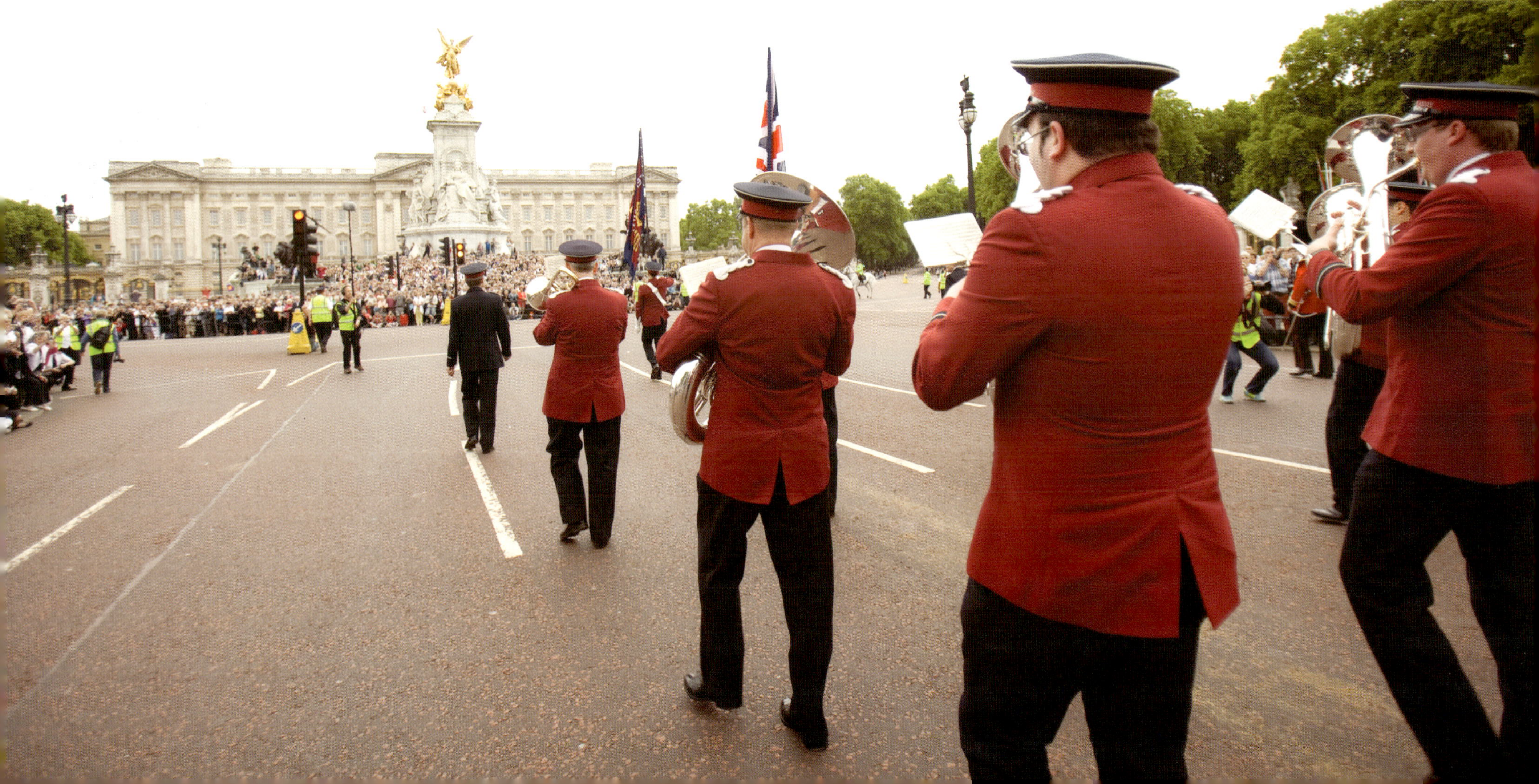

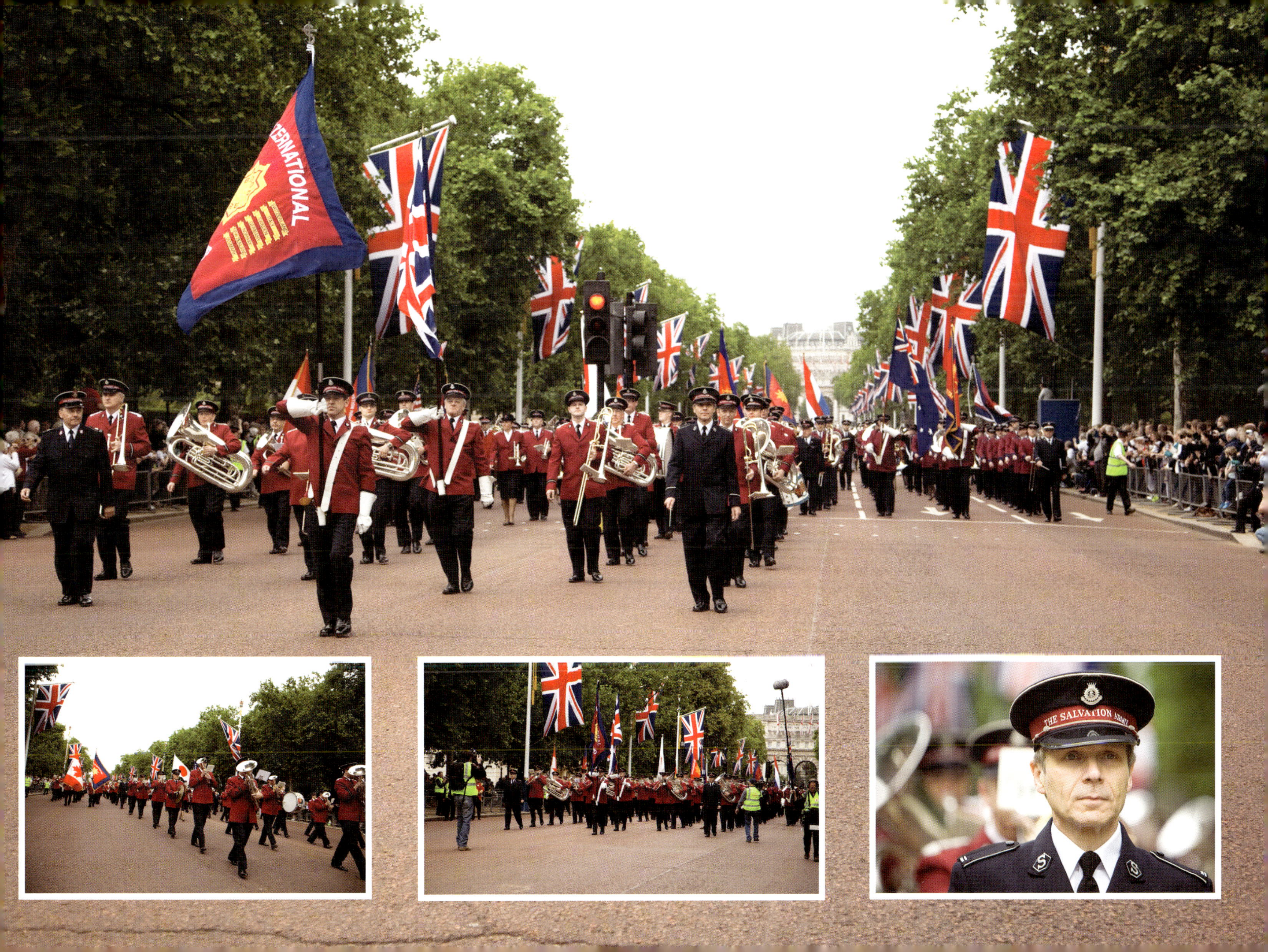
ERNATIONAL
THE SALVATION ARMY

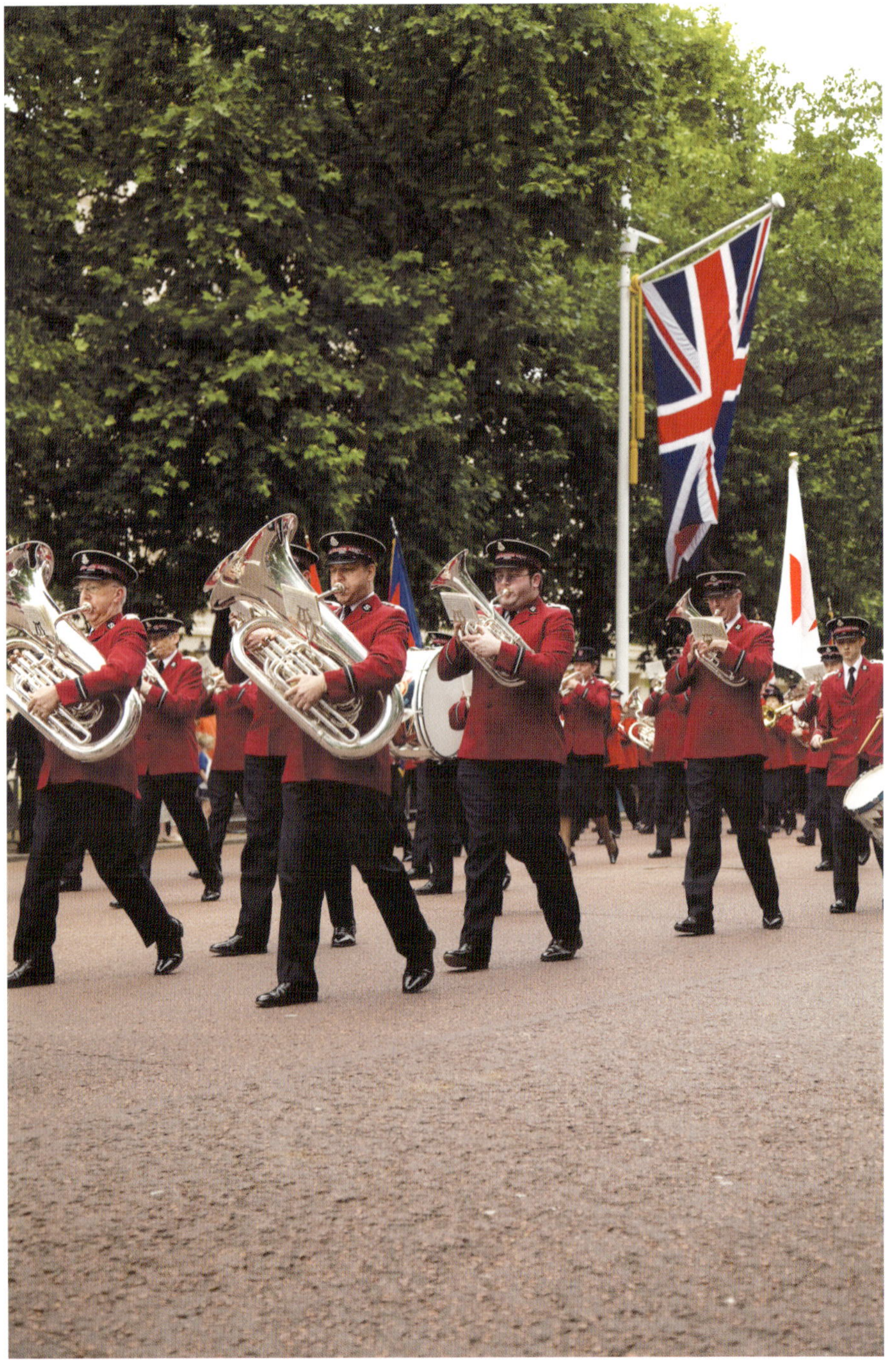

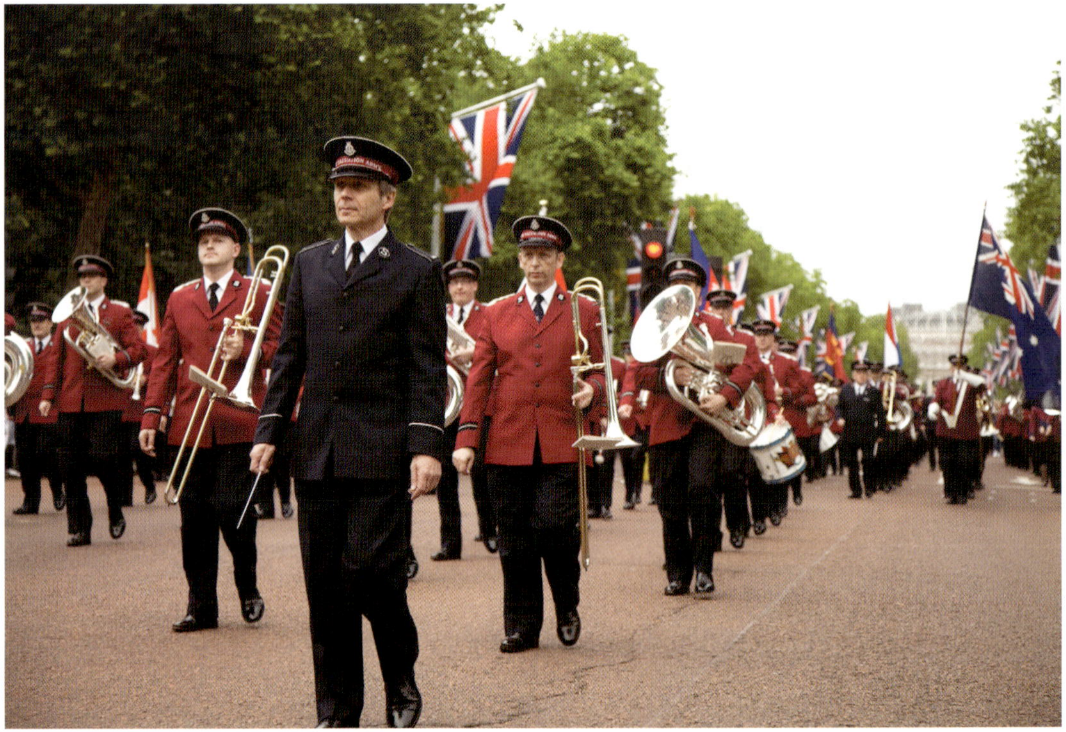

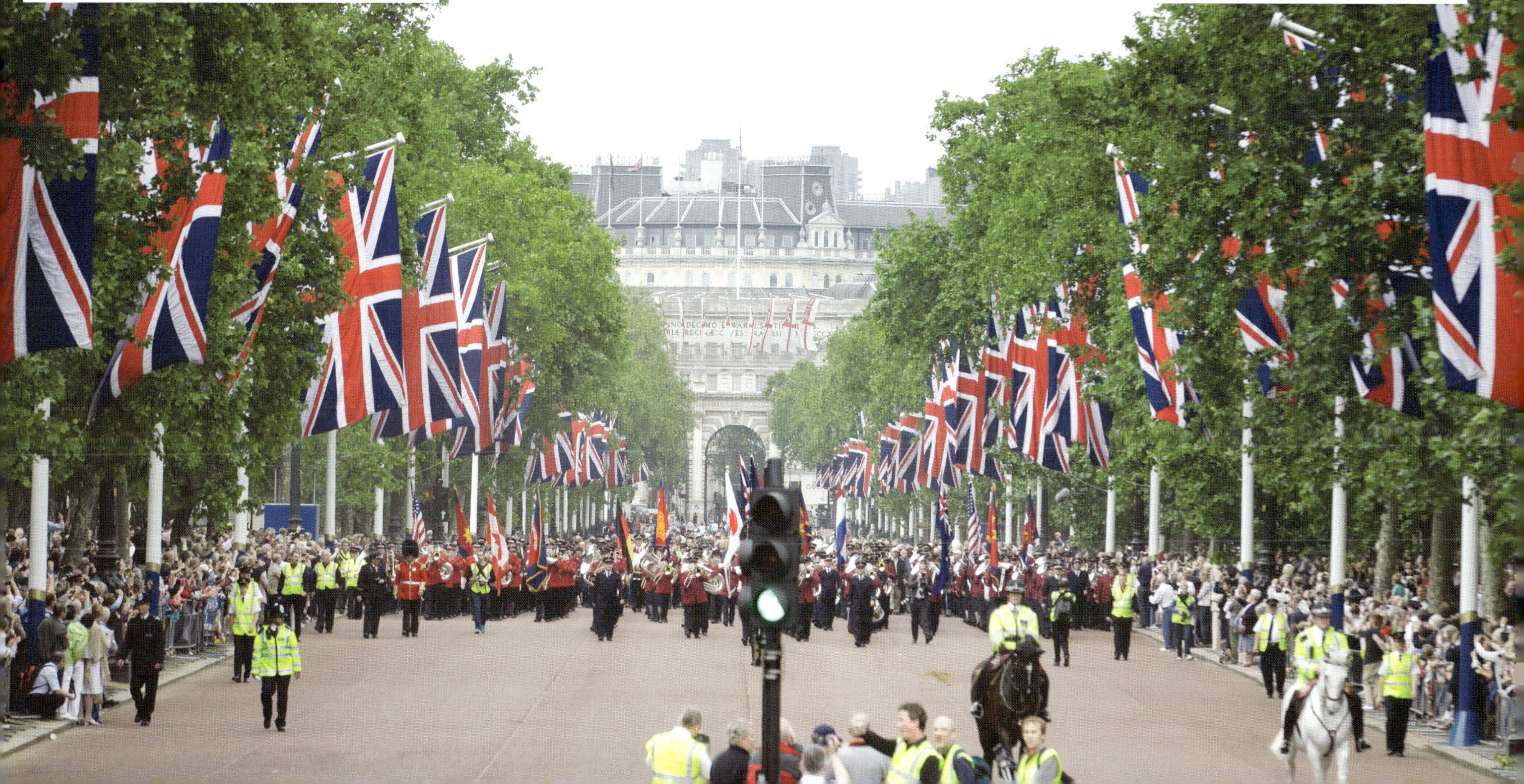
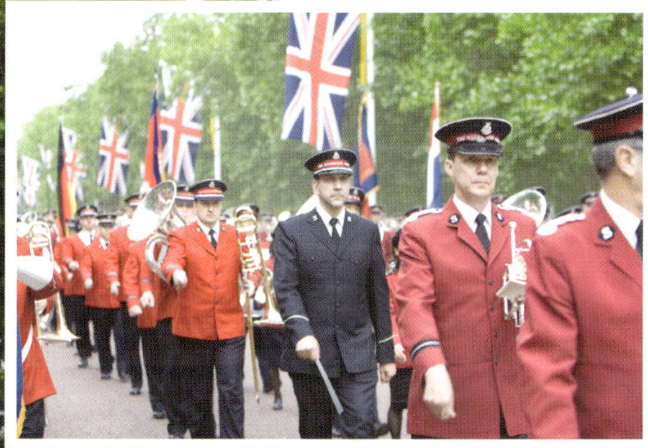
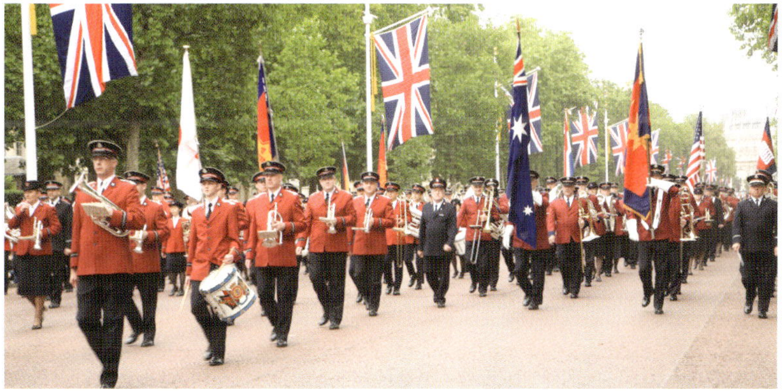
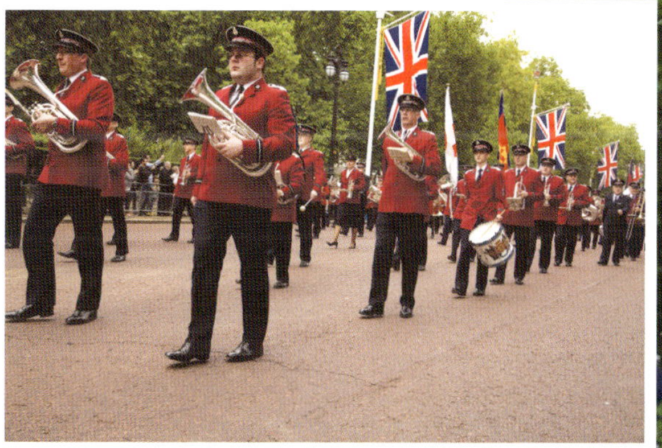

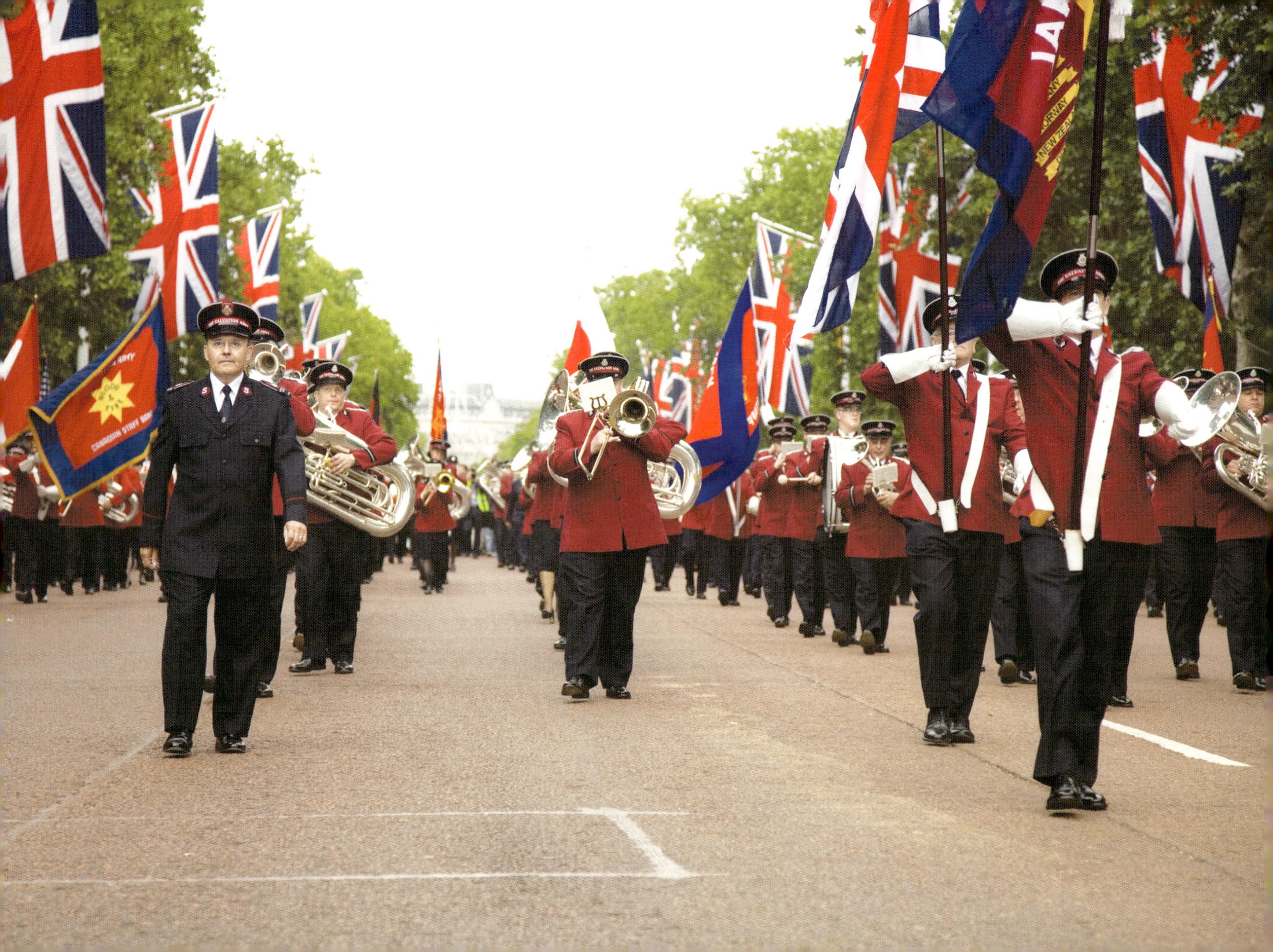

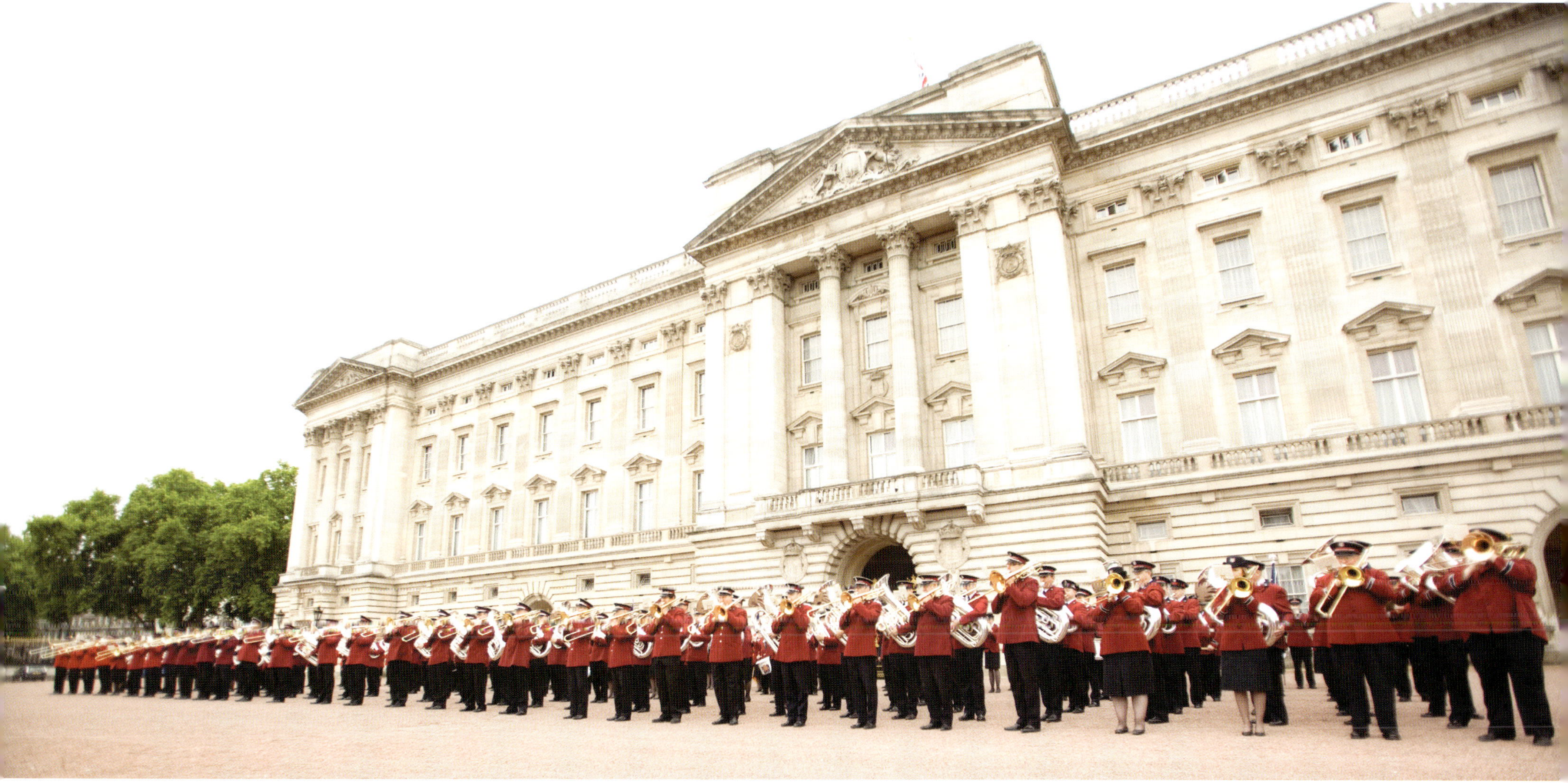

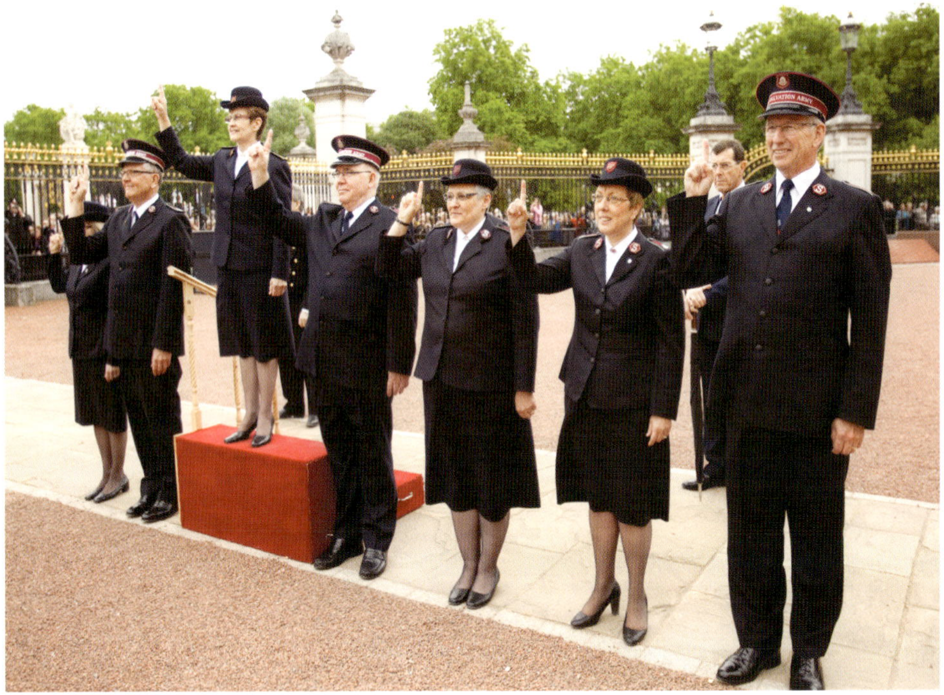

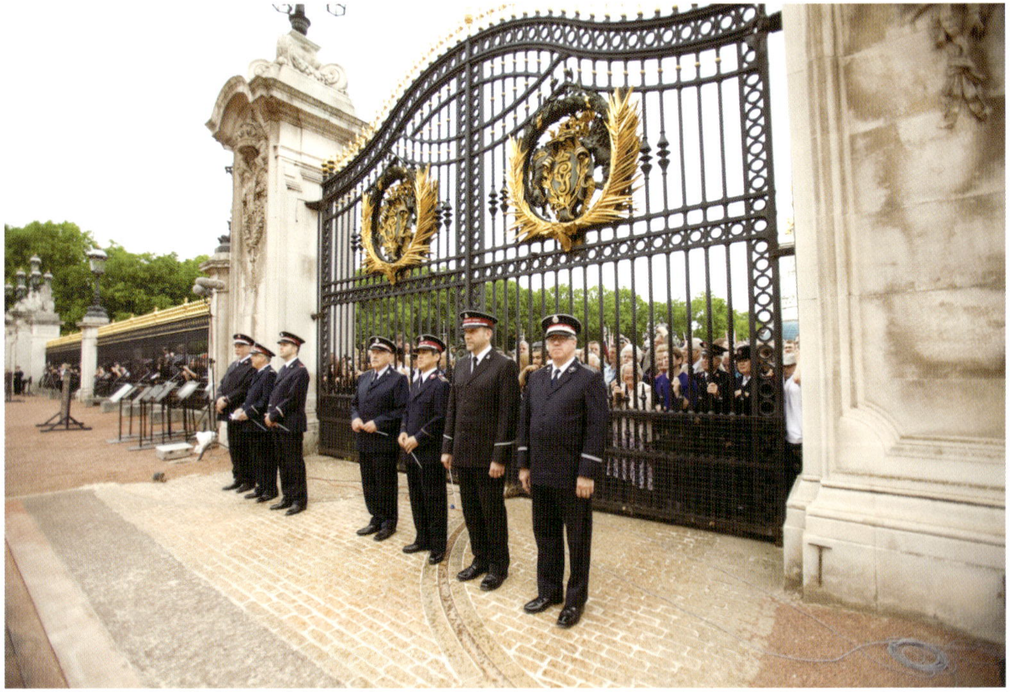

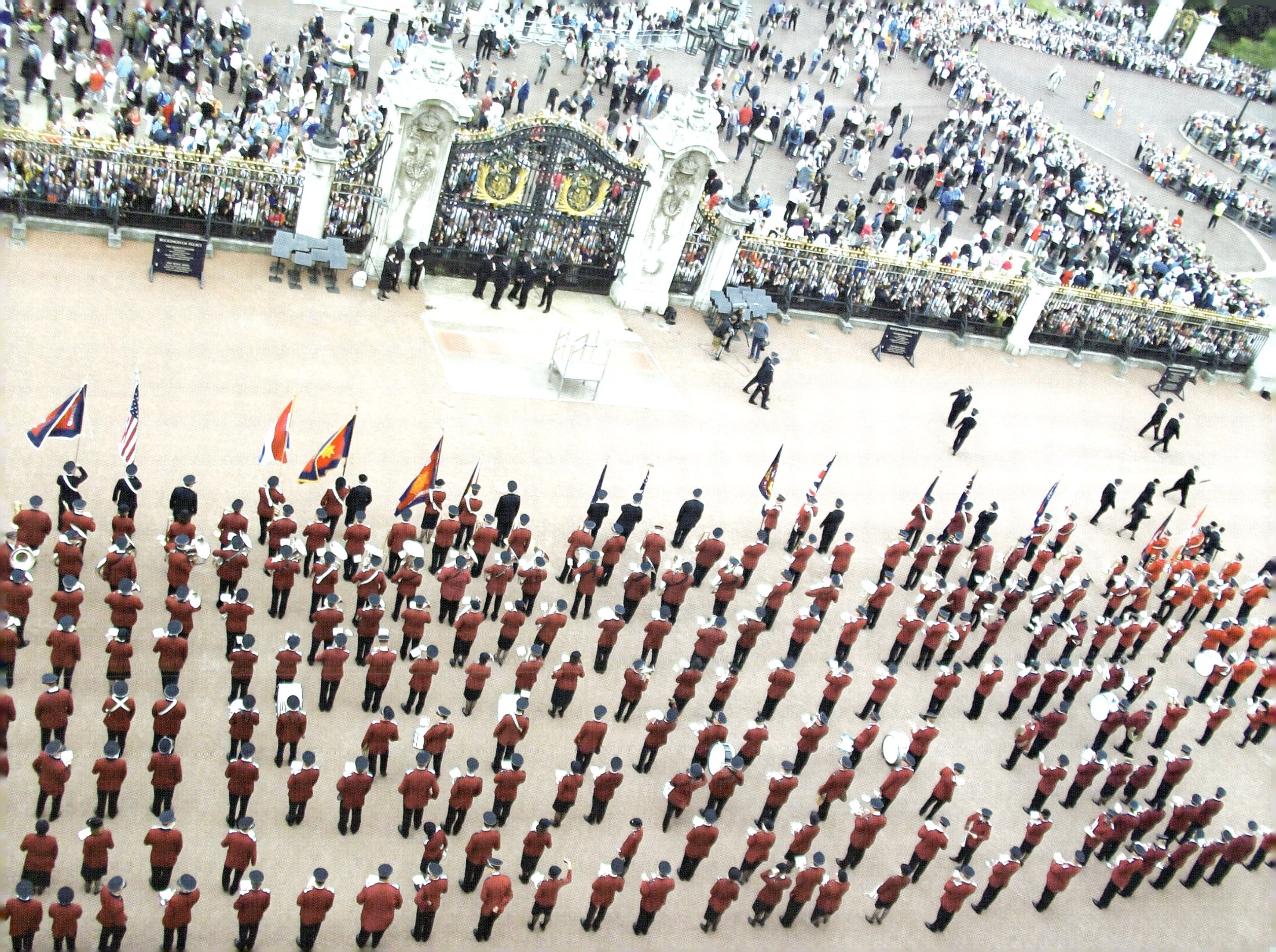

Staff Bands relax at Wellington Barracks after the march

231

From top to bottom: Sopranos, Principal Cornets and Flugel Horns from all eight Staff Bands

From top to bottom: Horns, Basses, Euphoniums and Baritones

Ladies from all eight Staff Bands, led by Chicago Staff Band Deputy Bandmaster Peggy Thomas, the very first lady to join a Staff Band over 35 years ago

The national and band flags of all eight Staff Bands

Clockwise from left: Derick and Stephen Kane (ISB and German Staff Band), Amsterdam and Canadian Staff Band friends and Chris, Gordon and Tim Ward (New York Staff Band)

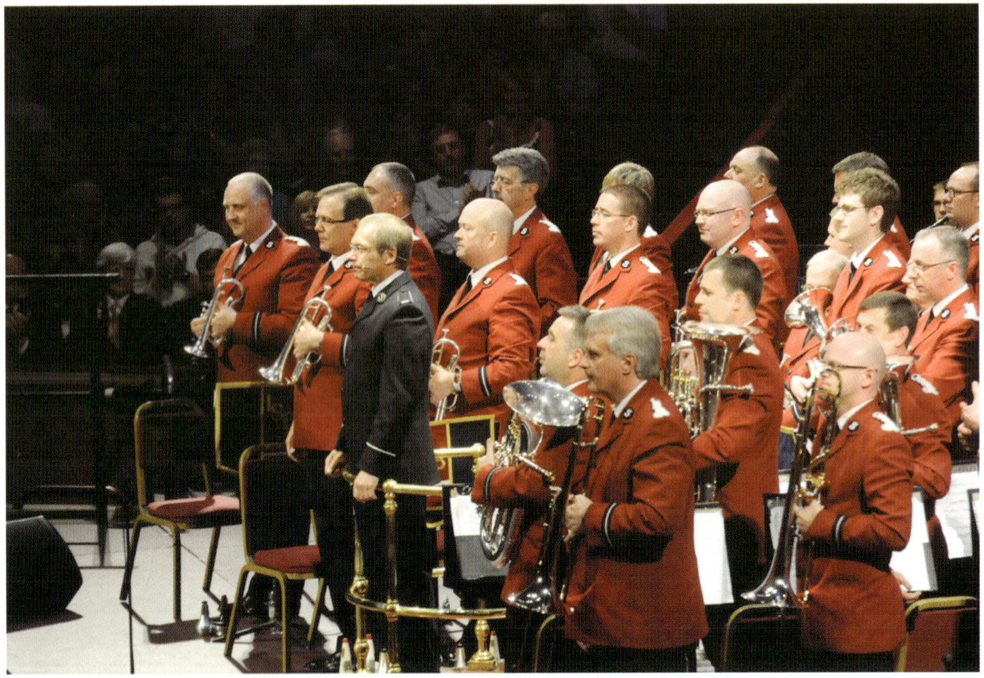

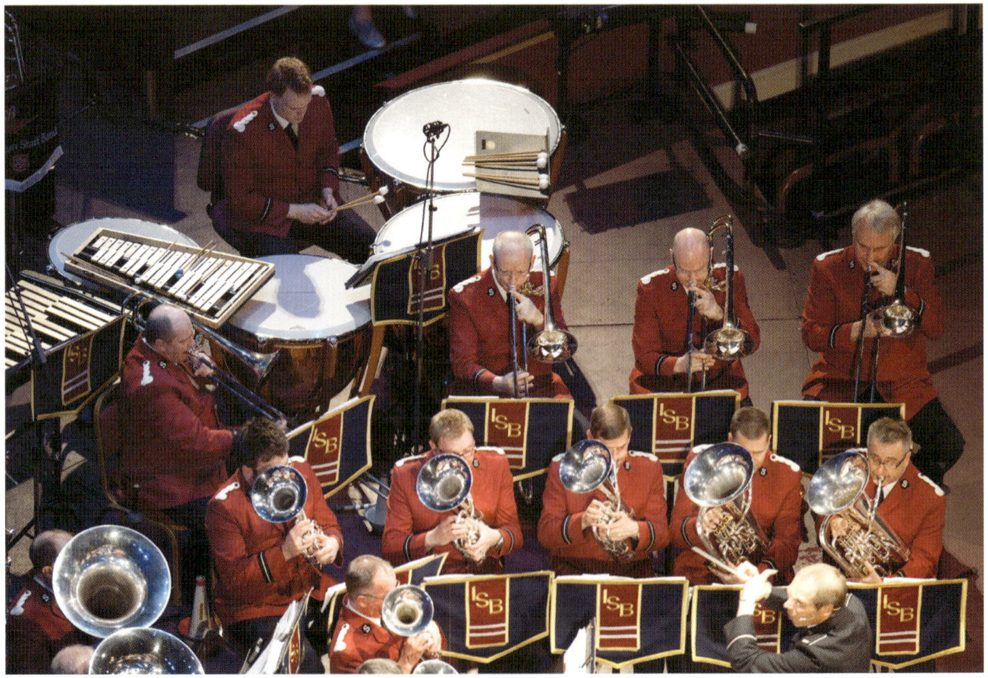

ISB

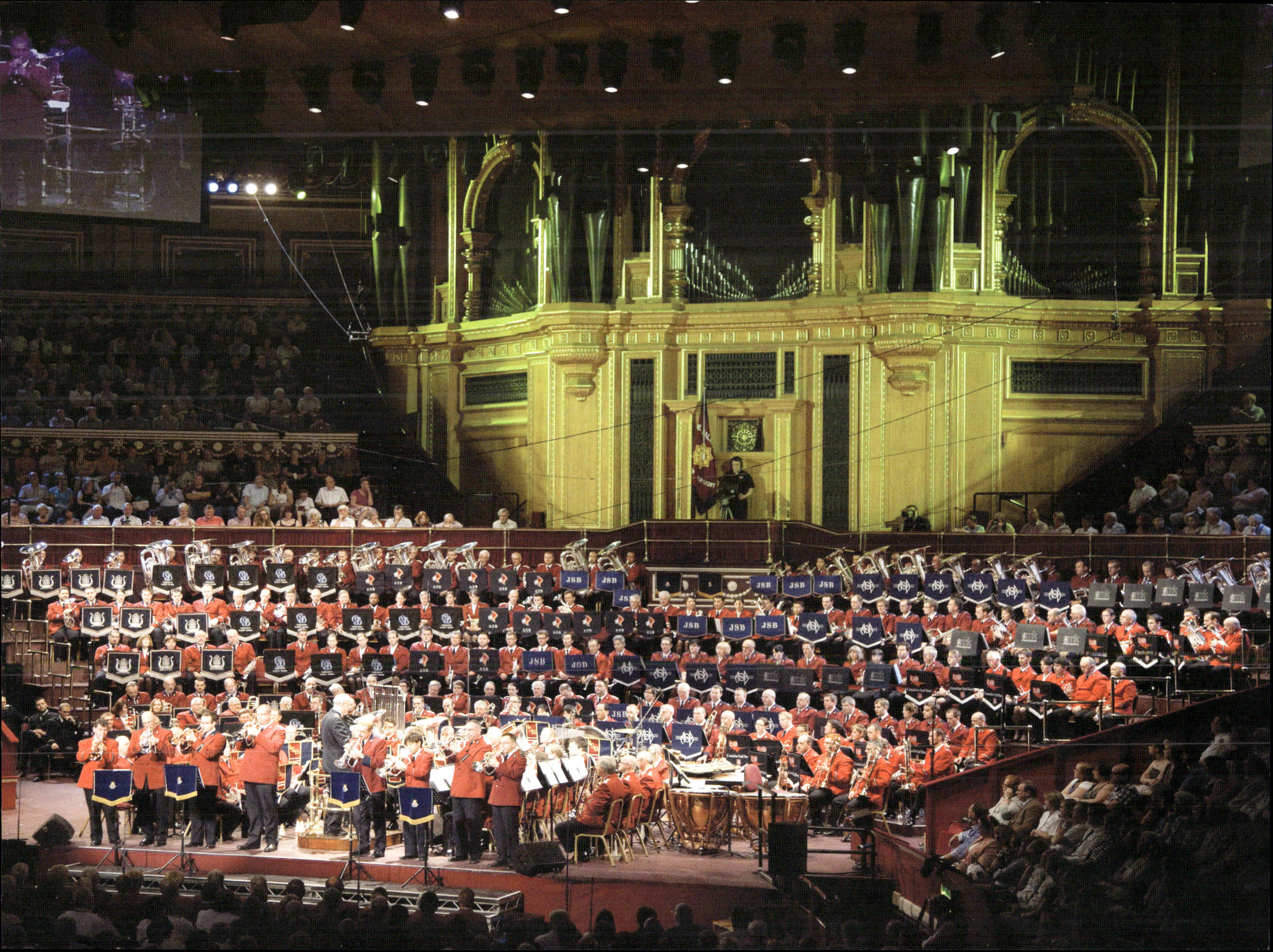
JSB

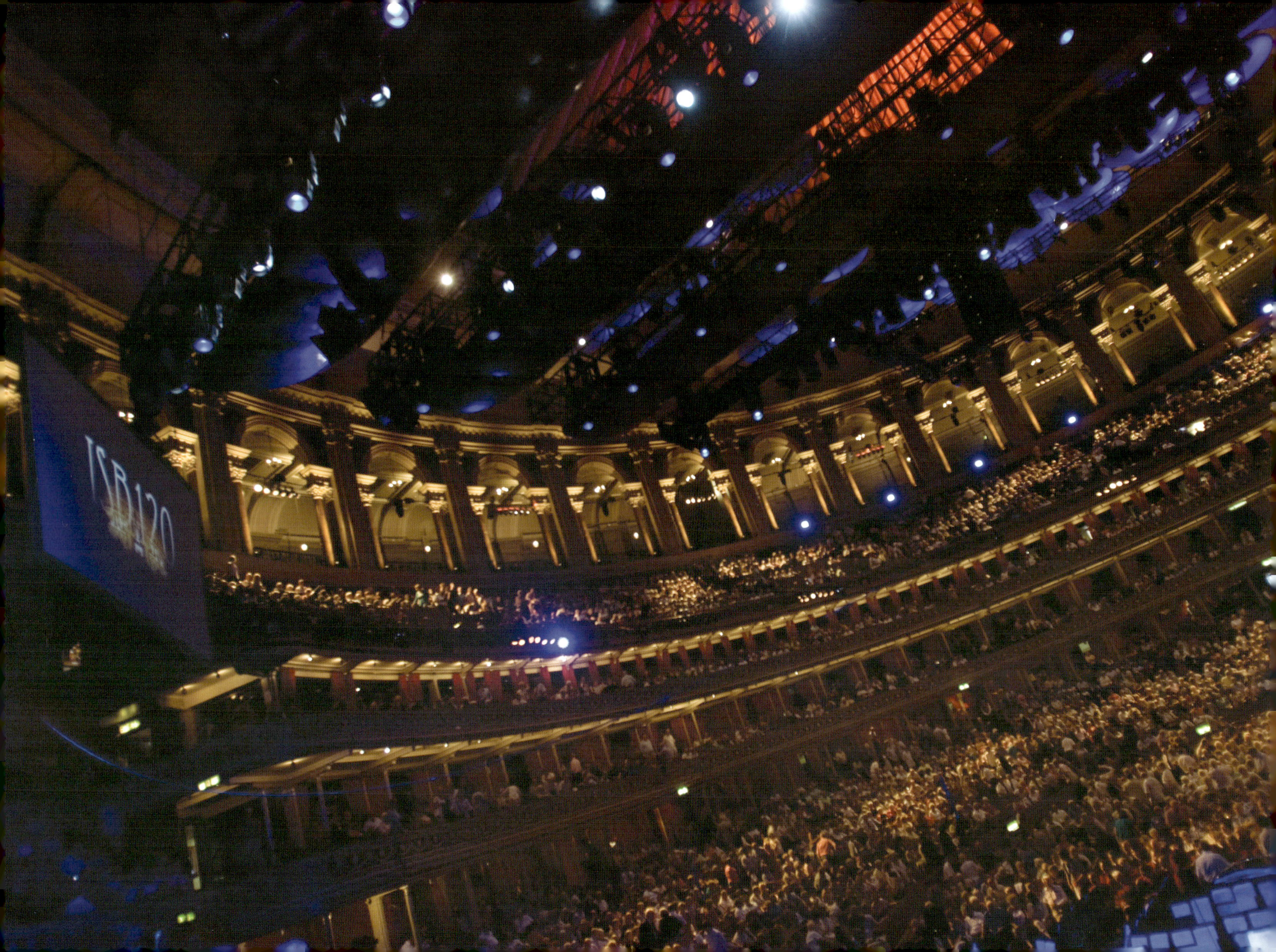

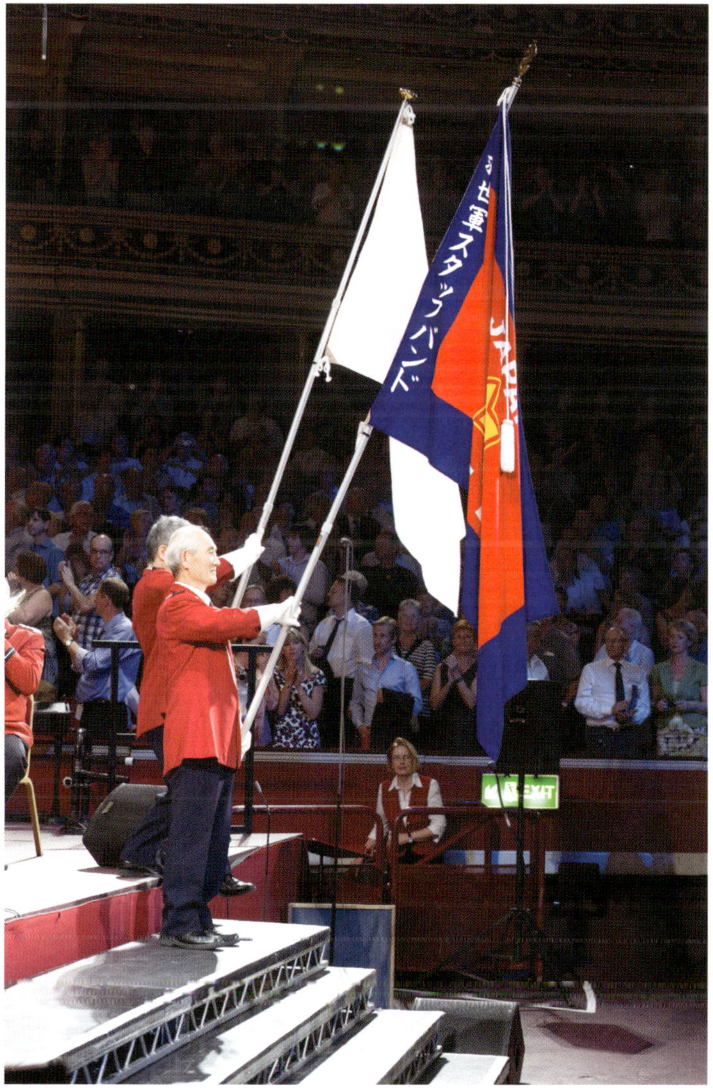

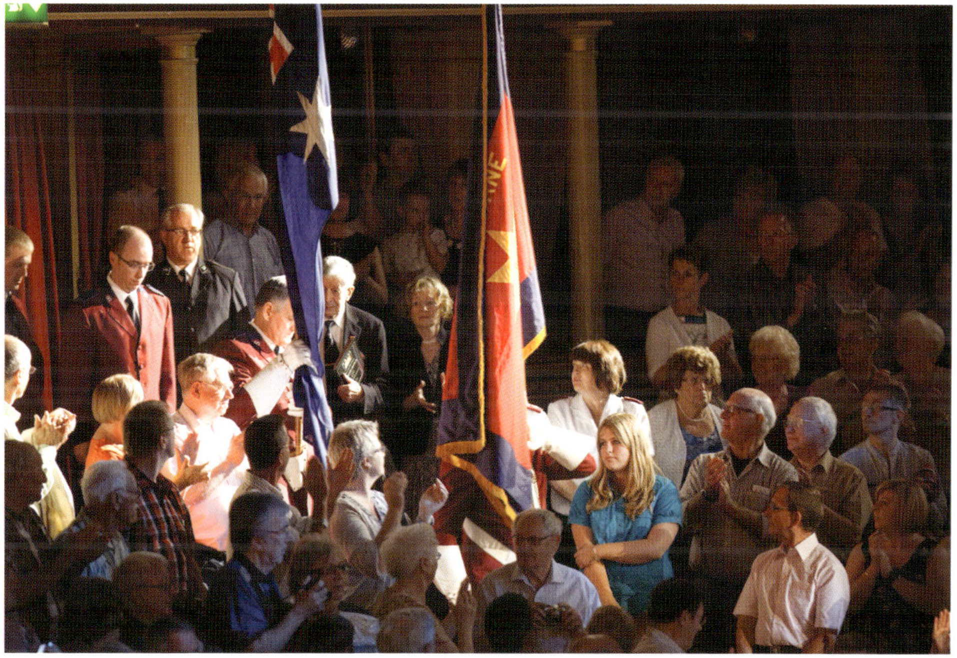

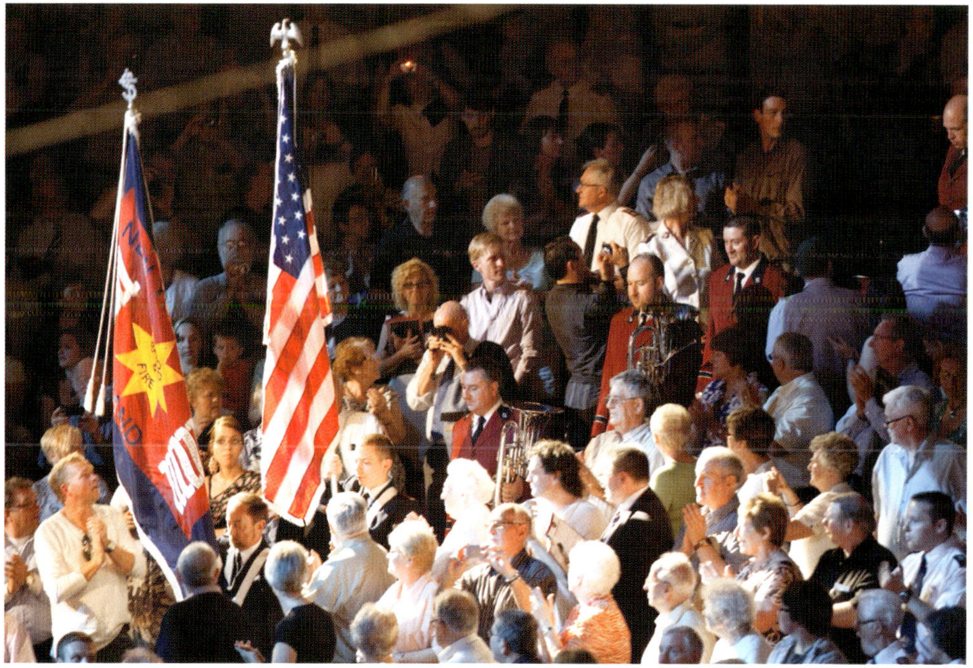

The Royal Box relaxing between the Saturday afternoon and evening programmes

Left: Commissioner John Matear shares scripture
Above: 'The World' welcomes General Linda Bond, Commissioner John Matear and Commissioner Betty Matear

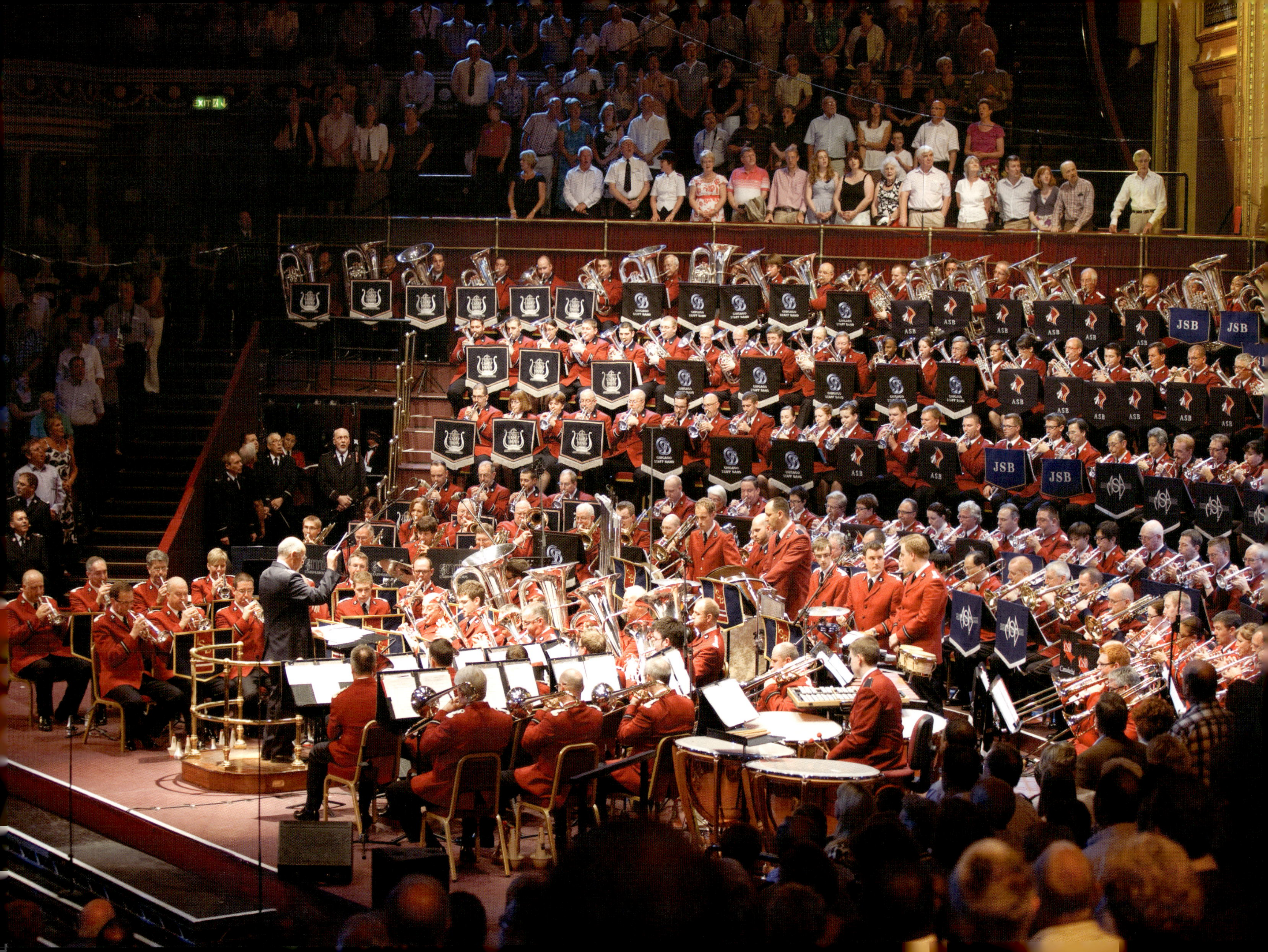
JSB
ASB

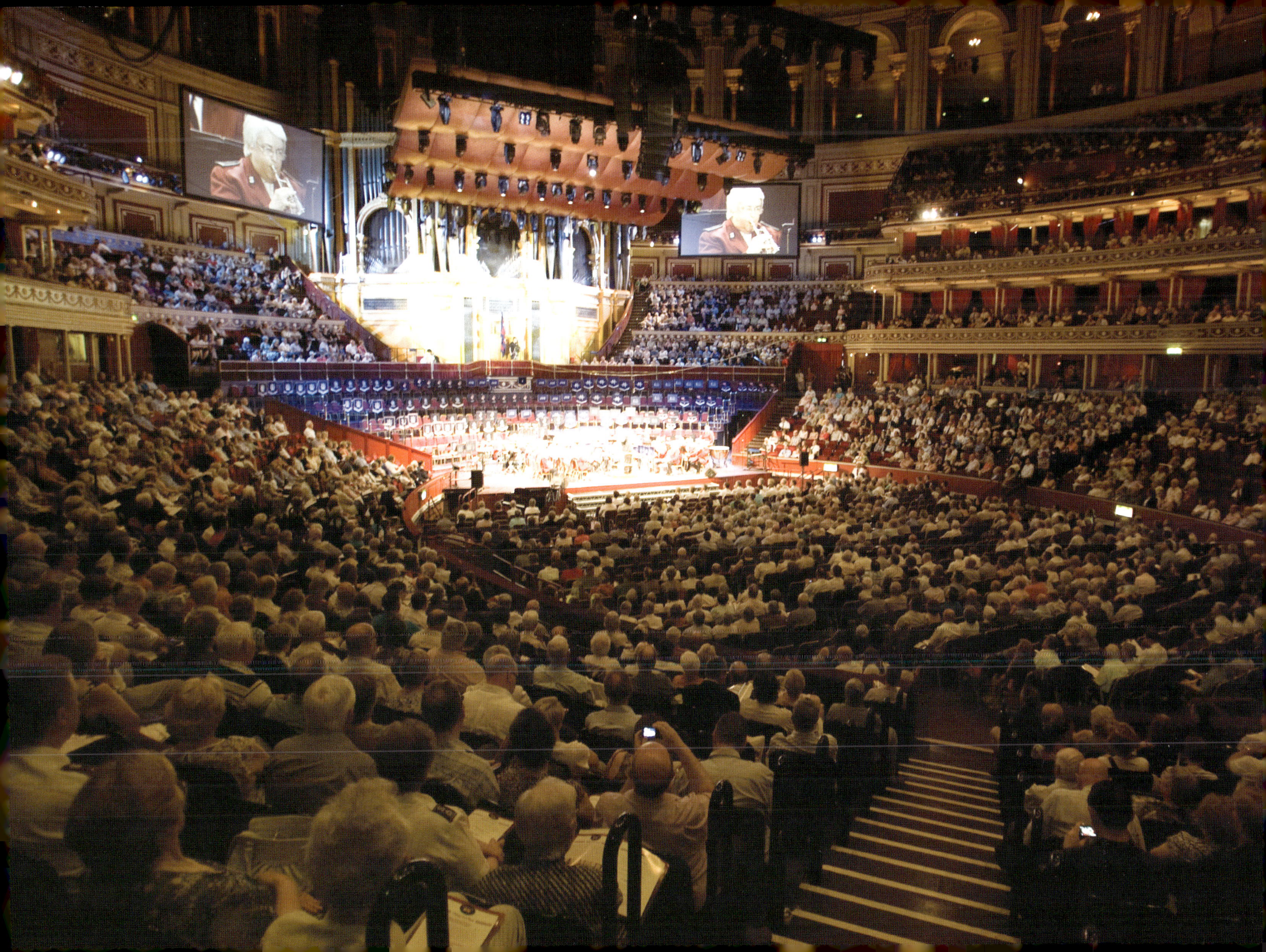

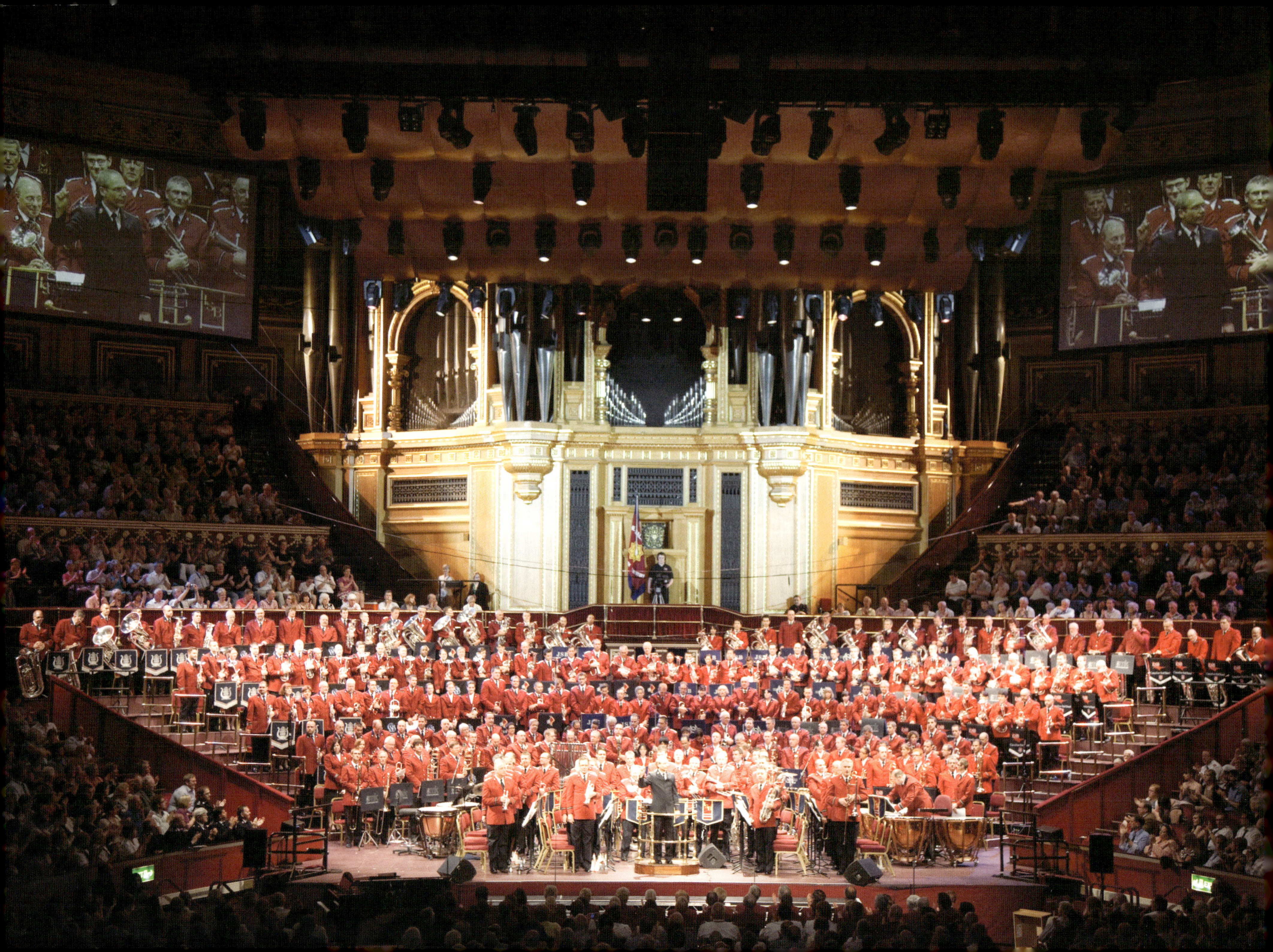

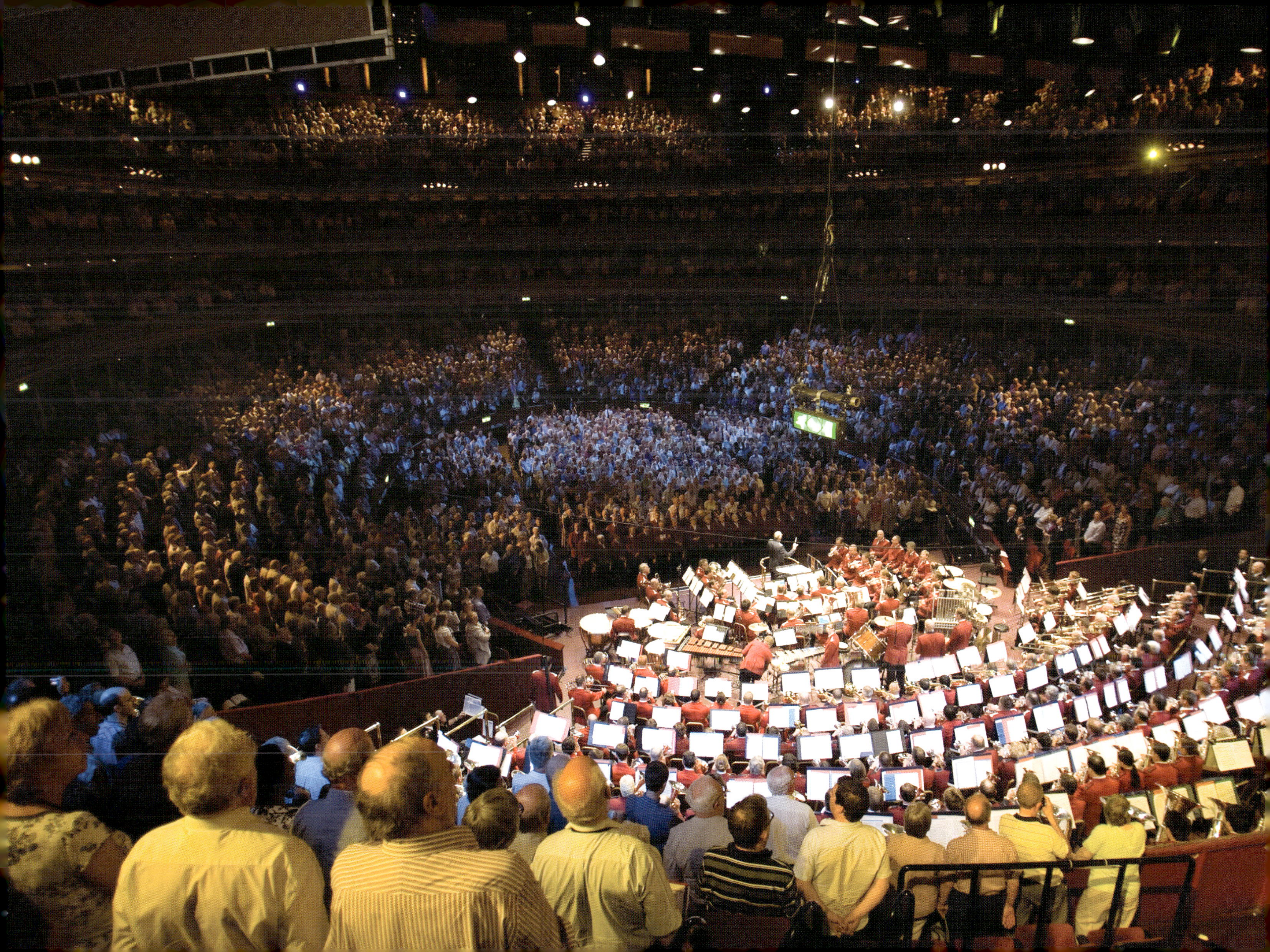

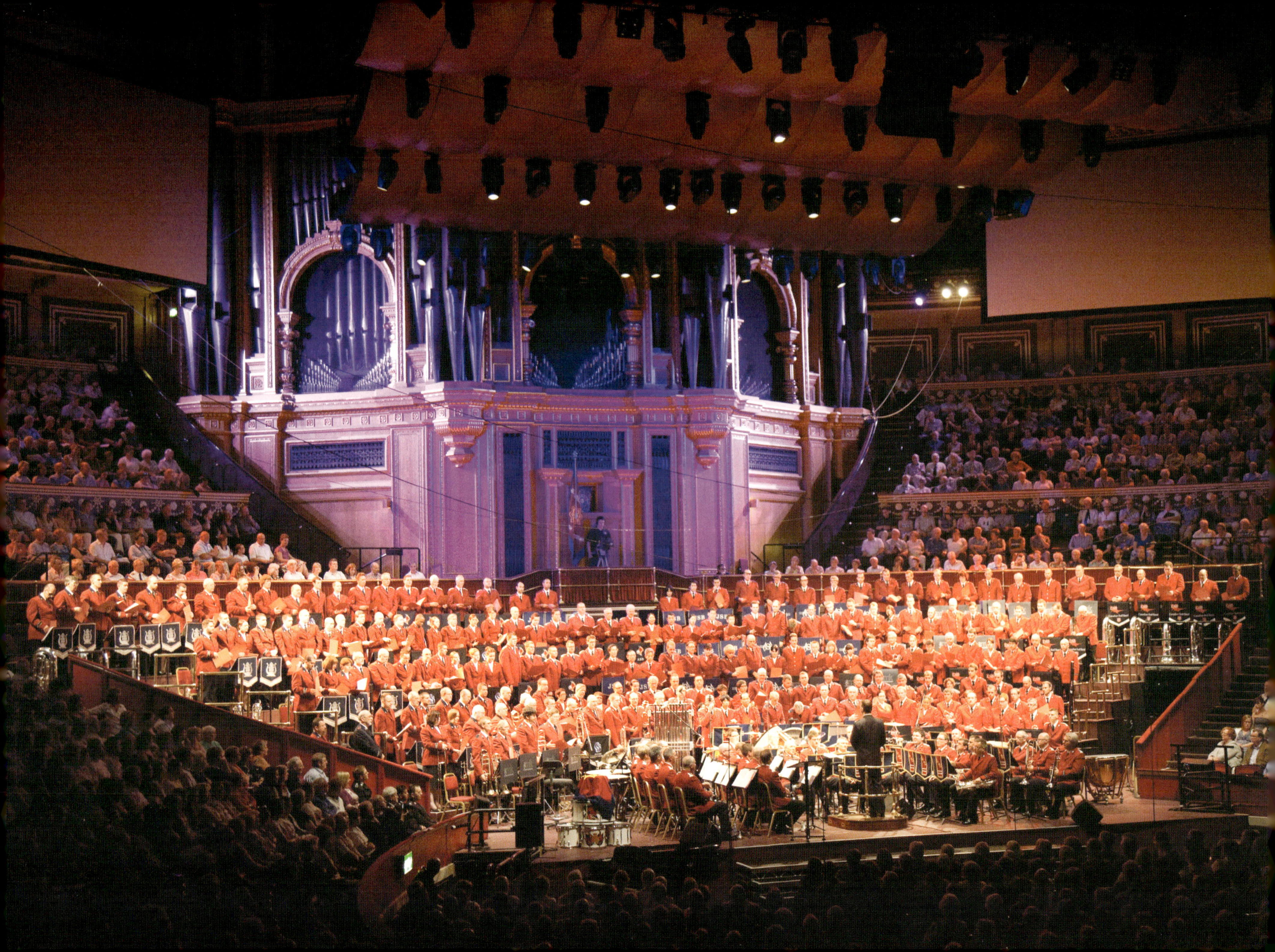

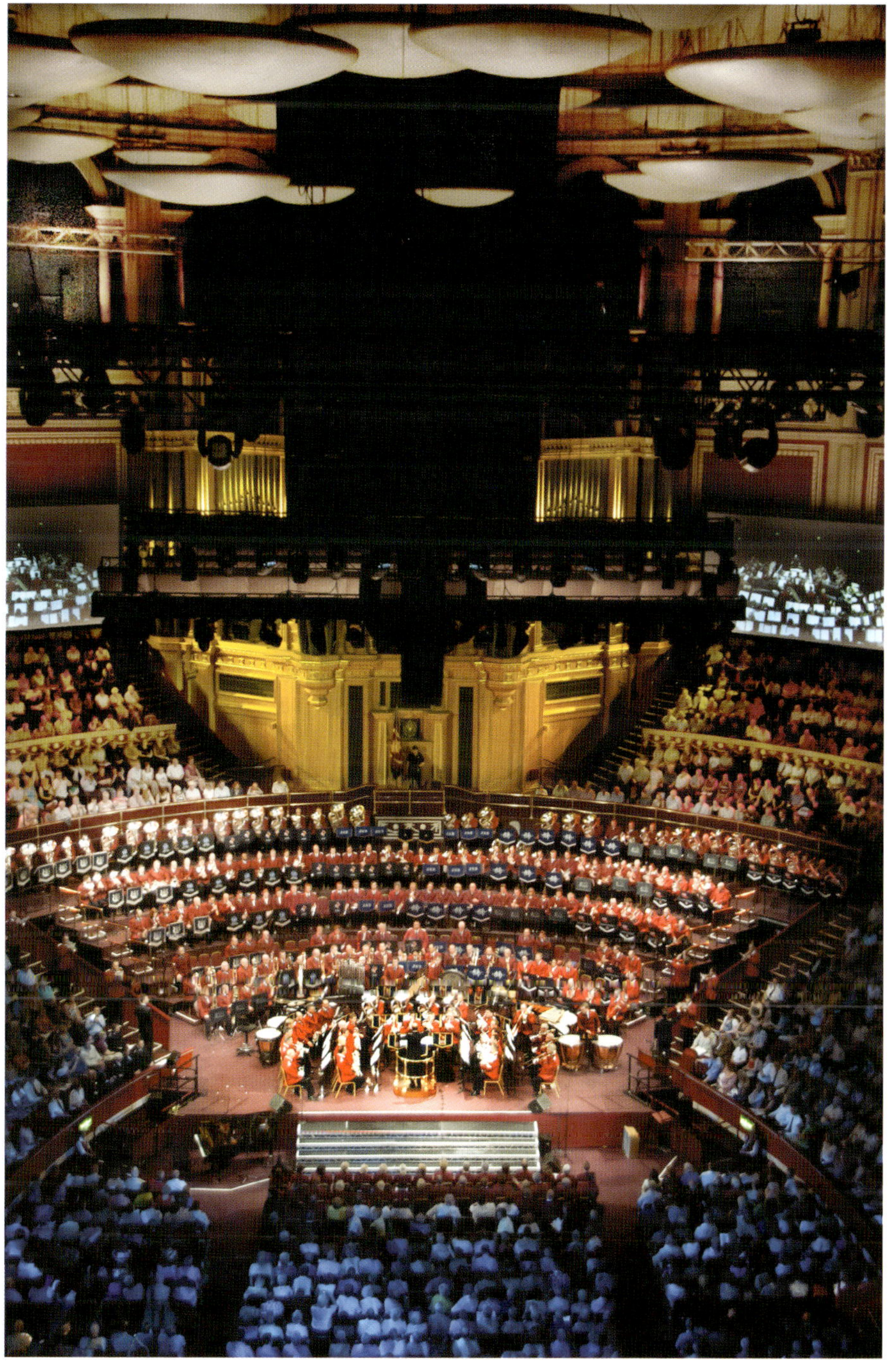

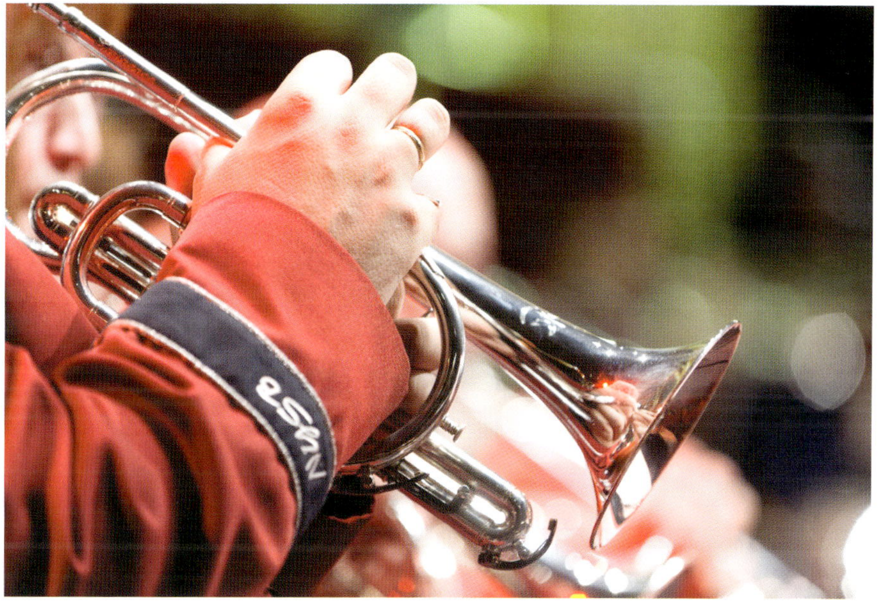

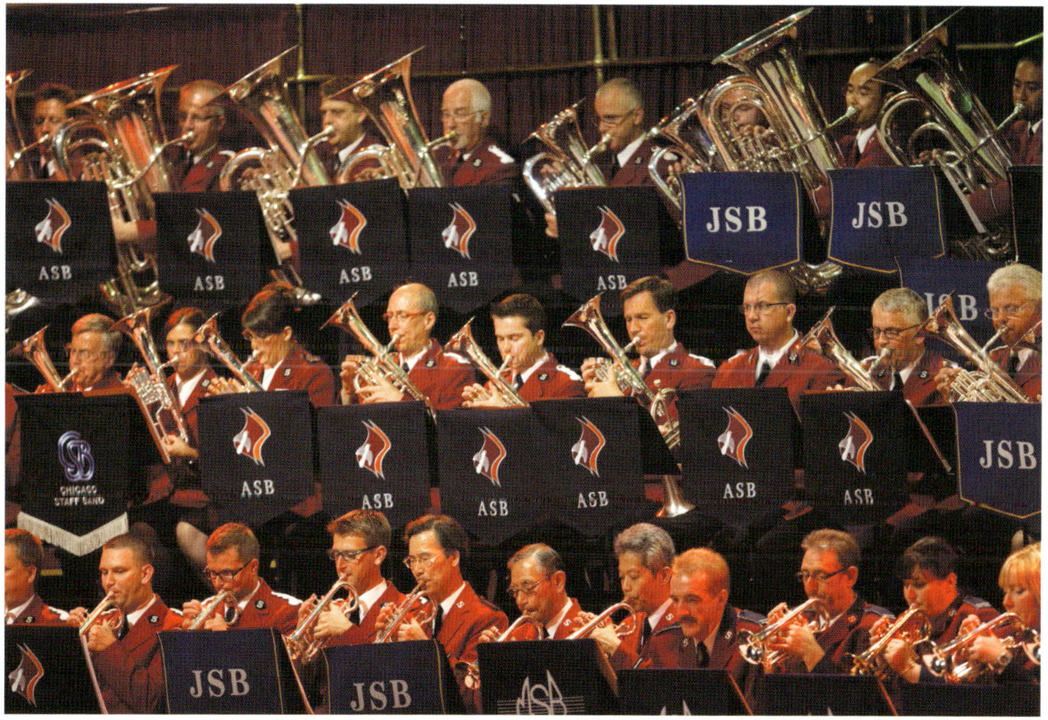
ASB
JSB
CHICAGO STAFF BAND

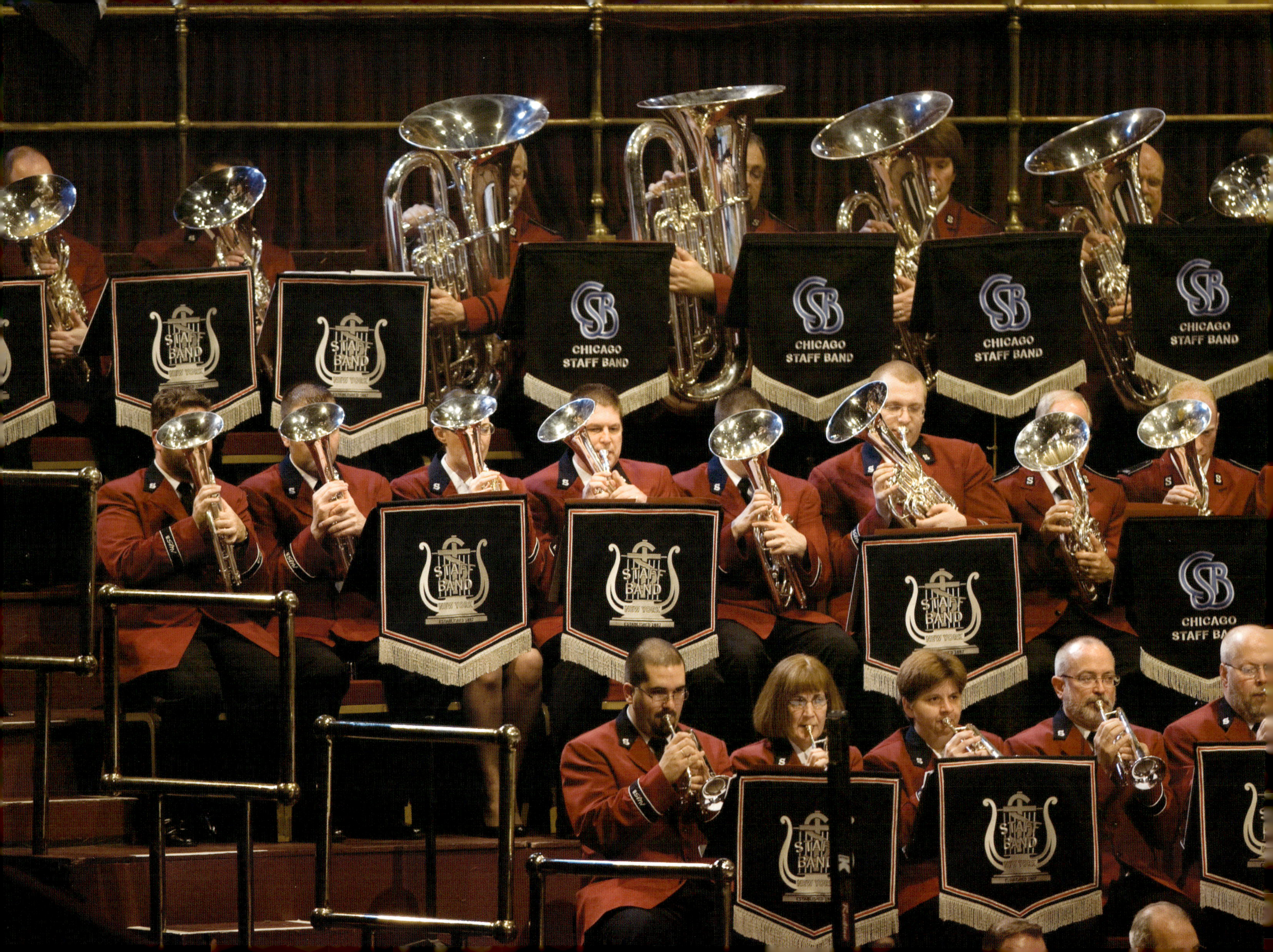
STAFF BAND
NEW YORK
CSB
CHICAGO
STAFF BAND

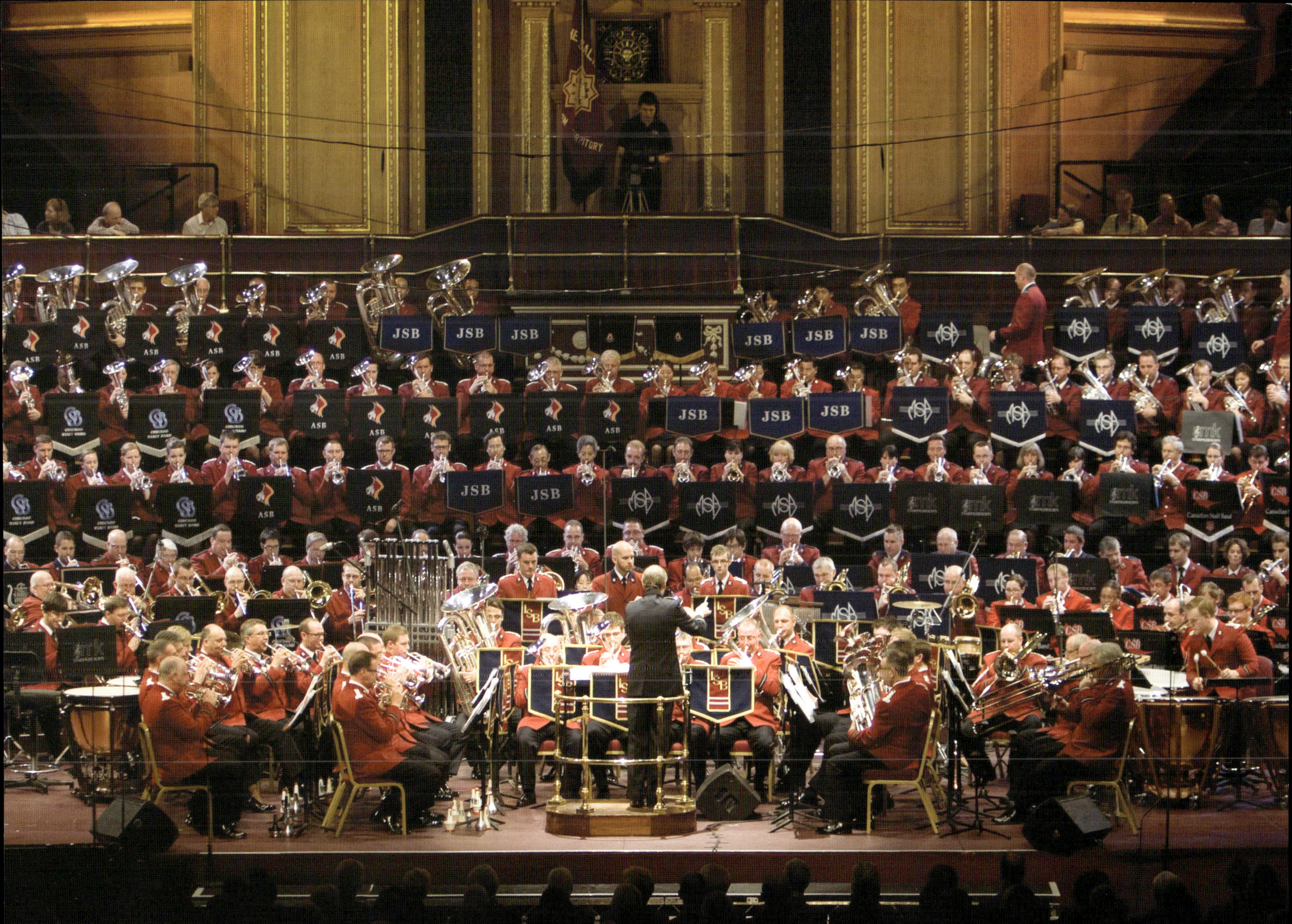
JSB
ASB

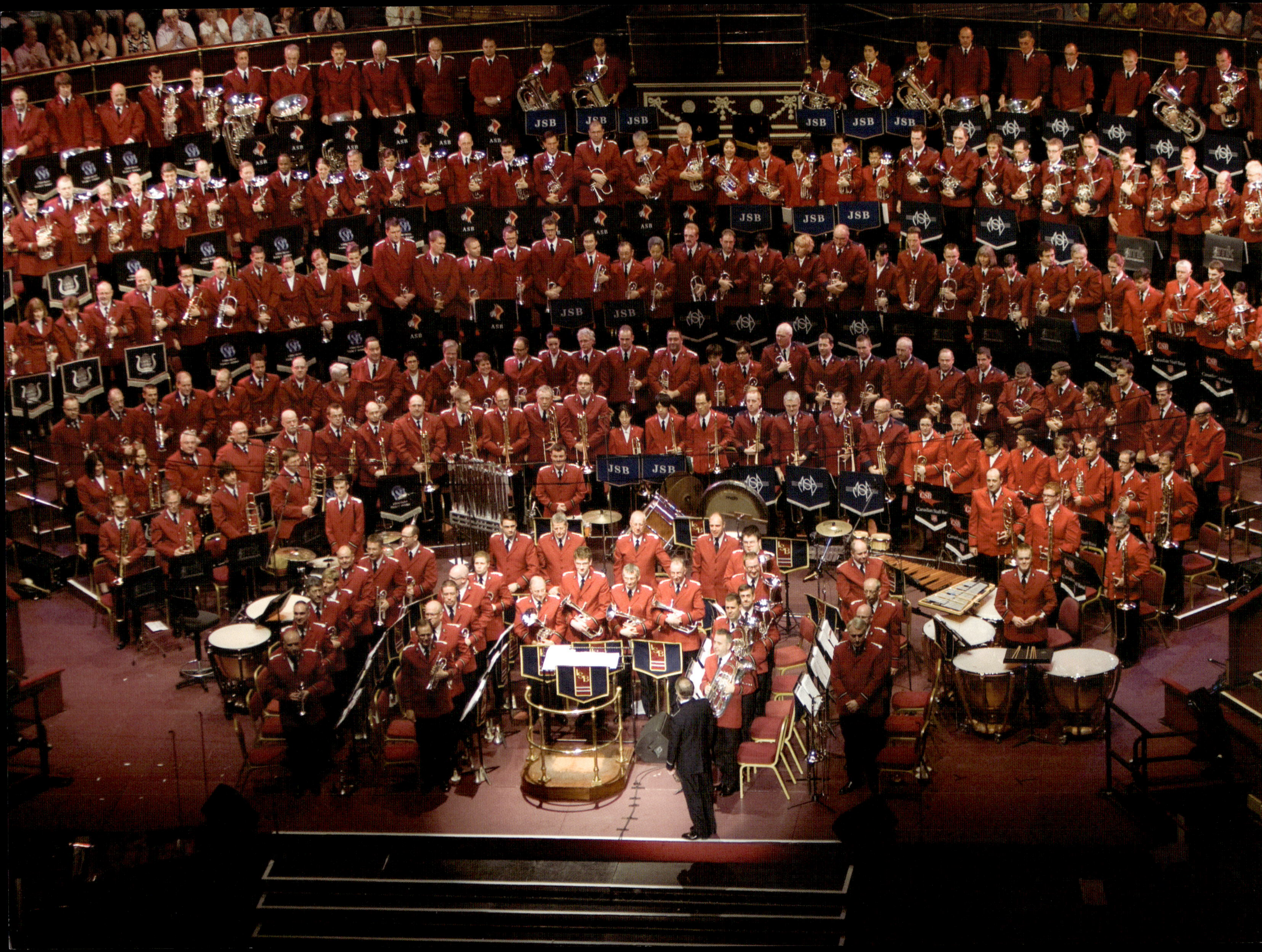
JSB

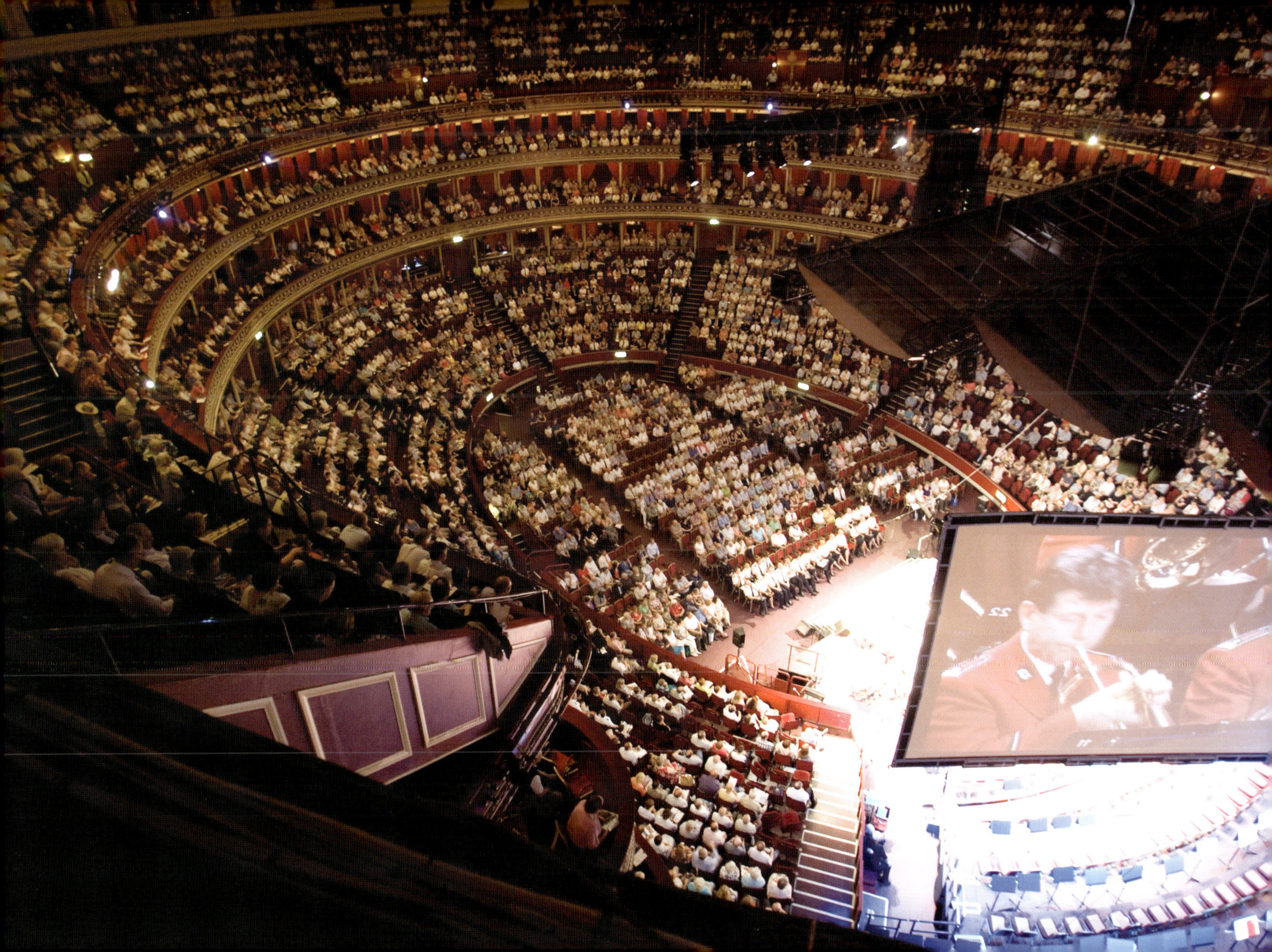

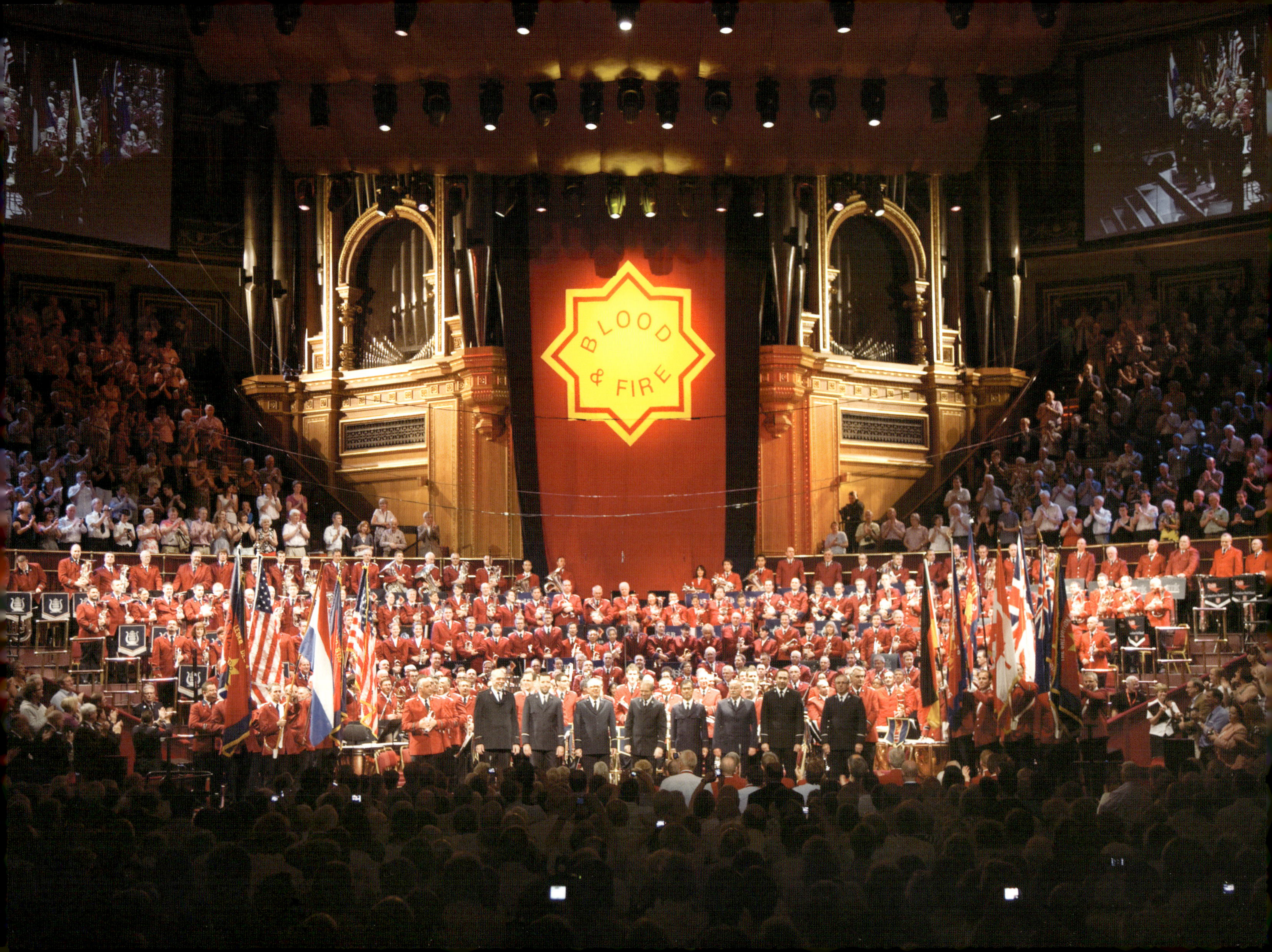
BLOOD & FIRE

The eight Staff Bandmasters of the world

William Flinn shares a final prayer at the end of *Brass Spectacular*

FINAL REFLECTIONS

As we reflect on ISB120, we can clearly see that the sentiments of Salvationism and Internationalism have caught on like wildfire, both in our own territories and around the world, with technology allowing us to relive and share these moments on demand. In the words of Staff Bandsman Stephen Mansfield, "I feel blessed to have been a part of such a wonderful experience; God was evident throughout the events in so many ways". For some of us, ISB120 was a watershed moment. A time that reaffirmed for us the value of our ministry in brass bands. It was a celebration of our past, but more importantly, it was a positioning for the future. It has served to challenge and inspire. Its legacy will not be measured in months or years, but in decades. In the days immediately after ISB120, I penned this short paragraph which is now my official mantra. It serves as a fitting summary of this great experience:

I am a Salvation Army bandsman. I can go halfway around the world, walk into a hall full of strangers and instantly have good friends. I can make music with someone who doesn't speak the same language yet communicate the same message. I can be moved to tears without a single word being spoken. I can share the joy of knowing Jesus by blowing through a brass instrument.

I am a Salvation Army bandsman!

Craig S Lewis – Canadian Staff Band

As I reflect back on ISB120, I've been reminded of the common bond that each of us as Salvation Army band members enjoy. God has given us talents that are offered to Him not only as a witness and testimony to His faithfulness in our lives, but also as a way of bringing those who hear us into a closer relationship with our Lord and Saviour. To be able to do it in a way that provides a message of hope through uplifting music is indeed a privilege. Each Staff Band member who was part of ISB120 has his or her own personal memories of this once-in-a-lifetime experience. If you see me with a smile on my face chances are I'm reliving that glorious weekend which will stay with me for as long as I live.

Lindsay R Evans – New York Staff Band